8

IMPRINT

PROJECT MANAGEMENT
Florian Kobler, Cologne

COLLABORATION
Harriet Graham, Turin

PRODUCTION
Thomas Grell, Cologne

DESIGN
Sense/Net Art Direction
Andy Disl and Birgit
Eichwede, Cologne
www.sense-net.net

GERMAN TRANSLATION
Kristina Brigitta Köper, Berlin

FRENCH TRANSLATION
Jacques Bosser, Paris

© VG BILD-KUNST
Bonn 2012, for the works of
Odile Decq, Benoît Cornette,
Jean Nouvel and Ben van
Berkel

PRINTED IN ITALY
ISBN 978–3–8365–2681–4

© 2012 TASCHEN GMBH
Hohenzollernring 53
D–50672 Cologne
www.taschen.com

ARCHITECTURE NOW!

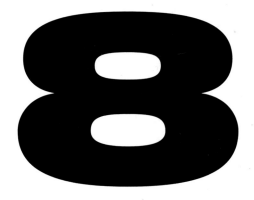

Architektur heute / L'architecture d'aujourd'hui
Philip Jodidio

TASCHEN

CONTENTS

INTRODUCTION

HOW THIN THE EDGE

Imagine a time of contradictions and conflicts, of the Arab world rising, and a wave of destruction ten meters high in Japan. This is early 2011, with most major economies still in the grips of a recession. Whether the news is political, geological, or economic, it brings with it a message of fragility. Wooden houses may have been shattered by the tsunami in Japan, but the far more solid concrete of the Fukushima Daiichi reactors was also no match for the power of nature. The Japanese have a history of earthquakes, wars, destruction, and reconstruction, one reason perhaps that their contemporary architecture shows such vitality. When Frank Lloyd Wright built the Imperial Hotel in Tokyo (1915–23), he imagined incorrectly that the structure would float on the site's alluvial mud "like a battleship floats on water." Despite reports to the contrary, the Imperial Hotel was severely damaged by the Great Kantō earthquake (September 1, 1923, 7.9 on the Richter scale) that devastated Tokyo and Yokohama. Imagine a city that is so seriously damaged in 1923, only to rebuild and to be firebombed in February and March of 1945. In one raid, during the night of March 9–10, 1945, more than 200 B-29s destroyed 41 square kilometers of the Japanese capital and killed 100 000 people.

THE NEW INSTABILITY

It is curious today that the wrath of nature and the unpredictability of the economy should have similar results, making fragility a word for the times. Surely many architects will take these events as an occasion to tread lightly, to build more ephemeral structures. With radiation falling from the sky, perhaps, too, ecology may finally have its say. A number of the projects published in this book take fairly radical or completely new approaches to environmental sustainability. Renovations and temporary structures would also seem to be on the rise, taking advantage of the solidity of an old building on the one hand or the chance to just appear and fade away far faster than the average nuclear power plant on the other. When Francis Fukuyama proclaimed the "end of history" (*The End of History and the Last Man*, 1992), some thought "globalization" or rather global capitalism was just beginning its reign of uncontested superiority. Might it be that the times of the Cold War, heyday of rampant modernism, were far more stable for architecture than the atmosphere of failure and collapse that has accompanied the early 21st century? When two vast political and economic blocks stared each other down, as postwar reconstruction made it seem the world could be built anew, there was often optimism and faith in the future. Gone now, and with the Berlin Wall gone as well, how curious that more walls should spring up all over the world, from Gaza to the border between Mexico and the United States.

LIFE IN THE EMERALD CITY

What if the new masters of the world—billionaires and dictators—were to be exposed for the frauds they are, Wizards of Oz in their Emerald Cities? Adrian Smith, the designer of Burj Khalifa (2004–10), admits that he was thinking of the towers of the Emerald City in the film version of *The Wizard of Oz*. "That was in my mind as I was designing Burj Dubai," he said, "although in a subliminal way. I didn't research the way it looked. I just remembered the glassy, crystalline structure coming up in the middle of what seemed like nowhere. The funny thing is, I didn't remember it being green." And so the tallest man-made structure ever built (828 meters) remains largely empty, a victim of Dubai's fall

1
24H Architecture, Panyaden School,
Chiang Mai, Thailand, 2010–11

from grace. As hubris is far more durable than buildings, someone will surely build a higher tower one day quite soon, but can the dreams of limitless wealth and brave new frontiers in architecture survive the age of fragility? When asked how Japan would change after the real-estate bubble broke in 1991, the noted architect Arata Isozaki said with a smile: "No more crazy little buildings!" Though this prediction was not fully validated, it is true that restricted funds bring austerity to architecture while freely flowing money encourages more excess. With natural and economic disaster going hand in hand with social upheaval, will inventive architects be forced to drive New York cabs? Or will ecological nightmares and failing banks make some look for saner ways to design and build, and perhaps to find a calmer, greener future?

OUT OF CONTROL

A prescient article published in the London daily newspaper the *Guardian* on March 18, 2011,[1] summed up events related to the Japanese earthquake and hinted at solutions that such cataclysms can lead to: "What the events reveal is the thinness of the margin on which modernity lives. There's not a country in the world more modern and civilized than Japan; its building codes and engineering prowess kept its great buildings from collapsing when the much milder quake in Haiti last year flattened everything. But clearly, it's not enough. That thin edge on which we live, and which at most moments we barely notice, provided nowhere near enough buffer against the power of the natural world." The writer makes a link, tenuous as it may seem, between such a natural event and the man-made dangers posed by global warming, while suggesting that we may have reached the limits of the science of engineering in the broadest sense. "Maybe this isn't the week to trust the grandest promises of engineers, not when they've all but lost control of the highest technology we've ever built, there on the fluff at Fukushima. The other possibility is to try to build down a little to focus on resilience, on safety; and to do that—there's the controversial part—decide that the human enterprise (at least in the West) has got big enough, that our appetites need not grow, but shrink a little, in order to provide us more margin."

Architecture, too, has in general followed the arc of consumer societies, ever more, ever higher. Curiously, spurred on by society and economics, architects have handily given up their old dream of building "eternal" structures, one that could last like a Gothic cathedral. They have been happy to build more and more cheap and flimsy buildings, now convinced that durability is not one of the qualities the world needs today. The *Guardian* takes the opposite tack and writes: "Suddenly squat and plain words—'durable,' 'stable,' 'robust,'—sound sweeter to the ear."

THE WAY IT IS

The *Architecture Now!* series offers a broad panorama of contemporary architecture. Architectural criticism in the past has sought to define and support a school, as Philip Johnson and Henry-Russell Hitchcock did in the celebrated Museum of Modern Art show—"Modern Architecture: International Exhibition"—in 1932. Focusing on work by Le Corbusier, Mies van der Rohe, Neutra, Gropius, and Wright, the show was accompanied by the influential book *The International Style*. More recently (and less durably), Charles Jencks sang the praises of a post-

2
Foster + Partners, Spaceport America, New Mexico, USA, 2009–12

2

modernism that turned out to be nothing more than cosmetic and superficial. Rather than promoting one trend, *Architecture Now!* shows recent buildings from around the world, in a willful mixture of styles and types. Quite simply put, that is the way architecture is now. Nor are times of upheaval and questioning likely to make that any less the case in the years to come. When anyone can see plenty of architecture on the Internet, *Architecture Now!* is about making choices, about showing what is good, without reference to schools and without being subjected to pressures or undue influences. This is a critical choice without any predetermined agenda. This is how it is.

RAMMED EARTH AND BAMBOO POLES

What if environmentally sustainable architecture was to be found less in the sophisticated laboratories that conceive the latest photovoltaic cells and more in the parts of the world where people must be ecologically aware in order to survive? Maartje Lammers and Boris Zeisser from the Rotterdam firm 24H Architecture have delved wholeheartedly into this perception with their Panyaden School (Chiang Mai, Thailand, 2010–11, page 50), with its rammed-earth walls and bamboo roof design, intended for a school that teaches such subjects as cloth weaving and local agricultural methods as part of an approach that links Buddhist principles and common sense. Where some architects vaunt designs that reduce emissions by a few percentage points, 24H finds a route to a "negligible" carbon footprint via methods that appear largely traditional.

The Indonesian architect Effan Adhiwira, based in Bali, is the designer of the Green School published here (Badung, Bali, Indonesia, 2007, page 64). Unrelated to the Panyaden School, this initiative, too, seeks to teach children about sustainable life patterns. Bamboo columns set on top of natural river stones or considerable roof overhangs to protect from sunlight characterize this design. The architect states: "Our architecture is inspired by the inherent characteristics of the bamboo pole itself. We strive to maximize the span of the bamboo structure, optimize the natural 'curve/flex' in the pole allowing us to design and construct organic, natural-shaped buildings." As is the case of a number of other projects published here, the Green School was identified by the Aga Khan Award for Architecture as a significant structure and shortlisted for the 2010 Award. The Award assessment of this project affirms: "Local bamboo, grown using sustainable methods, is used in innovative and experimental ways that demonstrate its architectural possibilities. The result is a holistic green community with a strong educational mandate that seeks to inspire students to be more curious, more engaged, and more passionate about the environment and the planet."

POWER DOWN

In another interesting relay created between Europe and the Muslim world Christian Félix and Laetitia Delubac (FELIX-DELUBAC) designed the 390-square-meter Ecolodge in Siwa, Egypt (2006–07, page 110). This is a desert retreat built with *kershef*, which is to say mud, sand, and sun-dried salt. Even more "radical" in a sense, the Ecolodge has a wind tower inspired by traditional Persian ventilation structures, and has no electricity. The same architects are currently working on a Passive House in Normandy that makes use of a wood structure and thatched roof. Those who know Normandy will immediately identify such roofs with a rather picturesque impression of this northern French area. Yet, there too, traditional materials and methods obviously appeal to a pair of architects born in the mid 1970s who graduated from the Paris Villemin School just over ten years ago. It would seem that it must be quite fashionable to be traditional.

The Aga Khan Award for Architecture and its sister organization, the Historic Cities Programme, have singled out the work of the architect Diébédo Francis Kéré, born in Burkina Faso, as being worthy of interest. His Primary School (Gando, 2001), located in the village where he was born, was the winner of a 2004 Aga Khan Award. The description made at the time of the project for the Award states: "To achieve sustainability, the project was based on the principles of designing for climatic comfort with low-cost construction, making the most of local materials and the potential of the local community, and adapting technology from the industrialized world in a simple way. It was also conceived as an exemplar that would raise awareness in the local community of the merits of traditional materials." Diébédo Francis Kéré was the first person in Gando, a town of 3000, to receive higher education, and he studied at the Technische Universität Berlin. While his sensibility is rooted in African traditions, it is to be clearly noted that a Western, technology-oriented architectural education is compatible with working in a sustainable, traditionally inspired vocabulary. Kéré's Earthen Architecture Center (Mopti, Mali, 2010, page 37) is a 476-square-meter structure built by the Aga Khan Trust for Culture's Historic Cities Programme subsequent to their efforts concerning the restoration of the mosque and construction of a new sewage system in Mopti. Compressed earth blocks and overhanging roofs are part of the design whose ventilation is achieved without recourse to mechanical systems.

DUSTY FUTURE

Far from the down-to-earth approach used in the projects in Mali, Egypt, or Bali, the Emirate of Abu Dhabi had dreamed of an opposite approach to sustainability and energy consumption. Granted, the climate of the Gulf is a harsh one that apparently requires the consumption of a great deal of electricity. By 2016 Masdar City was to be a $22 billion, six-square-kilometer city for 45 000 residents and 1500 businesses. Masdar aimed to use only renewable energy sources and to generate zero carbon emissions and no waste. The Masdar Institute of Science and Technology working with MIT would produce solar energy, in particular with photovoltaic panels manufactured on site. A first surprising problem arose when it was discovered that Abu Dhabi's frequent dust storms reduce the performance of photo voltaic cells by 40%. In the midst of resignations and bad press, Masdar saw its completion date pushed back to 2020, with electricity after all to be imported.

It is in this atmosphere that Foster + Partners completed the first large structure there, the Masdar Institute (Abu Dhabi, UAE, 2008–10, page 118). Nobody will doubt the efficiency of the passive strategies employed, such as orientation and contemporary versions of the wind tower, but then, these existed centuries ago. The photovoltaic systems employed remain to prove their long-term efficiency, and so, too, the dream of a zero carbon city in the desert may prove to be more of a mirage than it is a contemporary reality. Imagine a country that has no fresh water, 50°C summer heat, and inhabitants whose carbon footprint per capita is the highest in the world.

LOCATION IS EVERYTHING

The architects Studio Mumbai led by Bijoy Jain completed the 300-square-meter Palmyra House in 2007 (Nandgaon, Maharashtra, India, page 412). This is another project that was shortlisted for the 2010 Aga Khan Award for Architecture. The description of the residence made by the Award emphasizes its sustainability, which relies much more on tradition and "authentic" materials than it does on any complex technological attempt to reduce the carbon footprint. "The functions of the house are placed within two oblong masses slightly offset from one another, whose façades are predominantly characterized by louvers made from the trunks of the local palmyra palm. The structure is made of ain wood; local basalt was used to make boundary walls, plinths, and paving. Plaster finishes were pigmented with sand from the site. The development of the design and detail, which resulted from collaboration between the architect and the craftsmen, took on tested techniques, both local and foreign, and raised them to a finer construction resolution. The house is well-adapted to its environment: the louvers on the elevations enable passive cooling, as does the extensive shade provided by the coconut trees above; water for the house is harvested from three on-site wells, filtered and stored at the top of a water tower and fed by gravity to the house. The result of these measures is a quietly compelling project that is fully integrated into its landscape."[2]

Though readers may have the impression that some of the projects cited here are coming from rather far afield, or that they are in the "third world," the truth is that some very talented younger architects are turning to the resources of traditional architecture and realizing that the issues posed by contemporary society, developed or less so, may be better addressed by looking to the past with modern eyes than by seeking at all costs to be at the technological cutting edge. As the *Guardian* points out, the Fukushima Daiichi power plant in some ways represents the highest point of engineering knowledge, and that has been proven woefully inadequate. Well then?

ASHES TO ASHES

Vo Trong Nghia is, in fact, not only an architect but also an engineer, holder of a Master's of Civil Engineering degree from Tokyo University, born in 1976 in Vietnam. His wNw Bar (Binh Duong, Vietnam, 2008, page 454) makes use of a structural bamboo arch system that allowed him to create a dome 10 meters high and 15 meters wide. Set next to the architect's wNw Café, the Bar shows that architecture made of bamboo can be as exciting as anything you have seen in glass and steel. "The two wNw buildings originated from nature," says Vo Trong Nghia. "They now merge in harmony with nature. With time they will return to nature." This emphasis on the natural cycle, which still controls every living creature, immediately differentiates this architecture from most modern buildings. Be they nuclear reactors (the worst example) or downtown steel-and-glass towers, the works of contemporary architects and engineers are often erected as though they would never have to be torn down.

A willful call on traditional materials and methods surely characterizes a large number of the innovative architectural projects of the moment. A variant on this drive is the desire to find a proximity with nature, even if the building techniques concerned are not necessarily

3
al bordE, Atelier–Greenhouse,
Machachi, Ecuador, 2007

3

fully sustainable. The Berlin architects AFF created their 70-square-meter Protective Hut on Fichtelberg Mountain ("Hutznhaisl", Teller-häuser, Oberwiesenthal, Germany, 2008–09, page 72) in a marked effort to distance themselves from modern urban life. They made use of recycled materials and concrete forms that include casts of the former wooden hut on the site. Isolation from the modern world, even if it is formed in today's concrete shows a rejection of the systems and methods that have led to what can only be qualified as a certain architectural impasse.

AIR BETWEEN THE WALLS

The Ecuadorian architects al bordE also combine a sensitivity to the modern with traditional methods or, rather, questions about the directions of modern design. Two of their projects are published in this book. The first, the Entre Muros House (Tumbaco, Quito, Ecuador, 2007–08, page 78) is a 180-square-meter residence that cost just $50 000. It is built of rammed earth, wood, and stone, and incarnates a "search for living in harmony with nature." Gray water is used for irrigation, and solar energy to heat water. The raw materials of the adobe walls come from the site itself. The architects have also paid careful attention to customs such as a ceremony requesting the permission of the volcano to build on the site, and cutting wood and reeds at the appropriate phase of the moon. Here the forms are in harmony not only with nature, but also with modernity. This is also true of al bordE's Atelier–Greenhouse (Machachi, Ecuador, 2007, above), which measures just 47 square meters and cost only $16 200. This unusual structure combines stone, rammed earth, and a greenhouse, pitched above a solid base, a haven for flowers. The sun heats the gap between stone and earth, while other local materials like pine and eucalyptus provide not only economical solutions but also a firm and real connection to the earth and to this site.

The South African architects dhk completed the Ahmed Baba Institute (Sankore Precinct, Timbuktu, Mali, 2006–09, page 26) using an unusual combination of sun-baked mud-brick walls and concrete, glass, and metal. The 4800-square-meter structure was a gift to Mali from the Presidency of South Africa, decided under the rule of Thabo Mbeki. The architects have succeeded in demonstrating that a certain modernity is fully compatible with the use of more traditional materials and, above all, a site oriented on the Sankore Mosque. Far less heralded than such projects as Masdar City, this type of structure achieves a kind of equilibrium between worlds—between Africa and the West, but also between modernity and the very deep traditions that run through the architecture of the past in most of the world.

ROOM WITH A VIEW

The talented Japanese architect Kengo Kuma has sought in a very different way to adapt local architectural tradition to a contemporary building. His Yusuhara Marché (Yusuhara, Kochi, Japan, 2009–10, page 222) is a market building intended for the sale of local products that includes a small hotel. Kuma had the unexpected idea of creating a "curtain wall" formed with modules made of straw. He also made use of cedar logs, in both instances calling on locally produced materials that hark back to the traditions of the place. Imagine thinking carefully about how traditions and materials can be brought up to date for the purposes of a building completed in 2010.

4
*Massimiliano and Doriana Fuksas,
Admirant Entrance Building, Eindho-
ven, The Netherlands, 2008–10*

4

Two of the projects published here concern the observation of nature more than a specifically "natural" conception. The first of these is the Jübergtower (Hemer, Germany, 2010, page 96) by Stephan Birk (born in 1975) and Liza Heilmeyer (born the same year). Architecture, unlike art, usually requires a certain maturity and experience, and, thus, architects who are under 40 are the "youngsters" of the profession. The contribution of Birk & Heilmeyer Architekten is thus all the more interesting. Their 23.5-meter-high tower is intended as a landmark for a local garden and flower festival. A bit like the trees that visitors can observe as they ascend the structure, the mesh design becomes lighter and lighter as it rises to the nine-meter-wide, 360° observation deck. Like the concrete form of a mathematical formula, this structure has a natural but predictable progression, highlighted by the use of Siberian larch beams.

Hardly older than their colleagues, Klaus Loenhart and Christoph Mayr (from the German firm Terrain) conceived and built the Mur River Nature Observation Tower, completed in 2009 (Southern Styria, Austria, page 418). Built with a complex system of nodes and load-bearing tube-shaped members, the structure required 3D models and CNC manufacturing. In this instance, nature is approached through a product of contemporary technology—the proof that the only way forward is not to look back. The proximity to nature in this instance is the link between this and many other recent buildings that have sought the way to reestablish the bonds between human beings and nature that seem to have been diluted if not broken by the onslaught of modern engineering, and the consumer society.

BACK TO THE BLOB

So, ok, there are those who are with it and those who are not. There are architects who are out there trying to deal with the way the world turns and changes, and others who seem to be caught in a kind of time warp where the 1980s are still here. But they are real architects, and talented ones at that, sometimes as famous as they come. The Admirant Entrance Building (Eindhoven, The Netherlands, 2008–10, page 142) by Massimiliano and Doriana Fuksas is definitely a blast from the past, from the good old days of the blob. The architects describe the design of the Admirant Entrance Building as "fluid and amorphous" and compare it to a "marine mammal that erupts for air." It has no front or back, but rather a continuous building envelope wrapped around a five-story concrete structure. It is true that blob forms "erupted" on the architectural scene just as computers started to allow the machine to take precedence over more "standardized" forms of conception, and there is no real reason that such shapes should be totally abandoned. There is, indeed, no more reason for buildings to be rectilinear than there is for them to be fluid in their shapes, except that straight buildings make for straight indoor spaces, which can be an advantage when you are trying to put a desk against a wall presumably. In all due fairness to the architects, the Peres Peace House (Jaffa, Israel, 2005–09, page 136) has all the straight lines that didn't make it into the Eindhoven project. The difference between the two structures by the same architects might well be described as the reason that Massimiliano and Doriana Fuksas remain interesting and that their new work continues to attract attention and interest.

5
Frank O. Gehry, Cleveland Clinic
Lou Ruvo Center for Brain Health,
Las Vegas, Nevada, USA, 2005–10

ART IN VEGAS

Frank O. Gehry can be credited with inventing the building as sculpture with the Guggenheim Bilbao. Of course, there had been many sculptural buildings before this one, but the success of the Bilbao structure, made it the great architectural fantasy of the late 20th century. How to bring a city to life with a single, daring building—a conundrum that has been confronted by various provincial centers, at least since Gehry did the Nervion (River). It would seem high time that Gehry and Las Vegas got together, and that is just what happened in the Cleveland Clinic Lou Ruvo Center for Brain Health (Las Vegas, Nevada, USA, 2005–10, page 158). Though it is an eminently practical structure with all the facilities that one might expect in a high-end clinic, the Lou Ruvo Center takes Gehry's sculptural instincts a step further, where the geometric volumes of modernism have been put in a blender turned on "high." And out pops a remarkable jumble of forms, more art than architecture, unless Gehry has actually redefined the term and brought architecture far closer to art than it ever has been. The speculation should be left there, and the spectacle enjoyed for its intrinsic values.

Just as the Fuksas showed themselves capable of going from Admirant to Peres, Gehry, too, struck out in a markedly different direction with the Orchestral Academy (Miami Beach, Florida, USA, 2003–11, page 42), built in close discussion with the conductor Michael Tilson Thomas. Here Gehry has worked with the man of music to redefine the performance, surrounding it with banks of great large screens, allowing the seated performance to be carried elsewhere and higher, full not only of sound, but of images. Recalling certain other buildings like his American Center in Paris or his DG Bank Headquarters (Berlin, Germany, 2001), this home for the New World Symphony is less astonishing from the outside than the Lou Ruvo Center; it is inside that the break occurs. Like the gigantic horse head sculptural shape that confronts those who walk in from the staid Pariser Platz in Berlin to the DG Bank, the Orchestral Academy truly integrates large screens into its function and existence, bringing new dimensions to the musical performance, not a small feat for an architect.

SOMEWHERE, OVER THE RAINBOW

What is so interesting about *Architecture Now!* is that it comes in many different shapes, sizes, and types. The interest in sustainability may well be on the rise, but it is unlikely to become the real driving force of inventive architecture for the moment. There are still many architects who engage in form-giving, the traditional creative role of builders. True, the success of an architect like Frank Gehry has given great freedom to "artistic" architects, and those younger than him have taken full advantage. One of the best known of these is Zaha Hadid, whose quest has long been to break out of the box and through the glass ceiling that has constrained not only the forms of contemporary architecture, but also the role of women. The Pritzker Prize winner has achieved both of these marks of change, and one of her most recent works shows both her persistence and her ability to make "art" with her creative gestures. The 842-meter-long spans of the Sheikh Zayed Bridge in Abu Dhabi (UAE, 2003–11, page 166) were more than 13 years in the making. The astonishing, asymmetrical curves of the bridge posed significant engineering issues, but when the bridge opened to automobile traffic, it instantly became a landmark on the horizon of this Gulf emirate. Set not far from the great domes of the Sheikh Zayed Grand Mosque on the way into the city, Hadid's bridge stands out in the day-

6
*Jean Nouvel, Sofitel Vienna
Stephansdom-Stilwerk, Vienna,
Austria, 2006–10*

6

light, but also at night, when its colors change in a subtle chromatic progression. Hadid has long imagined and built her flowing curves in buildings new and old, but this is a first attempt to rethink one of the most basic of building types. Such unusual forms may not sweep the world of bridge design, but, in Abu Dhabi, she has posed the kinds of radical questions that have always characterized her work. Why does a bridge have to be dull when it can be a work of art in its own right?

A THOUSAND LINES OF VARIABLE ORIENTATION

Jean Nouvel has in many ways become the most outstanding international architect of the time, building from New York to Doha with equal inventiveness and enthusiasm. His Sofitel Vienna Stephansdom-Stilwerk in Vienna (Austria, 2006–10, page 310) shows in many respects why his work is so sought after. Like the Japanese architects of SANAA, he has taken on the realm of appearances, and used space, reflections, and color to create buildings that are on the fine edge between art and practicality. As is often the case, Nouvel wrote a brief introductory text about this hotel. His terms might well have been chosen to describe a complex sculpture, though it is true that he collaborated with the Swiss artist Pipilotti Rist for the back-lit ceiling paintings that participate actively in the overall impression of design that goes beyond the ordinary. Nouvel wrote: "So just imagine that starting with these curious constructible prisms, their planes begin to slide; intersections are created; one plane begins to tilt under the magnetic deviance of Hans Hollein while another decides to light the city from a ceiling made of furtive images. Imagine that the other planes begin to vibrate with a thousand lines of variable orientation and reflectivity, that gray sometimes melts into gray squares on a gray background. It is not surprising then to find that the oblique plan of the roof becomes hatched, weaving a tight, random pattern of parallelograms and lozenges, that the planes to the North take the form of granited glass for transparence; that the planes to the West cloak themselves in variations of black to display their shadows. At the limit between building and sky there is another, flat plane that reveals the appearance–disappearance of changing faces, an evocation of the multiple faces forever linked to the depth of imagery born of this city."

ENVIRONMENT, ART, ARCHITECTURE

Ryue Nishizawa, one of the principals of SANAA, has also completed a work that is very much at the frontier between art and architecture, realized in this instance in collaboration with the noted artist Rei Naito. His Teshima Art Museum (Teshima Island, Kagawa, Japan, 2009–10, page 304) is a 2300-square-meter free-form curve of a building. The vast thin concrete shell of the structure, open in places to the sky, is, indeed, precisely the "powerful architectural space" that Nishizawa speaks about. When Nishizawa states "our goal is to generate a fusion of the environment, art, and architecture, and we hope these three elements work together as a single entity," he renders explicit the ambition that is latent or stated in so much of contemporary architecture. The difference between Nishizawa and some others is that he has succeeded in crossing the invisible threshold between mere ambition and success.

7
*Ryue Nishizawa, Teshima Art
Museum, Teshima Island, Kagawa,
Japan, 2009–10*

7

Two other interesting projects published here flirt with the limits between art and architecture, or rather seek to use architecture in a symbolic and essentially minimal way. Arata Isozaki's Obscured Horizon (Pioneertown, California, USA, 2008–10, page 196) project for Eba and Jerry Sohn in the Mojave Desert consists in a series of three, very reduced structures that are related to the seasons. Like other noted Japanese architects including the younger Shigeru Ban, Isozaki has long been interested in the very definitions of architecture. Just what constitutes a building? Might it be a simple concrete slab as is the case here? And when is a building "as high as the sky"? In a powerful natural setting, Isozaki's nine-square-meter structures are just about as close to nature as one can get, despite being made with modern materials.

NEVER-ENDING JOURNEY

On a more ambitious scale, the Ruta del Peregrino (Route of the pilgrim) from Ameca to Talpa de Allende (Jalisco, Mexico, 2009–11, page 446), curated by the architects Tatiana Bilbao and Derek Dellekamp, is a group of very interesting and essentially minimal and sculptural interventions by Tatiana Bilbao (Mexico), Christ & Gantenbein AG Architekten (Switzerland), Dellekamp Arquitectos (Mexico), Elemental (Chile), Godoylab (Mexico), Fake Design (China), HHF architects (Switzerland), Periférica (Mexico), and Taller TOA (Mexico). These works are located along a 117-kilometer-long pilgrimage route that attracts tens of thousands every year. The Gratitude Open Chapel (Dellekamp Arquitectos, Tatiana Bilbao, 2009) is located near the beginning of the route. According to the architects: "The four walls evoke an unfinished Chapel creating a continuously changing scenario of shadows cast on this landscape otherwise filled with sun; spaces created by moving shadows hold the pilgrims to allow them to pause and rest." A second almost purely abstract structure on the route is the Void Temple (Dellekamp Arquitectos, Periférica, 2009), described by its architects in the following terms: "The circle is a universal symbol of unity, a meaning that transcends cultures, borders, and languages. It appears time and time again within the religious rituals and depictions, from the halo of holy figures to the shape of the host given during communion. It also represents a cycle, a never-ending journey that symbolizes the faith of the pilgrims that travel. The circle offers a place of reflection, for the pilgrim to look back upon his journey, before continuing on to his final destination." These forms, the circle of the Void Temple, the uplifting walls of the Gratitude Open Chapel, show that architecture that is not specifically "useful" can attain a kind of spirituality which is certainly what the many pilgrims seek on the Ruta.

RGB LED

The question of just where art and architecture meet, or indeed of when one becomes the other, has long preoccupied architects (and artists). One unusual example seen here is the work of the Brazilian illustrator and designer Muti Randolph. His works "Tube" (The Creators Project, Galeria Baró, São Paulo, Brazil, 2010, page 344) and "Deep Screen" (The Creators Project, Beijing, China, 2010, page 346) make use of the most basic of architectural devices—the grid—combined with devices such as RGB LED clusters to create illusions of space and movement that are intimately related with the built form. With these small works, of less than 20 square meters, Muti Randolph boldly proposes to the spectator to put himself inside the work, all the better to experience its explosions of color and change. When sound synthesized

8

8
*Maurer United, Indemann Watchtower,
Inden, Germany, 2009*

in conjunction with the light display is added to the mix, Randolph succeeds in creating a complete environment. In this instance, it might be admitted that there is more art than architecture; nonetheless, the perception of these pieces does rely on a certain familiarity with the grid as it were.

The idea of the light show as an architectural expression takes a different turn with the Indemann Watchtower (Inden, Germany, 2009, page 264) by the Dutch architects Maurer United. Located near the A4 motorway between Aachen and Cologne, the work is no less than 36 meters tall and holds an array of 40 000 LEDs that can be programmed by a computer. The architects call this "social media architecture" as it is located in a former mining area that is due for redevelopment. Though both works, those of Muti Randolph and of Maurer United, seek to combine essentially architectural forms with massive accumulations of LEDs, it is clear that the Indemann Tower comes closer to the usual definition of buildings. In both instances, despite the difference of scale, the idea of sculpture is not far from the works concerned. A modest and completely ephemeral one in Brazil, a rather massive and robotic piece in Germany.

SPICING UP THE RUINS

Economics and the realization that many older buildings were probably more solid than today's "modern" ones have led to a logical rise in the number of renovations that are being made for various purposes. Two examples published here concern hotels. Both make use of the preexisting structures in interesting ways that probably say a good deal about the spirit of the times. In Shanghai, local architects Neri & Hu completed The Waterhouse at South Bund in 2010 (China, page 290). With just 19 rooms, this trendy boutique hotel makes use of what was left of a 1930s three-story Japanese Army headquarters building. In a sense taking a page from David Chipperfield's work on the Neues Museum (Museum Island, Berlin, Germany, 1997–2009), where the ruins of the existing building were reinstated and subtle restauration work kept traces of past events legible, Neri & Hu have left quite a bit of the rough surfaces of the "host" building much as they were. Adding an unexpected touch of a sort of voyeurism that allows peeks into private rooms from public spaces, they also made additions using the kind of Cor-ten steel that a sculptor like Richard Serra employs. This is not what the French call *misérabiliste*—it is a very hip take on what it requires to be contemporary today, especially in a design hotel.

Michel da Costa Conçalves (born in 1973) and Nathalie Rozencwajg (born in 1975) are the cofounders of the London-based firm rare architecture. Their Town Hall Hotel (Patriot Square, London, UK, 2008–10, page 352) is a larger (98-room) hotel built in the old Bethnal Green Town Hall in London's East End. In this instance, a contemporary wing and a top floor were added at the same time as the Grade II listed 1910 Edwardian building was restored. The new spaces are wrapped in a patterned laser-cut aluminum skin with no windows or doors visible. This restoration and updating is by no means as "rough-edged" as The Waterhouse project, but it proceeds from many of the same ideas, bringing a real presence of the spirit of the times to an old building, and, above all, giving it a new, productive life.

9
REX, Museum Plaza, Louisville,
Kentucky, USA, 2007–

9

In a city such as Paris, where architecturally interesting new construction within the historic perimeter is relatively rare, Manuelle Gautrand has successfully undertaken the renovation of the historic Théâtre de la Gaîté Lyrique (France, 2007–10). With a large €62 million budget, Gautrand completely refitted the 19th-century structure to make it viable for 21st-century performances. The flexibility and technological adaptation of the building allows its program, "dedicated to digital culture and music," to be generously housed in the 9500-square-meter facility. Just as she did with her Citroën building on the Champs-Élysées (the Avenue itself and the Citroën brand), Gautrand here shows her capacity to fit into a sensitive historic environment and in a sense to make old France new again.

ONCE AND FUTURE KING

A completely different kind of use of an existing structure was imagined by one of the rising stars of architecture in the United States, Joshua Prince-Ramus. Prince-Ramus was the founding partner of OMA (Rem Koolhaas) in New York and partner in charge of such significant projects as the Seattle Central Library. The architect created his present firm REX out of the former OMA New York office. His Vakko Fashion Center (Istanbul, Turkey, 2008–10, page 366) involved the complete conversion of the concrete skeleton of an unfinished and abandoned hotel into a headquarters of two related firms working in the fashion and music industries. The client needed a very fast delivery for the project, and REX actually managed to commence construction four days after being approached by Vakko and Power Media. With such complex problems as the seismic resistance of the existing skeleton to consider, Joshua Prince-Ramus conceived a steel-box system that allowed for considerable variety in the final design of interior spaces, dubbed the "Showcase." Wrapping the whole in a thin glass envelope likened to "Saran Wrap," REX met the unusual requirements of the client for this 9000-square-meter structure while creating one of the most frequently published buildings of the past two years. OMA and Koolhaas, through their Rotterdam office in particular, have been the source of a number of rising talents in contemporary architecture. Because of his own background, Joshua Prince-Ramus, formerly identified with OMA, has come forward as a major new independent talent on the US scene; this at a time when the fading stars of another generation were not being replaced in any obvious way.

YOUNG AND RESTLESS

Though not every architect can appear to spring onto the world scene as a star like Joshua Prince-Ramus, there continue to be very gifted younger talents that come to the fore every year, in spite of the economic difficulties that have been a part of the equation since 2008. These architects either turn such problems to their advantage, or simply make do with a harsh environment for anything that goes beyond ordinary "functional" buildings. Three examples from different horizons can be cited here. Todd Saunders was born in 1969 in Gander, Newfoundland. He studied at McGill University (Montreal, Canada, 1993–95) and the Nova Scotia College of Art and Design (1988–92). Based in Bergen, Norway, he recently returned to his native Canada to design a number of artist's studios for the Shorefast Foundation and the Fogo Island Arts Corporation. The Long Studio (Fogo Island, Newfoundland, Canada, 2010, page 382), designed for an artist's residency program on an isolated site, shows how architecture can make a difference in a building that might otherwise have been quite ordinary. Though only

120 square meters in size, the building's long black silhouette voluntarily contrasts with its shoreline site. The white interior contrasts with this dark skin. Set partially up on thin pilotis, the Long Studio is something of an alien presence here, and yet it allows artists to live very much in the midst of a powerful natural setting.

The Swiss architect Laurent Savioz was born in 1976 and received his degree in architecture from the Haute École Spécialisée (HES) of Fribourg (1998). He created his present firm in 2005 with Claude Fabrizzi, who was born in 1975 in Sierre, Switzerland. The pair's most recent work, a school and a house in the valleys leading up to Verbier in the Valais region of Switzerland, shows a powerful originality within relatively strict parameters. Their Primary School (Vollèges, Switzerland, 2009–10, page 394) is a powerful concrete building whose faceted, slightly angled exterior surfaces seem to obviate its mass and to allow it to shift slightly even as it is being observed. Concrete, also, is nearly omnipresent inside, though wood floors and generous windows soften stony hardness. Their Val d'Entremont House (Val d'Entremont, Switzerland, 2009–10, page 398) would appear to be even harder, with its ample use of concrete, stainless steel, and glass. Set in a traditional mountain village, this house has an undeniable coldness that allows its residents to observe the natural and architectural environment from a certain remove. The participation of the house in its architectural context is one of observation and penetration, in an almost voyeuristic way. This house seems to be both powerful and vulnerable because of its openness, its nudity as it were. Angles and space are often unexpected. These young architects give the already time-worn concept of the Swiss Box (a concrete, geometric type of architecture) new meaning.

Kulapat Yantrasast, born in 1968 in Thailand, received his M.Arch degree and Ph.D degrees from the University of Tokyo. He created wHY Architecture in 2003 in Culver City, California, with Yo-ichiro Hakomori. Yantrasast might in some sense be compared to Prince-Ramus because he made a considerable reputation for himself as one of the main collaborators of Tadao Ando in Osaka, but also on the Japanese architect's US projects, such as the Modern Art Museum of Fort Worth. The L&M Arts Los Angeles gallery in Venice, California, (USA, 2009–10, page 19) designed by wHY Architecture, is an intriguing contrast between the refurbishment of a 1929 power station and the construction of a strongly geometric, recycled brick gallery with an exposed timber roof. Between renovation and new construction, Yantrasast succeeds in blurring the boundaries that normally separate the old and the new, in itself a considerable architectural achievement. Whereas Joshua Prince-Ramus appears to have handily adopted the heroic approach of Koolhaas, it can be said that Yantrasast has learned greatly from the modesty that inhabits Tadao Ando's best work. Savioz on the other hand is firmly anchored in his native Switzerland, which does not keep him from being simultaneously strong and subtle in his realizations. With creators such as these, the next generation of major contemporary architects already appears to be coming to the fore.

REASON AND MODESTY

Times of upheaval and change will surely have their influence on contemporary architecture. Ecological catastrophe such as that engendered by the failure of the Fukushima Daiichi nuclear reactors certainly drives home the point that the possibilities of technology and

10
*wHY Architecture, L&M Arts
Los Angeles, Venice, California,
USA, 2009–10*

engineering are not limitless. Quite the contrary, as the *Guardian* suggested in March 2011, the havoc wrought by the Japanese earthquake shows how thin an edge we live on. Rather than expansion and rising consumption, reason and modesty may well be the key words of years to come. And architecture must surely be in the forefront of the massive adjustment that will be imposed by nature if it is not grasped in time by those who design and build. Nor do mud bricks and bamboo need to be restricted to the third world. Americans and Emiratis, to cite just two examples, might do well to reduce their carbon footprints, and not just with sand-covered photovoltaic cells. And so the old guard of architectural heroes is starting to pass and a new generation is rising, with a different agenda and a different understanding. This does not make for any less excitement and sense of discovery in contemporary architecture, quite the contrary. This is *Architecture Now!*

EINLEITUNG

EIN SCHMALER GRAT

Stellen Sie sich eine Zeit der Widersprüche und Kriege vor, Tumulte in der arabischen Welt und eine zehn Meter hohe Welle der Zerstörung in Japan. Wir schreiben Anfang 2011, und die meisten großen Wirtschaftsstaaten haben nach wie vor mit der Rezession zu kämpfen. Die Nachrichten, ganz gleich ob politischer, geologischer oder wirtschaftlicher Art, zeugen kaum von Stabilität. Der Tsunami in Japan hat viele Holzhäuser zerstört, doch selbst die ungleich massiveren Betonbauten der Reaktoren des Atomkraftwerks Fukushima Daiichi waren den Naturgewalten nicht gewachsen. Vielleicht ist eine Geschichte der Erdbeben, Kriege, Zerstörung und des Wiederaufbaus in Japan einer der Gründe, warum die zeitgenössische Architektur hier so besonders lebendig ist. Als Frank Lloyd Wright das Imperial Hotel in Tokio (1915–23) baute, glaubte er fälschlicherweise, sein Bau würde auf dem Schwemmgrund „wie ein Schlachtschiff auf dem Wasser treiben". Nach dem Großen Kantō-Erdbeben vom 1. September 1923 (7,9 auf der Richterskala), das Tokio und Yokohama verwüstete, wurde das Hotel jedoch trotz anfänglich gegenteiliger Versicherungen schwer beschädigt. Und nun stelle man sich vor, dass eine Stadt, die bereits 1923 so schwer durch ein Erdbeben zerstört und wieder aufgebaut worden war, im Februar und März 1945 mit Brandbomben überzogen wurde. Allein in der Nacht vom 9. auf den 10. März 1945 zerstörten 200 B-29-Bomber 41 km² der japanischen Hauptstadt, über 100 000 Menschen kamen ums Leben.

DIE NEUE INSTABILITÄT

Wie eigenartig, dass heute Naturgewalten und wirtschaftliche Unwägbarkeiten ähnliche Folgen haben – Unsicherheit ist zum Schlagwort unserer Zeit geworden. Zweifellos begreifen viele Architekten das als Impuls, flüchtigere Spuren zu hinterlassen und stärker auf ephemere Bauweisen zu setzen. Seit radioaktive Strahlung mit dem Regen auf die Erde fällt, ist sogar denkbar, dass ökologische Überlegungen endlich Gehör finden. Einige in diesem Band vorgestellte Projekte sind recht radikal und umfassend in ihrem Bemühen um ökologische Nachhaltigkeit. Auch Sanierungen und temporäre Bauten scheinen auf dem Vormarsch zu sein. Sie profitieren einerseits von der soliden Bauweise von Altbauten, andererseits von der Option, sich schneller errichten zu lassen und wieder zu verschwinden, als ein durchschnittliches Atomkraftwerk. Als Francis Fukuyama das „Ende der Geschichte" verkündete (*The End of History and the Last Man*, 1992), dachten manche, die „Globalisierung" oder vielmehr der globale Kapitalismus trete ihre bzw. seine unangefochtene Vormachtstellung an. Doch könnte es sein, dass sich der Kalte Krieg, Höhepunkt einer sich rasend verbreitenden Moderne, von nachhaltigerer Bedeutung für die Architektur erweisen sollte als die Säumnisse und Niederlagen des frühen 21. Jahrhunderts? Als sich zwei mächtige politische und wirtschaftliche Blöcke unversöhnlich gegenüberstanden und der Wiederaufbau nach dem Zweiten Weltkrieg suggerierte, die Welt ließe sich neu erfinden, herrschte oft Optimismus, gab es Glauben an die Zukunft. Dies alles ist verschwunden, ebenso wie die Berliner Mauer. Wie eigenartig, dass jetzt wieder neue Mauern in aller Welt errichtet werden, von Gaza bis zur Grenze zwischen Mexiko und den Vereinigten Staaten.

LEBEN IN DER SMARAGDSTADT

Was wäre, wenn die neuen Herrscher der Welt – Milliardäre und Diktatoren – enthüllt würden als die Hochstapler, die sie tatsächlich sind: als *Zauberer von Oz* in der Smaragdstadt? Der für den Entwurf des Burj Khalifa (2004–10) verantwortliche Architekt Adrian Smith gesteht, dass bei seinem Konzept die Türme der Smaragdstadt aus der Filmversion des Zauberer von Oz Pate gestanden haben. „Das hatte ich im Kopf, als ich am Entwurf für den Burj Khalifa arbeitete", erzählt Smith, „wenn auch eher unbewusst". „Ich habe nicht recherchiert, wie [die Smaragdstadt] aussieht. Ich erinnerte mich nur an die gläserne, kristalline Struktur, die scheinbar aus dem Nichts heraus in die Höhe wuchs. Das Seltsame ist, dass ich mich offenbar nicht daran erinnert habe, dass die Stadt grün war." Inzwischen steht das höchste je von Menschenhand errichtete Bauwerk (828 m) überwiegend leer, ein Opfer der Krise in Dubai. Doch da Hybris gemeinhin wesentlich langlebiger ist als jedes Bauwerk, wird sicher bald jemand ein noch höheres Gebäude errichten. Dennoch bleibt die Frage: Werden die Träume von grenzenlosem Wohlstand und von immer neuen Grenzüberschreitungen in der Architektur die heutige Zeit der Instabilität überleben? Als man den bedeutenden Architekten Arata Isozaki 1991 nach dem Platzen der Immobilienblase fragte, was sich in Japan ändern würde, antwortete er mit einem Lächeln: „Keine verrückten kleinen Häuser mehr!" Auch wenn sich seine Vorhersage nicht gänzlich bewahrheiten sollte, trifft sicher zu, dass begrenzte Mittel zu größerer architektonischer Strenge führen, während beliebig verfügbare Gelder eher zur Opulenz ermutigen. In Zeiten, in denen Naturkatastrophen und wirtschaftliche Krisen Hand in Hand gehen, mag man sich fragen, ob innovative Architekten bald als Taxifahrer in New York arbeiten werden. Oder werden ökologische Desaster und kollabierende Banken manche dazu veranlassen, bei ihren Entwürfen und Bauvorhaben nach größerer Besonnenheit zu streben und uns womöglich eine ruhigere, grünere Zukunft bescheren?

AUSSER KONTROLLE

Ein weitsichtiger Artikel, erschienen am 18. März 2011 in der Londoner Tageszeitung *The Guardian*[1], brachte die Ereignisse um das Erdbeben in Japan auf den Punkt und deutete an, wozu solche Katastrophen mitunter führen können: „Was diese Ereignisse deutlich machen ist, auf welch schmalem Grat die Moderne sich bewegt. Kein Land der Welt ist moderner und zivilisierter als Japan; die dortigen Bauvorschriften und ingenieurtechnische Leistungsfähigkeit haben große Bauten vor dem Zusammensturz bewahrt, während das wesentlich schwächere Erdbeben in Haiti letztes Jahr so gut wie alles zerstört hat. Doch offenbar reicht das nicht. Der schmale Grat, auf dem wir leben, und den wir zumeist nicht einmal bewusst wahrnehmen, bietet nicht annähernd genügend Schutz vor den Gewalten der Natur." Der Autor stellt, wenn auch nur andeutungsweise, eine Verbindung zwischen Naturkatastrophen wie diesen und den vom Menschen ausgelösten Folgen der globalen Erwärmung her. Er impliziert, wir könnten die Grenzen der menschlichen Bautechnik im weitesten Sinne erreicht haben. „Vielleicht ist dies nicht die richtige Woche, um den großartigen Versprechungen von Ingenieuren Glauben zu schenken – nicht jetzt, wo wir gerade fast jede Kontrolle über die hoch entwickeltste Technologie verloren haben, die wir je entwickelt haben, dort in Fukushima. Die Alternative ist, kleiner zu bauen und auf Stabilität zu setzen, auf Sicherheit. Und um das zu tun – jetzt wird es kontrovers – müssten wir beschließen, dass unser menschliches Streben (zumindest im Westen) inzwischen weit genug gegangen ist, dass unser Appetit nicht größer, sondern kleiner werden muss, um uns ein wenig mehr Spielraum zu verschaffen."

Die Architektur ist im Großen und Ganzen der Wachstumskurve der Konsumgesellschaften gefolgt: immer mehr, immer höher. Erstaunlicherweise jedoch haben Architekten, angestoßen durch Impulse aus Gesellschaft und Wirtschaft, ihren alten Traum vom Errichten „ewiger" Bauwerke aufgegeben, die eine Lebensdauer gotischer Kathedralen versprachen. Sie waren bereit, immer billigere und instabilere Bauten zu entwerfen, überzeugt, dass Langlebigkeit nichts sei, was die Welt heute braucht. Der *Guardian* jedoch argumentiert genau entgegengesetzt und schreibt: „Plötzlich klingen gesetzte und hausbackene Schlagworte – ‚langlebig', ‚stabil', ‚robust' – wieder attraktiver in unseren Ohren."

SO WIE ES IST

Die Reihe *Architecture Now!* präsentiert ein breites Spektrum zeitgenössischer Architektur. In der Vergangenheit hat die Architekturkritik immer wieder versucht, Schulen zu definieren und zu fördern, so etwa, als Philip Johnson und Henry-Russell Hitchcock 1932 ihre berühmte Ausstellung *Modern Architecture: International Exhibition* am Museum of Modern Art konzipierten. Im Mittelpunkt der Ausstellung standen Entwürfe von Le Corbusier, Mies van der Rohe, Neutra, Gropius und Wright, begleitend erschien die einflussreiche Publikation *The International Style*. In jüngerer Zeit (und von ungleich kürzerer Lebensdauer) war das Loblied, das Charles Jencks auf die Postmoderne sang, die sich letztlich als kosmetisches, oberflächliches Phänomen erweisen sollte. Und so vertritt *Architecture Now!* keine spezifischen Trends, sondern präsentiert vielmehr neue Bauten aus aller Welt, bewusst eine Mischung verschiedener Stile und Bautypen. Auf eine einfache Formel gebracht: Architektur, so wie sie heute ist. Zeiten der Unruhe und des Fragens dürften dafür sorgen, dass dies in den kommenden Jahren kaum anders sein wird. Heute kann jeder jede Menge Architektur im Internet finden, weshalb es bei *Architecture Now!* um Auswahl geht, darum zu zeigen was gut ist, ohne Festlegung auf bestimmte Schulen, ohne dabei Zwängen oder Einflüssen entsprechen zu müssen. Dies ist eine kritische Auswahl ohne zwingende Prämissen: Ganz einfach so, wie es ist.

STAMPFLEHM UND BAMBUSPFÄHLE

Was wäre, wenn sich ökologisch nachhaltige Architektur weniger in aufwendigen Labors fände, in denen die neuesten Solarzellen entwickelt werden, sondern vielmehr in Teilen der Welt, in denen Menschen ökologisch handeln, um überleben zu können? Maartje Lammers und Boris Zeisser vom Rotterdamer Büro 24H Architecture haben sich mit ihrem Projekt für die Panyaden School (Chiang Mai, Thailand, 2010–11, Seite 50) ganz diesem Ansatz verschrieben und bauten Wände aus Stampflehm und Dächer aus Bambus. Unterrichtet werden hier Fächer wie Weben oder lokale Techniken des Landbaus, es ist ein Ansatz, der buddhistische Philosophie und gesunden Menschenverstand verbindet. Während sich manche Architekten damit brüsten, die Emissionen ihrer Bauten um wenige Prozentpunkte gesenkt zu haben, gelingt es 24H, einen „kaum merklichen" ökologischen Fußabdruck zu hinterlassen, und das dank überwiegend traditioneller Bautechniken.

Die ebenfalls hier vorgestellte Green School (Badung, Bali, Indonesien, 2007, Seite 64) ist ein Entwurf des indonesischen Architekten Effan Adhiwira, der sein Büro auf Bali hat. Die hinter der Schule stehende Initiative hat es sich zur Aufgabe gemacht, Kindern die Grundsätze einer nachhaltigen Lebensweise zu vermitteln. Der Entwurf zeichnet sich besonders durch seine Bambussäulen aus, deren Sockel Natursteine aus einem Flussbett sind, und durch sein mächtiges, überhängendes Dach, das vor der Sonne schützt. Der Architekt erklärt: „Unsere Architektur lässt sich von den natürlichen Eigenschaften der Bambuspfähle inspirieren. Wir wollen die Spannweite von Bambuskonstruktionen maximieren und die natürliche ‚Biegungs-/Spannungs'-Ratio der Pfähle optimieren, um organisch-natürlich anmutende Bauten entwerfen zu können." Wie etliche der hier vorgestellten Projekte wurde auch die Green School von der Jury des Aga-Khan-Preises für Architektur als

11
Effan Adhiwira, Green School,
Badung, Bali, Indonesia, 2007

bedeutendes Bauwerk eingestuft und auf die Shortlist für den Aga-Khan-Preis 2010 aufgenommen. Die Einschätzung der Jury bekräftigt: „Hier kommt lokal und nachhaltig angebauter Bambus zum Einsatz, der auf innovative und experimentelle Weise verwendet wird und belegt, welches architektonische Potenzial das Material birgt. So entstand eine ganzheitliche, grüne Gemeinschaft mit dem wichtigen pädagogischen Anliegen, Schüler zu Neugier anzuregen und sich engagierter und leidenschaftlicher für die Umwelt und den Planeten einzusetzen."

RUNTERSCHALTEN

Ein weiterer interessanter Brückenschlag zwischen Europa und der islamischen Welt ist die 390 m² große Ecolodge in Siwa, Ägypten (2006–07, Seite 110), von Christian Félix und Laetitia Delubac (FELIX-DELUBAC). Das Wüstenhotel wurde aus *kershef* gebaut, einer Mischung aus Lehm, Sand und sonnengetrocknetem Salz. „Radikaler" jedoch ist in gewisser Weise der Windfänger des Belüftungssystems und die Tatsache, dass es im Hotel keinen Strom gibt. Zurzeit arbeiten die Architekten an einem Passivhaus in der Normandie – einem Holzhaus mit Reetdach. Wer die Normandie kennt, wird diese Dächer unmittelbar mit der pittoresken Region in Nordfrankreich in Verbindung bringen. Die Architekten, beide Mitte der 1970er-Jahre geboren, haben vor gut zehn Jahren ihr Studium an der Architekturfakultät Villemin in Paris abgeschlossen und zeigen sich auch in der Normandie fasziniert von traditionellen Materialien und Baumethoden. Offenbar ist es in Mode, traditionell zu sein.

Der Aga-Khan-Preis für Architektur und seine Schwesterorganisation, das Aga-Khan-Programm für historische Städte, haben das Interesse auf die Entwürfe von Diébédo Francis Kéré gelenkt, einem in Burkina Faso geborenen Architekten. Die von ihm in seinem Heimatort geplante Grundschule (Gando, Burkina Faso, 2001) wurde 2004 mit dem Aga-Khan-Preis ausgezeichnet. Die Projektbeschreibung zur Preisverleihung fasst zusammen: „Um Nachhaltigkeit zu erzielen, folgte das Projekt dem Prinzip, klimatischen Komfort mithilfe kostengünstiger Baumethoden zu erreichen. Hierfür wurden lokal verfügbare Materialien und Fachkenntnisse der Anwohnerschaft vor Ort bestmöglich genutzt; Technologien der industrialisierten Welt kamen in vereinfachter Form zum Einsatz. Zugleich war der Entwurf ein Musterbeispiel, das bei der lokalen Bevölkerung ein Bewusstsein für die Vorzüge traditioneller Baumaterialien schaffen sollte." Diébédo Francis Kéré war der Erste in seinem Heimatort Gando, einer Kleinstadt mit 3000 Einwohnern, der eine höhere Ausbildung absolvierte; er studierte an der Technischen Universität Berlin. Kérés Formensprache wurzelt in afrikanischen Traditionen, wobei auffällt, dass ein technisch orientiertes, westliches Architekturstudium durchaus kompatibel mit einem nachhaltigen, von traditionellen Formen inspirierten Stil ist. Das von Kéré entworfene Earthen Architecture Center (Zentrum für Lehmbauarchitektur, Mopti, Mali, 2010, Seite 37) ist ein 476 m² großer Komplex. Realisiert wurde der Bau mit Unterstützung des Aga-Khan-Programms für Kultur und historische Städte im Anschluss an die Sanierung einer Moschee und eines neuen Abwassersystems für Mopti. Elemente des Entwurfs sind u.a. Stampflehmziegel und eine schwebende Dachkonstruktion. Die Belüftung des Gebäudes erfolgt ohne technische Systeme.

STAUBIGE ZUKUNFT

In den Emiraten von Abu Dhabi sah der Traum von Nachhaltigkeit ganz anders aus als bei diesen Projekten. Zugegeben, das Klima am Golf ist eine Herausforderung, die offenbar hohen Stromverbrauch mit sich bringt. Dort sollte bis 2016 Masdar City als 22 Milliarden Dollar teure, 6 km² große Stadt für 45 000 Einwohner und 1500 Unternehmen entstehen. Ziel war es, ausschließlich erneuerbare Energien zu nutzen und keine CO_2-Emissionen und Abfälle zu erzeugen. In Zusammenarbeit mit dem MIT sollte das Masdar Institute of Science & Technology Solarenergie produzieren, vorwiegend mit vor Ort produzierten Photovoltaikelementen. Ein erstes überrraschendes Problem ergab sich, als man herausfand, dass Abu Dhabis häufige Staubstürme die Leistung der Solarzellen um 40% reduzieren würden. Es kam zu zahlreichen Rücktritten und schlechter Presse; der Termin der Fertigstellung für Masdar wurde auf 2020 verschoben, Strom wird man letztlich doch importieren müssen.

In dieser Atmosphäre haben Foster + Partners den ersten großen Bau der Stadt fertiggestellt, das Masdar Institute (Abu Dhabi, VAE, 2008–10, Seite 118). Niemand wird die Effizienz der hier angewandten Passivstrategien, wie Ausrichtung und zeitgenössische Varianten von Windfängertürmen anzweifeln, doch diese gibt es schon seit Jahrhunderten. Die eingesetzten Photovoltaiksysteme werden ihren langfristigen Nutzen noch unter Beweis stellen müssen. Auch der Traum von einer Stadt mit einer CO_2-Nullbilanz mitten in der Wüste könnte sich mehr als Fatamorgana denn als heute realisierbares Phänomen erweisen. Man muss sich nur vorstellen, dass dieses Land keinen Zugang zu Frischwasser hat, Sommertemperaturen von 50°C und einen ökologischen Fußabdruck pro Kopf, der weltweit der höchste ist.

LAGE IST ALLES

2007 konnte das 300 m² große Palmyra House (Nandgaon, Maharashtra, Indien, 2006–07, Seite 412) von Studio Mumbai unter der Leitung von Bijoy Jain fertig gestellt werden. Auch dieses Projekt kam 2010 auf die Shortlist für den Aga-Khan-Preis für Architektur. Die anlässlich des Preises verfasste Projektbeschreibung betont besonders die Nachhaltigkeit des Wohnhauses, das eher auf Tradition und „authentische" Materialien setzt als auf komplexe Technologien und damit seinen ökologischen Fußabdruck minimieren will. „Die Funktionen des Hauses sind in zwei gegeneinander versetzten, rechteckigen Baukörpern untergebracht, deren Fassaden besonders durch die Sonnenschutzblenden aus dem Holz der heimischen Palmyra-Palme geprägt sind. Das Tragwerk besteht aus Ain-Holz [einem lokalen Hartholz]; die Einfassungsmauern, Fundamente und Wege aus heimischem Basalt. Dem Putz wurde Sand vom Bauplatz als farbiges Pigment zugeschlagen. Entwurf und bauliche Details – Ergebnis einer Kollaboration zwischen Architekt und ortsansässigen Handwerkern – setzte auf bewährte (lokale und auswärtige) Techniken und adaptierte sie für technisch aufwändigere Bauformen. Das Haus fügt sich optimal in sein Umfeld: die Sonnenschutzlamellen sorgen für passive Kühlung, ebenso wie der Schatten der Kokosnusspalmen. Wasser für das Haus wird auf dem Gelände in drei Brunnen gesammelt, gefiltert und in einem Wasserturm gespeichert, der das Haus durch natürlichen, gefällebedingten Wasserdruck versorgt. Resultat dieser Maßnahmen ist ein Projekt, das auf stille Weise zu faszinieren weiß und umfassend in die Landschaft integriert ist."[2]

Vielleicht gewinnt der eine oder andere Leser den Eindruck, viele der hier vorgestellten Projekte lägen in weiter Ferne oder der „Dritten Welt", dabei ist es vielmehr so, dass sich einige sehr talentierte junge Architekten mit traditioneller Architektur und deren Potenzial befassen. Schließlich wird mehr und mehr deutlich, dass zahlreiche Probleme unserer heutigen Gesellschaften – ob nun industrialisiert oder nicht – womöglich besser zu lösen sind, indem man mit modernen Augen in die Vergangenheit blickt, statt um jeden Preis immer auf dem neusten Stand der Technik sein zu wollen. Wie der *Guardian* anmerkte, war das Kernkraftwerk Fukushima Daiichi in mancherlei Hinsicht der Inbegriff höchster Ingenieurleistung und hat sich dennoch als erschütternd unzulänglich erwiesen. Was sagt uns das?

12
Studio Mumbai, Palmyra House,
Nandgaon, Maharashtra, India,
2006–07

12

ASCHE ZU ASCHE

Vo Trong Nghia, geboren 1976 in Vietnam, ist nicht nur Architekt, sondern auch Ingenieur. Sein Studium der Bauingenieurwissenschaften absolvierte er an der Universität Tokio. Die wNw Bar (Binh Duong, Vietnam, 2008, Seite 454) ist eine Bogenkonstruktion aus Bambus, die ihm erlaubte, eine 10 m hohe Kuppel mit einem Durchmesser von 15 m zu realisieren. Die neben dem wNw Café gelegene Bar ist der Beleg, dass Bambusarchitektur ebenso aufregend sein kann wie Bauten aus Glas und Stahl. „Die beiden wNw-Bauten entwickelten sich aus der Natur", erklärt Vo Trong Nghia. „Inzwischen verschmelzen sie absolut harmonisch mit ihr. Mit der Zeit werden sie wieder zu Natur werden." Diese Betonung des Naturkreislaufs, der nach wie vor alle Lebewesen bestimmt, unterscheidet diese Art von Architektur unmittelbar von den meisten modernen Bauten. Ob es sich nun um Atomkraftwerke handelt (das wohl negativste Beispiel) oder um Hochhäuser aus Glas und Stahl, oft wirken die Entwürfe zeitgenössischer Architekten und Ingenieure, als ginge man davon aus, sie nie wieder abreißen zu müssen.

Ohne Frage zeichnen sich zur Zeit eine Vielzahl innovativer Architekturprojekte durch Rückgriffe auf traditionelle Baumaterialien und -methoden aus. Eine weitere Spielart dieser Tendenz ist der Wunsch nach mehr Nähe zur Natur, auch bei Bautechniken, die nicht zwingend nachhaltig sind. Die 70 m² große Schutzhütte auf dem Fichtelberg („Hutznhaisl", Tellerhäuser, Oberwiesenthal, Deutschland, 2008–09, Seite 72) des Berliner Büros AFF Architekten ist die bewusste Suche nach Distanz zum modernen urbanen Leben. Die Architekten verwendeten recycelte Bauteile und nutzten Wände des Vorgängerbaus – einer Holzhütte – als Schalungselemente für den Neubau aus Beton. Der Rückzug aus der modernen Welt, selbst in Form von zeitgenössischem Beton, signalisiert eine Ablehnung von Systemen und Methoden, die in gewisser Weise in eine architektonische Sackgasse geführt haben.

ZWISCHEN DEN WÄNDEN LUFT

Auch das ecuadorianische Architektenteam al bordE verbindet sein Gespür für moderne Formen mit dem Einsatz traditioneller Methoden und hinterfragt darüber hinaus die Zielsetzungen moderner Architektur an sich. Zwei ihrer Projekte sind in diesem Buch vorgestellt. Das erste Projekt, ihre Casa Entre Muros (Tumbaco, Quito, Ecuador, 2007–, Seite 78) ist ein 180 m² großes Wohnhaus, das mit einem Budget von 50 000 Dollar realisiert wurde. Der Bau aus Stampflehm, Holz und Stein steht für die „Suche nach einem Leben in Harmonie mit der Natur". Für die Bewässerung wird Grauwasser genutzt, Warmwasser wird durch Solarenergie erzeugt. Das Material für die Lehmziegelmauern stammt vom Grundstück. Auch traditionelle Bräuche wurden von den Architekten respektiert, wie etwa eine Zeremonie, in der der Vulkan um Erlaubnis gebeten wurde, auf dem Grundstück bauen zu dürfen, oder das Schlagen von Holz und das Schneiden von Reet zu entsprechenden Mondphasen. Doch der Entwurf fügt sich nicht nur harmonisch in die Natur, sondern harmoniert auch mit einer modernen Formensprache.

Dasselbe gilt für al bordEs Atelier und Gewächshaus (Machachi, Ecuador, 2007), ein nur 47 m² großer Bau, der für nur 16 200 Dollar realisiert wurde. Das ungewöhnliche Gebäude besteht aus Stein und Stampflehm und einem auf dem massiven Sockel aufgestockten Gewächshaus, einem Paradies für Blumen. Der Hohlraum zwischen Stein und Lehm erwärmt sich durch Sonneneinwirkung; weitere lokale Baumaterialien wie Kiefer und Eukalyptusholz sind nicht nur ökonomische Lösungen, sondern stehen auch für eine enge und höchst greifbare Bindung an die Erde und das Grundstück.

13

13
*dhk Architects, Ahmed Baba Institute,
Sankore Precinct, Timbuktu, Mali,
2006–09*

Das Ahmed Baba Institute (Bezirk Sankore, Timbuktu, Mali, 2006–09, oben) des südafrikanischen Büros dhk Architects hingegen ist eine ungewöhnliche Kombination aus sonnengetrockneten Lehmziegeln, Beton, Glas und Metall. Der 4800 m² große Komplex war ein Geschenk des südafrikanischen Präsidenten an Mali und wurde während der Amtszeit Thabo Mbekis beschlossen. Die Architekten stellen unter Beweis, dass Modernität absolut mit traditionellen Baumaterialien und dem traditionsreichen Standort neben der Sankore-Moschee vereinbar ist. Bei Projekten wie diesem, obwohl ungleich geringer beachtet als etwa Masdar City, gelingt ein harmonischer Brückenschlag zwischen den Welten – zwischen Afrika und dem Westen, ebenso wie zwischen der Moderne und jenen tief verwurzelten Traditionen, die die Architekturgeschichte fast überall auf der Welt prägen.

ZIMMER MIT AUSSICHT

Der renommierte japanische Architekt Kengo Kuma wiederum entschied sich für einen völlig anderen Weg, um lokale bauliche Traditionen für ein zeitgenössisches Gebäude nutzbar zu machen. Das Yusuhara Marché (Yusuhara, Präfektur Kochi, Japan, 2009–10, Seite 222) ist ein Marktgebäude für den Verkauf lokaler Produkte, in dem auch ein kleines Hotel untergebracht ist. Kuma hatte den ungewöhnlichen Einfall, eine vorgehängte „Curtain Wall" aus Strohballen zu realisieren. Außerdem arbeitete er mit Zedernholzstämmen – beides lokal verfügbare Baumaterialien, die auf traditionelle Bauformen anspielen. Dies zeigt, wie sich Traditionen und Bauformen durch sensible Einfühlung aktualisieren und für ein 2010 fertiggestelltes Gebäude nutzen lassen.

Bei zwei Projekten in diesem Band geht es eher um den Blick in die Natur als um „natürliche" Konzepte. Das erste Beispiel ist der Jübergturm (Hemer, Deutschland, 2010, Seite 96) von Liza Heilmeyer und Stephan Birk, beide 1975 geboren. Anders als Kunst erfordert Architektur in der Regel eine gewisse Reife und Erfahrung, weshalb Architekten unter 40 oft als die „jungen Vertreter" der Branche gelten. Der Entwurf von Birk & Heilmeyer Architekten ist deshalb umso interessanter. Der 23,5 m hohe Turm wurde als Landmarke für eine regionale Landesgartenschau geplant. Wie bei Bäumen, auf die die Besucher beim Besteigen des Turms Ausblick haben, wird das Stabgeflecht offener und leichter, je weiter es sich der 9 m großen Aussichtsplattform nähert, von der aus sich ein 360°-Panoramablick bietet. Die Konstruktion aus sibirischem Lärchenholz wirkt wie die dreidimensionale Umsetzung einer mathematischen Formel. Die natürliche, berechenbare Progression wird durch die Materialwahl zusätzlich betont.

Klaus Loenhart und Christoph Mayr vom Büro Terrain, kaum älter als ihre Kollegen, entwarfen und realisierten den Murturm, der 2009 fertiggestellt wurde (Südsteiermark, Österreich, Seite 418). Die Konstruktion, ein komplexes System aus Knotenverbindungen und tragenden Formrohren, wurde mithilfe von 3D-Modellen und CNC-Fertigung realisiert. Hier nähert man sich der Natur mittels zeitgenössischer Technologie – der Beweis, dass der Blick in die Vergangenheit nicht die einzige Option ist. Die augenfällige Nähe zur Natur verbindet diese und zahlreiche weitere Bauwerke: Hier wie dort der Versuch, die Verbindung zwischen Mensch und Natur wiederherzustellen, die durch die Reizüberflutung moderner Technik und unsere Konsumgesellschaften gestört, wenn nicht gar abgerissen ist.

ZURÜCK ZUM BLOB

Ganz offensichtlich gibt es also jene, die mit der Zeit gehen, und jene, die es lassen. Es gibt Architekten, die versuchen auf die Welt mit all ihren Wandlungen und Veränderungen zu reagieren, und andere, die offenbar in einer Zeitkapsel leben, in der nach wie vor die 1980er-Jahre regieren. Und doch sind dies durchaus versierte Architekten, renommierte noch dazu, manchmal so berühmt, wie Architekten nur sein können. Zweifellos ist das Zugangsgebäude zum Komplex De Admirant (Eindhoven, Niederlande, 2008–10, Seite 142) von Massimiliano und Doriana Fuksas eine solche Reise in die Vergangenheit – zurück zu den guten alten Tagen des Blobs. Die Architekten bezeichnen den Bau als „fließend und amorph" und vergleichen ihn mit einem „Wal, der zum Luftholen auftaucht". Hier gibt es keine Vorder- oder Rückseite, sondern eine kontinuierliche Gebäudehülle, die den fünfstöckigen Betonbau umschließt. Natürlich kamen Formen wie der Blob auf, als Computer erlaubten, sich von „Standard"-Entwurfsmustern zu lösen und stattdessen maschinell generierten Formen den Vorrang zu geben. Und selbstverständlich gibt es keinen Grund, warum man solche Formen vollständig vernachlässigen sollten. Es gibt sicher nicht mehr oder weniger handfeste Gründe für rechtwinklige Bauten als für fließende Formen, außer vielleicht der Überlegung, dass geradlinige Bauten auch geradlinige Innenräume haben, was durchaus von Vorteil ist, wenn man einen Schreibtisch an eine Wand stellen will. Doch der Fairness halber sollte man den Architekten zugute halten, dass ihr Peres Friedenszentrum (Jaffa, Israel, 2005–09, Seite 136) eben jene Geradlinigkeit aufweist, die man in Eindhoven vergeblich sucht. Vielleicht ist der auffällige Unterschied zwischen diesen Bauten der Architekten der Grund, warum Fuksas nach wie vor interessant ist und weshalb die Bauten des Teams nach wie vor Aufmerksamkeit erregen und Interesse wecken.

KUNST IN VEGAS

Man darf Frank O. Gehry zweifellos zuschreiben, mit seinem Guggenheim Bilbao das Gebäude als Skulptur erfunden zu haben. Zwar hat es schon früher skulpturale Bauten gegeben, doch der Erfolg des Museums in Bilbao hat gerade dieses Gebäude zu einer der großen architektonischen Fantasien des späten 20. Jahrhunderts werden lassen. Wie kann man eine Stadt mit einem einzigen, gewagten Bauwerk zum Leben erwecken – mit dieser Frage haben sich viele Provinzstädte auseinandersetzen müssen, spätestens seit Gehry sein Museum am Nervion (Bilbao) verwirklicht hat. Vor diesem Hintergrund war ein Zusammenschluss zwischen Gehry und Las Vegas eigentlich überfällig, und genau hierzu kam es mit dem Bau des Lou Ruvo Center for Brain Health der Cleveland Clinic (Las Vegas, 2005–10, Seite 158). Das Lou Ruvo Center ist ohne Frage ein ausgesprochen funktionaler Bau mit sämtlichen Einrichtungen, die man von einer anspruchsvollen Klinik erwarten darf. Zugleich geht Gehry hier skulptural noch einen Schritt weiter – es scheint fast, als habe jemand die geometrischen Formen der Moderne in einen Mixer gefüllt und ihn auf höchste Stufe gestellt. Das Ergebnis ist ein erstaunliches Konglomerat von Formen, mehr Kunst als Architektur. Denkbar ist jedoch auch, dass Gehry den Begriff Architektur hier neu definiert und näher an die Kunst heranführt als jemals zuvor. Vielleicht sollten wir diese Frage im Raum stehen lassen. Das architektonische Schauspiel lässt sich dennoch um seiner selbst willen genießen.

Ebenso wie Fuksas bewiesen haben, dass der Sprung vom Admirant zum Peres möglich ist, hat auch Gehry mit seiner Orchestral Academy (Miami, Florida, 2003–11, Seite 42) eine bemerkenswert andere Richtung eingeschlagen. Realisiert wurde das Bauwerk in intensiven Gesprächen mit Michael Tilson Thomas, dem Dirigenten der dort beheimateten New World Symphony. Im Zuge seiner Zusammenarbeit mit

14
Zaha Hadid, Sheikh Zayed Bridge,
Abu Dhabi, UAE, 2003–10

dem Musiker gelang es Gehry, die Aufführungspraxis neu zu definieren: Um die Bühne herum ließ er großformatige Projektionswände installieren, durch die das sitzende Orchester gewissermaßen in höhere Regionen versetzt wird, nicht allein durch Klang, sondern auch durch Bilder. Der neue Sitz der New World Symphony erinnert an andere Bauten Gehrys, darunter sein American Center in Paris oder seine DG Bank in Berlin (2001), und ist von außen weniger ungewöhnlich als das Lou Ruvo Center; im Innern jedoch zeigt sich der gewollte Bruch. Wie die gewaltige Pferdekopfskulptur in der DG Bank in Berlin, mit der die Besucher konfrontiert werden, sobald sie vom gesetzten Pariser Platz in das Gebäude treten, werden die großen Projektionswände der Orchestral Academy integraler Bestandteil des Bauwerks und seiner Funktion. Diese Bereicherung eines Musiktheaters um eine neue Dimension ist keine geringe Leistung für einen Architekten.

SOMEWHERE, OVER THE RAINBOW

Was die zeitgenössische Architektur – und damit *Architecture Now!* – so interessant macht, sind ihre vielfältigen Formen, Dimensionen und Typologien. Sicherlich ist nachhaltige Architektur ein wachsender Bereich, dennoch ist es unwahrscheinlich, dass sie die entscheidende Triebfeder für innovative Architektur der Gegenwart wird. Nach wie vor gibt es zahlreiche Architekten, die sich als Formgeber verstehen, sich in der kreativen Rolle des traditionellen Baumeisters sehen. Zweifellos haben „künstlerische" Architekten durch den Erfolg solcher Gestalter wie Frank Gehry erhebliche Freiheiten gewonnen – eine Freiheit, die jüngere Kollegen durchaus zu nutzen wissen. Eine der bekanntesten ist Zaha Hadid, die schon lange nach Wegen aus der Konformität sucht und jene unsichtbaren Barrieren überwindet, die nicht nur die Formen in der zeitgenössischen Architektur, sondern auch die herrschenden Rollenbilder von Frauen einengen. Beides ist der Gewinnerin des Pritzker-Preises gelungen. Einer ihrer jüngsten Entwürfe belegt ihre Beharrlichkeit und ihre Fähigkeit, mit kreativen Gesten „Kunst" zu schaffen. Die Realisierung der 842 m langen Scheich-Zajed-Brücke in Abu Dhabi (2003–11, Seite 166) zog sich mehr als 13 Jahre hin. Die erstaunlichen, asymmetrischen Bögen der Brücke waren bautechnisch eine erhebliche Herausforderung, doch schon direkt nach ihrer Öffnung für den Autoverkehr erwies sich die Brücke als Wahrzeichen am Horizont des Emirats am Golf. Hadids Brücke zeichnet sich unweit der großen Kuppeln der Großen Scheich-Zajed-Moschee auf dem Weg in die Stadt ab, und auch nachts fällt sie durch dezente chromatische Farbwechsel auf. Hadid entwirft und realisiert schon lange ihre typischen fließenden Kurven, in Neubauten ebenso wie als Bestandteile bestehender Altbauten. Die Brücke jedoch ist ihr erster Versuch, eine der grundlegendsten baulichen Typologien neu zu erfinden. Auch wenn ihre ungewöhnlichen Formen die Welt des Brückenbaus kaum im Sturm erobern dürften, so hat Hadid in Abu Dhabi doch jene radikalen Fragen aufgeworfen, die ihr Werk von Anfang an kennzeichnen. Warum sollte eine Brücke langweilig sein, wenn sie ein regelrechtes Kunstwerk sein kann?

TAUSENDE LINIEN

Jean Nouvel hat sich in vielerlei Hinsicht zum herausragendsten Architekten unserer Zeit entwickelt; von New York bis Doha baut er mit gleichbleibendem Innovationsgeist und Engagement. Sein Sofitel Vienna Stephansdom-Stilwerk in Wien (2006–10, Seite 310) macht in mehrfacher Hinsicht deutlich, warum er so gefragt ist. Wie die japanischen Kollegen von SANAA, so befasst sich auch Nouvel mit der Welt der Erscheinungen und arbeitet mit Raum, Spiegeleffekten und Farbe. Die so entstehenden Bauten bewegen sich auf dem feinen Grat zwischen

15
Arata Isozaki, Obscured Horizon,
Pioneertown, California, USA,
2008–10

15

Kunst und Funktionalität. Wie so oft bei seinen Bauten, hat Nouvel auch zu diesem Hotel einen kurzen Text verfasst, wobei seine Wortwahl sicher auch einer komplexen Skulptur gerecht würde. Allerdings arbeitete Nouvel hier auch mit der Schweizer Künstlerin Pipilotti Rist zusammen, um die hinterleuchteten Deckenmotive zu realisieren, was maßgeblich dazu beiträgt, diesen Entwurf vom Mainstream abzuheben. Nouvel schrieb: „Stellen Sie sich vor, wie alles mit eigentümlichen konstruierbaren Prismen beginnt, wie sich ihre Ebenen zu verschieben beginnen; Überschneidungen entstehen; eine Ebene kippt durch Hystereseeffekte, während eine andere die Stadt vom Dach aus mit flüchtigen Bildern in Licht taucht. Stellen Sie sich vor, wie die übrigen Ebenen durch Tausende Linien unterschiedlichster Ausrichtung und Reflexivität zu vibrieren beginnen, wie Grau mitunter zu grauen Quadraten vor grauem Hintergrund verschmilzt. Jetzt überrascht es nicht mehr, dass der schiefe Grundriss des Dachs schraffiert wirkt, gewebt wie ein dichtes Zufallsmuster aus Parallelogrammen und Rhomben, dass die Ebenen im Norden transparent, aus Strukturglas sind, während sich die Ebenen im Westen in Abstufungen von Schwarz zeigen, um Schatten zu werfen. An der Grenze zwischen Bauwerk und Himmel präsentiert eine weitere, flache Ebene einen Wechsel aufscheinender und wieder verschwindender Gesichter, eine Anspielung auf die zahlreichen Gesichter, die für immer mit der vielschichtigen Bildsprache verknüpft sein werden, die diese Stadt hervorgebracht hat."

UMWELT, KUNST, ARCHITEKTUR

Auch Ryue Nishizawa, einer der Partner bei SANAA, realisierte ein Projekt an der Schnittstelle von Kunst und Architektur – zusammen mit der renommierten Künstlerin Rei Naito. Das Teshima Art Museum (Insel Teshima, Kagawa, Japan, 2009–10, Seite 304) ist im Prinzip eine 2300 m² große, frei geformte Kurve. Die ausgreifende, dünnwandige Betonschale des Bauwerks öffnet sich zum Teil dem Himmel und überzeugt als „eindringlicher architektonischer Raum", wie Nishizawa ihn beschreibt. Wenn der Architekt erklärt, „unser Ziel ist eine Verschmelzung von Umwelt, Kunst und Architektur; wir hoffen, diese drei Elemente zu einer Einheit zusammenzuführen", formuliert er im Grunde ein Ziel, das direkt oder indirekt in einem Großteil zeitgenössischer Architektur zum Ausdruck kommt. Der Unterschied zwischen Nishizawa und manchen anderen ist jedoch, dass es ihm gelingt, die unsichtbare Schwelle zwischen Ambition und Gelingen tatsächlich zu überschreiten.

Auch zwei weitere hier vorgestellte Projekte spielen mit den Grenzen zwischen Kunst und Architektur, oder versuchen vielmehr, Architektur als Metapher minimalistisch zu interpretieren. Arata Isozakis Projekt Obscured Horizon (Pioneertown, Kalifornien, USA, 2008–10, Seite 196), das er für Eba und Jerry Sohn in der Mojave-Wüste realisierte, besteht aus drei reduzierten Elementen, die den Jahreszeiten gewidmet sind. Wie andere japanische Architekten, darunter auch der jüngere Shigeru Ban, beschäftigt sich Isozaki schon lange mit Definitionen von Architektur. Was macht ein Gebäude aus? Könnte es nicht auch eine einfache Betonplatte sein, wie hier? Und wann ist ein Bauwerk „so hoch wie der Himmel"? Isozakis 9 m² große Pavillons sind der Natur so nah wie nur irgend möglich, ihren modernen Baumaterialien zum Trotz.

DIE UNENDLICHE REISE

Die Ruta del Peregrino (Pilgerweg) von Ameca nach Talpa de Allende (Jalisco, Mexiko, 2009–11, Seite 446), wurde von den Architekten Tatiana Bilbao und Derek Dellekamp kuratiert und ist in ihren Dimensionen ungleich ambitionierter. Hier finden sich eine Reihe zumeist mini-

16

malistischer, skulpturaler Interventionen von Tatiana Bilbao (Mexiko), Christ & Gantenbein AG Architekten (Schweiz), Dellekamp Arquitectos (Mexiko), Elemental (Chile), Godoylab (Mexiko), Fake Design (China), HHF architects (Schweiz), Periférica (Mexiko) und Taller TOA (Mexiko). Die Arbeiten entlang des 117 km langen Pilgerwegs ziehen jedes Jahr Zehntausende von Besuchern an. Die Gratitude Open Chapel (Dellekamp Arquitectos, Tatiana Bilbao, 2009) liegt am Anfang des Pilgerwegs. Die Architekten schreiben: „Die vier Wände wirken wie eine unvollendete Kapelle und lassen durch das sich kontinuierlich wandelnde Schattenspiel in der Landschaft, die sonst voller Sonnenlicht ist, Räume aus wandernden Schatten entstehen. Sie gestatten den Pilgern zu verweilen und zu rasten." Eine zweite, fast vollkommen abstrakte Struktur auf dem Weg ist der Void Temple (Dellekamp Arquitectos, Periférica, 2009), den die Architekten wie folgt beschreiben: „Der Kreis ist ein universelles Symbol der Einheit; eine Bedeutung, die Kulturen, Grenzen und Sprachen transzendiert. In religiösen Ritualen und Bildern taucht er immer wieder auf, vom Nimbus der Heiligen bis hin zur Oblate in der heiligen Kommunion. Darüber hinaus steht er für den Kreislauf, ein unendliche Reise als Symbol für den Glauben der wandernden Pilger. Der Kreis gibt Raum für Reflexion, lässt den Pilger auf seine Reise zurückblicken, bevor er sein Ziel schließlich erreicht." Die Formen des Void Temple und auch die feierlichen Wände der Gratitude Open Chapel belegen, dass Architektur, die nicht rein „zweckdienlich" ist, Spiritualität vermitteln kann – wonach viele Pilger auf ihrem Weg suchen.

RGB-LEUCHTDIODEN

Die Frage nach dem Punkt, an dem sich Kunst und Architektur treffen, oder das eine gar zum anderen wird, beschäftigt Architekten (und Künstler) schon lange. Ein ungewöhnliches Beispiel ist das Werk des brasilianischen Illustrators und Designers Muti Randolph. Für seine Projekte *Tube* (The Creators Project, Galeria Baró, São Paulo, 2010, Seite 344) und *Deep Screen* (The Creators Project, Peking, China, 2010, Seite 346) arbeitete er mit dem grundlegendsten architektonischen Hilfsmittel überhaupt – dem Raster – und kombinierte es mit technischen Elementen wie Clustern aus RGB-LEDs. So entstehen Illusionen von Raum und Bewegung, die eng an ihr bauliches Umfeld anknüpfen. Mit seinen räumlich bescheidenen Arbeiten von weniger als 20 m² lädt Muti Randolph die Besucher ein, in die Installation hineinzutreten, um die Farbexplosionen und -wechsel umso besser erleben zu können. Durch synthetische Klänge, die mit den Lichteffekten synchronisiert sind, gelingt es Randolph, eine totale Umgebung zu schaffen. Vielleicht ist dies eher Kunst als Architektur, dennoch setzt die Wahrnehmung der Installationen eine gewisse Vertrautheit mit dem Raster voraus.

Eine andere Wendung nimmt das Konzept der Lichtinstallation als Architektur mit einem Projekt des niederländischen Büros Maurer United, dem Aussichtsturm Indemann (Inden, Deutschland, 2009, Seite 264). Der Turm liegt unweit der A4 zwischen Aachen und Köln, ist ganze 36 m hoch und mit 40 000 LEDs ausgestattet, die sich per Computer programmieren lassen. Die Architekten verstehen ihr Projekt als „Social-Media-Architektur", das inmitten einer ehemaligen Braunkohle-Tagebau-Region liegt, die zur Umnutzung als Naherholungsgebiet vorgesehen ist. Auch wenn beide Projekte darauf setzen, architektonische Formen mit einer gewaltigen Anzahl von LED-Leuchten zu kombinieren, liegt auf der Hand, dass der Indemann-Turm mehr mit landläufigen Definitionen von Gebäuden gemein hat als Randolphs Installationen. Doch trotz ihrer unterschiedlichen Dimensionen sind beide Arbeiten nicht weit vom Konzept der Skulptur entfernt: das bescheidene, ganz und gar flüchtige Projekt in Brasilien ebenso wie die monumentale, an einen Roboter erinnernde Arbeit in Deutschland.

ALTBAUTEN NEU BELEBT

Ökonomische Zwänge und das Bewusstsein dafür, dass viele Altbauten vermutlich wesentlich solider als heutige „moderne" Gebäude sein dürften, haben zu einer nachvollziehbaren Zunahme von Sanierungen aus den unterschiedlichsten Gründen geführt. Zwei in diesem Band vorgestellte Projekte sind Hotels. Beide integrieren bestehende Altbauten auf interessante Weise, was einiges über den Zeitgeist sagt. In Shanghai konnten die Architekten Neri & Hu 2010 das Hotel The Waterhouse im Stadtteil South Bund (Seite 290) fertigstellen. Das trendbewusste Boutique-Hotel mit nur 19 Zimmern integriert die baulichen Überreste eines dreistöckigen Hauptquartiers der japanischen Armee aus den 1930er-Jahren. Neri & Hu ließen sich in gewisser Weise von David Chipperfields Arbeit am Neuen Museum (Museumsinsel, Berlin, 1997–2009) inspirieren, der die Ruinen des Altbaus erhielt und behutsam so sanierte, dass die Spuren der Vergangenheit lesbar blieben. Entsprechend beließen auch Neri & Hu einen Großteil der rauen Oberfläche des „Wirts"-Gebäudes mehr oder weniger unverändert. Ein überraschendes, fast „voyeuristisches" Element sind die Anbauten aus Corten-Stahl, wie ihn auch der Künstler Richard Serra verarbeitet: Durch sie ergeben sich Einblicke aus den öffentlichen Bereichen in die privaten Hotelzimmer. Dies ist ganz und gar nicht, was die Franzosen „misérabiliste" nennen würden – vielmehr ist es genau das, was es braucht, um heute hip und zeitgemäß zu sein, besonders in einem „Designhotel".

Michel da Costa Conçalves, geboren 1973, und Nathalie Rozencwajg, geboren 1975, gründeten gemeinsam das Londoner Büro rare architecture. Ihr Town Hall Hotel (Patriot Square, London, 2008–10, Seite 352) ist ein größeres Hotel mit 98 Zimmern, das im ehemaligen Rathaus von Bethnal Green im Londoner East End eröffnet wurde. Hier wurde nicht nur der denkmalgeschützte Edwardianische Altbau von 1910 saniert, sondern auch ein moderner Flügel und ein neues Obergeschoss aufgestockt. Die Neubaubereiche sind von einer Haut aus lasergeschnittenem Aluminium umfangen und lassen von außen weder Fenster noch Türen erkennen. Die Sanierung und Modernisierung ist zwar keineswegs so „rau" wie das Waterhouse in Shanghai, entstand jedoch aus ähnlichen Motiven: Dem Wunsch, in einem Gebäude authentisch die Atmosphäre vergangener Zeiten aufleben zu lassen und ihm zugleich eine neue, produktive Bestimmung zu geben.

In einer Stadt wie Paris, in der architektonisch interessante Neubauten (zumindest im historischen Zentrum) eher selten sind, hat Manuelle Gautrand das historische Théâtre de la Gaîté Lyrique auf gelungene Weise saniert (2007–10). Dank des Budgets von 62 Millionen Euro konnte Gautrand das alte Gebäude aus dem 19. Jahrhundert umfassend neu ausstatten und als Kunstzentrum des 21. Jahrhunderts nutzbar machen. Die Flexibilität und technische Modernisierung des Gebäudes ermöglicht ein Programm, das „der digitalen Kultur und Musik gewidmet" ist und großzügig in den 9500 m² großen Räumlichkeiten Platz findet. Wie schon bei ihrem Citroën-Showroom auf den Champs-Élysées beweist Gautrand einmal mehr die Fähigkeit, sich in ein historisches Umfeld einzufühlen und das alte Frankreich neu aufleben zu lassen.

DER ALTE UND DER NEUE KÖNIG

Einer der neuen Stars der amerikanischen Architekturszene, Joshua Prince-Ramus, entwickelte einen vollkommen anderen Ansatz, um ein bestehendes Gebäude in seinen Entwurf zu integrieren. Prince-Ramus war einer der Gründungspartner von OMA/Rem Koolhaas in New York und verantwortlicher Partner bei so bedeutenden Projekten wie der Seattle Central Library. Sein Büro REX entstand aus der ehemaligen OMA-Niederlassung in New York. Für sein Vakko Fashion Center (Istanbul, Türkei, 2008–10, Seite 366) musste das bestehende Betonskelett eines

17

17
*Todd Saunders, The Long Studio,
Fogo Island, Newfoundland, Canada,
2010*

nicht fertiggestellten, verlassenen Hotels integriert werden, um die Zentrale zweier miteinander assoziierter Firmen aus der Mode- und Musik-branche bauen zu können. Der Auftraggeber hatte ein extrem kleines Zeitfenster für die Realisierung des Projekts vorgegeben, und REX gelang es, nur vier Tage nachdem sie von Vakko und Power Media kontaktiert worden waren, mit den Bauarbeiten zu beginnen. Da auch so komplexen Fragen wie die Erdbebensicherheit des bestehenden Skeletts zu berücksichtigen waren, entwarf Joshua Prince-Ramus ein Stahlboxsystem, das große Flexibilität bei der Gestaltung der Innenräume erlaubte, die scherzhaft „Showcase" genannt wurden. Den ungewöhnlichen Anforderungen des Auftraggebers des 9000 m² großen Gebäudes wurde REX auch dadurch gerecht, dass er den gesamten Bau mit einer dünnen Glashülle überzog, die an Schrumpffolie erinnert. Auf diese Weise entstand eines der meistpublizierten Gebäude des vergangenen zwei Jahre. OMA und Koolhaas haben, insbesondere mit ihrem Büro in Rotterdam, zahlreiche neue Talente der zeitgenössischen Architekturszene hervorgebracht. Dank seines Hintergrunds konnte sich Prince-Ramus, früher assoziiert mit OMA, inzwischen als bedeutendes unabhängiges Talent in den USA etablieren, und dies zu einer Zeit, in der sich für die schwindenden Stars einer älteren Generation keine Nachfolger aufzudrängen scheinen.

JUNG UND RASTLOS

Auch wenn nicht alle Architekten so plötzlich auf der internationalen Bühne auftauchen wie Joshua Prince-Ramus, gibt es doch hoch-begabte jüngere Talente, die von sich Reden machen – trotz der wirtschaftlichen Schwierigkeiten seit 2008. Entweder machen sie aus dieser Not eine Tugend oder sie arrangieren sich ganz einfach mit einem Umfeld, das für alles, was über das baulich rein „Funktionale" hinausgeht, ausgesprochen unwirtlich ist. Hier lassen sich drei Architekten mit verschiedenen Hintergründen nennen. Todd Saunders wurde 1969 in Gan-der, Neufundland, geboren. Er studierte an der McGill University (Montreal, Kanada, 1993–95) sowie am Nova Scotia College of Art and Design (1988–92). Saunders, der sein Büro in Bergen, Norwegen, hat, kehrte unlängst in sein Heimatland Kanada zurück, um Künstlerateliers für die Shorefast Foundation und die Fogo Island Arts Corporation zu realisieren. Das Long Studio (Fogo Island, Neufundland, 2010, Seite 382), ent-worfen für ein Stipendiatenprogramm an einem entlegenen Standort, zeigt, wie sehr Architektur einen Unterschied machen kann – mit einem Gebäude, das ebensogut völlig nichtssagend hätte ausfallen können. Die lang gestreckte schwarze Silhouette des nur 120 m² großen Gebäu-des sucht bewusst den Kontrast zur Küstenlandschaft. Die weißen Innenräume kontrastieren mit der dunklen Gebäudehaut. Das teilweise auf *pilotis* aufgeständerte Long Studio wirkt fremd und erlaubt den Künstlern doch, inmitten der beeindruckenden Landschaft zu wohnen.

Der Schweizer Architekt Laurent Savioz, geboren 1976, schloss sein Studium der Architektur an der Haute École Spécialisée (HES) in Fribourg ab (1998). Sein derzeitiges Büro gründete er 2005 mit Claude Fabrizzi, geboren 1975 in Sierre. Die jüngsten Projekte des Teams, eine Schule und ein Wohnhaus in der Nähe von Verbier im Schweizer Kanton Wallis sind von ausdrucksstarker Originalität, realisiert innerhalb vergleichsweise strenger Parameter. Ihre Grundschule (Vollèges, 2009–10, Seite 394) ist ein markanter Betonbau, dessen facettierte, leicht winklig versetzten Fassadenflächen die Massigkeit des Gebäudes zu negieren scheinen. Betrachtet man sie, scheinen sie sich fast zu bewe-gen. Auch im Innern des Gebäudes ist Beton allgegenwärtig, wenngleich Holzböden und großzügige Fensteröffnungen die steinerne Härte mil-dern. Der Hausentwurf des Teams in Val d'Entremont (2009–10, Seite 398) scheint auf den ersten Blick gar noch härter: Beton, Edelstahl und Glas kamen erschöpfend zum Einsatz. Das in einem traditionellen Bergdorf gelegene Haus hat zweifellos eine gewisse Kühle, die den Eigentü-

18
Savioz Fabrizzi, Primary School,
Vollèges, Switzerland, 2009–10

18

mern erlaubt, ihr natürliches und bauliches Umfeld mit einer gewissen Distanz zu betrachten. An seinem architektonischen Kontext nimmt das Haus nur durch Beobachten und Eindringen teil, auf nahezu voyeuristische Weise. Durch seine Offenheit, ja beinahe Nacktheit, ist das Haus ebenso eindrücklich wie verletzlich. Winkel und Räume wirken oft überraschend. Die jungen Architekten geben dem in die Jahre gekommenen Konzept der „Swiss Box" (eine sich durch Beton und geometrische Formen auszeichnenden Architektur) neue Bedeutung.

Kulapat Yantrasast, 1968 in Thailand geboren, absolvierte seinen M.Arch und seinen Ph.D an der Universität Tokio. Gemeinsam mit Yoichiro Hakomori gründete er 2003 das Büro wHY Architecture in Culver City, Kalifornien. In gewisser Hinsicht lässt sich Yantrasast mit Prince-Ramus vergleichen, denn seinen Ruf baute er sich maßgeblich als einer der wichtigsten Mitarbeiter von Tadao Ando in Osaka auf, ebenso wie als Mitarbeiter Andos bei dessen Projekten in den USA, wie dem Modern Art Museum of Fort Worth. Die Galerie L&M Arts Los Angeles in Venice, Kalifornien (2009–10, Seite 19), ein Entwurf von wHY, ist ein faszinierender Kontrast zwischen dem sanierten Elektrizitätswerk von 1929 und dem streng geometrischen Backstein-Neubau mit einer freiliegenden Dachkonstruktion aus Holz. Yantrasast gelingt es, die Grenzen zwischen saniertem Altbau und Neubau zu verwischen, was an und für sich schon eine architektonische Leistung ist. Während sich Joshua Prince-Ramus den für Koolhaas typischen heroischen Ansatz zu eigen gemacht hat, ist bei Yantrasast zu erkennen, dass er stark von der Bescheidenheit gelernt hat, die Tadao Andos beste Arbeiten auszeichnet. Savioz Fabrizzi wiederum ist ein Büro, das erkennbar in der Schweiz verwurzelt ist, was die Architekten nicht daran hindert, sich in ihren Projekten ebenso ausdrucksstark wie subtil zu zeigen. Mit Gestaltern wie diesen scheint die nächste Generation großer zeitgenössischer Architekten auf dem Vormarsch zu sein.

VERNUNFT UND BESCHEIDENHEIT

Zweifellos werden die heutigen Zeiten des Umbruchs und der Veränderung Einfluss auf die zeitgenössische Architektur haben. Ökologische Katastrophen wie das Versagen der Reaktoren des Atomkraftwerks Fukushima Daiichi machen ohne Frage deutlich, dass Technik und Ingenieurskunst ihre Grenzen haben. Wie der *Guardian* im März 2011 anmerkte, zeigt die Zerstörung des Erdbebens in Japan, wie schmal der Grat ist, auf dem wir leben. Statt Expansion und steigendem Konsum dürften die Schlüsselbegriffe der nächsten Jahre wohl eher Vernunft und Bescheidenheit lauten. Sicherlich wird die Architektur Vorreiter jenes einschneidenden Wandels sein müssen, den uns die Natur aufzwingen wird, sofern Planer und Baumeister nicht rechtzeitig reagieren. Gleichwohl werden Lehmziegel und Bambus als Baumaterialien keineswegs auf die „Dritte Welt" beschränkt sein. Amerika und die Emirate, um nur zwei Beispiele zu nennen, tun gut daran, ihren ökologischen Fußabdruck zu reduzieren, und das nicht nur mithilfe sandverkrusteter Solarpaneele. Die alte Garde der Architekturhelden tritt langsam ab und eine neue Generation wächst heran – mit anderen Zielen und neuen Einsichten. Dies bedeutet wohl kaum weniger Spannung und Entdeckungen in der zeitgenössischen Architektur, im Gegenteil: Das ist *Architecture Now!*

[1] Bill McKibben, "Japan Reveals How Thin Is the Edge We Live On," *The Guardian*, 18. März 2011.
[2] http://www.akdn.org/architecture/project.asp?id=3754, Zugriff am 20. März 2011.

INTRODUCTION

UNE MARGE ÉTROITE

Pouvait-on imaginer cette période de contradictions et de conflits, de soulèvements dans le monde arabe et de tsunami de dix mètres de haut ravageant les côtes du Japon ? Et pourtant nous en sommes là, en ce début d'année 2011, alors que la plupart des grandes économies sont encore aux prises avec la récession économique. Qu'il vienne de la politique, de l'économie ou de la géologie, le message est le même : nous sommes fragiles. Les maisons en bois ont certes été mises en pièces par le séisme japonais, mais le béton réputé si solide des réacteurs de Fukushima n'a pu résister aux déferlements de la nature. Les Japonais savent depuis toujours ce que sont les séismes, les guerres, les destructions et la reconstruction, raison expliquant peut-être la vitalité de leur architecture contemporaine. Lorsque Frank Lloyd Wright construisit l'Imperial Hotel à Tokyo (1915–23), il imaginait à tort qu'il flotterait à la surface des boues alluviales comme « un bateau de guerre sur les eaux ». Malgré ce que l'on a pu dire, l'hôtel fut gravement endommagé par le grand tremblement de terre de Kantō du 1er septembre 1923 (7,9 sur l'échelle de Richter) qui dévasta Tokyo et Yokohama. Pensez aussi à cette ville ravagée en 1923, qui se reconstruisit pour être la cible de bombes incendiaires en février et mars 1945. Au cours du seul raid de la nuit du 9 au 10 mars 1945, plus de 200 avions B-29 anéantirent 41 kilomètres carrés de la capitale japonaise et provoquèrent la mort de 100 000 personnes.

UNE NOUVELLE INSTABILITÉ

Force est de constater aujourd'hui que le courroux de la nature et les errements de l'économie aboutissent à un résultat similaire : la fragilité. Beaucoup d'architectes vont sans doute profiter de ces événements pour adopter un profil bas et penser à des bâtiments plus éphémères. Les nuages radioactifs retombant sur terre permettront peut-être aux thèses écologistes de se faire mieux entendre. Un certain nombre de projets publiés dans cet ouvrage montrent des approches globales ou assez radicales du développement durable. Les rénovations et les constructions temporaires semblent également plus nombreuses, profitant parfois de la solidité de bâtiments anciens, ou de la chance de pouvoir apparaître et disparaître nettement plus vite qu'une centrale nucléaire. Lorsque Francis Fukuyama proclama « la fin de l'histoire » (*La fin de l'histoire et le dernier homme*, 1992), certains pensèrent que la « globalisation » ou une forme globale de capitalisme allait imposer sa supériorité incontestable. Mais il semblerait que la période de la guerre froide – qui vit le triomphe du modernisme – représente dans le domaine de l'architecture une parenthèse beaucoup plus stable que l'atmosphère d'échec et de déclin de ce début de XXIe siècle. Quand les deux grands blocs politico-économiques se faisaient face et que le monde s'efforçait de se reconstruire, régnaient souvent un grand optimisme et une foi dans le futur. Tout ceci n'existe plus, et alors que le mur de Berlin a disparu, il est curieux que de nouveaux murs s'élèvent dans le monde, de la zone de Gaza à la frontière entre le Mexique et les États-Unis.

DANS LA VILLE D'ÉMERAUDE

Et si l'imposture des nouveaux maîtres du monde – milliardaires et dictateurs – ces magiciens d'Oz trônant dans leurs villes d'émeraude, nous était soudain révélée en ce début de siècle ? Adrian Smith, l'architecte de la tour Burj Khalifa (2004–10), admet s'être inspiré des tours de la Cité d'émeraude de la version filmée du *Magicien d'Oz* : « Je l'avais en tête quand je concevais le projet, explique-t-il, mais de

20
FELIX-DELUBAC, Ecolodge,
Siwa, Egypt, 2006–07

façon subliminale… Je ne suis pas allé voir à quoi cela ressemblait. Je me souvenais seulement de constructions cristallines s'élevant au milieu de nulle part. Ce qui est amusant, c'est que je ne me rappelais pas leur couleur verte. » Aujourd'hui, la plus haute construction jamais érigée par l'homme (828 mètres) reste en grande partie vide, victime de la chute de Dubaï. Comme l'orgueil est beaucoup plus résistant que les bâtiments, quelqu'un construira sans doute bientôt une tour encore plus haute, mais les rêves de richesse illimitée et de nouvelles frontières de l'architecture survivront-ils à l'âge de la fragilité ? Lorsqu'après l'explosion de la bulle immobilière japonaise en 1991, l'on demanda au célèbre architecte Arata Isozaki comment son pays pourrait changer, il répondit dans un sourire : « Plus jamais ces petites constructions stupides ! » Bien que cette prédiction n'ait pas été vraiment confirmée par la réalité, il est vrai que la diminution des moyens financiers incite l'architecture à l'austérité, alors que l'argent qui coule à flots encourage les excès. Si les désastres naturels et économiques s'ajoutent aux soulèvements sociaux, les architectes créatifs devront-ils se reconvertir en chauffeurs de taxi à New York ? Ou ces cauchemars écologiques et la chute des banques pousseront-ils certains à trouver des modes de conception et de construction plus sains, et peut-être à œuvrer pour un futur apaisé et plus « vert » ?

HORS DE CONTRÔLE

Un article prémonitoire publié par le quotidien londonien *The Guardian* le 18 mars 2011[1] reliait les événements liés au séisme japonais et indiquait certaines solutions auxquelles ce type de cataclysme pourrait conduire: « Ces événements révèlent combien la marge sur laquelle s'appuie la modernité est étroite. Il n'y a pas dans le monde de pays plus moderne et plus civilisé que le Japon. Grâce à sa règlementation de la construction et aux performances de ses ingénieurs, les immeubles de grande hauteur ne se sont pas effondrés, alors que le séisme beaucoup moins fort d'Haïti, l'an dernier, avait tout anéanti. Mais il est évident que cela ne suffit pas. Ce fil du rasoir sur lequel nous vivons, et qu'à certains moments nous ne remarquons même pas, ne procure pas une protection suffisante contre les forces de la nature. » L'auteur fait le lien, aussi ténu puisse-t-il paraître, entre un événement naturel de ce type et les dangers dus au réchauffement climatique provoqué par les activités humaines et suggère que nous avons peut-être atteint les limites de l'ingénierie au sens large. « Ce n'est sans doute pas le moment de faire confiance aux superbes promesses des ingénieurs alors qu'ils ont pratiquement perdu le contrôle d'une des technologies les plus sophistiquées jamais inventées, là-bas sur la côte de Fukushima. L'autre possibilité est de tenter de réduire un peu nos ambitions constructives, pour nous concentrer sur la résilience, sur la sécurité, et pour ce faire – et c'est là que s'ouvre la controverse – décider que les entreprises humaines (au moins en Occident), se sont assez développées, que nos appétits ne doivent plus croître, mais au contraire diminuer afin de nous offrir une marge de sécurité plus grande. »

L'architecture a suivi la courbe de croissance des sociétés de consommation pour faire toujours plus, aller toujours plus haut. Curieusement, aiguillonnés par la société et l'économie, les architectes ont aisément délaissé leur vieux rêve de réaliser des œuvres « éternelles », qui dureraient autant que les cathédrales gothiques. Ils se sont contentés d'édifier des bâtiments de plus en plus bon marché et légers, convaincus que la durabilité n'est plus ce que le monde attend aujourd'hui. *The Guardian* prend la position opposée et écrit : « Brusquement, des mots tout simples comme durable, stable, ou robuste, sonnent plus agréablement à nos oreilles. »

L'ARCHITECTURE D'AUJOURD'HUI

La collection *Architecture Now!* a pour objectif d'offrir à ses lecteurs un panorama de l'architecture contemporaine. Dans le passé, la critique architecturale a cherché à définir et soutenir des écoles, comme le firent Philip Johnson et Henry-Russel Hitchcock lors de la célèbre exposition du Musée d'art moderne de New York, « Modern Architecture : International Exhibition » en 1932. Se concentrant sur les travaux de Le Corbusier, Mies van der Rohe, Neutra, Gropius et Wright, l'exposition s'accompagnait d'un livre qui exerça une grande influence : *The International Style*. Plus récemment (et moins durablement), Charles Jencks a chanté les louanges d'un postmodernisme qui finit par n'être rien de plus qu'un habillage cosmétique et superficiel. Plutôt que de promouvoir une tendance, *Architecture Now!* présente des réalisations récentes, choisies dans le monde entier, dans un mélange voulu de styles et de typologies. En d'autres termes, c'est l'architecture telle qu'elle est aujourd'hui et l'on ne voit guère la situation changer dans les années à venir, malgré les bouleversements et les remises en question du moment. Alors que tout le monde peut trouver de multiples exemples d'architecture contemporaine sur Internet, *Architecture Now!* veut faire des choix, montrer ce qui est intéressant, sans référence aux écoles et sans soumission à de quelconques pressions ou influences indues. C'est un choix critique, sans objectifs prédéterminés. C'est l'architecture telle qu'elle est aujourd'hui.

PISÉ ET PILIERS DE BAMBOU

Et si l'architecture environnementale durable se préparait moins dans les laboratoires sophistiqués qui conçoivent les derniers modèles de cellules photovoltaïques que dans les régions du monde où la conscience écologique est une condition de survie ? Maartje Lammers et Boris Zeisser de l'agence de Rotterdam 24H Architecture explorent avec enthousiasme cette piste dans leur école de Panyaden (Chiang Mai, Thaïlande, 2010–11, page 50) à murs de pisé et toit de bambou. L'établissement enseigne des matières comme le tissage de vêtements et les méthodes agricoles locales selon une approche centrée sur des principes bouddhistes et bon sens. Alors que certains architectes vantent des projets qui réduisent les émissions de CO_2 de quelques points, 24H Architecture ouvre la voie à des empreintes carbone « négligeables » par des méthodes en grande partie traditionnelles.

L'architecte indonésien Effan Adhiwira, basé à Bali, a conçu l'École verte publiée dans ces pages (Green School, Badung, Bali, Indonésie, 2007, page 64). Sans lien avec l'école de Panyaden, elle enseigne aux enfants des modes de vie durables. Les colonnes en bambou appuyées sur des pierres tirées de la rivière ou les vastes toits en surplomb qui protègent du soleil sont les traits caractéristiques de ce projet. Pour l'architecte : « Notre architecture s'inspire des caractéristiques inhérentes à la tige de bambou. Nous nous efforçons d'optimiser la portée de la structure en bambou, d'optimiser l'effet de "courbure/flexion" naturel de ces piliers pour concevoir et construire des bâtiments de formes organiques et naturelles. » Comme dans un certain nombre d'autres projets publiés ici, l'École verte a été remarquée par le Prix Aga Khan d'architecture et retenue parmi les présélections du prix 2010. Le communiqué du prix précise : « Le bambou local, cultivé selon des méthodes durables, est utilisé ici d'une façon expérimentale et novatrice qui démontre ses possibilités architecturales. Cette approche a permis de faire naître une communauté écologique holistique fortement axée sur l'enseignement, qui cherche à inciter les élèves à être plus curieux, plus engagés et davantage passionnés par l'avenir de l'environnement et de la planète. »

21
*Diébédo Francis Kéré, Earthen Archi-
tecture Center, Mopti, Mali, 2010*

21

RETOURS

Dans un autre exemple intéressant de lien entre l'Europe et le monde musulman, Christian Félix et Laetitia Delubac (FELIX-DELUBAC)
ont conçu leur Ecolodge de 390 mètres carrés (2006–07, page 110) à Siwa en Égypte. Retraite isolée en plein désert, elle est en *kershef*,
c'est-à-dire un mélange de boue séchée, de sable et de sel. Encore plus « radical » en un sens, l'Ecolodge possède une tour à vent inspirée
des anciennes techniques de ventilation traditionnelles perses et n'est pas équipé de l'électricité. Les mêmes architectes travaillent actuellement au projet d'une maison passive à ossature en bois et toit de chaume en Normandie. Ceux qui ont parcouru cette région du nord-ouest
de la France connaissent depuis toujours ces toits typiques. Pourtant, ces matériaux et ces méthodes traditionnelles peuvent de nouveau
séduire des architectes nés au milieu des années 1970, diplômés de l'École d'architecture de Paris-Villemin il y a juste un peu plus de dix
ans. La tradition redeviendrait-elle à la mode ?

Le Prix Aga Khan d'architecture et son organisation-sœur, le Programme Aga Khan en faveur des villes historiques, ont salué le travail
de l'architecte Diébédo Francis Kéré, né au Burkina Faso. Son école primaire construite pour son village natal (Gando, 2001) a remporté le
prix Aga Khan 2004. La description qui en était donnée par les organisateurs du prix précisait : « Pour atteindre ses objectifs de développement durable, le projet s'appuie sur des principes de confort climatique obtenu par une construction économique, tirant parti au maximum
des matériaux et du potentiel humain locaux en adaptant de façon simple les technologies du monde industriel. Il a également été conçu
comme un exemple destiné à faire prendre conscience aux habitants des mérites des matériaux traditionnels. » Diébédo Francis Kéré a été la
première personne originaire de Gando, un village de 3000 habitants, à recevoir une éducation supérieure. Il a étudié à l'Université technique
de Berlin. Ce parcours montre qu'une formation occidentale sophistiquée n'empêche pas de travailler à partir d'un vocabulaire d'inspiration
traditionnelle durable. Le Centre d'architecture en terre de Kéré (Mopti, Mali, 2010) est une construction de 476 mètres carrés édifiée par le
Trust Aga Khan pour la culture à la suite de ses efforts en faveur de la restauration de la mosquée locale et la construction d'un nouveau
réseau d'égouts à Mopti. Des pavés de terre compressée et des toits en surplomb caractérisent ce projet dont la ventilation ne fait appel à
aucun système mécanique.

UN FUTUR SANS VISIBILITÉ ?

Loin de la voie très réaliste des projets du Mali, d'Égypte ou de Bali, l'Émirat d'Abou Dhabi (EAU) a rêvé d'une approche opposée du
développement durable et de la consommation énergétique. Réalisée sous un climat entraînant une importante consommation électrique, la
ville nouvelle de Masdar devait, en 2016, regrouper 45 000 habitants et 1500 entreprises sur six kilomètres carrés, pour un budget de
22 milliards de dollars. Elle devait ne faire appel qu'à des sources d'énergies renouvelables, ne générer aucun déchet et ne pas émettre un
seul gramme d'oxyde de carbone. L'Institut des sciences et de la technologie de Masdar, en collaboration avec le MIT, était censé produire de
l'énergie solaire, notamment grâce à des panneaux photovoltaïques fabriqués sur place. Un premier problème s'est posé lorsqu'on a constaté
que les fréquentes tempêtes de sable d'Abou Dhabi réduisaient de 40 % les performances de ces panneaux. Dans un contexte de démissions
et de critiques médiatiques, la date d'achèvement de Masdar a été repoussée à 2020, et son énergie électrique va devoir être importée.

22

C'est dans cette atmosphère que Foster + Partners a achevé le premier grand immeuble de la ville, le Masdar Institute (2008–10, page 118). Personne ne met en doute l'efficacité des stratégies passives utilisées, telles l'orientation et les versions contemporaines des tours à vent, mais elles existent depuis des siècles. Les systèmes photovoltaïques utilisés doivent prouver leur efficacité à long terme et le rêve d'une ville zéro émission dans le désert risque bien d'être plus un mirage qu'une réalité, même future. Actuellement, Abou Dhabi ne dispose pas de ressources aquifères suffisantes, la température s'élève à 50 °C en été et l'empreinte carbone par tête y est la plus élevée au monde.

LA SITUATION, UN ÉLÉMENT ESSENTIEL

C'est en 2007 que l'agence d'architecture Studio Mumbai, dirigée par Bijoy Jain, a livré la maison Palmyra – 300 mètres carrés – à Nandgaon (Maharashtra, Inde, page 412), projet également présélectionné en 2010 par le Prix Aga Khan pour l'architecture. La description de cette résidence par l'institution de l'Aga Khan met l'accent sur les qualités du projet en matière de développement durable, qui s'appuie d'avantage sur la tradition et les matériaux « authentiques » que sur des approches technologiques complexes pour diminuer l'empreinte carbone. « Les fonctions de la maison sont réparties en deux volumes oblongs, légèrement décalés l'un par rapport à l'autre. Leurs façades se caractérisent par des persiennes en bois local, le palmier de Palmyre, et la structure est faite dans un autre bois dur de la région. Les murs du terrain, les socles et les pavements sont en basalte. Les plâtres sont pigmentés au sable trouvé sur place. Le projet et son exécution, résultat d'une collaboration entre les architectes et les artisans de la région, a fait appel à des techniques éprouvées, aussi bien locales qu'étrangères, mais portées à un niveau d'exécution supérieur. La maison est bien adaptée à son environnement : les persiennes des façades en facilitent le rafraîchissement passif, de même que les cocotiers qui la surplombent. L'eau est tirée de trois puits voisins et stockée dans un château d'eau avant d'alimenter les installations par gravité. Ce projet serein et séduisant est pleinement intégré à son cadre naturel [2]. »

Le lecteur peut avoir le sentiment que certains des projets cités viennent de bien loin, ou sont situés dans ce que l'on appelait le « tiers-monde ». La vérité est qu'une nouvelle génération d'architectes de talent se tourne vers les ressources de l'architecture traditionnelle et a compris que les enjeux de la société contemporaine, développée ou en voie de l'être, seront peut-être mieux relevés si l'on regarde vers le passé avec un œil neuf plutôt qu'en cherchant à tout prix à se placer à l'avant-garde technologique. Comme le note *The Guardian*, la centrale nucléaire de Fukushima représente peut-être le sommet de nos connaissances technologiques, mais elles se sont révélées insuffisantes. Que faire alors ?

LE CYCLE DU RETOUR

Né au Vietnam en 1976, Vo Trong Nghia est non seulement architecte, mais aussi ingénieur, titulaire d'un mastère en ingénierie civile de l'université de Tokyo. Son wNw Bar (Binh Duong, Vietnam, 2008, page 454) utilise un système d'arcs structurels en bambou qui soutient une coupole de 10 mètres de haut et 15 mètres de diamètre. Proche du wNw Café (du même architecte), ce bar montre qu'une architecture en bambou peut-être aussi formidable que toute construction de verre et d'acier. « Le café et le bar wNw sont issus de la nature, explique

Vo Trong Nghia, ils fusionnent avec elle, en harmonie. Avec le temps, ils retourneront à la nature. » Cet accent mis sur le cycle naturel qui détermine la vie sur terre différencie cette architecture de la plupart des constructions modernes. Que ce soit des réacteurs nucléaires (le pire exemple) ou des tours de verre et d'acier en centre-ville, les réalisations des architectes et des ingénieurs contemporains sont souvent conçues comme si elles ne devaient jamais disparaitre.

Le recours volontaire aux matériaux et méthodes traditionnelles caractérise un grand nombre de projets architecturaux novateurs actuels. Une variante de cette orientation est le désir de retrouver une proximité avec la nature, même si les techniques de constructions utilisées ne sont pas pleinement durables. L'agence berlinoise AFF a créé un refuge de 70 mètres carrés sur le Fichtelberg (« Hutznhaisl », Tellerhäuser, Oberwiesenthal, Allemagne, 2008–09, page 72), dans une tentative voulue de s'éloigner de la vie urbaine moderne. Les architectes ont utilisé des matériaux recyclés et des formes en béton reprenant pour certaines des moulages d'un refuge en bois qui existait préalablement sur le site. L'isolement du monde moderne, même sous forme bétonnée, montre un rejet des systèmes et des méthodes qui ont conduit à ce que l'on pourrait appeler une impasse architecturale.

DE L'AIR ENTRE LES MURS

L'agence équatorienne al bordE combine elle aussi une sensibilité à la modernité et aux méthodes traditionnelles, ou plutôt interroge les orientations de la conception contemporaine. Deux de ses projets sont publiés dans ce livre. Le premier, la maison Entre Muros (Tumbaco, Quito, Équateur, 2007–08, page 78), est une résidence de 180 mètres carrés qui n'a coûté que 50 000 $. Elle est en pisé, bois et pierre et représente « une recherche de vie en harmonie avec la nature ». Les eaux usées servent à l'irrigation et l'énergie solaire chauffe l'eau sanitaire. La terre des murs d'adobe a été prélevée sur le site même. Les architectes ont également respecté des coutumes locales consistant à demander la permission au volcan de construire sur ses flancs ou couper du bois et des roseaux pendant certaines phases de la lune. Ici, les formes sont non seulement en harmonie avec la nature mais aussi avec la modernité. C'est également vrai de l'atelier-serre d'al bordE (Machachi, Équateur, 2007) de 47 mètres carrés seulement, réalisé pour un budget de 16 200 $. Cette curieuse construction associe la pierre, le pisé et une serre, petit paradis pour les fleurs qui s'élève sur un socle plein. Le soleil chauffe le vide entre la pierre et la terre. D'autres matériaux locaux comme le pin et l'eucalyptus apportent non seulement des solutions économiques mais aussi un lien réel avec la terre et le site.

L'agence sud-africaine dhk a réalisé l'Institut Ahmed Baba (quartier de Sankoré, Tombouctou, Mali, 2006–09, page 26) à partir d'une combinaison peu courante de briques de terre cuites au soleil, de béton, de verre et de métal. Cette construction de 4800 mètres carrés est un cadeau fait au Mali par la présidence de l'Union sud-africaine sous le mandat de Thabo Mbeki. Les architectes ont réussi à démontrer qu'un certain degré de modernité est parfaitement compatible avec le recours à des matériaux plus traditionnels et par-dessus tout avec le site, orienté vers la mosquée de Sankoré. Beaucoup moins repris par la presse que la ville de Masdar, ce type de construction atteint à une sorte d'équilibre entre deux mondes – l'Afrique et l'Occident – mais aussi entre la modernité et les traditions très anciennes qui irriguent l'architecture du passé dans la plupart des pays du monde.

23
*Terrain, Mur River Nature Observation
Tower, Southern Styria, Austria, 2009*

23

CHAMBRE AVEC VUE

Le célèbre architecte japonais Kengo Kuma cherche à adapter la tradition architecturale locale à la contemporanéité de façon très différente. Son marché de Yusuhara (Yusuhara, Kochi, Japon, 2009–10, page 222) est un bâtiment consacré à la vente de produits locaux, qui comprend également un petit hôtel. Kuma a eu l'idée surprenante d'un « mur-rideau » en modules de paille. Il a également utilisé des grumes de cèdre, autre matériau local qui renvoie aux traditions anciennes de cette région. C'est une réflexion imaginative sur la manière dont les traditions et les matériaux peuvent être remis au goût du jour pour les besoins du XXIe siècle.

Deux des projets publiés dans ces pages concernent davantage l'observation de la nature qu'une approche spécifiquement « naturelle ». Le premier est la tour Jüberg (Jübergturm, Hemer, Allemagne, 2010, page 96) signée Liza Heilmeyer et Stephan Birk, tous deux nés en 1975. À la différence de l'art, l'architecture demande une forme de maturité et un certain degré d'expérience. Les architectes de moins de quarante ans apparaissent ainsi comme les « jeunes » de la profession. La contribution de Birk & Heilmeyer Architekten en est d'autant plus intéressante. Leur tour de 23,50 mètres de haut est un signal pour un festival local consacré aux jardins et aux fleurs. Un peu comme les arbres que les visiteurs voient en montant dans la tour, la structure en treillis s'allège de plus en plus jusqu'à la plate-forme d'observation panoramique de neuf mètres de diamètre. Traduction en béton d'une formule mathématique, cette construction se développe selon une progression naturelle et prévisible, que met en valeur l'utilisation d'un lattis en mélèze de Sibérie.

À peine plus âgés que leurs confrères précédemment cités, Klaus Loenhart et Christoph Mayr (de l'agence allemande Terrain) ont conçu et édifié le la tour d'observation de la nature de la Mur, achevée en 2009 (Murturm, Styrie méridionale, Autriche, page 418). Construite selon un système complexe de nodules et de poutres porteuses tubulaires, cette structure a fait l'objet de recherches sur maquettes en 3D et a été réalisée à l'aide de techniques de fabrication à commande numérique. Ici, la nature est observée grâce à un objet architectural issu de la technologie contemporaine, preuve que la seule façon d'avancer est de ne pas regarder en arrière. La proximité de la nature est le point commun entre cette réalisation et de nombreuses autres constructions récentes qui ont cherché à rétablir les liens entre l'homme et la nature si souvent relâchés, si ce n'est rompus par les assauts de l'ingénierie moderne et de la société de consommation.

RETOUR AU BLOB

Certains architectes s'efforcent de composer avec le monde tel qu'il est et évolue, d'autres semblent rester captifs d'une sorte de parenthèse spatiale, quelque part dans les années 1980. Mais pour autant, ce sont de vrais architectes, et de talent, parfois célèbres à juste titre. L'immeuble d'entrée du centre commercial Admirant (Eindhoven, Pays-Bas, 2008–10, page 142) de Massimiliano et Doriana Fuksas est définitivement un rappel du passé, de l'âge d'or du *blob*. Les architectes qui décrivent leur projet comme « fluide et amorphe » le comparent à « un mammifère marin surgissant à la surface pour respirer ». Il n'a ni avant ni arrière, mais se présente plutôt comme une enveloppe continue qui habille une construction en béton de cinq niveaux. La forme de *blob* a fait irruption sur la scène architecturale au moment où les ordinateurs commençaient à prendre le pas sur les méthodes plus « standardisées » de conception et il n'y a pas vraiment de raisons pour que ces formes soient totalement abandonnées. Il n'y en a d'ailleurs pas davantage pour qu'un bâtiment soit rectiligne plutôt que fluide, sauf que les constructions orthogonales déterminent des volumes intérieurs qui le sont aussi, ce qui est sans doute un avantage lorsque vous voulez appuyer un meuble contre un mur. Pour rendre justice aux architectes, leur Centre Peres pour la Paix (Jaffa, Israël, 2005–09, page 136) possède toutes les lignes droites que l'on ne trouve pas à Eindhoven. La différence entre ces deux réalisations des mêmes architectes est peut-être justement ce qui explique que le travail de Massimiliano et Doriana Fuksas reste intéressant et continue à retenir l'attention.

L'ART À LAS VEGAS

Le musée Guggenheim de Bilbao a valu à Frank O. Gehry d'être crédité de l'invention de l'immeuble-sculpture. Certes, de nombreuses constructions sculpturales existaient avant lui, mais le succès de Bilbao en a fait le grand « caprice » de la fin du XXe siècle. Comment revitaliser une ville par un bâtiment audacieux reste une énigme à laquelle plusieurs grandes villes de province ont essayé de répondre depuis l'intervention de Gehry sur la rive du Nervion. Une rencontre Gehry/Las Vegas s'imposait et c'est ce qui vient de se produire avec le Centre de santé mentale Lou Ruvo de la Cleveland Clinic (Lou Ruvo Center for Brain Health, Las Vegas, 2005–10, page 158). Bien que ce soit certainement un bâtiment fonctionnel disposant de tous les équipements attendus d'une clinique de haut niveau, le Centre Lou Ruvo pousse les ambitions sculpturales de Gehry encore plus loin. Il semblerait que les volumes géométriques modernistes aient été jetés dans un mixer en position « maxi ». Il en a jailli un remarquable méli-mélo de formes, relevant plus de l'art que de l'architecture, à moins que Gehry ne cherche à redéfinir ce terme et ne se rapproche plus que jamais de la création artistique. Les spéculations doivent peut-être s'arrêter là et le spectacle être admiré pour sa seule valeur intrinsèque.

De même que les Fuksas sont capables de réaliser aussi bien l'Admirant que le Centre Peres pour la Paix, Gehry a choisi une orientation assez différente pour son Académie orchestrale (Orchestral Academy, Miami, Floride, 2003–11, page 42), conçue en échange étroit avec le chef d'orchestre Michael Tilson Thomas. Gehry a donc travaillé avec un homme de l'art musical pour redéfinir ce qu'était un concert, entourant sa salle d'énormes écrans qui permettent de diffuser le programme hors de l'enceinte de la salle. Rappelant certains autres bâtiments comme l'American Center à Paris ou la DG Bank à Berlin (2001), ce siège de l'orchestre New World Symphony est moins étonnant vu de l'extérieur que le Centre Lou Ruvo. C'est à l'intérieur que la surprise se produit. Comme la gigantesque forme en tête de cheval qui accueille les visiteurs de la DG Bank berlinoise, l'Orchestral Academy intègre la présence de ces vastes écrans et donne de nouvelles dimensions à la performance musicale, tâche non sans difficulté pour un architecte.

SOMEWHERE, OVER THE RAINBOW

Ce qui est intéressant dans l'architecture contemporaine – et dans *Architecture Now!* –, c'est qu'elle emprunte de multiples formes, types et échelles. L'intérêt pour le développement durable est certes en pleine ascension, mais il est peu probable qu'il devienne la force d'impulsion essentielle de l'architecture créative d'aujourd'hui. De nombreux architectes réfléchissent encore à des recherches formelles autour de leur rôle traditionnel de constructeur. Il est vrai que le succès d'un Frank Gehry a apporté une plus grande liberté aux architectes « artistiques » et de nouvelles générations en ont beaucoup bénéficié. L'une des bénéficiaires les plus connues est Zaha Hadid, qui a mis

24

24 + 25
Frank O. Gehry, Orchestral Academy,
Miami, Florida, USA, 2003–11

longtemps à faire éclore ses recherches et à traverser le plafond de verre qui s'oppose aux formes contemporaines, mais aussi au rôle des femmes. Titulaire du Prix Pritzker, elle a relevé ce double défi et l'une de ses plus récentes réalisations montre à la fois la continuité de son travail et sa capacité à faire de « l'art » à travers de grands gestes créatifs. Il a fallu plus de treize ans pour mener à bien le projet du pont Sheikh Zayed, 842 mètres de portée, à Abou Dhabi (EAU, 2003–11, page 166). Les étonnantes courbures asymétriques de cet ouvrage ont posé de réels problèmes à ses ingénieurs, mais dès son ouverture à la circulation, il est devenu un des points de repère sur l'horizon de l'État du Golfe. Non loin des coupoles de la Grande Mosquée Sheikh Zayed, le pont d'Hadid se détache dans la lumière du jour, mais tout autant la nuit lorsque ses couleurs changent selon une progression chromatique subtile. Depuis longtemps, l'architecte imagine des courbes fluides pour ses constructions nouvelles ou ses interventions dans des bâtiments existants, mais c'est là sa première tentative de repenser l'un des types constructifs les plus basiques. Ces formes étonnantes ne s'imposeront peut-être pas dans la conception des ouvrages d'art, mais à Abou Dhabi elles reposent les questions radicales qui depuis toujours caractérisent son travail. Pourquoi un pont devrait-il être d'aspect ennuyeux quand il peut être une œuvre d'art ?

MILLE LIGNES À ORIENTATIONS ET RÉFLEXIONS VARIABLES...

À de nombreux égards, Jean Nouvel est devenu l'un des plus brillants architectes internationaux de notre temps, construisant de New York à Doha avec la même inventivité et la même passion. Son immeuble mixte Sofitel Vienna Stephansdom-Stilwerk à Vienne (2006–10, page 310), montre bien pourquoi ses interventions sont si recherchées. Comme l'agence japonaise SANAA, l'architecte français maîtrise les apparences et utilise l'espace, les reflets et la couleur pour créer des bâtiments à la frontière de l'art et du fonctionnalisme. Comme souvent, Nouvel a rédigé un bref texte explicatif sur cet hôtel. Ses termes auraient pu être choisis pour décrire une sculpture complexe, et il a d'ailleurs collaboré avec l'artiste suisse Pipilotti Rist pour les plafonds peints rétroéclairés qui participent activement aux impressions extraordinaires que suscite son projet. Nouvel écrit ainsi : « Étonnez-vous qu'à partir des prismes constructibles inattendus, les plans de ces prismes aient glissé, qu'ils aient fabriqué des intersections, que sous le magnétisme des déviances de Hans Hollein, l'un deux ait fini par s'incliner, un autre se soit décidé à éclairer la ville d'un plafond aux images furtives. Imaginez que d'autres plans se soient mis à vibrer de mille lignes à orientations et réflexions variables, que le gris se noie de temps en temps dans des carrés gris sur fond gris. Rien de plus normal dans ce cas qu'un plan oblique de toiture se soit hachuré pour tisser une trame aléatoire trop serrée de parallélogrammes et de losanges, que les plans du Nord déclinent le verre granité pour construire un peu leur transparence pendant que les plans Ouest se cachent dans de noires variations pour illustrer leurs ombres. À la limite du ciel un plan plane pour révéler l'apparition-disparition de visages mutants, évocation de multiples visages à jamais attachés à la profondeur des images nées de cette ville. »

ENVIRONNEMENT, ART, ARCHITECTURE

Ryue Nishizawa, l'un des deux partenaires de SANAA a récemment achevé une réalisation elle aussi à la frontière entre l'art et l'architecture, en collaboration avec la célèbre artiste Rei Naito. Son Musée d'art de Teshima (île de Teshima, Kagawa, Japon, 2009–10, page 304)

25

est un bâtiment incurvé de forme libre de 2300 mètres carrés. Sa vaste coque mince en béton, ouverte sur le ciel à certains endroits, est précisément ce « puissant espace architectural » auquel se réfère Nishizawa. Lorsqu'il écrit que « notre but est de générer la fusion de l'environnement, de l'art et de l'architecture, et nous espérons que ces trois éléments fonctionneront ensemble comme une entité unique », il explicite une ambition latente ou déclarée d'une bonne partie de l'architecture contemporaine. La différence entre cet architecte et d'autres est qu'il a réussi à franchir le seuil invisible entre la simple ambition et la réussite.

Deux autres projets de valeur publiés plus loin flirtent avec les limites de l'art et de l'architecture, ou plutôt cherchent à se servir de l'architecture de manière symbolique et quasi minimale. Le projet Horizon obscurci d'Arata Isozaki (Obscured Horizon, Pioneertown, Californie, 2008–10, page 196) pour Eba et Jerry Sohn dans le désert de Mojave, consiste en une série de trois très petites constructions liées aux saisons. Comme d'autres grands architectes japonais, dont son cadet Shigeru Ban, Isozaki s'est longtemps intéressé aux définitions même de l'architecture. Qu'est-ce qui constitue un bâtiment ? Une simple plaque de béton comme ici ? Et quand peut-on dire d'une construction qu'elle est « aussi haute que le ciel » ? Dans ce cadre naturel majestueux, les structures de neuf mètres carrés d'Isozaki sont aussi proches de la nature qu'il est possible de l'être, bien qu'elles soient réalisées en matériaux modernes.

UN PARCOURS SANS FIN

À une échelle plus ambitieuse, la route du Pèlerin d'Ameca à Talpa de Allende (Ruta del Peregrino, Jalisco, Mexique, 2009–11, page 446), pilotée par les architectes Tatiana Bilbao et Derek Dellekamp, est un ensemble d'interventions très intéressantes et essentiellement minimalistes et sculpturales signées Tatiana Bilbao (Mexique), Christ & Gantenbein AG Architekten (Suisse), Dellekamp Arquitectos (Mexique), Elemental (Chili), Godoylab (Mexique), Fake Design (Chine), HHF architects (Suisse), Periférica (Mexique) et Taller TOA (Mexique). Ces œuvres se répartissent le long d'une route de pèlerinage de 117 kilomètres de long qui attire des dizaines de milliers de participants chaque année. La chapelle ouverte de la Gratitude (Capilla Abierta la Gratitud, Dellekamp Arquitectos, Tatiana Bilbao, 2009), se dresse à proximité du point de départ de la route. Selon ses architectes : « Les quatre murs qui évoquent une chapelle non achevée créent un scénario d'ombres en mouvement constant qui se projettent sur le paysage par ailleurs ensoleillé ; les espaces délimités par ces ombres mouvantes offrent aux pèlerins un endroit pour s'arrêter et se reposer. » Presque purement abstrait, le Temple vide (Vacio Circular, Dellekamp Architectos, Periférica, 2009) est décrit par ses auteurs dans les termes suivants : « Le cercle est un symbole universel d'unité, signification qui transcende les cultures, les frontières et les langues. Il apparaît et réapparaît dans les rituels religieux et leurs représentations, de l'auréole des saints jusqu'à l'hostie donnée aux catholiques lors de la communion. Il représente également un cycle, un parcours sans fin qui symbolise la foi des pèlerins. Le cercle est aussi un lieu de réflexion dans lequel les pèlerins se remémorent leur voyage avant de le poursuivre jusqu'à sa destination finale. » Ces formes – le cercle du Temple vide ou les murs dressés de la chapelle ouverte de la Gratitude – montrent que l'architecture qui n'est pas spécialement « utile » peut atteindre à une sorte de spiritualité, répondant certainement aux attentes des pèlerins sur cette « ruta ».

26

DEL RVB

Le moment de la rencontre de l'art et de l'architecture, ou plutôt le moment où l'un devient l'autre, a longtemps préoccupé les archi-tectes (et les artistes). Un exemple surprenant nous en est donné par l'œuvre de l'illustrateur et designer brésilien Muti Randolph. Ses œuvres *Tube* (The Creators Project, Galeria Baró, São Paulo, 2010, page 344) et *Deep Screen* (The Creators Project, Pékin, 2010, page 346) font appel aux procédés architecturaux les plus basiques, une trame associée à divers procédés techniques comme des ensembles de DEL RVB, pour créer l'illusion de l'espace et du mouvement intimement liés à la forme construite. À travers ces petites interventions (moins de 20 mètres carrés), Muti Randolph propose au spectateur de se placer à l'intérieur même de l'œuvre pour faire l'expérience d'une explosion de couleurs et de mouvements. Lorsque le son de synthèse s'ajoute aux effets lumineux, se crée un environnement intégral. Il s'agit ici da-vantage d'art que d'architecture néanmoins, la perception de ces pièces s'appuie sur une certaine maîtrise du principe de trame.

L'idée de *light show* en tant qu'expression architecturale prend un sens tout différent dans la tour d'observation Indemann (Aussichts-turm Indemann, Inden, Allemagne, 2009, page 264) des architectes néerlandais Maurer United. Érigée à proximité de l'autoroute A4 entre Aix-la-Chapelle et Cologne, l'œuvre qui ne mesure pas moins de 36 mètres de haut est recouverte d'un réseau de 40 000 ampoules à DEL programmées par ordinateur. Les architectes parlent de cette œuvre située dans une ancienne zone minière en reconversion comme d'une « architecture médiasociale ». Bien que ces deux œuvres – une sculpture modeste et entièrement éphémère au Brésil et une œuvre assez massive et robotisée en Allemagne – remplissent une fonction et cherchent à combiner des formes essentiellement architecturales et des accumulations massives de DEL, il est clair que la tour Indemann reste plus proche de la définition habituelle du bâti. Dans les deux cas, malgré les différences d'échelle, l'idée de sculpture n'est cependant pas très loin.

RELEVER LES RUINES

La situation économique et le constat que beaucoup d'immeubles anciens sont probablement plus solides que les « modernes » ont augmenté le nombre des projets de rénovation et de réhabilitation. Deux exemples retenus ici concernent des hôtels. Tous deux utilisent des constructions antérieures d'une manière qui jettent un éclairage sur l'esprit du temps. À Shanghai, des architectes locaux, Neri & Hu, ont achevé en 2010 The Waterhouse at South Bund (Chine, page 290). De 19 chambres seulement, cet hôtel-boutique à la mode s'est logé dans les vestiges d'un ancien quartier général de l'armée japonaise des années 1930. Reprenant d'une certaine façon l'approche de David Chipperfield pour le Neues Museum (île des musées, Berlin, 1997–2009) qui a réinvesti les ruines de bâtiments existants sans effacer la totalité des traces du bombardement de la ville, Neri & Hu ont laissé apparentes un certain nombre de surfaces brutes de l'immeuble « hôte ». En ajoutant une touche inattendue de « voyeurisme » qui permet de regarder à l'intérieur des chambres à partir des espaces communs, ils ont également réalisé des extensions en acier Corten, un des matériaux favoris du sculpteur Richard Serra. Ce n'est pas ce que les Français appellent du « misérabilisme », mais une récupération très tendance de l'esprit contemporain d'aujourd'hui, en particulier dans le secteur des hôtels « design ».

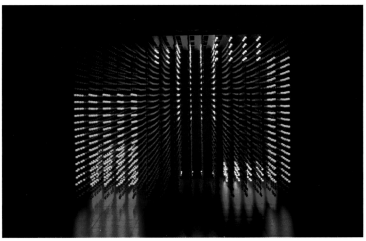

27
Muti Randolph, "Deep Screen," The
Creators Project, Beijing, China, 2010

27

Michel da Costa Conçalves, né en 1973, et Nathalie Rozencwajg, née en 1975, ont fondé ensemble l'agence londonienne rare architecture. Leur Town Hall Hotel (Patriot Square, Londres, 2008–10, page 352) est un établissement de 98 chambres aménagé dans l'ancien hôtel de ville de Bethnal Green dans le quartier de l'East End. Parallèlement à la restauration de ce bâtiment de style édouardien datant de 1910 et classé monument historique, une aile contemporaine et un étage ont été ajoutés. Les nouveaux volumes sont enveloppés d'une peau d'aluminium découpée au laser. Ni les portes, ni les fenêtres ne sont visibles. Cette restauration-modernisation n'est en aucun cas aussi « brute » que le projet The Waterhouse mais procède en grande partie des mêmes idées : insuffler un esprit contemporain dans un bâtiment ancien et, surtout, lui offrir une existence nouvelle et productive.

Dans une ville comme Paris où les créations architecturales contemporaines sont relativement rares dans le périmètre historique, Manuelle Gautrand a entrepris avec succès la restauration du Théâtre de la Gaîté lyrique (2007–10). Pour un budget de 62 millions d'euros, elle a entièrement rénové ce bâtiment du XIXe siècle pour l'adapter à de nouvelles fonctions. La souplesse et la capacité à suivre l'évolution technologique caractérisent ce programme consacré à la culture et à la musique numériques, logé à l'aise dans 9500 mètres carrés. De même que pour l'immeuble Citroën sur les Champs-Élysées, Gautrand montre ici sa capacité à s'adapter à un environnement historique sensible et à rajeunir une certaine image passéiste de la France.

FUTUR ROI ?

L'une des étoiles montantes de l'architecture américaine, Joshua Prince-Ramus, a imaginé utiliser de façon radicalement différente un bâtiment existant. Prince-Ramus a été cofondateur d'OMA (Rem Koolhaas) à New York et partenaire en charge de projets aussi importants que la bibliothèque centrale de Seattle. Il a créé son agence actuelle REX à partir de l'ancienne agence new-yorkaise d'OMA. Son Centre de la mode de Vakko (Istanbul, 2008–10, page 366) est la reconversion d'une ossature de béton prévue pour un hôtel jamais construit pour en faire le siège de deux entreprises liées intervenant dans les domaines de la mode et de la musique. Le client était extrêmement pressé et REX a débuté les travaux de construction quatre jours après avoir été contacté par Vakko et Power Media. Face à des problèmes complexes comme la résistance sismique de l'ossature, Joshua Prince-Ramus a conçu un système de boîte d'acier offrant de considérables facilités d'aménagement des espaces intérieurs, appelée la « Vitrine ». Enveloppant le tout d'une fine peau de verre, REX a réussi à répondre aux attentes du client de ce bâtiment de 9000 mètres carrés et à créer l'une des réalisations architecturales les plus publiées de ces deux dernières années. L'agence OMA et Koolhaas, en particulier à travers l'agence de Rotterdam, a été une véritable ruche de nouveaux talents de l'architecture contemporaine. Par sa propre formation, Joshua Prince-Ramus, longtemps identifié à OMA, a réussi à se faire reconnaître comme un nouveau talent majeur sur la scène américaine, à un moment où les stars des générations antérieures, ne semblaient pas pouvoir être remplacées.

JEUNE ET SANS RÉPIT

Si tout le monde ne peut répéter l'exploit de Joshua Prince-Ramus et s'imposer rapidement sur la scène mondiale, de nombreux jeunes talents arrivent à se faire connaître chaque année, malgré les difficultés économiques qui font partie de l'équation de l'architecture

28

contemporaine depuis 2008. Ces architectes tournent parfois ces difficultés à leur avantage, ou s'adaptent à un environnement devenu diffi-cile pour tout ce qui n'est pas un simple projet « fonctionnel ». Trois exemples de cette situation peuvent être cités. Todd Saunders, né en 1969 à Gander (Terre-Neuve, Canada) a étudié à l'université McGill (Montréal, 1993–95) et au Collège d'art et de design de la Nouvelle-Écosse (NSCAD, 1988–92). Basé à Bergen (Norvège), il est récemment revenu au Canada pour concevoir un ensemble d'ateliers d'artistes destiné à la Fondation Shorefast et la Société des arts de l'île de Fogo. L'Atelier en longueur (Long Studio, île de Fogo, Terre-Neuve, 2010, page 382) conçu pour un programme de résidence d'artistes dans un lieu reculé montre de quelle façon une architecture de qualité peut faire la différence avec une réalisation ordinaire. De 120 mètres carrés de surface seulement, la longue silhouette noire du petit bâtiment contraste avec la ligne de côte. Alors que sa peau extérieure est noire, son intérieur est entièrement blanc. L'atelier, qui repose en partie sur de fins pilotis, est certes une présence étrangère, mais qui permet à des artistes de vivre au cœur même d'un cadre naturel sauvage.

L'architecte suisse Laurent Savioz, né en 1976, est diplômé en architecture de la Haute École spécialisée (HES) de Fribourg (1998). Il a créé son agence actuelle en 2005 avec Claude Fabrizzi, né en 1975 à Sierre. Leurs réalisations les plus récentes, une école et une maison dans les vallées conduisant à Verbier dans le canton du Valais, témoignent d'une originalité puissante mais contenue dans un cadre de contraintes assez strictes. Leur école primaire (Vollèges, 2009–10, page 394) est un petit bâtiment de béton dont les murs extérieurs facet-tés légèrement inclinés semblent compenser la masse et donnent une légère impression de mouvement. Le béton est également omniprésent à l'intérieur, même si des planchers en bois et de généreuses ouvertures atténuent sa rigueur minérale. La maison du Val d'Entremont (2009–10, page 398) semble encore plus rigide, par la forte présence du béton, de l'acier inoxydable et du verre. Située dans un village de montagne traditionnel, elle est indéniablement d'apparence froide, mais permet à ses occupants d'observer le cadre naturel et architectural qui les entoure avec une certaine distance. Dans ce contexte architectural la maison est un objet d'observation mais qui se laisse aussi péné-trer de façon presque voyeuriste. Elle semble à la fois solide et vulnérable par son ouverture et sa nudité même. Les volumes et certaines pentes ou inclinaisons sont inattendus. Ces jeunes architectes donnent au concept déjà un peu fatigué de la boîte suisse (type d'architecture géométrique en béton) un nouveau sens.

Kulapat Yantrasast, né en 1968 en Thaïlande, a obtenu son M. Arch. et son Ph. D. à l'université de Tokyo. Il a fondé l'agence wHY Ar-chitecture en 2003 à Culver City en Californie, avec Yo-ichiro Hakomori. Il peut en un sens être comparé à Prince-Ramus puisqu'il s'est déjà fait une réputation déjà considérable en tant que principal collaborateur de Tadao Ando à Osaka, mais aussi sur les projets américains du maître japonais dont le Musée d'art moderne de Fort Worth. Leur galerie L&M Arts Los Angeles à Venice (Californie, 2009–10, page 19) pré-sente un contraste curieux entre la rénovation d'une station d'électricité de 1929 et la construction d'une galerie en brique recyclée de style fortement géométrique à charpente de bois apparente. Entre la rénovation et la construction à neuf, Yantrasast a réussi à brouiller les frontiè-res entre ce qui sépare habituellement l'ancien du nouveau, ce qui est déjà une réussite considérable. Alors que Joshua Prince-Ramus sem-ble avoir adopté l'approche héroïque de Koolhaas, on peut dire que Yantrasast a beaucoup appris de la modestie des meilleures œuvres de Tadao Ando. Savioz, quant à lui, est fermement ancré dans sa Suisse natale, ce qui ne l'empêche pas d'être à la fois solide et subtil dans ses réalisations. Avec de tels créateurs, la prochaine génération d'architectes contemporains semble déjà s'avancer vers la première ligne.

*29
Savioz Fabrizzi, Val d'Entremont
House, Val d'Entremont, Switzerland,
2009–10*

29

RAISON ET MODESTIE

Cette époque de soulèvements et de changement exercera certainement une influence sur l'architecture contemporaine. Une catastrophe écologique comme celle de la centrale nucléaire de Fukushima révèle cruellement les limites des technologies. Bien au contraire, comme *The Guardian* le suggérait en mars 2011, les ravages du séisme japonais montrent à quel point nous vivons sur le fil du rasoir. Plutôt que de rêver d'expansion et de consommation toujours accrue, la raison et la modestie pourraient bien devenir les mots-clés des années à venir. L'architecture sera certainement au premier rang des ajustements massifs qu'imposera la nature s'ils ne sont pas compris à temps par ceux qui conçoivent et construisent. Les briques de terre et le bambou ne sont peut-être plus réservés aux pays en voie de développement. Les Américains et les habitants des Émirats, pour ne citer que deux exemples, feraient sans doute bien de réduire leur empreinte carbone, et pas seulement en les remplaçant par des cellules photovoltaïques sensibles aux vents de sable. La vieille garde des stars de l'architecture commence à passer la main et une nouvelle génération apparaît, dont les objectifs et la compréhension du monde où nous vivons sont différents. Ceci ne réduit en rien l'excitation intellectuelle et le plaisir des sens de découvrir une nouvelle architecture, bien au contraire. C'est le propos d'*Architecture Now!*

[1] Bill McKibben, « Japan reveals how thin is the edge we live on », *The Guardian*, 18 mars 2011.
[2] http://www.akdn.org/architecture/project.asp?id=3754, consulté le 20 mars 2011.

24H ARCHITECTURE

24H Architecture
Hoflaan 132
3062 JM Rotterdam
The Netherlands

Tel: +31 10 411 10 00
Fax: +31 10 282 72 87
E-mail: info@24h.eu
Web: www.24h.eu

MAARTJE LAMMERS was born in 1963 and graduated from the Technical University of Delft in 1988. **BORIS ZEISSER**, born in 1968, graduated from the same institution in 1995. The pair worked in several architectural offices before founding 24H Architecture on January 1, 2001, such as (EEA) Erick van Egeraat Associated Architects, Mecanoo, and the Office for Metropolitan Architecture (Rem Koolhaas). Describing their work as inspired by the forms of nature and Art Deco, the firm currently employs 16 people. Their work includes the Ichthus Business Center (Rotterdam, The Netherlands, 2002); Dragspelhuset Holiday House (Arjang, Sweden, 2004); Soneva Kiri, Eco Holiday Resort (Koh Kood, Thailand, 2009); Panyaden School (Chiang Mai, Thailand, 2010–11, published here); Rijkswaterstaat Office (Assen, The Netherlands, 2011); and the Environmental Education Center (Assen, The Netherlands, 2012). Ongoing work includes Salt Cay Resort for Six Senses (Turks and Caicos Islands, 2013); and the Cité des Deux Mers (Morocco, 2013).

MAARTJE LAMMERS wurde 1963 geboren und schloss ihr Studium 1988 an der Technischen Universität Delft ab. **BORIS ZEISSER**, geboren 1968, absolvierte seinen Abschluss 1995 an derselben Hochschule. Bevor sie am 1. Januar 2001 ihr eigenes Büro 24H Architecture gründeten, arbeiteten die beiden für verschiedene Büros, darunter für (EEA) Erick van Egeraat Associated Architects, Mecanoo und das Office for Metropolitan Architecture (Rem Koolhaas). Als Einflüsse nennt das Team die Formen der Natur und den Art Déco, das Büro beschäftigt derzeit 16 Mitarbeiter. Zu ihren Projekten zählen das Ichthus Business Center (Rotterdam, Niederlande, 2002), das Ferienhaus Dragspelhuset (Arjang, Schweden, 2004), die ökologische Ferienanlage Soneva Kiri (Koh Kood, Thailand, 2009), die Panyaden School (Chiang Mai, Thailand, 2010–11, hier vorgestellt), ein Bürogebäude für die Rijkswaterstaat-Behörde (Assen, Niederlande, 2011) sowie das Zentrum für Umwelterziehung (Assen, Niederlande, 2012). Aktuelle Projekte sind u.a. der Salt Cay Resort for Six Senses (Turks- und Caicosinseln, 2013) und die Cité des Deux Mers (Marokko, 2013).

MAARTJE LAMMERS, née en 1963, est diplômée de l'Université de technologie de Delft (1988), comme **BORIS ZEISSER**, né en 1968 et diplômé en 1995. Le couple a travaillé dans plusieurs agences, dont Erick van Egeraat Associated Architects (EEA), Mecanoo et l'Office for Metropolitan Architecture (Rem Koolhaas), avant de créer 24H Architecture le 1er janvier 2001. Le travail de l'agence, qui emploie 16 collaborateurs, s'inspire des formes de la nature et du style Art déco. Parmi leurs réalisations : l'Ichthus Business Center (Rotterdam, Pays-Bas, 2002) ; la maison de vacances Dragspelhuset (Arjang, Suède, 2004) ; le complexe d'écovacances Soneva Kiri (Koh Kood, Thaïlande, 2009) ; l'école de Panyaden (Chiang Mai, Thaïlande, 2010–11, publiée ici) ; les bureaux du Rijkswaterstaat (Assen, Pays-Bas, 2011) et un Centre d'éducation environnementale (Assen, Pays-Bas, 2012). Ils travaillent actuellement aux projets du Salt Cay Resort for Six Senses (îles Turks et Caicos, 2013) et de la Cité des Deux Mers (Maroc, 2013).

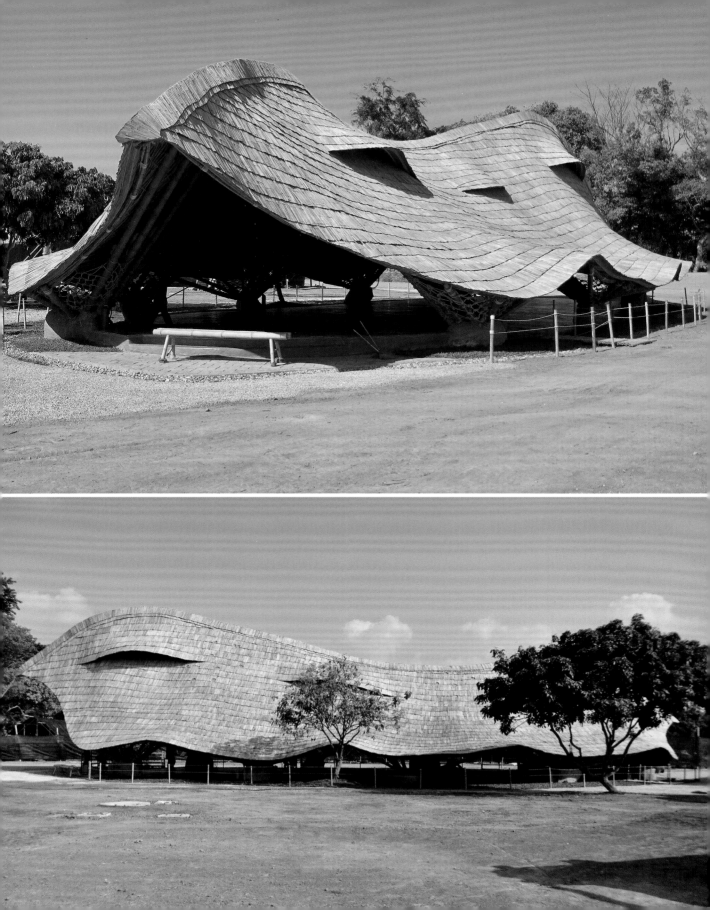

PANYADEN SCHOOL

Chiang Mai, Thailand, 2010–11

Address: 218 Moo 2, T. Namprae, A. Hang Dong, Chiang Mai 50230, Thailand, +66 5342 6618, www.panyaden.org
Area: 5000 m². Client: Yodphet Sudsawad. Cost: not disclosed
Collaboration: Olav Bruin, Andrew Duff

Built in a former orchard, the **PANYADEN SCHOOL** was conceived as a kindergarten and primary school for 375 students in a layout inspired by the shape "of the tropical antler horn fern." Classroom pavilions have load-bearing rammed-earth walls, which are connected by free-shaped adobe walls. All floors are of rammed earth and bamboo roof structures are related in their form to nearby mountains. The assembly hall and canteen are entirely made of bamboo with single bamboo or bundled bamboo columns, giving the feeling of walking through a bamboo forest. All materials are sourced locally and the overall carbon footprint of the project is a 10th of a comparable school. Panyaden School aims to deliver a holistic education that integrates Buddhist principles and environmental awareness with international academic standards.

Die **PANYADEN SCHOOL** wurde auf einer ehemaligen Obstplantage als Kindergarten und Grundschule für rund 375 Schülerinnen und Schüler geplant, ihr Grundriss ist der Form des „tropischen großen Geweihfarns" nachempfunden. Die tragenden Wände der Klassenraumpavillons wurden aus Stampflehm errichtet, zwischen ihnen verlaufen frei geformte Wände aus Lehmziegeln. Sämtliche Böden sind ebenfalls aus Stampflehm, während die Dachkonstruktion aus Bambus formal an die nahe Berglandschaft anknüpft. Aula und Kantine wurden mithilfe von Bambussäulen oder Säulenbündeln vollständig aus Bambus errichtet, sodass der Eindruck entsteht, durch einen Bambuswald zu laufen. Sämtliche Materialien sind lokalen Ursprungs, der gesamte ökologische Fußabdruck des Projekts beträgt rund ein Zehntel eines vergleichbaren Schulbaus. Die Panyaden School will ganzheitliche Bildung bieten und dabei buddhistische Prinzipien und Umweltbewusstsein mit internationalen akademischen Standards verbinden.

Établie dans un ancien verger, l'**ÉCOLE DE PANYADEN** est un jardin d'enfants et école primaire conçu pour recevoir 375 élèves. Son plan s'inspire de la forme d'une fougère tropicale, la *Platycerium superbum*. Les pavillons des classes ont des murs porteurs en pisé et des murs de façade de forme libre en adobe. Tous les sols sont en terre battue et les toitures en bambou rappellent le profil des montagnes avoisinantes. La salle de réunions et la cantine sont entièrement en bambou. La toiture est soutenue par des colonnes simples ou à fûts multiples réalisées dans ce même matériau, ce qui donne l'impression de se trouver dans une forêt de bambous. Tous les matériaux sont d'origine locale et l'empreinte carbone du projet n'est que le dixième de celle d'une école traditionnelle comparable. L'établissement délivre un enseignement holistique qui intègre à la fois des principes bouddhistes et des méthodes académiques internationales pour favoriser la prise de conscience environnementale des élèves.

The school blends into its jungle background in the image above. Right page, the undulating roof is seen in a closer image and in the elevation and section drawings below. A site plan shows the disposition of the elements of the complex.

Die Schule fügt sich harmonisch in die Dschungelkulisse (oben). Rechts das geschwungene Dach aus geringerer Distanz sowie auf Querschnitten unten. Ein Lageplan zeigt die Anordnung der baulichen Elemente des Komplexes.

Image ci-dessus : l'école se fond dans l'arrière-plan de la jungle. Page de droite : le toit ondulé en vue rapprochée et en élévation et en coupe dans les plans techniques. Un plan du site montre la disposition des diverses composantes du complexe.

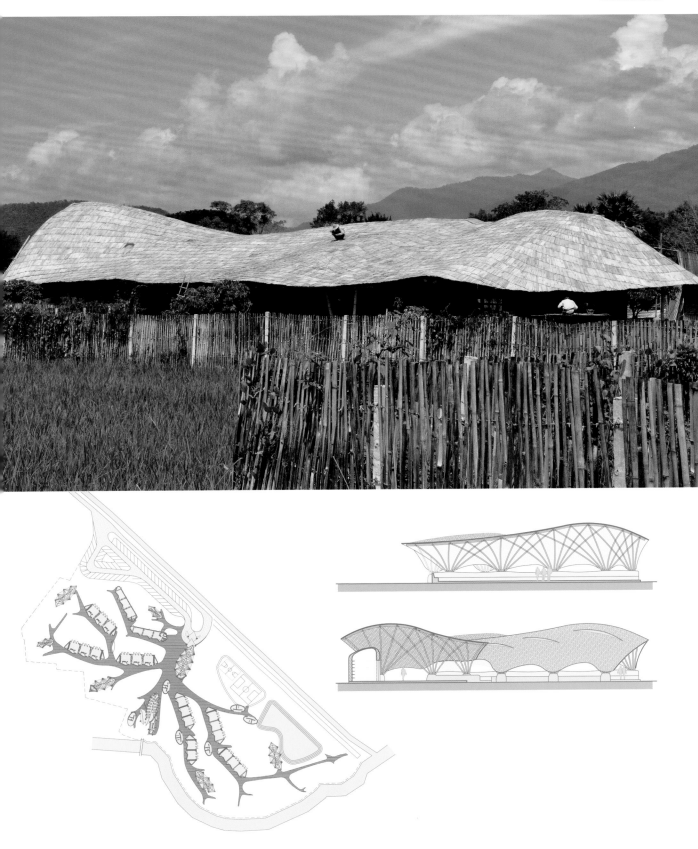

People gathered in the assembly hall with its bundled bamboo columns and low arching roof. Rammed-earth walls mark classroom areas. Local materials and a simple, intelligent form of construction make the carbon footprint of the complex very low.

Eine Versammlung in der „Aula" mit ihren gebündelten Bambusstützen und dem tief heruntergezogenen Dach. Wände aus Stampflehm markieren die Klassenräume. Lokale Materialien und einfache, intelligente Bauformen sorgen für eine ausgesprochen niedrige CO_2-Bilanz.

Assemblée dans la salle de réunions à colonnes à fûts multiples en bambou et à toiture à retombées surbaissées. Des murs en pisé délimitent les salles de classe. Grâce aux matériaux locaux et à un procédé de construction simple et intelligent, l'empreinte carbone du projet reste très basse.

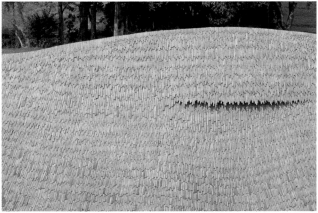

The design of the assembly hall, seen in plan and image (above), encourages the natural circulation of air and is inspired by the forms of local vegetation.

Die Konstruktion der Aula auf einem Grundriss und im Bild (oben). Die von regionaltypischen Pflanzen inspirierte Bauform fördert die natürliche Luftzirkulation.

La forme de la salle de réunions vue en plan et en image (ci-dessus) s'inspire des formes végétales locales et encourage la circulation naturelle de l'air.

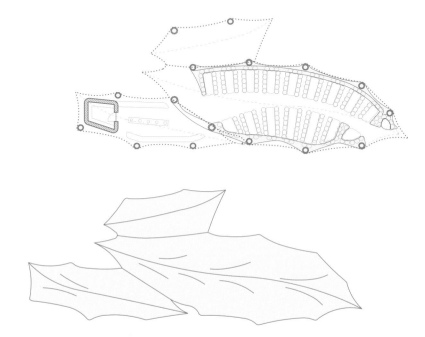

2012ARCHITECTEN

2012Architecten
Kruiskade 6
3056 AK Rotterdam
The Netherlands

Tel: +31 10 466 44 44
E-mail: pr@2012Architecten.nl
Web: www.2012Architecten.nl

JAN JONGERT was born in 1971 in Amsterdam and educated at the Technical University of Delft (TU; 1990–96) and the Academie van Bouwkunst (Rotterdam, 1998–2003). **JEROEN BERGSMA** was born in 1970, also in Amsterdam, and was educated at the TU Delft (1988–96). Their work includes the Wikado Playground (Rotterdam, 2006–07); Villa Welpeloo (Enschede, 2006–09, published here); the Kindervrijstaat, a reconstruction of a farm and interior for a children's art center (Utrecht, 2010); the DordtYart, the reconstruction of a former dock area into a contemporary art center (Rotterdam, 2009–12); and Cyclifer, a research project on energy, food, and water flows in the urban environment (2010–12), all in the Netherlands.

JAN JONGERT wurde 1971 in Amsterdam geboren und studierte an der Technischen Universität Delft (1990–96) sowie der Academie van Bouwkunst (Rotterdam, 1998–2003). **JEROEN BERGSMA** wurde 1970, ebenfalls in Amsterdam, geboren und studierte an der TU Delft (1988–96). Ihre Projekte sind u.a. der Wikado Spielplatz (Rotterdam, 2006–07), die Villa Welpeloo (Enschede, 2006–09, hier vorgestellt), der Kindervrijstaat, Umbau eines Bauernhofs zum Kinderkunstzentrum (Utrecht, 2010), DordtYart, Sanierung ehemaliger Hafenanlagen als Zentrum für zeitgenössische Kunst (Rotterdam, 2009–12), und Cyclifer, ein Forschungsprojekt zu Energie-, Nahrungs- und Wasserkreisläufen im urbanen Umfeld (2010–12), alle in den Niederlanden.

JAN JONGERT, né en 1971 à Amsterdam, a étudié à l'Université de technologie de Delft (1990–96) et à l'Académie de l'art de la construction (Academie van Bouwkunst, Rotterdam, 1998–2003). **JEROEN BERGSMA**, né en 1970 à Amsterdam, a aussi étudié à l'Université de Delft (1988–96). Parmi leurs réalisations, toutes aux Pays-Bas : le terrain de jeu Wikado (Rotterdam, 2006–07) ; la villa Welpeloo (Enschede, 2006–09, publiée ici) ; la Kindervrijstaat, reconstruction d'une ferme et aménagements intérieurs pour un centre d'art pour enfants (Utrecht, 2010) ; le DordtYart, reconversion d'anciens docks en Centre d'art contemporain (Rotterdam, 2009–12), et Cyclifer, projet de recherches sur l'énergie, l'alimentation et l'eau en environnement urbain (2010–12).

VILLA WELPELOO

Enschede, The Netherlands, 2006–09

Address: Bamshoevelaan 49, Enschede, The Netherlands
Area: 312 m². Client: not disclosed. Cost: €900 000

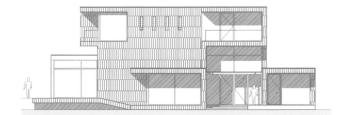

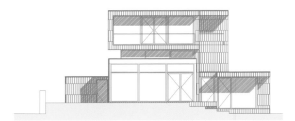

The combination of rough wooden surfaces and glazed walls gives the house an unusual appearance, although the elevations (above) show that its basic forms are strictly rectangular.

Durch die Mischung aus Holzverblendung und Verglasung wirkt das Haus ungewöhnlich, trotz seiner streng geradlinigen Grundformen, erkennbar auf den Aufrissen oben.

L'aspect étonnant de la maison doit beaucoup à la combinaison des plans en bois brut et des murs de verre car les élévations (ci-dessus) montrent la simplicité des articulations strictement orthogonales.

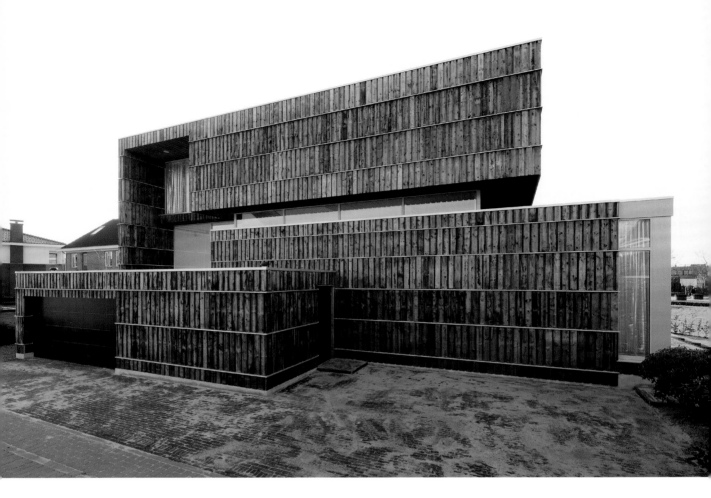

The reused wood employed for exterior cladding largely covers the surface of the building, as seen from the street side (above). Section drawings show the main stairway, living spaces, and the garage (below).

Fast die gesamte Außenfassade ist mit recyceltem Holz verblendet, wie auf der Straßenansicht zu sehen (oben). Querschnitte zeigen Treppenhaus, Wohnbereiche und Garage (unten).

Le bardage extérieur en bois de récupération recouvre une grande partie du bâtiment vu de la rue (ci-dessus). Les plans de coupe ci-dessous montrent l'escalier principal, les espaces de séjour et le garage.

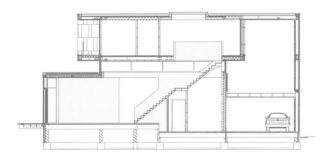

This villa was designed for a couple that collects drawings and graphic art by contemporary artists. It includes two bedrooms, a guesthouse, a studio/kitchen, and large reception area. The spaces of the villa are formed by surfaces extending out of a central element intended for the storage of the artworks. These surfaces in turn are used to display the art. The main structure is made of steel profiles that previously were part of a machine used for textile production, formerly an important local industry. Inside the house, the architects reused a building-site elevator. The façade and interior walls are clad with wooden slats from a thousand redundant cable reels collected at a local cable factory.

Die Villa wurde für ein Paar geplant, das zeitgenössische Zeichnungen und Druckgrafik sammelt. Zum Haus gehören zwei Schlafzimmer, ein Gästehaus, ein Atelier mit Küche sowie ein großer Empfangsbereich. Die Räume der Villa gruppieren sich um einen zentralen Magazinbereich, in dem die Kunstwerke gelagert werden, die Wandflächen dienen zur Präsentation ausgewählter Werke. Das Haupttragwerk wurde aus Stahlprofilen realisiert, die ursprünglich Teil einer Maschine für die Textilproduktion waren, einem vormals wichtigen Standbein der regionalen Industrie. Im Innern des Hauses fanden die Architekten neue Verwendung für einen alten Baustellenaufzug, während Fassaden und Teile des Innenausbaus mit Holzbrettern von Tausend ausgemusterten Kabelrollen verblendet sind, die von einem örtlichen Kabelhersteller stammen.

Cette villa a été conçue pour un couple de collectionneurs de dessins et d'estampes d'artistes contemporains. Elle comprend deux chambres, une maison d'amis, une cuisine-atelier et un vaste espace de réception. Les volumes se déploient à partir d'un bloc central prévu pour le stockage des œuvres d'art. Les différentes pièces permettent également d'exposer les œuvres. La structure principale est en profilés d'acier récupérés sur une vieille machine de fabrication de textiles (jadis importante industrie locale). Pour l'intérieur, les architectes ont de même réutilisé un élévateur de chantier. La façade et les murs intérieurs sont habillés de lattes de bois de milliers de bobines trouvées dans une usine de câbles locale.

As night falls, the house glows from within, making its modern character more evident than might be the case during the day.

In der Dämmerung leuchtet das Haus von innen, wodurch es noch moderner wirkt als vielleicht tagsüber.

À la nuit tombante, la maison brille de l'intérieur, ce qui renforce son caractère contemporain.

The interior of the house is quite simple and clean in order to give ample space to the works of art. Plans (below) show the orchestration of intersecting rectangular volumes that makes up the design.

Das Interieur ist schlicht und klar gehalten, um reichlich Platz für Kunst zu bieten. Grundrisse (unten) veranschaulichen die Verschränkung der rechteckigen Volumina im Entwurf.

L'intérieur de la maison, assez simplement traité et dégagé, laisse toute leur place aux œuvres d'art. Les plans ci-dessous montrent l'articulation des volumes rectangulaires dans la composition.

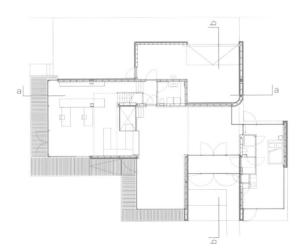

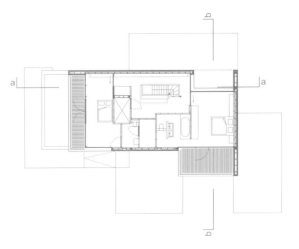

Open volumes with ample natural light allow for the display of art within the context of a house that is also livable.

In einem Haus, das durchaus wohnlich ist, bieten offene Bereiche mit Tageslicht viel Raum für die Präsentation von Kunst.

Des volumes très ouverts et un généreux éclairage naturel permettent la présentation de nombreuses œuvres d'art dans cette maison parfaitement habitable.

Artworks take center stage in a space that is essentially white and smooth, except where full-height glazing brings the exterior environment into the equation.

Kunst spielt die Hauptrolle in diesen vor allem weißen Räumen mit glatten Oberflächen – Ausnahme sind die deckenhohen Fenster, durch die auch das Umfeld Aufmerksamkeit fordert.

Les œuvres d'art tiennent le devant de la scène dans des espaces épurés en blanc. À certains moments, des vitrages toute hauteur laissent entrer le paysage dans cette équation.

EFFAN ADHIWIRA

Effan Adhiwira
PT Bamboo Pure
Br. Piakan, Sibang Kaja, Abiansemal
Badung
Bali 80352
Indonesia

Tel: +62 36 146 9874
E-mail: info@ibuku.com
Web: www.ibuku.com

EFFAN ADHIWIRA was born in 1982. He received his B.Arch degree from the Faculty of Engineering, Gadjah Mada University (Jogjakarta, Indonesia, 2000–05). He worked as an architect for the firm Toma House from 2005 to 2007. He has been the Senior Architect at PT Bamboo Pure since 2007. Recent work includes the Green School (Badung, Bali, 2007, published here); Kaba-Kaba house (Tabanan, Bali, 2009); VW House (Gianyar, Bali, 2009); and the Tanduk House (Payangan, Bali, 2010). Current work includes the Alphonse Island Resort (Alphonse Island, Seychelles, 2010–); Live Media Theater, a portable 30-meter-diameter bamboo dome theater; the Pemulung House(s) (Denpasar, Bali, 2010–); and the Green Village (Sibang, Bali, 2011–), all in Indonesia unless stated otherwise.

EFFAN ADHIWIRA wurde 1982 geboren und absolvierte seinen B.Arch an der Fakultät für Ingenieurwesen an der Universität Gadjah Mada (Jogjakarta, Indonesien, 2000–05). Von 2005 bis 2007 war er als Architekt bei Toma House tätig. Seit 2007 ist er leitender Architekt bei PT Bamboo Pure. Jüngere Projekte sind u.a. die Green School (Badung, Bali, 2007, hier vorgestellt), das Kaba-Kaba House (Tabanan, Bali, 2009), VW House (Gianyar, Bali, 2009) sowie das Tanduk House (Payangan, Bali, 2010). Derzeit in Arbeit sind u.a. das Alphonse Island Resort (Alphonse Island, Seychellen, 2010–), das Live Media Theater, ein mobiler Theater-Bambuskuppelbau mit einem Durchmesser von 30 m, die Pemulung House(s) (Denpasar, Bali, 2010–) sowie das Green Village (Sibang, Bali, 2011–), alle in Indonesien, sofern nicht anders angegeben.

EFFAN ADHIWIRA, né en 1982, a obtenu son B. Arch. à la faculté d'ingénierie de l'université Gadjah Mada (Jogjakarta, Indonésie, 2000–05). Il a travaillé pour l'agence Toma House de 2005 à 2007 et, depuis cette date, est architecte senior chez PT Bamboo Pure. Parmi ses réalisations récentes : l'École verte (Badung, Bali, 2007, publiée ici) ; la maison Kaba-Kaba (Tabanan, Bali, 2009) ; la maison VW (Gianyar, Bali, 2009) et la maison Tanduk (Payangan, Bali, 2010). Actuellement, il travaille sur les projets de l'Alphonse Island Resort (Alphonse Island, Seychelles, 2010–) ; du Live Media Theater, un théâtre mobile à coupole en bambou de 30 mètres de diamètre ; des Pemulung House(s) (Denpasar, Bali, 2010–) et du Village vert (Sibang, Bali, 2011–), tous en Indonésie sauf mention contraire.

GREEN SCHOOL

Badung, Bali, Indonesia, 2007

Address: Sibang Kaja, Abiansemal, Badung, Bali, Indonesia, +62 36 146 9875, www.greenschool.org
Area: 7542 m². Client: Yayasan Kulkul. Cost: $30 212 million

PT Bamboo and the related Meranggi Foundation were founded by John and Cynthia Hardy, designers and environmentalists from Bali. PT Bamboo is a design and construction company that uses bamboo, while the Meranggi Foundation seeks to develop bamboo timber plantations. They decided to build a school to demonstrate their interest in the use of sustainable materials for construction, and to educate children in sustainable life patterns. The bamboo used for the school was transformed by local artisans. Such materials as recycled rubble or car windshields are employed and landscaping includes an organic garden, a wastewater garden, and living tree fences. Bamboo columns are set on top of natural river stones to avoid insect and humidity related degradation of the wood. Steel bars drilled through the support rocks connect the columns to the foundation. Outward leaning columns and large roof overhangs reduce solar gain.

PT Bamboo und die mit dem Büro assoziierte Meranggi Foundation wurden von John und Cynthia Hardy gegründet, Designern und Umweltschützern auf Bali. Während PT Bamboo als Gestaltungs- und Baufirma mit Bambus arbeitet, bemüht sich die Meranggi Foundation um die Schaffung von Bambus-Bauholzplantagen. Die Entscheidung zum Bau der Schule entstand aus dem Interesse an der Verwendung von nachhaltigen Baumaterialien und dem Wunsch, Kindern nachhaltige Lebensweisen zu vermitteln. Der für den Schulbau verwendete Bambus wurde von ortsansässigen Kunsthandwerkern verarbeitet. Auch Materialien wie recycelter Bauschutt oder Auto-windschutzscheiben kamen zum Einsatz. Die Landschaftsgestaltung umfasst u.a. einen Biogarten, einen Brauchwassergarten und „lebende" Zäune. Um die Schädigung des Holzes durch Insektenbefall oder Feuchtigkeit zu verhindern, wurden die Bambusstützen auf Felssteine aus einem Flussbett gesetzt. Durch Stahlstäbe, die durch die Felssteine gebohrt wurden, sind die Stützen im Fundament verankert. Dank der Außenneigung der Stützen und dem großzügigen Dachüberhang wird die Erwärmung des Baus durch Sonneneinstrahlung reduziert.

PT Bamboo et la Meranggi Foundation affiliée ont été fondées par John et Cynthia Hardy, designers et écologistes installés à Bali. PT Bamboo est une agence de design et de construction qui utilise le bambou, tandis que la Meranggi Foundation cherche à en développer les applications. Ensemble, ils ont voulu construire une école pour illustrer l'intérêt de l'utilisation de matériaux durables dans la construction et former les enfants à des modes de vie durables. Le bambou a été transformé par des artisans locaux. D'autres matériaux comme des moellons ou des pare-brise d'automobiles de récupération ont été utilisés. L'aménagement paysager comprend un jardin biologique, un jardin de traitement des eaux usées et des haies vives. Les colonnes de bambou s'appuient sur des pierres trouvées dans la rivière pour éviter les attaques des insectes et les effets de l'humidité. Des tiges d'acier qui traversent ces supports en pierre solidarisent les colonnes aux fondations. Les importants débords de la toiture soutenue par des colonnes inclinées réduisent le gain solaire.

The school blends into the tropical vegetation much in the way that purely indigenous architecture might. Modulated building sizes and the materials employed assure this symbiotic appearance.

Die Schule verschmilzt mit der tropischen Vegetation, wie es authentische, indigene Architektur tun würde. Dieser symbiotische Eindruck wird besonders durch die Modulation unterschiedlicher Proportionen und Materialien erreicht.

L'école se fond dans la végétation tropicale à la manière de l'architecture indigène. La dimension raisonnable des constructions et les matériaux utilisés expliquent cette impression de symbiose.

Spiraling fernlike patterns mark the
plan and little distinction can be
made between interior and exterior
spaces, with bamboo columns offering ample ceiling heights.

Die Form des Grundrisses erinnert an
Farnwedel. Zwischen Außen- und
Innenraum ist dank der Bambusstützen und großzügigen Deckenhöhe
kaum zu unterscheiden.

Le plan en spirales rappelle le développement des fougères et la distinction entre les espaces intérieurs et
extérieurs est floue. Les colonnes de
bambou permettent de généreuses
hauteurs de plafonds.

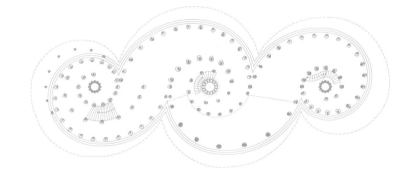

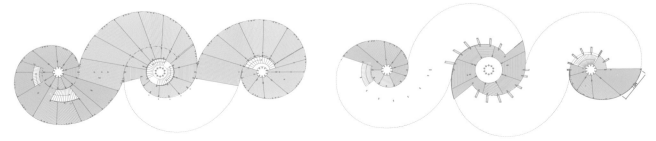

With its generous, open walls and high ceilings, the Green School certainly defies the usual image of sustainable architecture, which might be imagined as being dull and dark.

Mit ihren offenen Wänden und hohen Decken entspricht die Green School sicherlich nicht den üblichen Vorstellungen von nachhaltiger Architektur, die mitunter fälschlich für fade und dunkel gehalten wird.

Par ses ouvertures sur la nature et ses plafonds élevés, l'École verte est un défi à l'image habituelle des constructions durables, souvent jugées ennuyeuses et peu lumineuses.

The design of the large arching roof, seen in the images above and the drawing on the right, brings to mind very modern design, albeit here erected using only sustainable materials.

Das Design der hohen, geschwungenen Dachkonstruktion (Abbildungen oben und Zeichnung rechts) wirkt wie ein hochmoderner Entwurf, wurde jedoch ausschließlich mit nachhaltigen Materialien realisiert.

Le design de la vaste toiture en arc (photos ci-dessus et dessins de droite) rappelle des projets d'esprit contemporain, malgré l'utilisation exclusive de matériaux durables.

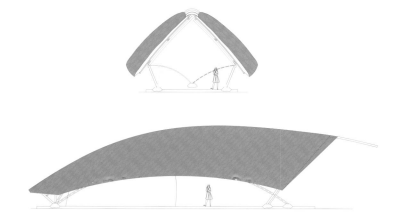

The curving roofs have large round openings that allow daylight into the interior spaces, while also protecting from sun and heat. Elevations (below) give an idea of the large scale of the buildings.

Die geschwungenen Dächer schützen vor Sonne und Hitze; durch große runde Öffnungen fällt Tageslicht ins Innere. Aufrisse (unten) vermitteln eine Vorstellung vom Maßstab der Gebäude.

Les toits incurvés sont interrompus par de vastes ouvertures qui laissent pénétrer la lumière du jour tout en protégeant l'intérieur du soleil et de la chaleur. Les élévations (ci-dessous) donnent une idée de l'importance de l'échelle de ces bâtiments.

Bundled and assembled in a spiraling
pattern, bamboo poles offer an obvious lightness and strength to the
building. Daylight and fresh air are
also omnipresent in this architecture.

Durch die spiralförmig angeordneten
Bambus-Säulenbündel wirkt der Bau
ausgesprochen hell und belastbar.
Allgegenwärtig in dieser Architektur
sind Tageslicht und frische Luft.

Liés et assemblés en torsades, les
piliers de bambou confèrent au bâtiment un sentiment de légèreté et de
solidité. La lumière et la ventilation
naturelles animent en permanence
l'architecture.

Curving desks echo the form of the buildings, while the curvature and slating of the roofs assures that potentially heavy monsoon rains can be carried off without overloading the structure.

Die geschwungenen Tische greifen die Form der Bauten auf. Schwung und Neigung der Dächer wiederum sorgen dafür, dass Wasser bei heftigen Monsunregen abfließen kann, ohne die Konstruktion zu überlasten.

Les bureaux incurvés rappellent la forme des bâtiments tandis que la courbure et l'inclinaison des toits protègent des fortes pluies de la mousson et assurent leur évacuation sans surcharger la structure.

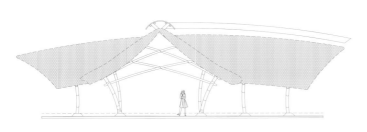

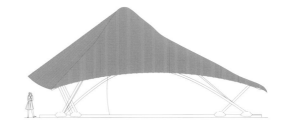

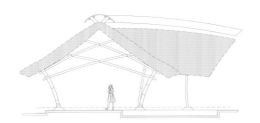

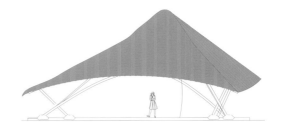

AFF

AFF Architekten
Wedekindstr. 24
10243 Berlin
Germany

Tel: +49 30 27 59 29 20
Fax: +49 30 275 92 92 22
E-mail: berlin@aff-architekten.com
Web: www.aff-architekten.com

AFF ARCHITEKTEN was founded in 1999 by Martin Fröhlich (born in 1968 in Magdeburg, Germany), Sven Fröhlich (born in 1974, also in Magdeburg), and Torsten Lockl (born in 1973 in Gotha, Germany), graduates of the Bauhaus University Weimar. They state that: "In accordance with the workshop tradition, we wanted to establish a firm that would produce architecture with character through the collaboration of committed architects." Their work includes Typological Houses (Weimar, 2006); Anna-Seghers Comprehensive School (Berlin, 2008); Freudenstein Castle (Freiberg, 2008); the exhibition "Terra Mineralia" (Freudenstein Castle, Freiberg, 2008); and the Protective Hut on Fichtelberg Mountain (Tellerhäuser, Oberwiesenthal, 2008–09, published here), all in Germany.

AFF ARCHITEKTEN wurde 1999 von Martin Fröhlich (1968 in Magdeburg geboren), Sven Fröhlich (1974 ebenfalls in Magdeburg geboren) und Torsten Lockl (geboren 1973 in Gotha) gegründet. Die Absolventen der Bauhaus-Universität Weimar erklären: „Im Sinne der Werkstättentradition wollten wir ein Büro gründen, das durch die Kollaboration engagierter Architekten Architektur mit Charakter entwirft." Zu ihren Projekten zählen Typologische Wohnhäuser (Weimar, 2006), die Gemeinschaftsschule Anna Seghers (Berlin, 2008), das Schloss Freudenstein (Freiberg, 2008), die Ausstellung *Terra Mineralia* (Schloss Freudenstein, Freiberg, 2008) sowie die Schutzhütte am Fichtelberg (Tellerhäuser, Oberwiesenthal, 2008–09, hier vorgestellt), alle in Deutschland.

L'agence **AFF ARCHITEKTEN** a été fondée en 1999 par Martin Fröhlich (né en 1968 à Magdeburg, Allemagne), Sven Fröhlich (né en 1974 à Magdeburg) et Torsten Lockl (né en 1973 à Gotha, Allemagne), diplômés de l'université Bauhaus à Weimar. « Dans l'esprit de la tradition de l'atelier, nous souhaitions créer une agence qui produise une architecture de caractère grâce à la collaboration active d'architectes engagés dans le projet », expliquent-ils. Leur œuvre comprend entre autres : les Maisons typologiques (Weimar, 2006) ; l'École secondaire Anna-Seghers (Berlin, 2008) ; le château Freudenstein (Freiberg, 2008) ; l'exposition « Terra Mineralia » (château Freudenstein, Freiberg, 2008) et le refuge de montagne du Fichtelberg (Tellerhäuser, Oberwiesenthal, 2008–09, publié ici), tous en Allemagne.

"HUTZNHAISL"

Protective Hut on Fichtelberg Mountain, Tellerhäuser, Oberwiesenthal, Germany, 2008–09

Address: Tellerhäuser Str. 5, Tellerhäuser, 09484 Oberwiesenthal, Germany
Area: 70 m². Client: not disclosed. Cost: €60 000

As befits this winter scene, the building exudes an austerity that is itself undeniably cold.

Passend zur winterlichen Szene ist der Bau formal von einer Strenge, die ohne Frage kalt wirkt.

Comme il convient sans doute à cette scène hivernale, le petit bâtiment exsude une austérité glaciale.

A photo and drawing sum up the extremely simple form of the architecture, cast in concrete with no visible frills.

Aufnahme und Zeichnung zeigen die extrem schlichte Architektur, die offenkundig ohne Extras auskommt und in Beton gegossen wurde.

Cette photo et le dessin ci-dessous illustrent l'extrême simplicité de l'architecture en béton coulé, sans le moindre ornement visible.

The architects state: "The hut appears to have been wrestled from the surrounding landscape, a concrete sculpture at the side of the road from Rittersgrün and Oberwiesenthal through the Ore Mountains in Saxony." The structure opens toward the forest "like a bus stop opens only to the street, always in the direction of the intended destination." Intended to accommodate six to eight people, the structure is spartan to say the least, with its concrete walls and ceilings and locally cut spruce floorboards. Recycled switches, lights, chairs, and washbasins are used. It has no "daring technical features" in a willful architectural distancing from modern urban life. The concrete of the structure bears the imprint of the former wooden hut that stood on the site, recalling work like that of the English sculptor Rachel Whiteread.

Die Architekten erklären: „Wie der Landschaft abgetrotzt erscheint die Hütte als Betonskulptur am Saum der erzgebirgischen Landstraße zwischen Rittersgrün und Oberwiesenthal." Der Bau öffnet sich zum Wald, „so wie sich eine Bushaltestelle ausschließlich zur Straße öffnet, immer in die Richtung des anvisierten Ziels". Der für sechs bis acht Personen ausgelegte Bau ist gelinde gesagt spartanisch mit seinen Wänden und Decken aus Beton und den Holzdielenböden aus vor Ort geschlagener Fichte. Schalter, Leuchten, Sessel, Stühle und Waschschüsseln sind recycelt. Hier gibt es keinerlei „gewagte technische Besonderheiten"; es ist die bewusste Distanzierung vom modernen, urbanen Leben durch Architektur. Auf dem Baukörper aus Beton zeichnet sich der Abdruck des Vorgängerbaus ab, ebenfalls eine Hütte – eine Reminiszenz an Arbeiten wie etwa die der englischen Künstlerin Rachel Whiteread.

« Sculpture en béton posée au bord de la route qui travers les monts Métallifères de Saxe, entre Rittersgrün et Oberwiesenthal, le refuge semble se mesurer au paysage qui l'environne », commentent les architectes. Il s'ouvre sur la forêt « comme un arrêt de bus s'ouvre sur la rue, toujours dans la direction de la destination supposée ». Prévu pour six à huit personnes, l'aménagement de ce refuge aux murs et plafonds en béton et sols en épicéa d'exploitation locale est pour le moins spartiate. Les éviers, les éclairages, les sièges et même les interrupteurs sont de récupération. Dans sa prise de distance par rapport à la vie urbaine moderne, ce refuge ne présente pas de « caractéristiques techniques audacieuses ». Le béton porte encore l'empreinte de l'ancien refuge en bois qui se trouvait sur le même site et rappelle le travail d'artistes comme la sculptrice britannique Rachel Whiteread.

The architects willfully eschew most comforts of modern life, while using casts of elements from the former wooden hut located on the same site, recalling work of artists such as Rachel Whiteread and her piece Ghost (1990).

Ganz bewusst verzichten die Architekten weitgehend auf modernen Komfort. Dank der Nutzung von Bauteilen des Vorgängerbaus, einer alten Holzhütte, als Schalungselemente, erinnert der Bau an Arbeiten der Künstlerin Rachel Whiteread wie etwa Ghost (1990).

Les architectes ont volontairement renoncé à la plupart des conforts de la vie moderne et utilisé des éléments moulés à partir de l'ancien refuge en bois qu'ils remplaçaient. Ces interventions rappellent certaines œuvres d'art comme la pièce Ghost (1990) de Rachel Whitehead.

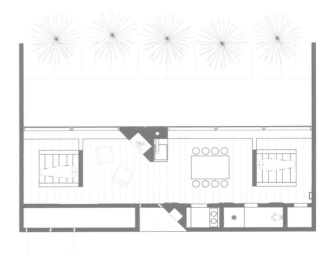

AL BORDE

al bordE
Los Ríos N9–35 y Esmeraldas
Quito
Pichincha
Ecuador

Tel: +593 8 463 6428
E-mail: contact@albordearq.com
Web: www.albordearq.com

Al bordE was founded in 2007 by **DAVID BARRAGÁN**, born in 1981, and **PASCUAL GANGOTENA**, born in 1971, in Quito, Ecuador. They both graduated from the Architecture School of the Catholic University of Ecuador, respectively in 2005 and 2006. Prior to creating their firm, David Barragán worked with the architect José María Sáez, and Pascual Gangotena was principal of the non-profit organization Un Techo Para Ecuador, whose main work was focused in design and construction of community infrastructure and low-income housing with the support of volunteers from all over the country. Their work includes the Pentimento House (Quito, 2006); the Atelier–Greenhouse (Machachi, 2007); Entre Muros House (Tumbaco, Quito, 2007–, published here); Kay Pacha Yaku Hukuma (Yasuni, 2009); the Itala House (Puembo, 2009); Nueva Esperanza School (Manabí, 2009); Houses 001 and 002 (Quito, 2010); and UEM North (Quito, 2011), all in Ecuador.

Gegründet wurde al bordE 2007 von **DAVID BARRAGÁN**, geboren 1981, und **PASCUAL GANGOTENA**, geboren 1971 in Quito, Ecuador. Beide schlossen ihr Studium 2005 bzw. 2006 an der Fakultät für Architektur der Katholischen Universität Ecuador ab. Vor der Gründung des eigenen Büros arbeitete David Barragán mit dem Architekten José María Sáez, während Pascual Gangotena sich als Direktor der Organisation „Un Techo Para Ecuador" engagierte, die sich vor allem für die Gestaltung und den Bau von Infrastruktur in kleineren Gemeinden und Wohnbauten für einkommensschwache Bürger einsetzt. Unterstützt wurde er von Freiwilligen aus dem gesamten Land. Zu den Projekten des Teams zählen die Casa Pentimento (Quito, 2006), ein Atelier und Gewächshaus (Machachi, 2007), die Casa Entre Muros (Tumbaco, Quito, 2007–, hier vorgestellt), Kay Pacha Yaku Hukuma (Yasuni, 2009), die Casa Itala (Puembo, 2009), die Schule Nueva Esperanza (Manabí, 2009), die Casa 001 und 002 (Quito, 2010) sowie UEM Nord (Quito, 2011), alle in Ecuador.

L'agence al bordE a été fondée en 2007 par **DAVID BARRAGÁN**, né en 1981, et **PASCUAL GANGOTENA**, né en 1971, à Quito (Équateur). Tous deux sont diplômés de l'École d'architecture de l'Université catholique de l'Équateur, respectivement en 2005 et 2006. Avant de créer cette agence, David Barragán avait travaillé avec l'architecte José María Sáez et Pascual Gangotena était un des dirigeants de l'association « Un Techo Para Ecuador » (Un toit pour l'Équateur) dont l'objectif principal est la conception et la construction d'infrastructures communautaires et de logements économiques avec l'aide de bénévoles de toutes les régions du pays. Parmi leurs réalisations : la maison Pentimento (Quito, 2006) ; un atelier-serre (Machachi, 2007) ; la maison Entre Muros (Tumbaco, Quito, 2007–, publiée ici) ; Kay Pacha Yaku Hukuma (Yasuni, 2009) ; la maison Itala (Puembo, 2009) ; l'école Nueva Esperanza (Manabí, 2009) ; les maisons 001 et 002 (Quito, 2010) et le projet UEM Nord (Quito, 2011), le tout en Équateur.

ENTRE MUROS HOUSE

Tumbaco, Quito, Ecuador, 2007–

*Address: 13ava Transversal e Intervalles S/N, Tumbaco, Quito, Ecuador
Area: 180 m². Client: Carla Flor. Cost: $50 400*

Built on a 5000-square-meter site on a hillside of the Ilaló volcano, the **ENTRE MUROS HOUSE** was built with rammed earth, wood, and stone. The architects describe it as the result of a "search for living in harmony with nature, the need of autonomy for each one of the three members of the family, the low budget," and the phrase: "There is always another way of doing things and another way for living." A long corridor was used as an element that isolates the project from neighbors and includes furniture "worked inside the thick adobe walls." Gray water is used for irrigation, and solar energy to heat water. The raw materials of the adobe walls come from the site itself. The architects have also paid careful attention to customs such as a ceremony requesting the permission of the volcano to build on the site, and cutting wood and reeds at the appropriate phase of the moon.

Die auf einem 5000 m² großen Grundstück am Abhang des Ilaló-Vulkans gelegene **CASA ENTRE MUROS** wurde aus Stampflehm, Holz und Stein gebaut. Die Architekten nennen es das Resultat einer „Suche nach einem Leben in Harmonie mit der Natur, dem Bedürfnis nach Unabhängigkeit für die drei Familienmitglieder und einem schmalen Budget". Außerdem sei es Folge des Leitsatzes: „Es gibt immer eine andere Art etwas zu machen, und eine andere Art zu leben." Ein langer Korridor dient als architektonisches Element, das den Bau von Nachbarn abschirmt; dort sind außerdem Einbauten „in die massiven Lehmziegelwände eingearbeitet". Für die Bewässerung wird Grauwasser genutzt, Warmwasser wird durch Solarenergie erzeugt. Das Material für die Lehmziegelmauern stammt vom Grundstück. Auch traditionelle Bräuche wurden von den Architekten respektiert, etwa eine Zeremonie, in der der Vulkan gebeten wurde, auf dem Grundstück bauen zu dürfen, oder das Schlagen von Holz und das Schneiden von Reet zu entsprechenden Mondphasen.

Construite sur un terrain de 5000 mètres carrés aux flancs du volcan Ilaló, la **MAISON ENTRE MUROS** est en adobe, bois et pierre. Les architectes la présentent comme « une recherche de vie en harmonie avec la nature, la réponse au besoin d'autonomie de chacun des trois membres de la famille et à un budget limité », et précise « qu'il y a toujours une autre façon de faire les choses et une autre façon de vivre ». Un long corridor qui isole la résidence du voisinage intègre des meubles « travaillés dans l'épaisseur des murs d'adobe ». Les eaux de récupération servent à l'irrigation et l'eau est chauffée par l'énergie solaire. Les matériaux ayant servi à fabriquer l'adobe viennent du site même. Les architectes ont porté la plus grande attention aux coutumes locales comme la cérémonie consistant à demander au volcan la permission de construire sur ses pentes ou d'abattre des arbres et des roseaux en fonction des phases de la lune.

Though composed of modern, geometric forms, in the image above the house appears to flow into its irregular site.

Trotz seiner modernen, geometrischen Formgebung scheint der Bau (oben) geradezu in das asymmetrische Grundstück hineinzufließen.

Composée de formes géométriques modernes, la maison (image ci-dessus) semble suivre le mouvement irrégulier de son terrain.

Though rammed earth was used in the construction, the house appears thoroughly modern in its setting at night and by day (below). Nor are its sustainable features readily apparent in these images.

Obwohl hier mit Stampflehm gebaut wurde, wirkt das Haus in seinem Umfeld absolut modern, sowohl auf der nächtlichen Ansicht als auch bei Tag (unten). Auch die ökologischen Aspekte des Baus drängen sich nicht auf.

Bien que la maison ait été partiellement construite en terre, elle paraît totalement actuelle, aussi bien la nuit que le jour (ci-dessous). Ses équipements pour les économies d'énergie n'apparaissent pas sur ces images.

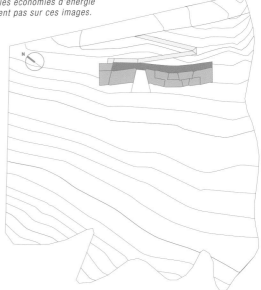

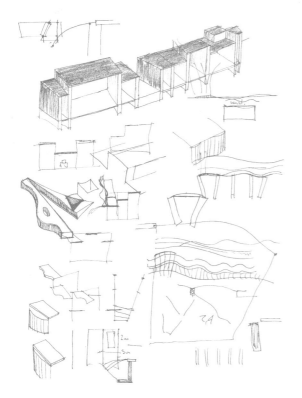

The sketch on the left and interior views make much more obvious the architects' concern with the use of sustainable materials and design. Roughness characterizes almost every surface.

Wesentlich augenfälliger sind die Bemühungen der Architekten um nachhaltige Materialien und nachhaltige Planung auf der Skizze links und den Innenansichten. Fast sämtliche Oberflächen sind rau und unbehandelt.

Les croquis de gauche et les vues de l'intérieur illustrent les préoccupations écologiques des architectes, aussi bien dans la conception que dans le choix des matériaux. Chaque surface ou presque présente un aspect brut et naturel.

APARICIO + DONAIRE

Jesús Mª Aparicio Guisado
Goya 39 4º, 28001 Madrid, Spain
Tel: +34 91 577 94 46, Fax: +34 91 576 07 96
E-mail: estudio@jesusaparicio.net
Web: www.jesusaparicio.net

Jesús Donaire García de la Mora
Parque de la Paloma 20, BJ-L, 28026 Madrid, Spain
Tel: +34 63 922 29 79
E-mail: jesus.donaire@jesusdonaire.com
Web: www.jesusdonaire.com

JESÚS Mª APARICIO GUISADO was born in Madrid, Spain, in 1960. He obtained his degree in Architecture from the Escuela Técnica Superior de Arquitectura de Madrid (ETSAM) in 1984. He then received his Ph.D. in Architecture and since 2009 has been a Full Professor of Building Design at ETSAM. In 2000 he represented Spain at the Architecture Biennale in Venice, Italy. **JESÚS DONAIRE GARCÍA DE LA MORA** was born in Ciudad Real, Spain, in 1974. He obtained his degree in Architecture from ETSAM in 2000. He then obtained a Master of Science in Advanced Architectural Design from the Graduate School of Architecture, Planning, and Preservation (GSAPP), Columbia University in New York. He worked with Alberto Campo Baeza in Madrid, and David Chipperfield in London, before the creation of his firm. Aparicio's work includes a Retirement Home in Santa Marta de Tormes (Salamanca, 2003); Architectural Archive and Lecture Hall in Nuevos Ministerios (Madrid, 2003); Meditel Headquarters (Casablanca, Morocco, 2006); House of the Horizon (Salamanca, 2007); House in an Oak Wood (Salamanca, 2010); House in an Olive Grove (Jaen, 2010). Donaire's work includes a House in Madroñera (Cáceres, 2005); and the "Young Architects of Spain" Exhibition (Madrid, 2008), all in Spain unless stated otherwise. The "DOMUS*ae* Spaces for Culture" (Madrid, 2010–11, published here) was a work of collaboration.

JESÚS Mª APARICIO GUISADO wurde 1960 in Madrid geboren. Sein Architekturstudium schloss er 1984 an der Escuela Técnica Superior de Arquitectura de Madrid (ETSAM) ab. Er promovierte in Architektur und lehrt seit 2009 als ordentlicher Professor für Entwerfen an der ETSAM. 2000 vertrat er Spanien auf der Architektur-biennale in Venedig. **JESÚS DONAIRE GARCÍA DE LA MORA** wurde 1974 in Ciudad Real, Spanien, geboren. Er schloss sein Architekturstudium an der ETSAM 2000 ab. Anschließend absolvierte er einen Master of Science in Advanced Architectural Design an der Graduate School of Architecture, Planning, and Preservation (GSAPP) der Columbia University New York. Vor der Gründung seines eigenen Büros arbeitete er bei Alberto Campo Baeza in Madrid und David Chipperfield in London. Zu Aparicios Projekten zählen: Seniorenheim in Santa Marta de Tormes (Salamanca, 2003), Architekturarchiv und Hörsaal in Nuevos Ministerios (Madrid, 2003), Zentrale für Meditel (Casablanca, Marokko, 2006), Casa del Horizonte (Salamanca, 2007), Haus in einem Eichenwald (Salamanca, 2010), Haus in einem Olivenhain (Jaen, 2010). Donaires Projekte sind u.a. ein Haus in Madroñera (Cáceres, 2005) sowie die Ausstellung *Young Architects of Spain* (Madrid, 2008), alle in Spanien, sofern nicht anders angegeben. *DOMUS*ae *Spaces for Culture* (Madrid, 2010–11, hier vorgestellt) war eine Kollaboration.

JESÚS MARIA APARICIO GUISADO, né à Madrid en 1960, est diplômé en architecture de l'École technique supérieure d'architecture de Madrid (ETSAM, 1984). Il est docteur en architecture et, depuis 2009, professeur de conception de bâtiments à l'ETSAM. En 2000, il a représenté l'Espagne à la Biennale d'architecture de Venise. **JESÚS DONAIRE GARCÍA DE LA MORA**, né à Ciudad Real (Espagne) en 1974, est diplômé en architecture de l'ETSAM (2000) et a obtenu son M. S. en conception architecturale de la Graduate School of Architecture, Planning, and Preservation (GSAPP) de l'université Columbia à New York. Il a travaillé avec Alberto Campo Baeza à Madrid et David Chipperfield à Londres avant de créer son agence. Aparicio a réalisé, entre autres une maison de retraite à Santa Marta de Tormes (Salamanca, 2003) ; les archives d'architecture et la salle de conférence des Nuevos Ministerios (Madrid, 2003) ; le siège de Meditel (Casablanca, Maroc, 2006) ; la Maison de l'horizon (Salamanca, 2007) ; la Maison dans la chêneraie (Salamanca, 2010) et la Maison dans une oliveraie (Jaen, 2010). Donaire a de son côté réalisé une maison à Madroñera (Cáceres, 2005) et l'exposition des « Jeunes architectes espagnols » (Madrid, 2008). Les « DOMUS*ae* espaces pour la culture » (Madrid, 2010–11, publiés ici) est un tra-vail en collaboration.

"DOMUSAE, SPACES FOR CULTURE"

Madrid, Spain, 2010–11

Address: Méndez Núñez, 1, Madrid, Spain, www.mcu.es
Area: 1700 m². Client: Gerencia de Infraestructuras y Equipamientos de Cultura, Ministry of Culture. Cost: not disclosed
Collaboration: Jesús Lazcano López, Aida González Llavona, Alberto Humanes Cisnal

Using the generous spaces of a former Army Museum, the designers insert colorful display cases (above) and large expanses of monochromatic bookshelves to integrate the temporary exhibition into the more permanent spaces.

In den weitläufigen Räumen des ehemaligen Armeemuseums platzierten die Architekten leuchtend farbige Vitrinen (oben) und großflächig installierte monochrome Regaleinheiten. So fügte sich die temporäre Ausstellung in die historischen Räume.

Dans les généreux espaces vides d'un ancien musée de l'armée, les designers ont inséré des vitrines de couleurs vives (ci-dessus) et d'immenses murs de rayonnages monochromes pour mieux intégrer l'exposition temporaire dans un cadre marqué par la permanence.

The exhibition **DOMUSAE, SPACES FOR CULTURE** was held in the Salón de Reinos, Madrid's former Army Museum, built between 1632 and 1640. The show concerned a representative group of recent Spanish cultural buildings. The architects state: "Having the opportunity to use an uninhabited historic building to house this exhibition has enabled us to construct an exhibition route through the building's empty spaces. This means that the visitor can simultaneously enjoy the content of the exhibition and experiment by way of spatial transition with new ways of seeing the original building. These interlinked spaces are underlined with the use of white flooring." On the main floor the exhibition is divided into three spaces. Plans, drawings, models, and other documents are presented in a first room, leading to the main space of the Salón de Reinos building, which was transformed into a library made with Ikea Expedit bookshelves. Reference books on each architect, together with models, photographs, films of the buildings, and interviews with the architects are presented here. The exhibition route ends in a space where cabinets from the old Army Museum display an index about the latest projects completed by the Gerencia de Infraestructuras y Equipamientos de Cultura and those that are still underway.

Die Ausstellung **DOMUSAE, SPACES FOR CULTURE** fand im historischen Salón de Reinos in Madrid statt, der zwischen 1632 und 1640 erbaut wurde. Hier befand sich früher das Museum der spanischen Armee. Die Ausstellung war einer repräsentativen Auswahl neuerer Kulturbauten in Spanien gewidmet. Die Architekten berichten: „Ein ungenutztes historisches Gebäude für die Ausstellung zu bespielen, gab uns die Gelegenheit, eine Route durch die leeren Säle des Gebäudes zu planen. Auf diese Weise konnten die Besucher die Ausstellung genießen, dabei zugleich mit den räumlichen Übergängen spielen und das historische Gebäude ganz neu erfahren. Das Ineinanderfließen der Räume wurde durch den durchgängig weißen Boden unterstrichen." Auf der Hauptebene gliederte sich die Ausstellung in drei Bereiche. Grundrisse, Zeichnungen, Modelle und weitere Dokumente waren im ersten Raum zu sehen, der in den zentralen Hauptraum des Salón de Reinos führte. Dieser war mit Expedit-Regalen von Ikea zur Bibliothek umfunktioniert worden. Hier war Literatur zu den einzelnen Architekten neben Modellen, Fotografien, Filmen der Bauten und Interviews mit den Architekten ausgestellt. Der Rundgang endete in einem Raum mit alten Kabinetten aus dem Armeemuseum, in denen ein Verzeichnis der Neubauten ausgestellt war, die mithilfe des spanischen Kultusministeriums bereits realisiert worden oder noch im Bau waren.

L'exposition **DOMUSAE, ESPACES POUR LA CULTURE** s'est tenue dans le Salón de Reinos, ancien Musée de l'armée de Madrid, construit de 1632 à 1640. Elle présentait un groupe de bâtiments culturels espagnols récents et représentatifs. « L'opportunité de disposer d'un bâtiment historique inutilisé pour abriter cette exposition nous a permis de construire un parcours à travers des volumes vides. Le visiteur pouvait ainsi à la fois apprécier le contenu de l'exposition et découvrir par des transitions spatiales de nouvelles façons de voir le bâtiment d'origine. Ces espaces reliés entre eux sont soulignés par un sol blanc », expliquent les architectes. Le niveau principal est divisé en trois espaces. Des plans, des dessins, des maquettes et autres documents sont présenté dans une première salle qui conduit vers l'espace principal du Salón de Reinos, transformé pour l'occasion en bibliothèque à l'aide de rayonnages Ikea Expedit. Des ouvrages de référence sur chaque architecte, des maquettes, des photographies, des films de leurs réalisations et des entretiens vidéo y étaient présentés. Le parcours se terminait dans une salle où des vitrines de l'ancien Musée de l'armée exposaient une liste des projets les plus récents de la Gerencia de Infraestructuras y Equipamientos de Cultura, et de ceux en cours.

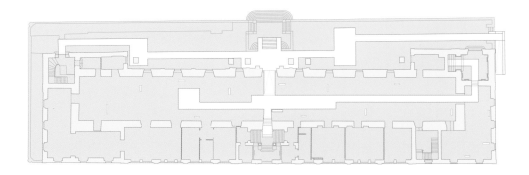

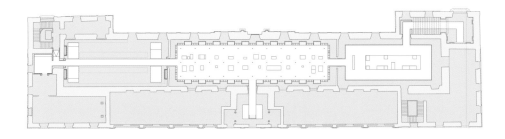

Within the large volumes, the designers carved out their exhibition sequences, in effect using the building exactly as they wanted to despite its historic weight and presence.

Die Architekten „schälten" die Ausstellungssequenz aus dem mächtigen Baukörper heraus und nutzten das Gebäude trotz seiner historischen Imposanz und Präsenz genau ihren Vorstellungen entsprechend.

Les designers ont découpé leur exposition en séquences pour utiliser les importants volumes des galeries comme ils le souhaitaient, malgré la présence et le poids du cadre historique.

The rather staid exterior of the building announces the exhibition with large white banners on either side of the entrance door.

An der Fassade des würdevollen Baus kündigen großformatige weiße Banner links und rechts des Portals die Ausstellung an.

Sur la façade assez sobre du bâtiment, de grandes bannières annoncent l'exposition de chaque côté de l'entrée.

Video images and a large transparent bookshelf create both spaces for the exhibits and the ambiance that accompanies the show effectively.

Mithilfe von Videos und einer großflächigen, transparenten Regalwand werden Räume und Stimmungen erzeugt, die die Ausstellung wirkungsvoll in Szene setzen.

Des écrans vidéo et un important mur de rayonnages quasi transparent sont autant d'espaces de présentation qui créent une intéressante atmosphère d'accompagnement de l'exposition.

RON ARAD

Ron Arad Architects
62 Chalk Farm Road
London NW1 8AN
UK

Tel: +44 20 72 84 49 63
Fax: +44 20 73 79 04 99
E-mail: info@ronarad.com
Web: www.ronarad.co.uk/architecture

RON ARAD was born in Tel Aviv in 1951. An industrial designer, artist, and architect, he attended the Jerusalem Academy of Art (1971–73) and the Architectural Association (AA) in London (1974–79), where he worked under Peter Cook and Bernard Tschumi. In 1981, he created One Off Ltd., a design studio, with Caroline Thorman. In 1989, the pair founded Ron Arad Associates. He has produced furniture and lighting design for several companies including Alessi, Vitra, Flos, Artemide, and Kartell, notably the Well-Tempered Chair (1987) and the Tom Vac stackable chair (1999) for Vitra, and the Book Worm for Kartell (1996). **ASA BRUNO** has been Co-Director of the firm since 2007. He was educated at the Bartlett School (London, 2002), Princeton University (M.Arch, 1998), and at the AA (London, 1993–98). He was the project architect for the Holon Museum. Aside from the Design Museum Holon (Holon, Israel, 2006–10, published here), the architectural work of the firm includes the Hotel Duomo (Rimini, Italy, 2006); and the Medicité Retail Center (Liege, Belgium, 2009). Ongoing work includes an apartment on the Place Vendôme in Paris (France, 2012); Shoreditch Hotel (London, UK, 2013); 154 Ha-Yarkon Street Residential Project (Tel Aviv, Israel, 2013); Villa Marrakech private residence (Marrakech, Morocco, 2013); and the Red Sea Concert Hall (Eilat, Israel), due for completion in 2014.

RON ARAD wurde 1951 in Tel Aviv geboren. Der Industriedesigner, Künstler und Architekt studierte an der Akademie der Künste Jerusalem (1971–73) und der Architectural Association (AA) in London (1974–79), wo er für Peter Cook und Bernard Tschumi arbeitete. 1981 gründete er mit Caroline Thorman sein Designstudio One Off. Die beiden gründeten 1989 Ron Arad Associates. Arad gestaltete Möbel und Leuchten für verschiedene Hersteller, darunter Alessi, Vitra, Flos, Artemide und Kartell. Am bekanntesten wurden der Well-Tempered Chair (1987) und der Tom Vac-Stapelstuhl (1999) für Vitra sowie der Book Worm für Kartell (1996). Seit 2007 unterstützt **ASA BRUNO** als Ko-Direktor das Büro. Bruno studierte an der Bartlett School (London, 2002), der Universität Princeton (M.Arch, 1998) und der AA (London, 1993–98). Er verantwortete die Projektleitung beim Museum in Holon. Zu den Architekturprojekten des Büros zählen neben dem Design Museum Holon (Holon, Israel, 2006–10, hier vorgestellt), das Hotel Duomo (Rimini, Italien 2006) sowie das Einkaufszentrum Medicité (Lüttich, Belgien, 2009). In Planung sind u.a. ein Apartment an der Place Vendôme in Paris (Frankeich, 2012), das Shoreditch Hotel (London, GB, 2013), ein Wohnbauprojekt an der Ha-Yarkon Street 154 (Tel Aviv, Israel, 2013), die private Villa Marrakech (Marrakesch, Marokko, 2013) und die Red Sea Concert Hall (Eilat, Israel), geplante Fertigstellung 2014.

RON ARAD est né à Tel-Aviv en 1951. Designer industriel, artiste et architecte, il a étudié à l'Académie de l'art de Jérusalem (1971–73) et à l'Architectural Association (AA) à Londres (1974–79), où il a travaillé pour Peter Cook et Bernard Tschumi. En 1981, il crée One Off Ltd., studio de design, avec Caroline Thorman et, en 1989, le couple fonde Ron Arad Associates. Il conçoit des meubles et des luminaires pour plusieurs éditeurs dont Alessi, Vitra, Flos, Artemide et Kartell, en particulier le Well-Tempered Chair (1987) et le siège empilable Tom Vac (1999) pour Vitra, ainsi que la bibliothèque Book Worm pour Kartell (1996). **ASA BRUNO** est codirecteur de l'agence depuis 2007. Il a étudié à la Bartlett School (Londres, 2002), à l'université de Princeton (M. Arch, 1998) et à l'AA (Londres, 1993–98) et a été architecte de projet du Holon Museum. En dehors du musée du Design de Holon (Holon, Israël, 2006–10, publié ici), les interventions architecturales de l'agence comprennent, entre autres, l'hôtel Duomo (Rimini, Italie, 2006) et le centre commercial Medicité (Liège, Belgique, 2009). Actuellement, l'agence travaille sur un appartement place Vendôme à Paris (2012) ; le Shoreditch Hotel (Londres, 2013) ; l'immeuble de logements 154 Ha-Yarkon Street (Tel-Aviv, 2013) ; une résidence privée, la villa Marrakech (Marrakech, 2013), et la salle de concert Red Sea (Eilat, Israël), prévue pour 2014.

DESIGN MUSEUM HOLON

Holon, Israel, 2006–10

Address: 8 Pinchas Eylon Avenue, Holon 58458, Israel, +972 7 32151515, www.dmh.org.il
Area: 3200 m². Client: Holon Development Corporation Ltd. Cost: €11 million
Collaboration: Asa Bruno (Project Architect), James Foster (Associate)

Sitting on the ground, almost as though it were not anchored in the earth, the Design Museum Holon contrasts with its environment, bringing brightly colored curves to the gray surroundings.

Das Designmuseum in Holon liegt auf dem Boden, als wäre es nicht in ihm verankert. Mit seinen leuchtend farbigen Kurven bildet es einen Kontrast zum eher grauen Umfeld.

Donnant l'impression d'être à peine ancré dans le sol, le musée du Design Holon contraste, par ses courbes aux couleurs vives, avec son environnement d'immeubles grisâtres.

Ron Arad was asked in 2003 to design the first Israeli national Design Museum. The facility opened in Holon, just south of Tel Aviv, in January 2010. Built on a rectangular 3700-square-meter site, the museum is located at the intersection of the city's main east–west and north–south avenues. A public plaza is set to the north, and the structure also has an internal courtyard between its two wings. Five Cor-ten steel bands (with a total length of one kilometer), which serve as a spine for the building, are the most visible exterior architectural gesture. On the north façade, an overhanging first-floor gallery provides a "protected opening." The museum café has a cedar façade. The two main galleries (500 m² and 200 m²) respectively provide naturally lit and "black box" spaces. The circulation routes offer further exhibition space.

2003 erhielt Ron Arad den Auftrag, das erste israelische Landesmuseum für Design zu entwerfen, das im Januar 2010 in Holon, unmittelbar südlich von Tel Aviv eröffnet wurde. Das Museum liegt auf einem 3700 m² großen Grundstück an der Kreuzung der ost-westlich und nord-südlich verlaufenden Hauptdurchgangsstraßen der Stadt. Neben einer Plaza an der Nordseite gibt es einen Innenhof zwischen beiden Flügeln des Komplexes. Markantestes Merkmal des Baus sind die fünf Bänder aus Cor-ten-Stahl (mit einer Gesamtlänge von einem Kilometer), die sein Rückgrat bilden. An der Nordfassade entsteht durch auskragende Ausstellungsräume im Obergeschoss ein „geschützter Durchgang". Das Museumscafé hat eine Fassade aus Zedernholz. Die beiden zentralen Ausstellungsbereiche (mit jeweils 500 m² bzw. 200 m²) bieten sowohl Räume mit Tageslicht als auch „Black Box"-Galerien. Die Verkehrsflächen können zusätzlich als Präsentationsflächen genutzt werden.

C'est en 2003 que Ron Arad a reçu commande du premier musée national israélien du design qui a ouvert ses portes à Holon, au sud de Tel-Aviv, en janvier 2010. Il a été édifié sur un terrain rectangulaire de 3700 mètres carrés, à l'intersection de deux axes majeur nord-sud et est-ouest. Au nord, il donne sur une place publique tandis qu'une cour intérieure s'étend entre ses deux ailes. Cinq grands bandeaux d'acier Corten (représentant au total un kilomètre de long) constituent l'épine dorsale du projet en un impressionnant geste architectural. Une galerie en saillie à l'étage offre une « ouverture protégée » sur la façade nord. Celle du café est habillée de bois. Les deux galeries principales (500 et 200 mètres carrés) sont traitées comme des « boîtes noires », mais à éclairage naturel. Le parcours que suivent les visiteurs sert également d'espace d'exposition.

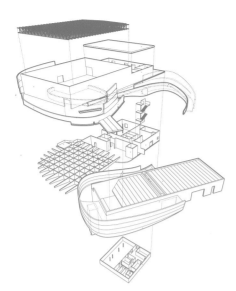

The arching Cor-ten steel bands that are the signature element of the design render the structure dynamic and inviting. Drawings show the inner workings of the museum and the relation of each part to the whole.

Dank seiner ausgreifenden Bänder aus Corten-Stahl – dem zentralen Element des Entwurfs – wirkt der Bau dynamisch und einladend. Zeichnungen illustrieren den funktionalen Innenaufbau des Museums sowie den Bezug der einzelnen Elemente zum Ganzen.

Les bandeaux incurvés en acier Corten sont l'élément fort de ce projet, lui conférant dynamique et aspect engageant. Les plans montrent l'organisation interne du musée et les relations de chaque partie au tout.

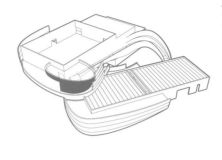

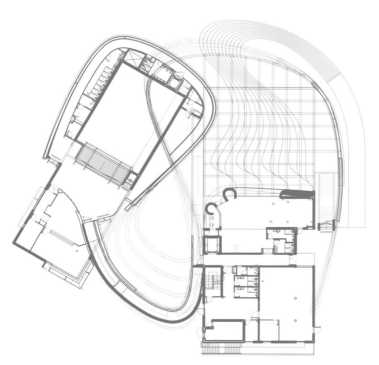

Using sculptural Cor-ten steel on a scale that even Richard Serra would find daunting, Ron Arad weaves these elements into the composition, seen in the plan on the left.

Skulpturale Corten-Stahlelemente, deren Dimensionen wohl selbst Richard Serra respekteinflößend finden würde, webt Ron Arad zu einer Gesamtkomposition, siehe Grundriss links.

Utilisant les possibilités sculpturales de l'acier Corten à une échelle que même Richard Serra aurait jugée audacieuse, Ron Arad a littéralement tissé sa composition de ces grands éléments (plan de gauche).

Exterior steel bands respond in the image selection below to the bands of lighting in a carefully designed display gallery.

Die Stahlbänder am Außenbau finden ihr Pendant in den Lichtbändern der sorgsam geplanten Ausstellungsräume, siehe Bildauswahl unten.

Les bandeaux d'acier de l'extérieur se retrouvent en écho dans les bandeaux d'éclairage de la galerie d'exposition ci-dessous.

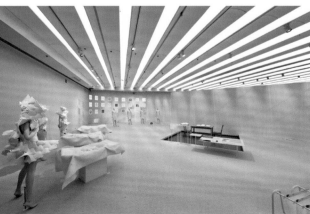

BIRK & HEILMEYER

Birk und Heilmeyer Architekten
Vogelsangstr. 9
70176 Stuttgart
Germany

Tel: +49 711 410 51 00
Fax: +49 711 410 51 01
E-mail: info@birkundheilmeyer.de
Web: www.birkundheilmeyer.de

STEPHAN BIRK was born in 1975 in Stuttgart. He studied architecture at the University of Stuttgart and worked for architects in Stuttgart, Boston, and London before cofounding Birk und Heilmeyer Architekten in Stuttgart in 2005 with his wife. **LIZA HEILMEYER** was born in 1975 in Freiburg im Breisgau, Germany. She studied architecture at the University of Stuttgart, and worked for architects in Stuttgart; Cambridge, Massachusetts; and London before cofounding the studio Birk und Heilmeyer. Their work includes a Glass Tube Bridge (prototype of a glass footbridge, 2003–04); a 500-car parking garage in Coesfeld-Lette (2005–07); Architecture Gallery am Weißenhof (Stuttgart, 2007); the Jübergtower (Hemer, 2010, published here); a modular system of ten new preschools / daycare centers (Frankfurt, 2010–13); and the Robotik and Mechatronic Center (Oberpfaffenhofen, 2011–14), all in Germany.

STEPHAN BIRK wurde 1975 in Stuttgart geboren. Er studierte Architektur an der Universität Stuttgart und arbeitete für verschiedene Architekturbüros in Stuttgart, Boston und London, bevor er 2005 mit seiner Frau das Büro Birk und Heilmeyer Architekten gründete. **LIZA HEILMEYER** wurde 1975 in Freiburg im Breisgau geboren. Sie studierte Architektur an der Universität Stuttgart und arbeitete vor der Gründung von Birk und Heilmeyer Architekten für verschiedene Büros in Stuttgart, Cambridge, Massachusetts und London. Projekte des Teams sind u.a. eine Rohrglasbrücke (Prototyp einer gläsernen Fußgängerbrücke, 2003–04), ein Parkhaus mit 500 Stellplätzen in Coesfeld-Lette (2005–07), die Architekturgalerie am Weißenhof (Stuttgart, 2007), der Jübergturm (Hemer, 2010, hier vorgestellt), ein Baukastensystem für zehn neue Kindertagesstätten (Frankfurt, 2010–13) sowie das Zentrum für Robotik und Mechatronik (Oberpfaffenhofen, 2011–14), alle in Deutschland.

STEPHAN BIRK, né en 1975 à Stuttgart, a étudié l'architecture à l'université de cette ville et travaillé en agence à Stuttgart, Boston et Londres avant de fonder Birk und Heilmeyer Architekten à Stuttgart avec son épouse en 2005. **LIZA HEILMEYER**, née en 1975 à Fribourg-en-Brisgau (Allemagne), a étudié l'architecture à l'université de Stuttgart et travaillé pour des agences à Stuttgart, Cambridge, Massachusetts et Londres avant de fonder leur agence. Parmi leurs réalisations, toutes en Allemagne, figurent : un pont en tubes de verre (prototype d'une passerelle de verre, 2003–04) ; un garage pour 500 voitures à Coesfeld-Lette (2005–07) ; la Galerie d'architecture am Weißenhof (Stuttgart, 2007) ; la tour Jüberg (Hemer, 2010, publiée ici) ; un système modulaire conçu pour dix nouvelles écoles maternelles et jardins d'enfants (Francfort, 2010–13) et le Centre de robotique et mécatronique (Oberpfaffenhofen, 2011–14).

JÜBERGTOWER

Hemer, Germany, 2010

Height: 23.5 meters. Client: Landesgartenschau Hemer 2010. Cost: €500 000
Collaboration: Knippers Helbig Advanced Engineering

This structure is a landmark for the regional garden and flower festival "Landesgartenschau Hemer 2010" in North Rhine–Westphalia. The architects used 240 Siberian larch square glulam beams (8 x 8 centimeters) in a hyperboloid pattern. Steel was used to anchor the tower six meters into the bedrock on which it stands. With its mesh structure expanding toward the top, the tower appears to be progressively lighter and lighter as visitors ascend past the five landing platforms on the way to the observation deck. Built in just six weeks, the structure has a six-meter-diameter base, and a nine-meter-diameter observation deck offering a 360° view.

Der Turm war eine der Landmarken der Landesgartenschau 2010 in Hemer, einer regionalen Blumen- und Gartenschau in Nordrhein-Westfalen. Die Architekten verarbeiteten 240 Brettschichthölzer aus Sibirischer Lärche (8 x 8 cm) zu einem Hyperbolid-Muster. Verankert wurde der Turm mit 6 m langen Stahlstäben im Felsgrund. Die sich nach oben erweiternde Netzstruktur wird lichter und lichter, je höher die Besucher die fünf Treppenabsätze bis zur Aussichtsplattform emporsteigen. Die Basis des in nur sechs Wochen erbauten Turms hat einen Durchmesser von 6 m, die Aussichtsplattform mit 9 m Durchmesser bietet eine 360° Rundumsicht.

Cette structure a été le centre d'attraction du Festival des jardins et des fleurs « Landesgartenschau Hemer 2010 » en Rhénanie-du-Nord-Westphalie. Les architectes ont utilisé 240 poutres en contrecollé de mélèze de Sibérie (de 8 x 8 cm de section) assemblées selon une forme hyperboloïde. Des ancrages en acier ont été scellés à six mètres de profondeur dans le rocher sur lequel repose la tour. Grâce à sa structure maillée qui s'évase en partie supérieure, celle-ci semble de plus en plus légère et transparente aux visiteurs qui escaladent ses cinq plates-formes intermédiaires avant d'accéder à l'observatoire. Construite en six semaines seulement, la tour possède un diamètre de six mètres à sa base et de neuf mètres pour la plate-forme du sommet qui offre une vue panoramique à 360°.

The use of larch to form the exterior mesh of the tower makes an interesting contrast between the essentially natural material and the specifically contemporary form of the structure.

Durch den Einsatz von Lärchenholz für das äußere Gitterwerk des Turms entstehen interessante Kontraste zwischen einem natürlichen Material und der dezidiert zeitgenössischen Formensprache des Baus.

Le bois de mélèze de la trame extérieure apporte un contraste intéressant avec la forme spécifiquement contemporaine de cette tour.

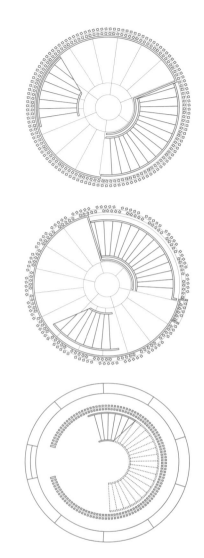

The density of the larch mesh cladding decreases as visitors rise up through the spiral steel staircase of the tower. Floor plans at various levels show the circular design with increasing diameters.

Das Gitternetz der Lärchenverkleidung wird lichter, je weiter die Besucher die stählerne Wendeltreppe im Turm hinaufsteigen. Etagengrundrisse verschiedener Ebenen zeigen den wachsenden Durchmesser der kreisrunden Konstruktion.

Les visiteurs qui empruntent l'escalier en spirale voient la densité de la trame du treillis de mélèze diminuer avec la hauteur. Les plans des niveaux montrent par ailleurs l'augmentation du diamètre des paliers.

ODILE DECQ BENOÎT CORNETTE

Odile Decq Benoît Cornette Architectes Urbanistes
11 Rue des Arquebusiers
75003 Paris
France

Tel: +33 1 42 71 24 51
Fax: +33 1 42 71 27 42
E-mail: odbc@odbc-paris.com
Web: www.odbc-paris.com

ODILE DECQ was born in 1955 in Laval, France, and obtained her degree in Architecture (DPLG) at UP6 in Paris in 1978. She studied urbanism at the Institut d'Études Politiques in Paris (1979) and founded her office in 1980. Her former partner Benoît Cornette died in 1998. She has designed a number of apartment buildings in Paris; the French Pavilion at the 1996 Architecture Biennale in Venice (Italy); three buildings for Nantes University (1993–99); a refurbishment of the Conference Hall of Unesco in Paris (France, 2001); renovation of the Cureghem Veterinary School in Brussels (Belgium, 2001); the Liaunig Museum (Neuhaus, Austria, 2004); and the MACRO in Rome (Italy, 2004–10, published here). Winner of the Golden Lion at the Venice Architecture Biennale (1996) and the 1999 Benedictus Award for the Faculty of Economics and the Law Library at the University of Nantes, she has just completed the Restaurant at Opéra Garnier in Paris (France, 2011) and is currently building the Flying Horse House (CIPEA, Nanjing, China); the FRAC Contemporary Art Center in Rennes (France); and Pavilion 8 in Lyon (France).

ODILE DECQ wurde 1955 in Laval, Frankreich, geboren und absolvierte ihr Architekturdiplom (DPLG) 1978 in Paris. Sie studierte Städtebau am Institut d'Études Politiques in Paris (1979) und gründete 1980 ihr Büro. Ihr Partner Benoît Cornette verstarb 1998. Sie entwarf eine Reihe von Apartmenthäusern in Paris, den französischen Pavillon auf der Architekturbiennale 1996 in Venedig, drei Gebäude für die Universität Nantes (1993–99), verantwortete die Sanierung des Kongresszentrums der Unesco in Paris (2001), die Sanierung der Fakultät für Veterinärmedizin Cureghem in Brüssel (2001), das Museum Liaunig (Neuhaus, Österreich, 2004) sowie das MACRO in Rom (2004–10, hier vorgestellt). Odile Decq wurde mit dem Goldenen Löwen der Architekturbiennale Venedig (1996) sowie dem Benedictus-Preis für die Fakultät für Wirtschaft und die Rechtsbibliothek der Universität Nantes (1999) ausgezeichnet. Kürzlich fertiggestellt werden konnte das Restaurant an der Opéra Garnier in Paris (2011), derzeit im Bau sind das Flying Horse House (CIPEA, Nanjing, China), das Zentrum für Zeitgenössische Kunst FRAC in Rennes (Frankreich) sowie der Pavilion 8 in Lyon (Frankreich).

ODILE DECQ, née en 1955 à Laval (France), est diplômée en architecture (DPLG) de l'UP6 (Paris, 1978). Elle a étudié l'urbanisme à l'Institut d'études politiques de Paris (1979) et créé son agence en 1980 avec son associé Benoît Cornette, décédé en 1998. Parmi ses réalisations figurent un certain nombre d'immeubles de logements à Paris ; le Pavillon de la France à la Biennale d'architecture de Venise 1996 ; trois immeubles pour l'université de Nantes (1993–99) ; la rénovation de la salle de conférence de l'UNESCO à Paris (2001) ; la rénovation de l'École vétérinaire de Cureghem à Bruxelles (2001) ; le musée Liaunig (Neuhaus, Autriche, 2004) et le Musée d'art contemporain MACRO à Rome (2004–10, publié ici). Elle a remporté le Lion d'or de la Biennale d'architecture de Venise 1996 et le prix Benedictus 1999 pour la faculté d'économie et la bibliothèque de droit de l'université de Nantes. Après avoir achevé le restaurant de l'Opéra Garnier à Paris (2011), elle construit actuellement la Maison du cheval volant (CIPEA, Nankin, Chine), le FRAC de Rennes et le Pavillon 8 à Lyon.

MACRO

Rome, Italy, 2004–10

Address: Via Nizza (corner Via Cagliari), Rome 00198, Italy, +39 06 671 07 04 00, www.macro.roma.museum
Area: 7000 m². Client: City of Rome. Cost: €22 million
Collaboration: Giuseppe Savarese, Valeria Parodi, Frederic Haesevoets

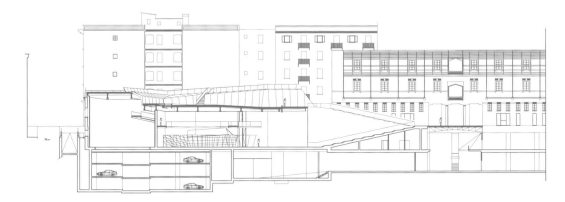

The new facility is skillfully inserted into an environment that is surrounded by much more traditional buildings. The molded façade (top image) added to the glass face of part of the structure furthers the impression of insertion and symbiosis.

Die neue Erweiterung wurde gelungen in ihr Umfeld mit traditionellerer Bebauung integriert. Die modellierte Fassade (Bild oben), eine Ergänzung der Glasfront, die Teile des Gebäudes umschließt, unterstreicht den Eindruck von Einschüben und Symbiose.

Ce nouveau musée s'insère habilement dans son environnement d'immeubles traditionnels. La façade à modénature rajoutée au mur de verre (image du haut) renforce l'impression d'insertion et de symbiose.

Set into an area of historic industrial buildings, the new museum of contemporary art of the city of Rome, Odile Decq's **MACRO**, has been hailed as a worthy competitor for Zaha Hadid's MAXXI in the same city. The architect explains that the architectural section of the building is expressed through "the translation from horizontal to vertical, from inside to outside, from the foyer to the roof-landscape-garden." Because of the complex location, she has developed the project as a series of transitions, or as an "abstract art garden," at least where the roof is concerned, and a "landscape." Although they are "non-regular," her interior spaces are nonetheless "simple spaces given to the artists," offering multiple exhibition possibilities.

Odile Decqs **MACRO**, das neue städtische Museum für Zeitgenössische Kunst in Rom, gelegen in einem Viertel mit historischen Industriebauten, wurde als ernstzunehmende Konkurrenz für Zaha Hadids MAXXI, ebenfalls in Rom, gefeiert. Die Architektin beschreibt den Aufriss ihres Baus als „eine Übersetzung vom Horizontalen ins Vertikale, von Innen nach Außen, vom Foyer bis in den Landschaftsgarten". Angesichts des komplexen baulichen Umfelds entwickelte sie das Projekt als Folge ineinander übergehender Zonen bzw. als „abstrakten Kunstgarten" – zumindest was das Dach angeht – sowie als „Landschaft". Obwohl die Räume „nicht regelmäßig bzw. konventionell" sind, sind es dennoch „schlichte Räume, die den Künstlern übergeben" werden und vielfältige Ausstellungsmöglichkeiten bieten.

Inséré dans un quartier de bâtiments industriels historiques, le nouveau Musée d'art contemporain de la ville de Rome, le **MACRO**, a été salué comme un sérieux concurrent du MAXXI construit par Zaha Hadid dans la capitale italienne. L'architecte explique que la coupe du bâtiment se révèle dans « une translation de l'horizontale vers le vertical, du dedans vers le dehors, depuis le foyer jusqu'au paysage du jardin sur le toit ». La situation dans un contexte complexe l'a poussée à traiter son projet en une série de transitions, comme un « jardin d'art abstrait » en toiture et un « paysage ». Bien que « non réguliers », les volumes intérieurs n'en sont pas moins « des espaces simples proposés aux artistes » qui offrent de multiples possibilités d'exposition.

The generous interior spaces allow natural light to enter. In the image above, angular forms are augmented with the use of a suspended steel walkway.

In die großzügigen Innenräume fällt Tageslicht. Die kantigen Formen werden durch einen abgehängten Stahlsteg zusätzlich betont (oben).

Les généreux volumes intérieurs bénéficient de la lumière naturelle. Dans l'image ci-dessus, la structure anguleuse d'une verrière de façade soutient une passerelle en acier.

Ample glazing offers views toward the surrounding buildings and brings daylight into the spaces. Below, a plan of the structures.

Großflächige Verglasung erlaubt den Blick auf Nachbarbauten und lässt Tageslicht in die Räume. Unten ein Grundriss des Komplexes.

D'importantes baies laissent apercevoir les immeubles environnants et pénétrer la lumière naturelle dans les galeries. Ci-dessous, plan du musée.

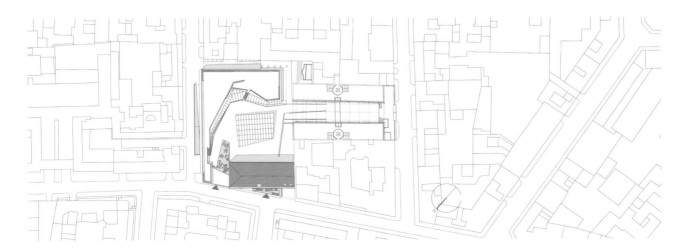

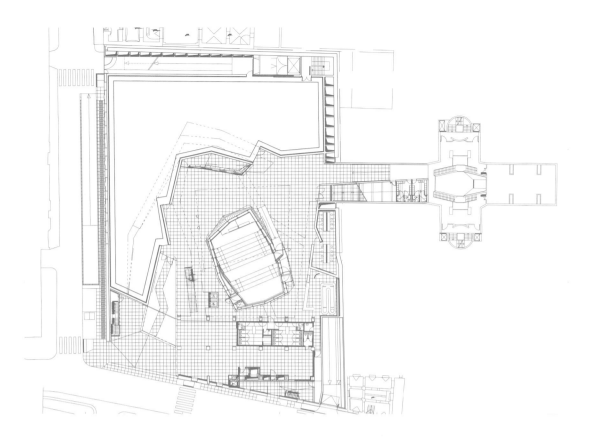

Despite the numerous angled irregularities in the plan (above), the building is carefully thought out to make usable, ample spaces.

Trotz der vielfältigen winkligen Asymmetrien im Grundriss (oben) wurde der Bau bewusst mit Blick auf großzügige, funktionale Räume geplant.

Malgré de nombreuses interventions de formes irrégulières (plan ci-dessus), le bâtiment offre de vastes espaces parfaitement utilisables.

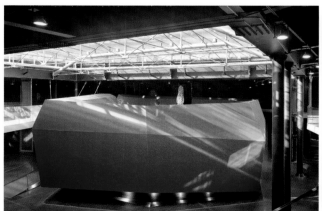

Contrasting with the usually gray or black tonalities employed by the architect, a bright red volume stands out, apparently floating inside the building.

Als Kontrast zur vorwiegend grauen bzw. schwarzen Farbpalette der Architektin sticht der leuchtendrote Raumkörper hervor und scheint geradezu im Gebäude zu schweben.

Contrastant avec les tons de gris ou de noir choisis par l'architecte, l'important volume rouge vif semble se tenir en suspension au milieu du musée.

FELIX-DELUBAC

FELIX-DELUBAC architectes
7 Rue Moncey
75009 Paris
France

Tel: +33 1 49 70 04 62
E-mail: contact@felix-delubac-architectes.com
Web: www.felix-delubac-architectes.com

CHRISTIAN FÉLIX was born in 1972 in Cholet, France. He obtained his diploma as an architect from the École d'architecture de Paris-Villemin in 1999 and went to work in the office of Christian Hauvette in Paris. **LAETITIA DELUBAC** was born in 1975 in Paris and also obtained her degree at Paris-Villemin (1999). She worked with Valode & Pistre and Christian Hauvette before the creation of their firm. Their work includes the Ecolodge (Siwa, Egypt, 2006–07, published here); Ferdinand apartment (Paris, 2008); Laboratories for the CNRS and the Cemagref (with Christian Hauvette, Lyon, 2009); and two projects that are still in progress, the Washington apartment (Paris, 2010–); and a Passive House built with wood and a thatched roof (Normandy, 2010–), all in France unless stated otherwise.

CHRISTIAN FÉLIX wurde 1972 in Cholet, Frankreich, geboren. 1999 absolvierte er sein Diplom an der École d'architecture de Paris-Villemin und arbeitete anschließend im Büro von Christian Hauvette in Paris. **LAETITIA DELUBAC** wurde 1975 in Paris geboren, auch sie machte ihren Abschluss in Paris-Villemin (1999). Vor der Gründung des gemeinsamen Büros arbeitete sie bei Valode & Pistre und Christian Hauvette. Zu ihren Entwürfen zählen die Ecolodge (Siwa, Ägypten, 2006–07, hier vorgestellt), das Apartment Ferdinand (Paris, 2008), Labors für das CNRS und Cemagref (mit Christian Hauvette, Lyon, 2009) sowie zwei Projekte in Planung, das Apartment Washington (Paris, 2010–) und ein Holz-Passivhaus mit Reetdach (Normandie, 2010–), alle in Frankreich, sofern nicht anders angegeben.

CHRISTIAN FÉLIX, né en 1972 à Cholet (France), est diplômé de l'École d'architecture de Paris-Villemin (1999) et a travaillé chez Christian Hauvette à Paris. **LAETITIA DELUBAC**, née en 1975 à Paris, est diplômée du même établissement (1999). Elle a travaillé chez Valode & Pistre et Christian Hauvette. Parmi les réalisations de leur agence figurent l'Ecolodge (Siwa, Égypte, 2006–07, publiée ici) ; l'appartement Ferdinand (Paris, 2008) ; des laboratoires pour le CNRS et le Cemagref (avec Christian Hauvette, Lyon, 2009) et deux projets en cours : l'appartement Washington (Paris, 2010–) et une maison passive en bois à toit de chaume (Normandie, 2010–).

ECOLODGE

Siwa, Egypt, 2006–07

Area: 390 m². Client: not disclosed. Cost: not disclosed

The sketch and the covered seating area with a view on the water (below) demonstrate the relative simplicity of the design, blending with a sense of local materials and traditions.

Die Skizze und der überdachte Sitz-bereich mit Blick aufs Wasser (unten) unterstreichen die Schlichtheit des Entwurfs, der von Gespür für lokale Materialien und Traditionen zeugt.

Le croquis et le séjour extérieur en bordure du lac (ci-dessous) illustrent la simplicité relative du projet qui fait appel à un sens certain des matériaux et des traditions locaux.

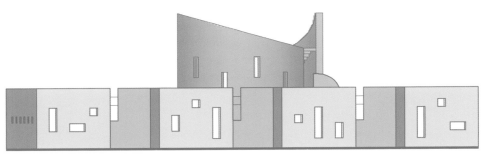

A drawing showing the emerging central volume and the image above with the colonnaded patio and basin again bring out the relation of the design to the regional use of courtyards in a similar vein.

Eine Zeichnung zeigt den aufragenden zentralen Baukörper, die Aufnahme oben den säulengesäumten Innenhof mit Wasserbecken. Beide belegen einmal mehr den Bezug des Entwurfs zu regionalen Bauformen mit ähnlichen Hofanlagen.

Élévation de façade montrant la manière dont le volume central semble jaillir. Au-dessus, le patio à péristyle et le bassin rappellent eux aussi des pratiques architecturales régionales.

The retreat and guesthouse in the desert is located on the peninsula of the Siwa Oasis on a 35 x 35-meter site. The architects state: "We have chosen to dilate the project in order to cover the plot completely. This allows us to provide as many patios as guest rooms, a closed courtyard, and garden; so many quiet places facing the desert." Four different façades offer four different points of view. The living room to the north opens onto a pergola that looks over the salt lake. Guest rooms on the west look out at the Adrere Amellal, while the southern façade with the staff quarters has minimal openings. The garden and swimming pool are located to the west. Walls are made of kershef, a local material made from mud, sand, and sun-dried salt. No electricity is used in the house, while a wind tower with a viewing terrace contains the owner's suite.

Das Feriendomizil und Gästehaus liegt auf einem 35 x 35 m großen Grundstück in der Wüste, auf der Halbinsel der Siwa-Oase. Die Architekten führen aus: „Wir haben uns entschieden, das Projekt zu erweitern, um die Gesamtfläche des Grundstücks vollständig zu nutzen. Das erlaubte uns, für jedes Gästezimmer eigene Terrassen anzulegen, einen geschlossenen Innenhof und einen Garten und damit eine Vielzahl stiller Orte mit Blick auf die Wüste." Vier verschiedene Fassaden bieten vier verschiedene Ansichten. Der nach Norden gelegene Wohnraum öffnet sich zu einer Pergola und überblickt den Salzsee. Die westlichen Gästezimmer haben Blick auf Adrere Amellal, während die Südfassade, hinter der die Personalräume liegen, nur minimale Öffnungen hat. Garten und Swimmingpool liegen nach Westen hin. Die Wände bestehen aus *kershef*, einem regionaltypischen Baumaterial aus Lehm, Sand und sonnengetrocknetem Salz. Im gesamten Haus gibt es keinen Strom, die Räume des Hausherrn mit Aussichtsterrasse liegen in einem Windfängerturm.

Cette maison d'hôtes dans le désert se trouve sur la péninsule de l'oasis de Siwa. Elle occupe un terrain de 35 x 35 mètres. « Nous avons choisi de dilater le projet afin d'occuper la totalité de la parcelle », expliquent les architectes, « ce qui nous a permis de créer un patio par chambres d'hôtes, une cour fermée et un jardin, autant de lieux tranquilles face au désert. » Les quatre façades différenciées offrent quatre points de vue différents. Le séjour au nord ouvre sur une pergola qui donne sur le lac salé. Les chambres d'hôtes situées à l'ouest regardent vers la butte calcaire de l'Adrere Amellal tandis que la façade sud, derrière laquelle se trouvent les installations pour le personnel, ne possède que peu d'ouvertures. Le jardin et la piscine sont à l'ouest. La tour du vent soutenant une terrasse d'observation abrite la suite du propriétaire. Les murs sont en *kershef*, matériau de la région fait de boue, de sable et de sel séchés au soleil. L'Ecolodge n'utilise pas d'électricité.

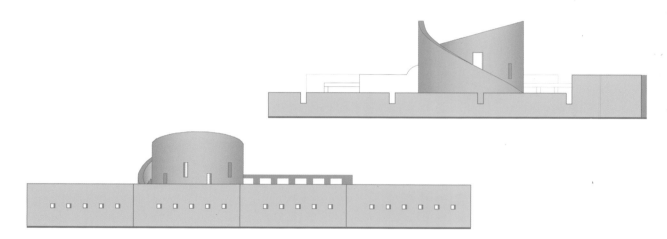

A plan (right) shows the angled, largely rectilinear forms of the design, centered on the circular, spiraling central element. Covered passages and numerous courtyards fill the allotted site, making use of materials that are typical in more rural Egyptian settings.

Der Grundriss rechts illustriert die schiefwinkligen, zumeist linearen Formen des Entwurfs, in dessen Zentrum ein spiralförmig-runder Baukörper steht. Laubengänge und Innenhöfe ziehen sich durch das gesamte Grundstück. Gearbeitet wurde mit Materialien, die typisch für ländlichere Gegenden Ägyptens sind.

Le plan de droite montre la répartition des chambres implantées en biais autour de l'élément central en spirale. Les différentes parties sont reliées par de nombreuses cours et passages couverts. Les matériaux sont typiques de l'Égypte rurale.

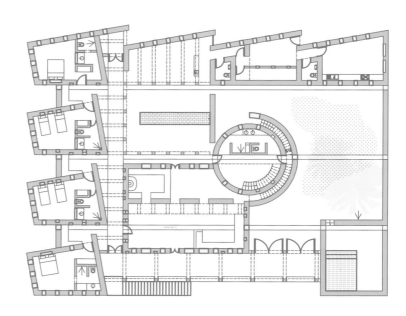

Shaded interior spaces provide comfortable refuge from the heat of the desert. Materials such as rope, earthen walls, and wooden furniture complement the natural aspect of the architecture.

Schattige Innenräume sind ein angenehmer Rückzugsort vor der Hitze der Wüste. Materialien wie Seile, Lehmwände oder Holzmöbel unterstreichen den natürlichen Charakter der Architektur.

Des espaces intérieurs abrités permettent de se protéger de la chaleur du désert. Les matériaux comme la terre des murs, le bois des meubles ou la corde participent à l'aspect naturel de cette architecture.

A dining area and pool on this page reflect the atmosphere of protected comfort that the architects have fashioned using simple and largely ecologically sensitive materials.

Essbereich und Pool auf dieser Seite sind Beispiele für den geschützten Komfort, den die Architekten mit schlichten und vorwiegend ökologischen Materialien geschaffen haben.

La salle à manger et la piscine sur cette page reflètent une atmosphère de confort protecteur que les architectes ont su créer en recourant à des matériaux simples et en grande partie écologiques.

FOSTER + PARTNERS

Foster + Partners
Riverside Three, 22 Hester Road
London SW11 4AN
UK

Tel: +44 20 77 38 04 55 / Fax: +44 20 77 38 11 07
E-mail: info@fosterandpartners.com / Web: www.fosterandpartners.com

Born in Manchester, UK, in 1935, **NORMAN FOSTER** studied architecture and city planning at Manchester University (1961). He was awarded a Henry Fellowship to Yale University, where he received his M.Arch degree and met Richard Rogers, with whom he created Team 4. He received the RIBA Gold Medal for Architecture (1983). He was knighted in 1990 and was honored with a Life Peerage in 1999. The American Institute of Architects granted him their Gold Medal for Architecture in 1994 and he was awarded the Pritzker Prize in 1999. Lord Norman Foster has notably built the IBM Pilot Head Office (Cosham, UK, 1970–71); Sainsbury Center for Visual Arts and Crescent Wing, University of East Anglia (Norwich, UK, 1976–77; 1989–91); Hong Kong and Shanghai Banking Corporation Headquarters (Hong Kong, 1981–86); Stansted Airport (Stansted, UK, 1987–91); the Commerzbank Headquarters (Frankfurt, 1994–97); Chek Lap Kok Airport (Hong Kong, 1995–98); the new German Parliament, Reichstag (Berlin, 1995–99); British Museum Redevelopment (London, 1997–2000); Millennium Bridge (London, 1996–2002); Petronas University of Technology (Seri Iskandar, Malaysia, 1999–2004); Millau Viaduct (Millau, France, 1993–2005); and Wembley Stadium (London, 1996–2006). More recent work includes Beijing Airport (China, 2003–08); Faustino Winery (Ribera del Duero, Spain, 2007–10); Masdar Institute (Abu Dhabi, UAE, 2008–10, published here); Sperone Westwater (New York, 2009–10, also published here); Spaceport America (New Mexico, USA, 2009–12); and the master plan for the West Kowloon Cultural District (Hong Kong, 2009–).

NORMAN FOSTER wurde 1935 in Manchester geboren, wo er später Architektur und Stadtplanung studierte (1961). Ein Henry Fellowship ermöglichte ihm das Studium in Yale, wo er seinen M.Arch absolvierte und Richard Rogers begegnete, mit dem er das Büro Team 4 gründete. Er wurde mit der RIBA-Goldmedaille für Architektur ausgezeichnet (1983), 1990 zum Ritter geschlagen und 1999 in den lebenslangen Adelsstand erhoben. 1994 verlieh ihm das American Institute of Architects die Goldmedaille für Architektur, 1999 erhielt er den Pritzker-Preis. Zu Lord Norman Fosters besonders hervozuhebenden Bauten zählen: der IBM-Hauptsitz in Cosham (Cosham, GB, 1970–71), das Sainsbury Center for Visual Arts und der Crescent Wing, Universität von East Anglia (Norwich, GB, 1976–77, 1989–91), der Hauptsitz der Hong Kong and Shanghai Banking Corporation (Hongkong, 1981–86), der Flughafen Stansted (1987–91), der Hauptsitz der Commerzbank (Frankfurt/Main, 1994–97), der Flughafen Chek Lap Kok (Hongkong, 1995–98), der Umbau des Reichstags (Berlin, 1995–99), der Umbau des British Museum (London, 1997–2000), die Millennium Bridge (London, 1996–2002), die Technische Universität Petronas (Seri Iskandar, Malaysia, 1999–2004), das Viadukt von Millau (Millau, Frankreich, 1993–2005) und das Wembley-Stadion (London, 1996–2006). Aktuelle Projekte sind der Flughafen Peking (China, 2003–08), das Weingut Faustino (Ribera del Duero, Spanien, 2007–10), das Masdar Institute (Abu Dhabi, VAE, 2008–10, hier vorgestellt), Sperone Westwater (New York, 2009–10, ebenfalls hier vorgestellt), der Spaceport America (New Mexico, USA, 2009–12) sowie der Masterplan für den Kulturbezirk in West Kowloon (Hongkong, 2009–).

Né à Manchester en 1935, **NORMAN FOSTER** a étudié l'architecture et l'urbanisme à l'université de Manchester (1961). Il a bénéficié d'une bourse d'études Henry Fellowship pour l'université Yale où il a obtenu son M. Arch. et rencontré Richard Rogers avec lequel il a créé l'agence Team 4. Titulaire de la médaille d'or du RIBA en 1983, il a été anobli en 1990 et fait pair à vie en 1999. L'American Institute of Architects lui a accordé sa médaille d'or en 1994 et il a reçu le prix Pritzker en 1999. Lord Foster a construit en particulier : le siège pilote d'IBM (Cosham, GB, 1970–71) ; le Sainsbury Center for Visual Arts et Crescent Wing de l'université d'East Anglia (Norwich, GB, 1976–77 ; 1989–91) ; le siège de la Hong Kong and Shanghai Banking Corporation (Hong-Kong, 1981–86) ; l'aéroport de Stansted (1987–91) ; le siège de la Commerzbank à Francfort (Allemagne, 1994–97) ; l'aéroport de Chek Lap Kok (Hong-Kong, 1995–98) ; le Parlement allemand, le Reichstag (Berlin, 1995–99) ; les nouveaux aménagements du British Museum (Londres, 1997–2000) ; le pont du Millennium (Londres, 1996–2002) ; l'Université de technologie Petronas (Seri Iskandar, Malaisie, 1998–2004) ; le viaduc de Millau (Millau, France, 1993–2005) et le stade de Wembley (Londres, 1996–2006). Plus récemment, il a réalisé l'aéroport de Pékin (2003–08) ; les chais Faustino (Ribera del Duero, Espagne, 2007–10) ; l'Institut Masdar (Abou Dhabi, UEA, 2008–10, publié ici) ; la galerie Sperone Westwater (New York, 2009–10, également publiée ici) ; le Spaceport America (Nouveau Mexique, 2009–12) et le plan directeur du quartier culturel de West Kowloon (Hong-Kong, 2009–).

MASDAR INSTITUTE

Abu Dhabi, UAE, 2008–10 (Phase 1A)

Area: 14 000 m² (Phase 1A). Client: Mubadala Development Company. Cost: not disclosed
Collaboration: PHA Consult (Sustainability MEP Engineer), Adams Kara Taylor (Structural Engineer)

The Masdar City Master Plan, developed by Foster + Partners, calls for the creation of a prototypical sustainable city in Abu Dhabi. The **MASDAR INSTITUTE** is the first part of the scheme to be realized, and is intended to provide context for the entire program. As the architects describe the ecological aspects of the institute: "The buildings are oriented to provide optimum shade and reduce cooling loads, and shaded colonnades at podium level exploit the benefits of exposed thermal mass. Façades are designed to respond to their orientation, and photovoltaic installations on every roof are combined with carefully positioned photovoltaic panels to shade streets and buildings. Cooling air currents are channeled through the public spaces using a contemporary interpretation of the region's traditional wind towers. The public spaces are further cooled by green landscaping and water to provide evaporative cooling." The complex includes laboratories, residences, and accompanying spaces.

Der von Foster + Partners entwickelte Masterplan für Masdar City sieht vor, den Prototyp einer nachhaltigen Stadt in Abu Dhabi zu realisieren. Das **MASDAR INSTITUTE** ist Teil des ersten Bauabschnitts und soll zugleich den Kontext für das gesamte Programm vorgeben. Die Architekten beschreiben die ökologischen Eigenschaften des Instituts: „Die Gebäude wurden nach optimaler Schattennutzung und mit Blick auf die Reduzierung des Kühlaufwands ausgerichtet; schattige Kolonnaden im Sockelgeschoss profitieren von der Wärmespeicherkapazität des Baus. Die Fassaden wurden entsprechend ihrer Ausrichtung geplant; Photovoltaikanlagen auf allen Dächern wurden kombiniert mit Solarpaneelen, die so positioniert wurden, dass sie Straßen und Gebäude beschatten. Dank einer zeitgenössischen Interpretation regionaltypischer, traditioneller Windfängertürme werden kühlende Luftströme erzeugt, die zur Kühlung der öffentlichen Bereiche beitragen. Zusätzliche Kühlung erfahren die öffentlichen Bereiche durch Begrünung und Wasser und die dadurch entstehende Verdunstungskühlung." Zum Komplex gehören Labors, Wohneinheiten und ergänzende Einrichtungen.

Conçu par Foster + Partners, le plan directeur de la ville de Masdar dessinait le prototype d'une ville durable à Abou Dhabi. Le **MASDAR INSTITUTE** qui représente la première partie de ce projet fournit un contexte de référence à l'ensemble du programme. «Les bâtiments sont orientés pour offrir le maximum d'ombre et réduire le gain solaire. Des colonnades qui apportent de l'ombre au niveau du podium bénéficient de la mise en exposition de leur masse thermique. Les façades sont conçues en fonction de leur orientation et sur chaque toit des équipements photovoltaïques sont alimentés par des panneaux photovoltaïques positionnés avec soin pour donner de l'ombre sur les rues et les bâtiments. Les courants d'air frais sont canalisés dans les espaces publics grâce à une version contemporaine des tours à vent traditionnelles locales. Les espaces publics sont également climatisés par des aménagements paysagers et des plans d'eau qui apportent une évaporation rafraichissante», expliquent les architectes. Le complexe comprend des laboratoires, des logements et leurs espaces attenants.

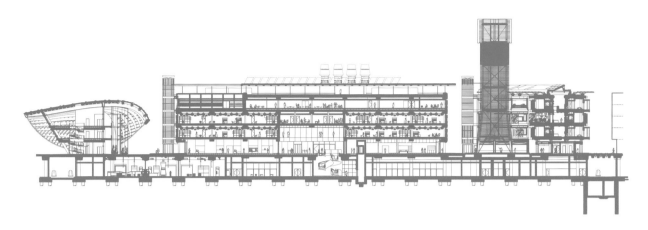

In the arid desert atmosphere of Abu Dhabi, Foster + Partners have created a kind of oasis of modern comfort with surprising forms and frequent touches of greenery.

Im trockenen Wüstenklima von Abu Dhabi haben Foster + Partners eine Oase modernen Komforts geschaffen – mit überraschender Formensprache und zahlreichen grünen Akzenten.

Sous le climat désertique d'Abou Dhabi, Foster + Partners ont créé une sorte d'oasis de confort contemporain marquée de formes surprenantes et de quelques touches de végétation.

SPERONE WESTWATER

New York, New York, USA, 2009–10

Address: 257 Bowery, New York, NY 10002, USA, +1 212 999 7337, www.speronewestwater.com
Area: 6096 m². Client: Sperone Westwater. Cost: not disclosed
Collaboration: Adamson Associates (Architects of Record), Buro Happold (Structural and MEP Engineers)

Located in the formerly destitute area of the Bowery in New York, now also home to the New Museum (SANAA), the Sperone Westwater Gallery stands out from its brick and stone-clad neighbors with a strongly vertical metal-and-glass presence.

Die Sperone Westwater Gallery liegt im ehemals heruntergekommenen Viertel Bowery in New York, wo heute auch das New Museum (SANAA) liegt. Mit markanten vertikalen Linien aus Metall und Glas hebt sie sich von ihren Nachbarbauten mit überwiegend roten Ziegel- oder Steinfassaden ab.

Située dans le quartier new-yorkais naguère misérable du Bowery qui a accueilli récemment le New Museum (SANAA), la galerie Sperone Westwater se singularise par rapport aux immeubles voisins en brique ou habillés de pierre par sa puissante verticalité exprimée dans le verre et le métal.

Located on the Bowery in Manhattan, **SPERONE WESTWATER** is known as one of New York's leading contemporary art galleries. Foster + Partners designed a nine-story building with five floors given over to the display of art. A significant architectural feature of the structure is a 3.65 x 6-meter "moving room." As this feature is explained: "At any given floor, the exhibition space can be extended by parking the moving room as required, by the use of an additional elevator and stairs which provide alternative access." A mezzanine floor and a double-height display area at street level, together with set-back offices and a top-floor library are other elements of the space, which is housed behind a CNC-milled glass façade.

SPERONE WESTWATER gilt als eine der führenden Galerien für zeitgenössische Kunst in New York und liegt an der Bowery in Manhattan. Foster + Partners entwarfen ein neunstöckiges Gebäude; fünf Etagen sind als Ausstellungsfläche für Kunst vorgesehen. Besonderes architektonisches Highlight des Baus ist ein 3,65 x 6 m großer *moving room* (beweglicher Raum). Diese technische Besonderheit funktioniert wie folgt: „Die Ausstellungsflächen lassen sich auf jeder Etage erweitern, indem der *moving room* entsprechend in Parkposition gebracht wird. Dies geschieht mithilfe eines Aufzugs, Treppen ermöglichen alternative Zugänge." Weitere Besonderheiten des Baus sind ein Mezzaningeschoss und ein Ausstellungsraum mit doppelter Geschosshöhe im Erdgeschoss sowie Büroräume, die in den hinteren Gebäudeteil verlegt wurden, und eine Bibliothek im Dachgeschoss. Dem Ganzen vorgeschaltet ist eine CNC-gefräste Glasfassade.

Située sur le Bowery à Manhattan, la galerie **SPERONE WESTWATER** est une des premières galeries d'art contemporain new-yorkaises. Foster + Partners ont dessiné un immeuble de neuf niveaux dont cinq sont consacrés à l'exposition d'œuvres d'art. Un des éléments les plus spectaculaires du projet est une « moving room », une salle mobile. « À n'importe quel étage, la surface d'exposition peut être agrandie en lui adjoignant cette salle, grâce à un ascenseur et des escaliers indépendants qui offrent une voie d'accès supplémentaire. » Derrière la façade en verre CNC se trouvent également une mezzanine, une salle d'exposition double hauteur au niveau de la rue, des bureaux en retraits et une bibliothèque au dernier étage.

Generous gallery spaces are largely closed off from the environment of the city, providing calm spaces to contemplate contemporary art.

Die großzügigen Ausstellungsräume sind weitgehend vom urbanen Umfeld abgeschirmt und damit stille Orte zur Betrachtung zeitgenössischer Kunst.

Les généreux volumes de la galerie sont en grande partie isolés de leur environnement urbain. Ils offrent des espaces sereins qui favorisent la contemplation de l'art contemporain.

To the right, a double-height gallery space, and below, a section drawing and image show the red elevator.

Rechts ein Ausstellungsraum mit doppelter Geschosshöhe. Unten ein Querschnitt und eine Aufnahme, auf der der rote Aufzug zu sehen ist.

À droite une galerie double hauteur et ci-dessous, un plan de coupe montrant en rouge l'ascenseur représenté sur la photographie de gauche.

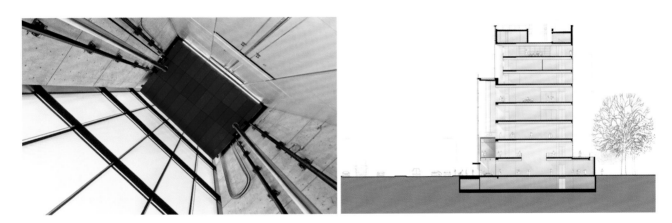

SOU FUJIMOTO

Sou Fujimoto Architects
10–3 Ichikawa-Seihon Building 6F
Higashi-Enoki-Cho Shinjuku
Tokyo 162–0807
Japan

Tel: +81 3 3513 5401
Fax: +81 3 3513 5402
E-mail: media@sou-fujimoto.net
Web: www.sou-fujimoto.net

SOU FUJIMOTO was born in 1971. He received a B.Arch degree from the University of Tokyo, Faculty of Engineering, Department of Architecture (1990–94). He established his own firm, Sou Fujimoto Architects, in 2000. He is considered one of the most interesting rising Japanese architects, and his forms usually evade easy classification. He has been a Lecturer at the Tokyo University of Science (2001–), Tokyo University (2004), and Kyoto University (2007–). His work includes the Industrial Training Facilities for the Mentally Handicapped (Hokkaido, 2003); Environment Art Forum, Annaka (Gunma, 2003–06); Treatment Center for Mentally Disturbed Children (Hokkaido, 2006); House O (Chiba, 2007); N House (Oita Prefecture, 2007–08); and the Final Wooden House (Kumamura, Kumamoto, 2007–08). Other recent work includes his participation in Toyo Ito's Sumika Project (House Before House, Utsunomiya, Tochigi, 2008); Musashino Art University Museum and Library (Tokyo, 2007–09, published here); House H (Tokyo, 2008–09); Tokyo Apartment (Itabashiku, Tokyo, 2009–10, also published here); and the Uniqlo store in Shinsaibashi (Osaka, 2010), all in Japan.

SOU FUJIMOTO wurde 1971 geboren. Sein Architekturstudium an der Fakultät für Bauingenieurwesen der Universität Tokio schloss er mit einem B.Arch ab (1990–94). Sein eigenes Büro, Sou Fujimoto Architects, gründete er 2000. Er gilt als einer der interessantesten jungen Architekten Japans, seine Formensprache entzieht sich einfachen Zuordnungen. Als Dozent lehrt er an der Tokioter Universität der Wissenschaften (2001–) sowie den Universitäten von Tokio (2004) und Kioto (2007–). Zu seinen Projekten zählen Ausbildungsstätten für geistig Behinderte (Hokkaido, 2003), das Umwelt-Kunst-Forum in Annaka (Gunma, 2003–06), ein Behandlungszentrum für psychisch erkrankte Kinder (Hokkaido, 2006), House O (Chiba, 2007), N House (Präfektur Oita, 2007–08) und das Final Wooden House in Kumamura (Kumamoto, 2007–08). Weitere jüngere Arbeiten sind u.a. seine Beteiligung an Toyo Itos Sumika-Projekt (House Before House, Utsunomiya, Tochigi, 2008), Museum und Bibliothek der Kunsthochschule Musashino (Tokio, 2007–09, hier vorgestellt), das House H (Tokio, 2008–09), das Tokyo Apartment (Itabashiku, Tokio, 2009–10, ebenfalls hier vorgestellt) und der Uniqlo Store in Shinsaibashi (Osaka, 2010), alle in Japan.

SOU FUJIMOTO, né en 1971, a obtenu son B. Arch. à l'université de Tokyo (faculté d'ingénierie, département d'architecture, 1990–94). Il crée sa propre agence, Sou Fujimoto Architects, en 2000. On le considère comme l'un des plus intéressants jeunes architectes japonais apparus récemment et son vocabulaire formel échappe à toute classification aisée. Il a été assistant à l'Université des sciences de Tokyo (2001–), à l'université de Tokyo (2004) et à l'université de Kyoto (2007–). Parmi ses réalisations : des installations de formation pour handicapés mentaux (Hokkaido, 2003) ; l'Environment Art Forum d'Annaka (Gunma, 2003–06) ; un Centre de traitement pour les enfants souffrant de troubles mentaux (Hokkaido, 2006) ; la Maison O (Chiba, 2007) ; la Maison N (préfecture d'Oita, 2007–08) ; la Maison de bois « définitive » (Kumamura, Kumamoto, 2007–08). Plus récemment, il a participé au projet Sumika de Toyo Ito (Maison d'avant la maison, Utsunomiya, Tochigi, 2008) ; le musée et la bibliothèque de l'Université d'art Musashino (Tokyo, 2007–09, publiés ici) ; la Maison H (Tokyo, 2008–09) ; l'appartement Tokyo (Itabashiku, Tokyo, 2009–10, également publié ici) et le magasin Uniqlo à Shinsaibashi (Osaka, 2010), tous au Japon.

MUSASHINO ART UNIVERSITY MUSEUM AND LIBRARY

Tokyo, Japan, 2007–09

Address: 1–736 Ogawa-cho, Kodaira-shi, Tokyo 187–8505, Japan, www.musabi.ac.jp
Area: 6419 m². Client: Musashino Art University. Cost: not disclosed

This is a new library for one of the most distinguished art universities in Japan. The project included the refurbishment of an existing building that now serves as an art gallery. The architect describes the library as an "ark" with a total of 200 000 books, half of which are in open stacks. "I imagined a place encircled by a single bookshelf in the form of a spiral. The domain encased within the infinite spiral itself is the library," says Fujimoto. The bookshelf spiral actually wraps around the site and the external wall. He sought to create the most "library-like" and "simplest" library possible, whence the idea of the building as bookshelves. The architect defines the act of using a library as a combination of "investigation" and "exploration"—"even in the age of Google." To achieve the coexistence of the two concepts, he continues: "Spatial and configuration logics beyond mere systematics are employed… One can faintly recognize the entirety of the library and at the same time imagine that there are unknown spaces that are rendered constantly imperceptible."

Die neue Bibliothek wurde für eine der renommiertesten Kunsthochschulen Japans gebaut. Teil des Projekts war die Sanierung eines älteren Gebäudes, in dem nun eine Kunstgalerie untergebracht ist. Der Architekt bezeichnet die Bibliothek mit ihrem Bestand von 200 000 Büchern, von denen die Hälfte in offenen Magazinen zugänglich ist, als „Arche". „Ich stellte mir einen Ort vor, der von einem durchgängigen spiralförmigen Regal umschlossen wird. Der von dieser unendlichen Spirale umfangene Bereich ist die Bibliothek", erklärt Fujimoto. Tatsächlich umschließt die Spirale das gesamte Gelände einschließlich der Außenmauern. Fujimoto ging es darum, eine Bibliothek zu gestalten, die so „bibliotheksmäßig" und „einfach" wie nur möglich ist: So entstand die Idee von einem Gebäude aus Bücherregalen. Für den Architekten ist das Nutzen einer Bibliothek eine Mischung aus „Forschen" und „Entdecken" – „selbst im Zeitalter von Google". Um beide Konzepte miteinander zu verbinden, führt er weiter aus: „Hier kamen räumliche und konfigurative Überlegungen zum Tragen, die weit über simple Systematik hinausgehen … Obwohl man die Gesamtheit der Bibliothek gerade noch ausmachen kann, kann man sich ebenso vorstellen, dass es auch unbekannte Räume gibt, die immer verborgen bleiben werden."

Cette nouvelle bibliothèque a été construite pour l'une des plus prestigieuses universités d'art du Japon. Le projet comprenait par ailleurs la rénovation d'un bâtiment existant, dorénavant utilisé comme galerie d'exposition. L'architecte décrit cette bibliothèque comme un « arche » abritant 200 000 livres, dont la moitié en rayonnages ouverts. « J'ai imaginé un lieu entouré d'un rayonnage l'enveloppant en spirale. L'espace pris à l'intérieur de cette spirale qui tend vers l'infini est la bibliothèque elle-même », explique Fujimoto. Ce rayonnage enveloppe le site et le mur extérieur. L'architecte a cherché à créer la bibliothèque la plus « bibliothèque » et la « plus simple » possible, d'où l'idée de ce bâtiment-rayonnage. Il définit l'utilisation d'une bibliothèque comme une combinaison « d'investigation » et « d'exploration », « même à l'âge de Google ». Pour faire coexister ces deux concepts : « … des logiques spatiales et de configuration qui vont au-delà d'une simple systématisation ont été utilisées… on peut vaguement appréhender la bibliothèque dans sa totalité et imaginer dans le même temps qu'il existe aussi, plus loin, d'autres espaces qui nous restent imperceptibles. »

A drawing shows the way the ample presence of books is alternated with openings and the unusual façade of the building itself. To the right, a drawing shows the idea of the "infinite spiral of books" evoked by the architect.

Eine Zeichnung illustriert den Wechsel zwischen dominierender Präsenz von Büchern, Öffnungen und ungewöhnlicher Fassade des Baus. Rechts eine Zeichnung, auf der die Vorstellung von einer „unendlichen Bücherspirale" des Architekten deutlich wird.

Cette illustration montre l'alternance des rayonnages de livres et des ouvertures de façade. À droite, dessin sur le concept de « spirale infinie de livres » évoqué par l'architecte.

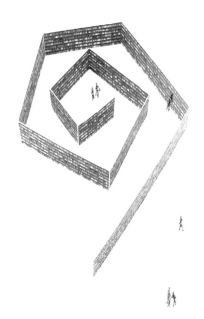

The entire inner structure of the library is marked by bookshelf space; largely empty here, and likely to remain empty in the future.

Der Innenraum ist vollständig von Büchermagazinen geprägt. Die hier noch weitgehend leeren Regalfächer werden wohl auch in Zukunft leer bleiben.

La totalité de la structure interne de la bibliothèque est habillée de rayonnages de livres, en grande partie vides et qui le resteront probablement.

Die Regaleinbauten reichen bis zur Decke und an den Treppen hinunter. Sie umfangen den Besucher und vermitteln den Eindruck eines allumfassenden Bücheruniversums.

Les rayonnages montent jusqu'au plafond et suivent les escaliers, pour donner aux visiteurs l'impression d'être entourés d'un univers de livres.

Bookshelves go up to the ceilings and down the steps, surrounding visitors and implying the presence of a whole world of books.

TOKYO APARTMENT

Itabashiku, Tokyo, Japan, 2009–10

Address: Komone, Itabashiku, Tokyo, Japan
Area: 181 m². Client: not disclosed. Cost: not disclosed

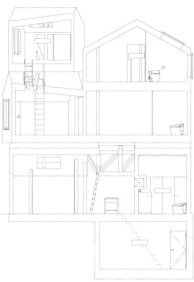

Apartment interiors are simple, but marked by unexpected features such as the window placement or the ladder seen above. The section drawing shows the relation of the units in the building.

Die Innenräume der Wohnungen sind schlicht gehalten, überraschen jedoch mit Details wie der Anordnung der Fenster oder der Leiter oben im Bild. Der Querschnitt illustriert das Verhältnis der Wohneinheiten zueinander.

L'intérieur des appartements est traité avec simplicité non sans quelques détails inattendus comme l'implantation des fenêtres ou d'une échelle (ci-dessus). Le plan de coupe montre la relation entre les unités qui composent le bâtiment.

This "apartment" is actually a group of four residences in the shape of houses that are accumulated on a single site. Rooms in the "houses" can be on different floors (first and third for example), connected by an outside stairway. "This collective housing is a miniature version of Tokyo," says the architect. "I meant to make an infinite, rich place that is crowded and disorderly." Indeed, most of those familiar with Tokyo would agree that it is often "crowded and disorderly." Further, the idea of having to pass outside to go from one part of a house to another is one that has often existed, even in small Japanese row houses for example. As is often the case, here Fujimoto challenges a basic concept of architecture, both in terms of the appearance of this apartment building, and in the way it functions.

Bei diesem „Apartment" handelt es sich im Grunde um vier gruppierte, wie einzelne Häuser gestaltete Wohneinheiten, die auf einem Grundstück gestapelt wurden. Die Zimmer in diesen „Häusern" liegen zum Teil auf verschiedenen Ebenen (so etwa bei Wohnung 1 und 3) und werden über Außentreppen erschlossen. „Diese kollektive Wohnanlage ist Tokio im Kleinformat", erklärt der Architekt. „Ich wollte einen vermeintlich unendlichen, facettenreichen Raum gestalten, der gedrängt und ohne jede Ordnung scheint." Fast alle, die Tokio kennen, würden zweifellos zustimmen, dass die Stadt oft „gedrängt und ohne jede Ordnung" wirkt. Auch das Prinzip, nach draußen gehen zu müssen, um von einem Teil des Hauses in einen anderen zu gelangen, ist etwas, das es oft gegeben hat, selbst in kleinen japanischen Reihenhäusern. Wie so oft, hinterfragt Fujimoto auch hier gängige architektonische Konzepte, sowohl im Hinblick auf das äußere Erscheinungsbild dieses Apartmenthauses, als auch auf seine Funktionalität.

Cet « appartement » est en fait un groupement de résidences en forme de maisons qui auraient été empilées sur un même terrain. Les pièces des « maisons » peuvent se trouver à différents niveaux (au premier et au troisième par exemple), reliées par un escalier extérieur. « Ce type de logement collectif est une version miniature de Tokyo », explique l'architecte. « Je voulais fabriquer un lieu riche, infini, surpeuplé et désordonné. » Ceux qui connaissent bien Tokyo pensent en effet que cette ville est « surpeuplée et désordonnée ». De plus, l'idée de passer par l'extérieur pour aller d'une partie de la maison à l'autre était chose courante, même dans les alignements de petites maisons japonaises, par exemple. Comme souvent, Fujimoto remet en question un concept de base de l'architecture, à la fois en termes d'aspect d'un immeuble d'appartements et de son fonctionnement.

On the right page, an exterior view that shows the typical web of above-ground electrical and telephone lines.

Rechts eine Außenansicht, auf der auch das typische Netzwerk von Strom- und Telefon-Oberleitungen zu sehen ist.

Page de droite : vue extérieure de l'immeuble derrière le réseau de câbles d'électricité et de téléphone typiques de Tokyo.

MASSIMILIANO AND DORIANA FUKSAS

Massimiliano and Doriana Fuksas
Piazza del Monte di Pietà 30
00186 Rome
Italy

Tel: +39 06 68 80 78 71
Fax: +39 06 68 80 78 72
E-mail: press@fuksas.com
Web: www.fuksas.com

MASSIMILIANO FUKSAS was born in 1944 in Rome. He received his degree in Architecture at the "La Sapienza" University of Rome in 1969. He founded a studio in Rome in 1967, and opened an office in Paris in 1989. He won the 1999 Grand Prix d'Architecture in France. He was the Director of the 7th Architecture Biennale in Venice (1998–2000). He has worked with **DORIANA MANDRELLI FUKSAS** since 1985. She attended the Faculty of Architecture at the "La Sapienza" University of Rome and has been responsible for design in the firm since 1997. They have completed the Ferrari Research Center (Maranello, Italy, 2001–04); Fiera Milano (Rho-Pero, Milan, Italy, 2002–05); Zenith Strasbourg (Eckbolsheim, Strasbourg, France, 2003–07); the Armani Ginza Tower (Tokyo, 2005–07); a church in Foligno (Italy, 2001–09); Peres Peace House (Jaffa, Israel, 2005–09, published here); Emporio Armani Fifth Avenue (New York, 2009); MyZeil Shopping Mall (Frankfurt, 2009); 18 Septemberplein (Eindhoven, The Netherlands, 2003–10); Lyon Confluence (Lyon, France, 2005–10); and the Admirant Entrance Building (Eindhoven, The Netherlands, 2008–10, also published here). Upcoming work includes the French National Archives (Paris, 2005–11); the Eur Congress Center (Rome, 1998–2012); Terminal 3, International Shenzhen Bao'an Airport (Shenzhen, China, 2008–12); and the House of Justice (Tbilisi, Georgia, 2010–).

MASSIMILIANO FUKSAS wurde 1944 in Rom geboren und schloss sein Architekturstudium 1969 an der Universität Rom „La Sapienza" ab. 1967 gründete er ein Studio in Rom, 1989 eröffnete er ein Büro in Paris. 1999 wurde er in Frankreich mit dem Grand Prix d'Architecture ausgezeichnet. Er war Direktor der 7. Architekturbiennale von Venedig (1998–2000). Seit 1985 arbeitet er mit **DORIANA MANDRELLI FUKSAS** zusammen. Sie studierte an der Fakultät für Architektur an der „La Sapienza" in Rom und ist seit 1997 verantwortlich für die Entwürfe des Büros. Fertigstellen konnte das Team das Ferrari-Forschungszentrum (Maranello, Italien, 2001–04), die Fiera Milano (Rho-Pero, Mailand, 2002–05), das Zenith Strasbourg (Eckbolsheim, Frankreich, 2003–07), den Armani Ginza Tower (Tokio, 2005–07), eine Kirche in Foligno (Italien, 2001–09), das Peres-Friedenszentrum (Jaffa, Israel, 2005–09, hier vorgestellt), Emporio Armani Fifth Avenue (New York, 2009), das Einkaufszentrum MyZeil (Frankfurt/Main, 2009), 18 Septemberplein (Eindhoven, 2003–10), Lyon Confluence (Lyon, Frankreich, 2005–10) und das Zugangsgebäude zum Komplex De Admirant (Eindhoven, 2008–10, ebenfalls hier vorgestellt). In Planung bzw. im Bau sind u.a. das Französische Nationalarchiv (Paris, 2005–11), das Kongresszentrum im Stadtteil Eur (Rom, 1998–2012), das Terminal 3 am Flughafen Shenzhen Bao'an (Shenzhen, China, 2008–12) und der Gerichtshof in Tblisi (Georgien, 2010–).

MASSIMILIANO FUKSAS, né en 1944 à Rome, est diplômé en architecture de l'université de Rome La Sapienza (1969). Il crée son agence à Rome en 1967 et ouvre un bureau à Paris en 1989. En 1999, il remporte le Grand Prix d'architecture français. Il a été directeur de la VIIe Biennale d'architecture de Venise (1998–2000) et travaille avec **DORIANA MANDRELLI FUKSAS** depuis 1985. Celle-ci a également étudié à la faculté d'architecture de l'université de Rome La Sapienza. Elle est responsable du design à l'agence depuis 1997. Ils ont réalisé : le Centre de recherches Ferrari (Maranello, Italie, 2001–04) ; les bâtiments de la Foire de Milan (Rho-Pero, Milan, 2002–05) ; le Zénith de Strasbourg (Eckbolsheim, Strasbourg, 2003–07) ; la tour Armani à Ginza (Tokyo, 2005–07) ; une église à Foligno (Italie, 2001–09) ; le Centre Peres pour la Paix (Jaffa, Israël, 2005–09, publié ici) ; l'Emporio Armani Fifth Avenue (New York, 2009) ; le centre commercial MyZeil (Francfort, 2009) ; l'immeuble 18 Septemberplein (Eindhoven, Pays-Bas, 2003–10) ; l'immeuble Lyon Confluence (Lyon, 2005–10) et l'immeuble d'entrée du centre commercial Admirant (Eindhoven, 2008–10, également publié ici). L'agence travaille également sur les projets des Archives nationales de France (Pierrefitte-sur-Seine, France, 2005–11) ; le Centre Eur Congress (Rome, 1998–2012) ; le Terminal 3 de l'aéroport international Bao'an (Shenzhen, Chine, 2008–12) et un palais de justice (Tbilissi, Georgie, 2010–).

PERES PEACE HOUSE

Jaffa, Israel, 2005–09

Address: 132 Kedem Street, Jaffa, Israel
Area: 2500 m². Client: Peres Center for Peace. Cost: $15 million

"Peace," says the architect, "cannot be enclosed in wrapping; it is, rather, a sensation of fullness and serenity that can be communicated through a place, or through architecture." The concept of this building relies on a series of layers that Fuksas equates to "time" and "patience." Concrete composed with different types of sand and aggregate constitutes these layers, together with a stone base. Translucent glass is also used in the design, both to bring natural light into the structure and to let it shine out in the evening. "This project represents the venue of an encounter, a debate, reasoning, and solutions," concludes the architect.

„Frieden", so der Architekt, „lässt sich nicht in einer Hülle einfangen, er ist vielmehr eine Fülle und Gelassenheit, die sich durch einen Ort oder Architektur vermitteln lässt." Das Konzept für den Entwurf entwickelte sich aus einer Abfolge von Schichten, die Fuksas als Symbole für „Zeit" und „Geduld" versteht. Die Schichten bestehen aus Beton mit verschiedenen Sandzuschlägen, ergänzt wird das Ganze durch einen Sockel aus Stein. Auch lichtdurchlässiges Glas kam hier zum Einsatz, das Tageslicht in den Bau einfallen und das Gebäude nachts leuchten lässt. Der Architekt fasst zusammen: „Dieses Projekt ist Ort der Begegnung, des Gesprächs, der Verhandlung und der Lösungen."

« La paix », explique l'architecte, « ne peut s'enfermer dans un habillage. C'est plutôt un sentiment de plénitude et de sérénité qui peut se communiquer à travers un lieu ou une architecture. » Le concept de ce bâtiment repose sur une succession de strates que Fuksas rapproche de notions de « temps » ou de « patience ». Elles sont faites d'un béton composé de différentes variétés de sable et d'agrégats, et reposent sur un socle en pierre. Le verre translucide qui facilite l'éclairage naturel de l'intérieur devient étincelant à la tombée du jour. « Ce projet offre l'occasion d'une rencontre, d'un débat, d'une réflexion et de solutions », conclut M. Fuksas.

With its strongly affirmed horizontal lines and hilltop position, the Peres Peace House stands out as it rightly should, glowing from within at night.

Mit seinen markanten horizontalen Linien und der erhöhten Lage auf einem Hügel ist das Peres-Friedenszentrum so prominent wie es verdient und leuchtet nachts von innen heraus.

Par sa position au sommet d'une colline et ses horizontales affirmées, le Centre Peres pour la Paix se détache de son environnement, en particulier la nuit quand il paraît illuminé de l'intérieur.

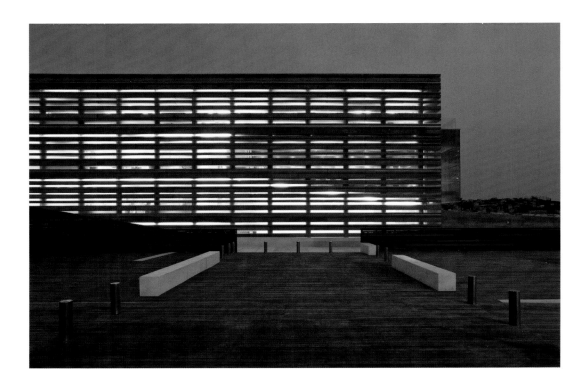

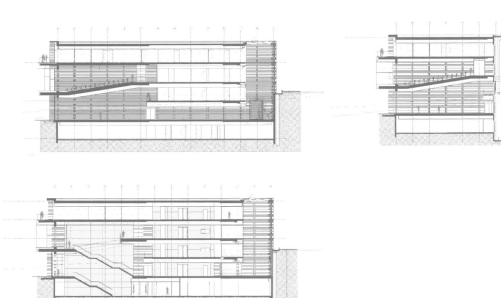

Drawings of the building show its strongly rectilinear design. It forms a strong block, as the interior view above also confirms with its simple concrete and steel design.

Zeichnungen des Gebäudes lassen das auffällig lineare Design des eindrucksvoll blockhaften Baukörpers deutlich werden, wie die Innenansicht oben mit ihren schlichten Formen aus Beton und Stahl belegt.

Les coupes du projet expriment la rectilinéarité de ce puissant bloc d'acier et de béton, comme le confirme la vue intérieure ci-dessus.

The architect's idea of the layering that occurs over time is expressed in these images, where concrete and steel are both layered in slightly irregular patterns, as if they had been put in place over a long period.

Auf den Ansichten ist zu erkennen, wie der Architekt historische Schichtungen visualisiert: Beton und Stahl sind in unregelmäßigen Lagen übereinandergeschichtet, als seien sie über lange Zeit gewachsen.

L'idée de Fuksas de couches qui se seraient développées avec le temps s'exprime dans ces images où les strates de béton et d'acier se superposent de façon légèrement irrégulière, comme si elles s'étaient mises en place sur une longue période.

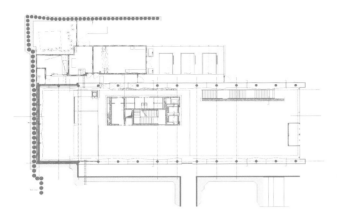

Fuksas is unusual in his lack of a signature style: instead here, as in his other work, he applies the distilled concept of the personality and work of Shimon Peres to the accumulated forms which, nonetheless, always leave space for openings and views to the exterior.

Ungewöhnlich ist, dass Fuksas keine typische Handschrift hat – vielmehr setzt er hier, ähnlich wie bei anderen Projekten, eine konzeptionelle Verdichtung der Persönlichkeit und des Lebenswerks von Shimon Peres um. So entstehen dichte Formen, die dennoch Raum lassen für Öffnungen und Blicke nach draußen.

Fuksas, qui ne se bat pas pour un style personnel identifiable, s'applique ici à exprimer la personnalité et l'œuvre de Shimon Peres à travers une accumulation de strates qui laissent cependant la place par moment à des ouvertures et des perspectives sur l'extérieur.

ADMIRANT ENTRANCE BUILDING

Eindhoven, The Netherlands, 2008–10

Address: Nieuwe Emmasingel 2, 5611 AM Eindhoven, The Netherlands
Area: 3000 m². Client: Rond de Admirant CV. Cost: not disclosed
Collaboration: Waagner Biro Stahlbau Ag (Façade Realization)

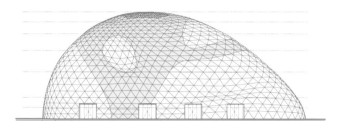 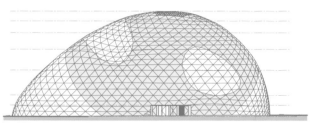

Affirming his own personality and thoughts, the architect here calls on a sort of extrusion from the earth that may recall the "blob" buildings that characterized the early period of the use of computers in design. The contrast with the Peres Peace Center could not be greater.

Hier zeigt der Architekt eigene Persönlichkeit und Ideen und gestaltet eine Art Extrusion aus dem Boden, die an typische „Blob"-Bauten aus der Frühzeit des digitalen Entwerfens erinnert. Der Kontrast zum Peres Peace Center könnte nicht größer sein.

Dans un geste d'affirmation de sa réflexion et sa personnalité, l'architecte a créé ici une sorte de protubérance qui rappelle les formes en blobs caractéristiques des débuts de la CAO en architecture. Le contraste avec le Centre Peres pour la Paix ne pourrait être plus grand.

Located in downtown Eindhoven, this project is part of a complex that also includes a large underground parking lot, the Piazza Shopping Mall, and a Media Market. The architects describe the design of the Admirant Entrance Building as "fluid and amorphous" and compare it to a "marine mammal that erupts for air." It has no front or back, but rather a continuous building envelope wrapped around a five-story concrete structure. Commercial spaces are located on the ground and first levels and office spaces on levels three and four, with a technical floor above. The structural system is "designed as a free-form steel grid with triangular mesh fixed to the building." Although "blob" forms were briefly popular at the beginning of the computer-design era, Fuksas seeks here to renew the genre.

Das mitten in Eindhoven gelegene Bauwerk ist Teil eines größeren Komplexes, zu dem auch eine große Tiefgarage, das Einkaufszentrum Piazza und ein Elektromarkt gehören. Die Architekten beschreiben den Zugangsbau zum Admirant-Gebäude als „fließend und amorph" und vergleichen ihn mit einem „Wal, der zum Luftholen auftaucht". Hier gibt es keine Vorder- oder Rückseite, sondern eine kontinuierliche Gebäudehülle, die den fünfstöckigen Betonbau umschließt. Während im Erdgeschoss und im ersten Stock Gewerbeflächen liegen, sind auf den Ebenen drei und vier Büros untergebracht, darüber liegt eine Etage mit Haustechnik. Das Tragwerk wurde „als frei geformter Stahlrahmen entworfen, ein Netzwerk aus Dreiecksformen zieht sich über den gesamten Gebäudekörper". Obwohl „Blob"-Formen schon zu Beginn der Ära des digitalen Entwerfens populär waren, geht es Fuksas hier darum, das Genre zu erneuern.

Construit dans le centre d'Eindhoven, ce projet fait partie d'un complexe comprenant par ailleurs un vaste parking souterrain, le centre commercial Piazza et un magasin d'électroménager et de matériel électrique. Les architectes qualifient cette construction de « fluide et amorphe » et la comparent à « un mammifère marin qui ferait surface pour respirer ». Il n'a ni avant, ni arrière. Il s'agit plutôt d'une enveloppe continue qui habille une construction en béton de cinq niveaux. Les espaces commerciaux sont implantés au rez-de-chaussée et au premier étage, des bureaux aux troisième et quatrième niveaux et un étage technique au sommet. Le principe structurel est celui « d'une trame en acier de forme libre à treillis triangulé fixé sur la façade ». Fuksas tente ici de renouveler la forme de « blob » qui connut une brève popularité aux débuts de l'ère de la conception assistée par ordinateur.

Eindhoven, heavily damaged during World War II, is a largely modern and quite staid city on the whole. The Admirant Entrance Building clearly stands out from its environment because of its shape, but also its unusual webbed, glazed design.

Eindhoven, im Zweiten Weltkrieg stark zerstört, ist eine weitgehend modern bebaute, wenn auch eher konservative Stadt. Das Admirant-Zugangsgebäude fällt aus seinem Umfeld nicht nur durch seine Form, sondern auch durch die ungewöhnliche, netzartig verglaste Fassade auf.

Très endommagée pendant la Seconde guerre mondiale, Eindhoven est une ville en grande partie moderne et assez ordonnée. Ce petit immeuble qui est l'entrée d'un centre commercial se détache fortement de son environnement par sa forme mais aussi par son habillage de verre.

The restaurant inside the Admirant Entrance Building offers views on the city but also provides spectacular, generous spaces for guests. To the right, a drawing of the overall shape of the building as seen from above.

Das Restaurant im Admirant-Komplex bietet seinen Gästen nicht nur Blick auf die Stadt, sondern auch spektakuläre, großzügige Räume. Rechts eine Zeichnung des Gebäudes in der Aufsicht.

Le restaurant offre à ses clients des perspectives sur la ville mais aussi des salles aux volumes spectaculaires et généreux. À droite, dessin de la forme d'ensemble de l'immeuble vue du dessus.

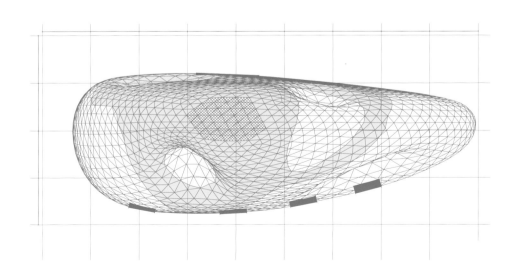

MANUELLE GAUTRAND

Manuelle Gautrand Architecture
36 Boulevard de la Bastille
75012 Paris
France

Tel: +33 1 56 95 06 46
Fax: +33 1 56 95 06 47
E-mail: contact@manuelle-gautrand.com
Web: www.manuelle-gautrand.com

Born in 1961, **MANUELLE GAUTRAND** received her degree in Architecture in 1985. She created her own office in 1991 in Lyon and moved it to Paris in 1994. She has been a teacher at the École Spéciale d'Architecture in Paris (1999–2000), at the École Nationale Supérieure d'Architecture Paris-Val-de-Seine (2000–03), and participates in numerous student workshops outside France. In 2001, she was selected to participate in the limited competition for the François Pinault Contemporary Art Museum that was to be located on the Île Seguin near Paris. Her built work includes a 72-meter-long pedestrian bridge (Lyon, 1993); five highway toll booths (in the Somme region on the A16 highway, 1998); and the Theater of the National Center for Dramatic Arts (Béthune, 1998). Her recent work includes "Solaris," a 100-unit sustainable apartment building and socio-cultural center in Rennes (2006); an administrative complex in Saint-Étienne (2005–07); Espace Citroën (Paris, 2007); the extension and restructuring of LaM, the Lille Museum of Modern, Contemporary and Outsider Art (Villeneuve d'Ascq, 2006–09, published here); and the Gaîté Lyrique Digital Arts and Music Center in Paris (2007–10), all in France.

MANUELLE GAUTRAND, geboren 1961, schloss ihr Architekturstudium 1985 ab. 1991 gründete sie ihr eigenes Büro in Lyon, mit dem sie 1994 nach Paris übersiedelte. Gautrand lehrte an der École Spéciale d'Architecture in Paris (1999–2000) sowie der École Nationale Supérieure d'Architecture Paris-Val-de-Seine (2000–03) und ist an zahlreichen Studentenworkshops außerhalb Frankreichs beteiligt. 2001 wurde sie zum Wettbewerb für das François-Pinault-Museum für zeitgenössische Kunst eingeladen, das auf der Île Seguin unweit von Paris gebaut werden sollte. Zu ihren realisierten Projekten zählen eine 72 m lange Fußgängerbrücke (Lyon, 1993), fünf Autobahn-Mautstationen (an der A16 in der Region Somme, 1998) sowie das Theater des staatlichen Zentrums für darstellende Künste (Béthune, 1998). Jüngste Projekte sind u.a. „Solaris", ein nachhaltiges Apartmentgebäude mit 100 Wohneinheiten und soziokulturellem Zentrum in Rennes (2006), ein Verwaltungskomplex in Saint-Étienne (2005–07), der Espace Citroën (Paris, 2007), die Erweiterung und Neustrukturierung des LaM, dem Museum für moderne, zeitgenössische und Outsider-Kunst in Lille (Villeneuve d'Ascq, 2006–09, hier vorgestellt) sowie die Gaîté Lyrique, das Zentrum für digitale Kunst und Musik in Paris (2007–10), alle in Frankreich.

Née en 1961, **MANUELLE GAUTRAND** a obtenu son diplôme d'architecte en 1985. Elle a créé son agence à Lyon en 1991 avant de s'installer à Paris en 1994. Elle a enseigné à l'École spéciale d'architecture de Paris (1999–2000), à l'École nationale supérieure d'architecture Paris Val de Seine (2000–03) et participe à de nombreux ateliers d'étudiants en dehors de la France. En 2001, elle a été sélectionnée pour participer au concours restreint organisé pour le Musée d'art contemporain François Pinault qui devait être édifié sur l'île Seguin aux portes de Paris. Parmi ses réalisations, toutes en France : une passerelle piétonnière de 72 mètres de long (Lyon, 1993) ; cinq péages d'autoroute (département de la Somme sur l'A16, 1998) et le théâtre du Centre dramatique national de Béthune (1998). Plus récemment, elle a réalisé « Solaris », un immeuble durable de 100 appartements et centre culturel à Rennes (2006) ; un complexe administratif à Saint-Étienne (2005–07) ; l'Espace Citroën (Paris, 2007) ; l'extension et la restructuration du LaM, Lille Métropole, Musée d'art moderne, d'art contemporain et d'art brut (Villeneuve d'Ascq, 2006–09, publié ici) et la Gaîté lyrique, Centre des arts numériques et des musiques actuelles (Paris, 2007–10).

LAM, LILLE MUSEUM OF MODERN CONTEMPORARY AND OUTSIDER ART

Villeneuve d'Ascq, France, 2006–09

Area: 11 600 m² (total); 3200 m² (new structure); 4000 m² (exhibition area)
Client: Lille Métropole Communauté Urbaine. Cost: €30 million. Collaboration: Yves Tougard (Project Architect)

The project involved the refurbishment and extension of the **LILLE MODERN ART MUSEUM**, located in a park at Villeneuve d'Ascq. The original building, designed by Roland Simounet in 1983, is already a listed structure. The architect states that the aim was to build up the museum "as a continuous and fluid entity," by adding new galleries dedicated to a collection of Art Brut (Outsider Art) works, and a complete refurbishment of the existing building. The extension wraps around the north and east sides of the existing building in a "fan-splay of long, fluid, and organic volumes." On one side, the ribs "stretch in close folds to shelter a café-restaurant that opens to the central patio; on the other, the ribs are more widely spaced to form the five galleries for the Art Brut collection." Gautrand states that her scheme meant to both engage and respect the older building, all the more so that Simounet's influence is still felt here and elsewhere.

Das Projekt umfasste die Sanierung und Erweiterung des **MUSEUMS FÜR MODERNE KUNST IN LILLE** im Park von Villeneuve d'Ascq. Der Altbau, entworfen 1983 von Roland Simounet, steht bereits unter Denkmalschutz. Die Architekten erklären, ihr Ziel sei gewesen, das Museum „als fließende Gesamtheit" zu konzipieren, als sie neue Ausstellungsräume für eine Sammlung mit Art Brut (Outsider Art) anbauten sowie das gesamte Gebäude einer Sanierung unterzogen. Der Anbau umfängt die Nord- und Ostseite des Altbaus wie ein „ausgebreiteter Fächer aus lang gestreckten, fließenden, organischen Baukörpern". Auf einer Seite bleiben die Rippen des Fächers „eng gefaltet und schützen ein Café und Restaurant, das sich zum zentralen Patio öffnet, auf der andere Seite sind die Rippen weiter gespreizt und bilden die fünf Ausstellungsräume für die Art-Brut-Sammlung". Gautrand betont, ihr Konzept sei darauf angelegt, den älteren Bau einzubinden und zu respektieren, zumal Simounets Einfluss hier wie andernorts noch immer spürbar ist.

Ce projet portait sur la rénovation et l'extension du **MUSÉE D'ART MODERNE DE LILLE**, situé dans le parc de Villeneuve d'Ascq. Le bâtiment d'origine, édifié par Roland Simounet en 1983, avait déjà été classé monument historique. L'objectif de l'architecte était de faire de ce musée « une entité fluide et continue » en ajoutant de nouvelles galeries consacrées à la collection d'art brut et en restaurant entièrement l'existant. L'extension enveloppe les ailes nord et est des installations antérieures en un « éventail de volumes organiques fluides et allongés ». D'un côté, ces plis « s'étirent sous forme fermée pour accueillir un café-restaurant s'ouvrant sur le patio central, de l'autre ils s'espacent davantage pour constituer les cinq galeries de la collection d'art brut ». Pour Gautrand, ce projet veut à la fois respecter l'ancien bâtiment et se confronter à lui, d'autant plus que l'influence de Simounet reste vivace, ici et ailleurs.

Gautrand took up the challenge of adding to a building by Roland Simounet—an architect respected in France—and came away from Lille with a triumph.

Gautrand stellte sich erfolgreich der Herausforderung, einen Erweiterungsbau für das Museum von Roland Simounet zu entwerfen, einen in Frankreich außerordentlich renommierten Architekten.

M. Gautrand a relevé avec succès le défi d'agrandir une réalisation de Roland Simounet, architecte très respecté en France.

The transition between the old building and the new is readily apparent in terms of surface treatment and the geometry of the blocks added by Gautrand, but the two elements now constitute a whole, as seen in the drawing below.

Der Übergang zwischen Alt- und Neubau ist dank Oberflächenbehandlung und Geometrie der von Gautrand entworfenen Volumina leicht zu erkennen. Dennoch bilden beide Bauabschnitte inzwischen ein Ganzes, wie die Zeichnung unten belegt.

La transition entre le bâtiment existant et le nouveau est marquée par les matériaux et la géométrie particulière des blocs créés par l'architecte, mais l'ensemble constitue néanmoins un tout comme le montre le dessin ci-dessous.

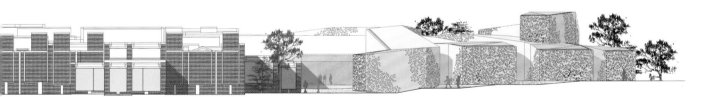

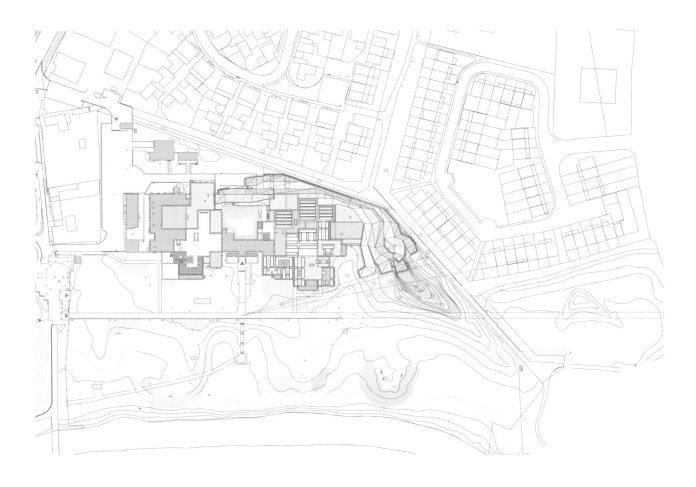

A site plan shows the juxtaposition of the older elements and the new. Below and on the right page, the cut-out pattern used by Manuelle Gautrand for the façades of her extension, and two exhibition galleries.

Auf dem Lageplan ist das Nebeneinander von alten und neuen Bauabschnitten zu erkennen. Unten und rechts im Bild das Scherenschnittmotiv, das Manuelle Gautrand für die Fassaden ihres Anbaus entwarf, sowie ein Blick in zwei Ausstellungsräume.

Le plan du site montre la juxtaposition des bâtiments anciens et nouveaux. Ci-dessous et page de droite, les effets lumineux du découpage des façades selon un motif dessiné par Manuelle Gautrand, et les deux nouvelles galeries d'exposition.

The architect uses an opaque screen to simultaneously block out natural light while leaving the patterns produced by her façade, and to provide a readily usable display surface.

Mit einer opaken Zwischenwand blendet die Architektin einerseits Tageslicht aus und schafft Ausstellungsfläche, lässt andererseits jedoch die Muster ihrer Fassade wirken.

L'architecte a dessiné ici un écran opaque servant à la présentation d'œuvres, et bloque l'éclairage naturel tout en laissant néanmoins apparaître la projection des motifs de la façade.

The façade patterns are frequently visible within the new galleries but only works that can withstand fairly high levels of natural light are exposed to incoming sunlight.

Das Muster der Fassadengestaltung taucht in den Ausstellungsräumen immer wieder auf, doch nur Kunstwerke, die vergleichsweise starke Helligkeit vertragen, werden dem einfallenden Tageslicht ausgesetzt.

Le motif en découpe de la façade réapparaît souvent dans les galeries, mais seulement près des œuvres qui peuvent supporter des niveaux assez élevés d'éclairage naturel, bien entendu.

FRANK O. GEHRY

Gehry Partners, LLP
12541 Beatrice Street
Los Angeles, CA 90066
USA

Tel: +1 310 482 3000 / Fax: +1 310 482 3006
E-mail: info@foga.com / Web: www.foga.com

Born in Toronto, Canada, in 1929, **FRANK GEHRY** studied at the University of Southern California, Los Angeles (1949–54), and at Harvard (1956–57). Principal of Frank O. Gehry and Associates, Inc., Los Angeles, since 1962, he received the Pritzker Prize in 1989. His early work in California included the redesign of his own house, and the construction of a number of others such as the Norton Residence (Venice, 1984) and the Schnabel Residence (Brentwood, 1989). His first foreign projects included Festival Disney (Marne-la-Vallée, France, 1988–92), and the Guggenheim Bilbao (Spain, 1991–97), which is felt by some to be one of the most significant build-ings of the late 20th century. Other work includes the DG Bank Headquarters (Berlin, Germany, 2001); the Fisher Center for the Performing Arts at Bard College (Annandale-on-Hudson, New York, USA, 2003); and the Walt Disney Concert Hall (Los Angeles, USA, 2003). More recent work includes a Maggie's Center (Dundee, Scotland, 1999–2003); the Jay Pritzker Pavilion in Millennium Park (Chicago, USA, 2004); the Hotel at the Marques de Riscal winery (Elciego, Spain, 1999–2007); his first New York building, the InterActiveCorp Headquarters (New York, New York, USA, 2003–07); an extension of the Art Gallery of Ontario (Toronto, Canada, 2000–08); Cleveland Clinic Lou Ruvo Center for Brain Health (Las Vegas, Nevada, USA, 2005–10, published here); and Orchestral Academy (Miami, Florida, USA, 2003–11). He is currently working on the Louis Vuitton Foundation for Creation in the Bois de Boulogne in Paris, France, and the Dwight D. Eisenhower Memorial in Washington, D.C., USA.

FRANK GEHRY wurde 1929 in Toronto, Kanada, geboren und studierte an der University of Southern California, Los Angeles (1949–51), sowie in Harvard (1956–57). Seit 1962 ist Gehry Direktor von Frank O. Gehry and Associates, Inc., in Los Angeles. 1989 wurde er mit dem Pritzker-Preis ausgezeichnet. Zu seinem Früh-werk in Kalifornien zählen der Umbau seines eigenen Wohnhauses und der Bau mehrerer Wohnbauten, darunter die Norton Residence (Venice, 1984) und die Schnabel Residence (Brentwood, 1989). Zu seinen ersten Projekten im Ausland gehören sein Bau für Festival Disney (Marne-la-Vallée, Frankreich, 1988–92) und das Guggenheim-Museum Bilbao (Spanien, 1991–97), das viele für eines der bedeutendsten Bauwerke des späten 20. Jahrhunderts halten. Andere Arbeiten sind u.a. die DG-Bank-Zentrale in Berlin (2001), das Fisher Center für Darstellende Künste am Bard College (Annandale-on-Hudson, New York, 2003) und die Walt Disney Concert Hall (Los Angeles, 2003). Zu seinen jüngeren Arbeiten zählen Maggie's Center (Dundee, Schottland, 1999–2003), der Jay-Pritzker-Pavillon im Millennium-Park in Chicago (2004), das Hotel am Weingut Marques de Riscal (Elciego, Spanien, 1999–2007), Gehrys erster Bau in New York, die Zentrale von InterActiveCorp an der West 19th Street in Manhattan (2003–07), die Erweiterung der Art Gallery of Ontario (Toronto, 2000–08), das Lou Ruvo Center for Brain Health der Cleveland Clinic (Las Vegas, 2005–10, hier vorgestellt) sowie die Orchestral Academy (Miami, 2003–11). Gegenwärtig arbeitet er an der Fondation Louis Vuitton pour la Création im Bois de Boulogne in Paris sowie dem Dwight D. Eisenhower Memorial in Washington, D.C.

Né à Toronto, Canada, en 1929, **FRANK GEHRY** étudie à l'USC (University of Southern California) à Los Angeles (1949–51) puis à Harvard (1956–57). Il dirige l'agence Frank O. Gehry and Associates, Inc., Los Angeles, depuis 1962, et a reçu en 1989 le Prix Pritzker. Ses premiers travaux en Californie comprennent la restructu-ration de sa propre maison et la construction d'un certain nombre de maisons dont la résidence Norton (Venice, 1984) et la résidence Schnabel (Brentwood, 1989). Ses premières réalisations à l'étranger furent le Festival Disney (Disney Village, Marne-la-Vallée, France, 1988–92) et le musée Guggenheim Bilbao (Espagne, 1991–97) jugé par beaucoup comme l'un des plus importants bâtiments de la fin du XXe siècle. Parmi ses projets remarqués figurent également le siège de la DG Bank (Berlin, 2001) ; le Fisher Center for the Performing Arts à Bard College (Annandale-on-Hudson, New York, 2003) et le Walt Disney Concert Hall (Los Angeles, 2003). Plus récemment, il a réalisé le Maggie's Center (Dundee, Écosse, 1999–2003) ; le pavillon Jay Pritzker dans le Millennium Park (Chicago, 2004) ; l'hôtel du domaine viticole Marques de Riscal (Elciego, Espagne, 1999–2007) ; son premier immeuble à New York, le siège d'InterActiveCorp (New York, 2003–07) ; une extension de la galerie d'art de l'Ontario (Toronto, 2000–08) ; le Centre de santé mentale Lou Ruvo de la Cleveland Clinic (Las Vegas, Nevada, 2005–10, publié ici) et l'Orchestral Academy (Miami, Floride, 2003–11). Il travaille actuellement sur le projet de la fondation Louis Vuitton pour la création dans le Bois de Boulogne à Paris et le mémorial Dwight D. Eisenhower à Washington.

CLEVELAND CLINIC LOU RUVO CENTER FOR BRAIN HEALTH

Las Vegas, Nevada, USA, 2005–10

*Address: 888 West Bonneville Avenue, Las Vegas, NV 89106-0100, USA, +1 702 483 6000,
http//my.clevelandclinic.org/brain_health/default.aspx
Area: 5600 m². Client: Keep Memory Alive. Cost: not disclosed*

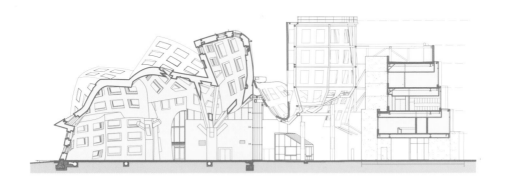

The Lou Ruvo Center is readily identifiable as a Frank Gehry building because of its exuberant curving forms. Indeed, this structure goes further in the direction of architectural sculpture than many other Gehry creations.

Dank der überbordenden geschwungenen Formensprache ist das Lou Ruvo Center unschwer als Gehry-Entwurf zu erkennen. Tatsächlich wirkt der Bau noch stärker wie eine architektonische Skulptur als andere Gehry-Schöpfungen.

Les courbes exubérantes des façades du Centre Lou Ruvo font indiscutablement penser à Frank Gehry. Ce nouveau bâtiment va encore plus loin dans l'approche sculpturale que nombre de créations antérieures de l'architecte.

This structure is part of the 24.7-hectare Symphony Park development area in downtown Las Vegas. It includes an outpatient clinic, research clinic, neuro-imaging suites, a reference library, community space, a multipurpose event/banquet center for 450 people, a catering kitchen, and offices for Keep Memory Alive. The research and clinical facilities, as well as the offices, are located in a four-story block "articulated as a series of offset rectangular shapes in white plaster and glass." The Event Center is marked by "a curvilinear metal façade and roof with punched-window/skylight openings." The integrated roofing system is made with a prefabricated structural steel shell. Stainless steel and thermoplastic membrane roofing are employed. In aesthetic terms, Gehry here seems to take his sculptural and artistic sense to new levels while still achieving the functionality required by the client.

Der Komplex ist Teil der 24,7 ha großen Bauerschließung des neuen Stadtteils Symphony Park im Zentrum von Las Vegas. Er umfasst eine Tagesklinik, eine Forschungsklinik, eine Fachbibliothek, Gemeinschaftsräume, ein Mehrzweck-/Bankettsaal für 450 Gäste, eine Großküche sowie Büros der Stiftung Keep Memory Alive. Forschungs- und klinische Einrichtungen sind, ebenso wie die Büros, in einem vierstöckigen Gebäude untergebracht, das „wie eine Reihe versetzter, rechtwinkliger Volumina aus weißem Putz und Glas erscheint". Das Veranstaltungszentrum zeichnet sich durch seine „geschwungene Metallfassade und ein Dach mit ausgestanzten Fenster- und Oberlichtöffnungen aus". Die in den Bau übergehende Dachkonstruktion wurde aus einer vorgefertigten, tragenden Stahlhülle realisiert. Neben Edelstahl kamen auch Dachelemente aus thermoplastischen Membranen zum Einsatz. Gehry scheint sein Gespür für skulpturale, künstlerische Formen hier auf neue Höhen zu treiben und wird dabei doch den funktionalen Anforderungen des Auftraggebers gerecht.

Ce bâtiment fait partie du Symphony Park, opération d'aménagement urbain de 24,7 hectares au centre de Las Vegas. Il comprend une clinique de consultations, une clinique de recherche, des installations d'imagerie neurologique, une bibliothèque de référence, un espace communautaire, un centre polyvalent pour événements et banquets de 450 personnes, une cuisine de traiteur et des bureaux pour l'association Keep Memory Alive. Les installations de clinique et de recherche ainsi que les bureaux sont logés dans un bloc de quatre étages « articulé en une série de formes rectangulaires en retrait, en verre et enduit blanc ». Le centre pour événements possède « une façade et une toiture métalliques curvilignes perforées de fenêtres ». Le système de toiture est une coque en acier structurel préfabriquée à couverture en acier inoxydable et membrane thermoplastique. Gehry semble porter ici son sens artistique et sculptural vers de nouveaux sommets tout en répondant aux nécessités fonctionnelles de son client.

The Center sits in an area that is currently not very built-up, but will surely be so in the future.

Das Center liegt in einer bislang nicht stark bebauten Gegend, was sich in Zukunft zweifellos ändern wird.

Le Centre est implanté dans une zone urbaine destinée à recevoir d'autres constructions dans un proche avenir.

An interior "street" recalls other buildings, such as the architect's Stata Center at MIT, but with an added dose of color. Right, a general plan shows the complexity of the facility.

Eine „Straße" im Innern des Gebäudes erinnert an andere Bauten Gehrys, etwa das Stata Center am MIT, ist jedoch von intensiverer Farbigkeit. Ein Überblicksplan (rechts) illustriert die Komplexität der Anlage.

Cette rue intérieure rappelle d'autres réalisations de l'architecte comme le Stata Center du MIT, mais selon un traitement plus coloré. À droite, plan d'ensemble montrant la complexité du Centre.

The apparent folded window pattern of the exterior façades gives an unusual and ever-changing orchestration of daylight within the facility.

Durch die wie gefaltet wirkende Fensterfront entsteht im Innern des Baus ein ungewöhnliches, sich beständig wandelndes Spiel von Tageslicht.

La composition des fenêtres sur les façades ondulées orchestre à l'intérieur un éclairage naturel qui change en permanence.

In this generous open space, the walls and the ceiling are one and the same, while windows that appear to have originally been aligned dance around the space, making it bright and airy.

In diesem großzügigen Raum gehen Wände und Decken nahtlos ineinander über. Fenster, von denen man zu glauben meint, sie seien ursprünglich geradlinig angeordnet gewesen, beginnen zu tanzen und lassen den Raum hell und luftig wirken.

Dans ce généreux espace ouvert, les murs et le plafond ne font qu'un. Les fenêtres alignées sur un seul plan dansent littéralement autour de cet espace lumineux et aérien.

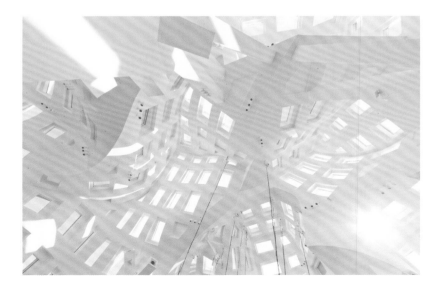

ZAHA HADID

Zaha Hadid Architects
Studio 9
10 Bowling Green Lane
London EC1R OBQ
UK

Tel: +44 20 72 53 51 47
Fax: +44 20 72 51 83 22
E-mail: press@zaha-hadid.com
Web: www.zaha-hadid.com

ZAHA HADID studied architecture at the Architectural Association (AA) in London, beginning in 1972, and was awarded the Diploma Prize in 1977. She then became a partner of Rem Koolhaas in OMA and taught at the AA. She has also taught at Harvard, the University of Chicago, in Hamburg, and at Columbia University in New York. In 2004, Zaha Hadid became the first woman to win the coveted Pritzker Prize. She completed the Vitra Fire Station (Weil am Rhein, Germany, 1990–94); and exhibition designs such as that for "The Great Utopia" (Solomon R. Guggenheim Museum, New York, USA, 1992). More recently, Zaha Hadid has entered a phase of active construction with such projects as the Lois & Richard Rosenthal Center for Contemporary Art (Cincinnati, Ohio, USA, 1999–2003); Phaeno Science Center (Wolfsburg, Germany, 2001–05); Ordrupgaard Museum Extension (Copenhagen, Denmark, 2001–05); the Central Building of the new BMW Assembly Plant in Leipzig (Germany, 2005); the Mobile Art, Chanel Contemporary Art Container (various locations, 2007–); and the MAXXI, the National Museum of 21st Century Arts (Rome, Italy, 1998–2009). Recent projects include the Sheikh Zayed Bridge (Abu Dhabi, UAE, 2003–10, published here); the Guangzhou Opera House (Guangzhou, China, 2005–10, also published here); and the Aquatics Center for the London 2012 Olympic Games (UK).

ZAHA HADID studierte ab 1972 an der Architectural Association (AA) in London und erhielt 1977 den Diploma Prize. Anschließend wurde sie Partnerin von Rem Koolhaas bei OMA und unterrichtete an der AA. Darüber hinaus lehrte sie in Harvard, an der Universität von Chicago, in Hamburg sowie an der Columbia University in New York. 2004 wurde Zaha Hadid als erste Frau mit dem begehrten Pritzker-Preis ausgezeichnet. Sie realisierte u.a. eine Feuerwache für Vitra (Weil am Rhein, Deutschland, 1990–94) und Ausstellungsarchitekturen wie *The Great Utopia* (Solomon R. Guggenheim Museum, New York, 1992). In Hadids aktiver Bauphase entstanden etwa das Lois & Richard Rosenthal Center for Contemporary Art (Cincinnati, Ohio, 1999–2003), das Phaeno Wissenschaftszentrum (Wolfsburg, 2001–05), der Anbau für das Museum Ordrupgaard (Kopenhagen, 2001–05), das Zentralgebäude des neuen BMW-Werks in Leipzig (2005), Mobile Art, Chanel Contemporary Art Container (verschiedene Standorte, 2007–) sowie das MAXXI Nationalmuseum für Kunst des 21. Jahrhunderts (Rom, 1998–2009). Ihre jüngsten Projekte sind u.a. die Scheich-Zajed-Brücke (Abu Dhabi, VAE, 2003–10, hier vorgestellt), das Opernhaus in Guangzhou (Guangzhou, China, 2005–10, ebenfalls hier vorgestellt) sowie das Aquatics Center für die Olympiade 2012 in London.

ZAHA HADID a étudié l'architecture à l'Architectural Association (AA) de Londres de 1972 à 1977, date à laquelle elle a reçu le prix du Diplôme. Elle est ensuite devenue partenaire de Rem Koolhaas à l'OMA et a enseigné à l'AA, ainsi qu'à Harvard, à l'université de Chicago, à Hambourg et à l'université Columbia à New York. En 2004, elle a été la première femme a remporter le très convoité Prix Pritzker. Parmi ses réalisations figurent un poste d'incendie pour Vitra (Weil am Rhein, Allemagne, 1990–94) et des projets pour des expositions comme *The Great Utopia* au Solomon R. Guggenheim Museum à New York (1992). Elle a également à son actif des projets comme le Centre Lois & Richard Rosenthal pour l'art contemporain (Cincinnati, Ohio, 1999–2003) ; le centre scientifique Phaeno (Wolfsburg, Allemagne, 2001–05) ; l'extension du musée Ordrupgaard (Copenhague, 2001–05) ; le bâtiment central de la nouvelle usine BMW de Leipzig (Allemagne, 2005) ; le Mobile Art, Chanel Contemporary Art Container (divers lieux, 2007–) et le Musée national des arts du XXIe siècle MAXXI (Rome, 1998–2009). Parmi ses projets récents figurent le pont Sheikh Zayed (Abou Dhabi, EAU, 2003–10, publié ici) ; l'Opéra de Guangzhou (Guangzhou, Chine, 2005–10, également publié ici) et le Centre des sports aquatiques pour les Jeux olympiques de Londres 2012.

SHEIKH ZAYED BRIDGE

Abu Dhabi, UAE, 2003–10

Length: 842 meters. Client: Abu Dhabi Municipality
Cost: not disclosed

Named after the founder of the United Arab Emirates (UAE), this bridge connects Abu Dhabi Island to the mainland. It is 842 meters long, 64 meters high, and 61 meters wide, carrying two segments of four-lane highway. As the architect describes the design: "A collection, or strands of structures, gathered on one shore, are lifted and 'propelled' over the length of the channel. A sinusoidal waveform provides the structural silhouette shape across the channel." Though others, such as Santiago Calatrava, have long designed asymmetrical bridges, this span represents a clear departure from common practice. Engineering proved very complex, and the overall time from design to opening early in 2011 was exceptionally long. With its slowly changing colors at night, the bridge represents a real landmark for those driving into Abu Dhabi.

Die nach dem Gründer der Vereinigten Arabischen Emirate (VAE) benannte Brücke verbindet Abu Dhabi Island mit dem Festland. Das 842 m lange, 64 m hohe und 61 m breite Bauwerk besteht aus zwei Segmenten mit einer jeweils vierspurigen Fahrbahntrasse. Die Architektin beschreibt ihren Entwurf wie folgt: „Eine Sammlung oder vielmehr verschiedene bauliche Stränge bündeln sich an einer Uferseite, werden angehoben und über die gesamte Breite des Wasserweges ‚geschleudert'. Eine sinusförmige Welle definiert die Silhouette des Tragwerks über dem Kanal." Obwohl längst andere, darunter auch Santiago Calatrava, asymmetrische Brücken entworfen haben, unterscheidet sich diese Spannkonstruktion zweifellos stark von der üblichen Brückenbaupraxis. Die ingenieurtechnische Planung erwies sich als hochkomplex, weshalb die Spanne zwischen Entwurfsbeginn und Eröffnung der Brücke Anfang 2011 ungewöhnlich lang war. Mit ihren langsamen Farbwechseln bei Nacht ist die Brücke ein echtes Wahrzeichen für alle, die Abu Dhabi per Auto erreichen.

Nommé en l'honneur du fondateur des Émirats arabes unis, ce pont relie l'île d'Abou Dhabi au continent. De 842 mètres de long, 64 de haut et 61 de large, il accueille huit voies d'autoroute. L'architecte présente ainsi le projet : « Un bloc ou écheveau de structures regroupées sur une rive est soulevé et propulsé à travers la largeur du chenal. La silhouette structurelle évoque une vague sinusoïdale… » Si d'autres architectes, comme Santiago Calatrava, ont depuis longtemps dessiné des ponts asymétriques, cet ouvrage représente néanmoins une rupture avec les pratiques traditionnelles. Son ingénierie s'est révélée très complexe et la durée de conception et du chantier ont été extrêmement longues. Changeant lentement de couleur pendant la nuit, ce pont est devenu un des monuments d'Abou Dhabi.

On the main road into Abu Dhabi Island, the bridge stands near the monumental Sheikh Zayed Mosque. Aside from its unusual asymmetric curves, the bridge boasts a changing nighttime color lighting pattern.

Die Brücke liegt an der zentralen Zufahrtsstraße zur Hauptinsel von Abu Dhabi, unweit der Scheich-Zajed-Moschee. Neben den asymmetrischen Bögen sind auch die farbigen Lichtwechsel bei Nacht ein besonderes Merkmal der Brücke.

Le pont se déploie à proximité de la monumentale mosquée Sheikh Zayed sur la route principale d'accès à l'île d'Abou Dhabi. En dehors de ses courbes asymétriques étonnantes, l'ouvrage se remarque par son éclairage nocturne changeant.

As seen from a distance, or from beneath its arches, the bridge has something of a living presence, perhaps like a great snake that undulates above and below the surface of the water.

Aus der Ferne und unterhalb der Bögen wirkt die Brücke fast wie ein Lebewesen, vielleicht wie eine große Schlange, die auf- und abtaucht, während sie sich durchs Wasser schlängelt.

Vu à distance, ou de sous son tablier, le pont prend une présence presque vivante, tel un énorme serpent qui ondulerait à la surface des eaux.

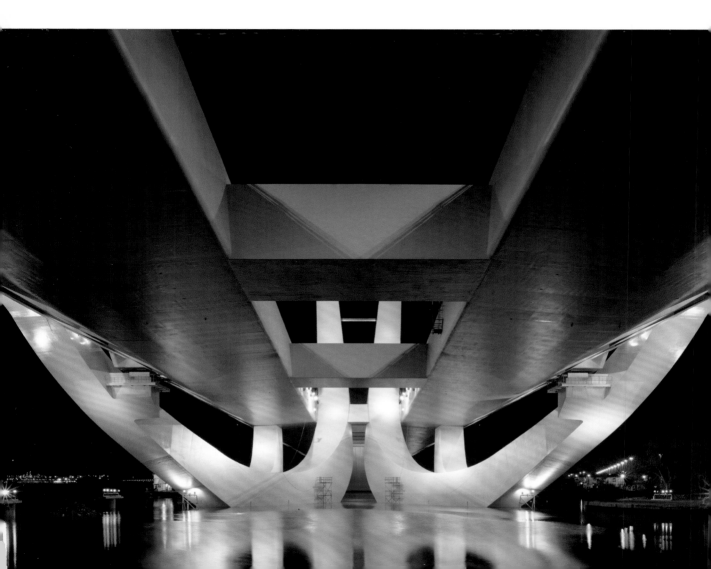

Despite its unusual and complex geometry, the bridge serves its automobile functions without any disturbance to the usual flow of traffic. Above, one of the bright colors that the bridge takes on during the night.

Trotz ihrer ungewöhnlichen und komplexen Geometrie wird die Brücke den Anforderungen des täglichen Verkehrsaufkommens vollauf gerecht. Oben eine der intensiven Farben, in die die Brücke nachts getaucht ist.

Malgré sa géométrie complexe et inhabituelle, le pont remplit parfaitement ses fonctions d'ouvrage de liaison. Ci-dessus, exemple de ses éclairages nocturnes de couleur vive.

GUANGZHOU OPERA HOUSE

Guangzhou, China, 2005–10

Address: 1 Zhujiang West Road, Pearl River New Town District, Guangzhou 510623, China
Area: 70 000 m². Client: Guangzhou Municipal Government. Cost: not disclosed

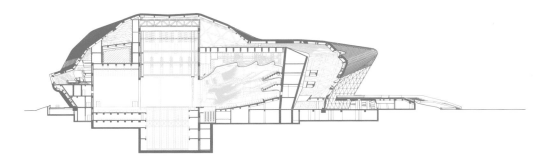

Though its spaces are astonishing and dramatic, the building actually has a readily comprehensible profile as seen, for example, in the section drawing above.

Trotz seiner erstaunlichen und dramatischen räumlichen Gestaltung erschließt sich das Profil des Baus sofort, wie etwa am Querschnitt oben zu sehen.

Sous ses aspects spectaculaires, le bâtiment reste aisément lisible comme le montre le dessin de coupe ci-dessus.

The irregular crystalline form of the building fits into its site as seen in the drawing to the right, but it stands out in a theatrical way from the otherwise rather conventional skyline of the city.

Die asymmetrischen, kristallinen Formen des Gebäudes fügen sich harmonisch in das Gelände, wie rechts auf der Zeichnung zu erkennen. Trotzdem hebt es sich dramatisch von der eher konventionellen Skyline der Stadt ab.

La forme de cristal irrégulier du bâtiment est adaptée à son site, comme le montre le dessin de droite, mais il se détache néanmoins de façon théâtrale sur le fond du panorama assez conventionnel de la ville.

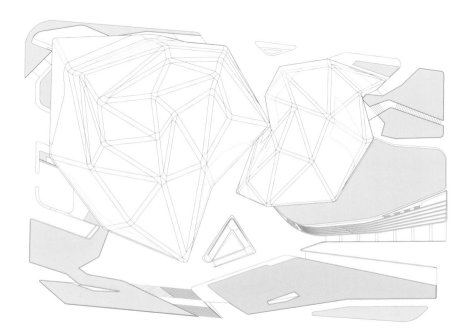

The site of the opera house, overlooking Pearl River, adjacent to a proposed municipal museum and a "metropolitan activities zone," is set against the background of the tall buildings of Zhujiang New Town, a spectacular location leading to the Haixinsha Tourist Park Island. The architect speaks of a "twin boulder design" and of landforms to describe the facility that includes a 1800-seat grand theater, entrance lobby, lounge, multifunction hall, and support facilities. An internal street leading to the future museum site has a café, bar restaurant, and retail areas on one side dividing the two main volumes. Inscribed in the urban context of the changing city in a strategic location at the foot of Zhujiang Boulevard, a central avenue of the city, the architectural design also adapts a variation on Hadid's theme of forms inspired by the land. The largest performing arts center in South China and one of the three biggest theaters in the country, the Guangzhou Opera House is Zaha Hadid's first completed work in China.

An seinem Standort mit Blick auf den Perlfluss, unmittelbar neben dem geplanten Stadtmuseum und einer „städtischen Freizeitzone", zeichnet sich das Opernhaus vor dem Hintergrund der Hochhäuser von Zhujiang New Town ab. Es ist ein spektakulärer Standort, in direkter Nachbarschaft zu einer geplanten Parklandschaft mit Freizeitanlagen auf der Insel Haixinsha. Die Architektin spricht von einem „Zwillings-Felsen-Motiv" und geologischen Formationen, wenn sie den Bau mit seinem großen Theatersaal mit 1800 Plätzen, Foyer, Lounge, Multifunktionssaal und Versorgungseinrichtungen beschreibt. Eine durch das Grundstück verlaufende Promenade, die die beiden zentralen Baukörper trennt, wird auf einer Seite von einem Café, einer Bar, einem Restaurant und Einkaufsmöglichkeiten gesäumt. Der Entwurf, eingeschrieben in den urbanen Kontext der sich wandelnden Stadt und strategisch gelegen unterhalb des zentralen Zhujiang Boulevard, ist darüber hinaus eine Variation landschaftlich inspirierter Formen, ein ständiges Thema bei Hadid. Das Opernhaus in Guangzhou, eines der größten Zentren für darstellende Künste in Südchina und zugleich eines der drei größten Theater des Landes, ist Hadids erster realisierter Bau in China.

Cet opéra qui domine la rivière des Perles à proximité d'un futur musée municipal et d'une « zone d'activités métropolitaines » se détache sur le fond du panorama des immeubles de grande hauteur du quartier des affaires de Zhujiang. Il occupe un site spectaculaire sur l'axe qui conduit à l'île du parc touristique de Haixinsha. L'architecte parle « d'un projet fait de rochers jumelés » et de formes naturelles pour décrire cet équipement culturel qui comprend une salle de 1800 places, un foyer, un salon, un hall polyvalent et tous les services nécessaires. La rue intérieure qui sépare les deux volumes et conduit au futur musée est animée d'un côté par un café, un bar-restaurant et des commerces. Dans le contexte urbain d'une ville en évolution rapide, occupant une situation stratégique sur le boulevard Zhujiang, principale avenue de la ville, cette réalisation est une variation sur la thématique d'Hadid inspirée des formes telluriques. Plus vaste salle de spectacle de la Chine du Sud et l'une des trois plus grandes salles du pays, cet opéra est la première œuvre achevée par Zaha Hadid en Chine.

The main concert hall with its gold finish is spectacular but obviously well conceived for acoustics and crowd movement.

Der große Konzertsaal mit seinem goldenen Anstrich wirkt spektakulär und wurde doch offenkundig im Hinblick auf Akustik und Verkehrsflüsse geplant.

De couleur or, la salle principale est spectaculaire. Bien étudiée pour canaliser le flux des spectateurs, elle offre une acoustique de qualité.

Interior and exterior forms echo each other and confirm the overall design coherence of the building. Below, even walkways are angled and form part of the landscape into which the building is ultimately inserted.

Innen- und Außenbau spiegeln einander formal und zeugen von der schlüssigen Gesamtgestaltung des Gebäudes. Selbst die Rampen (unten) wurden winklig angelegt und werden so zum Teil der Landschaft, in die der Komplex eingebettet ist.

Les formes intérieures et extérieures se font écho dans l'expression de la cohérence du projet. Ci-dessous, même les passerelles inclinées font partie du paysage dans lequel le bâtiment s'insère.

HAPSITUS

*Hapsitus
Almathaf Corm St. Khayat Bldg
Beirut 2064 2703
Lebanon*

*Tel/Fax: +961 1 615 374
E-Mail: info@hapsitus.com
Web: www.hapsitus.com*

NADIM KARAM was born in 1957 in Kaolack, Senegal. He received a B.Arch degree from the American University of Beirut, and a Master's followed by a Ph.D. in Architecture from Tokyo University in 1989. He founded Hapsitus, "a pluri-disciplinary company that focuses on the creation of an original urban vocabulary," in 1996 in Beirut, Lebanon. Hapsitus has designed large-scale urban art projects for cities including Beirut, Kwangju, Prague, London, Tokyo, Nara, and Melbourne. Nadim Karam has exhibited his artwork in different biennales, and curated the Lebanese participation for the first Rotterdam Architecture Biennale. He has taught design at the Shibaura Institute of Technology, Tokyo, the American University of Beirut, SCI-Arc Vico Morcote, and was Dean of the Faculty of Architecture, Art, and Design at Notre Dame University in Lebanon from 2000 to 2003. His work includes Villa Sehnaoui (Mansourieh, Lebanon, 2008); The Cloud of Dubai (Dubai, UAE, 2007–); The Dialogue of the Hills (Amman, Jordan, 2010–); Cadillac Showroom (Monza, Italy, 2011–); Casper & Gambini Restaurant chain (Amman, Damascus, Jeddah, and Khartoum, 2011–); and the BLC Bank Headquarters project (Beirut, Lebanon, 2011–, published here).

NADIM KARAM wurde 1957 in Kaolack, Senegal, geboren. Seinen B.Arch absolvierte er an der Amerikanischen Universität Beirut, seinen Master und seine Promotion in Architektur folgten 1989 an der Universität Tokio. Sein Büro Hapsitus, „ein pluri-disziplinäres Unternehmen, das sich auf das Entwerfen ungewöhnlicher urbaner Formensprachen spezialisiert hat", gründete er 1996 in Beirut, Libanon. Hapsitus entwarf urbane Kunst-Großprojekte für Städte wie Beirut, Kwangju, Prag, London, Tokio, Nara und Melbourne. Nadim Karams künstlerische Arbeiten waren auf mehreren Biennalen zu sehen, darüber hinaus kuratierte er den libanesischen Beitrag für die erste Rotterdamer Architekturbiennale. Er lehrte am Shibaura Institut für Technik, Tokio, der Amerikanischen Universität Beirut sowie am SCI-Arc Vico Morcote und war von 2000 bis 2003 Dekan der Fakultät für Architektur, Kunst und Design an der Notre-Dame-Universität im Libanon. Zu seinen Projekten zählen die Villa Sehnaoui (Mansourieh, Libanon, 2008), The Cloud of Dubai (Dubai, VAE, 2007–), The Dialogue of the Hills (Amman, Jordanien, 2010–), ein Showroom für Cadillac (Monza, Italien, 2011–), die Restaurantkette Casper & Gambini (Amman, Damaskus, Jeddah und Khartoum, 2011–) sowie die Zentrale der BLC Bank (Beirut, Libanon, 2011–, hier vorgestellt).

NADIM KARAM, né en 1957 à Kaolack (Sénégal), a obtenu son B. Arch. à l'Université américaine de Beyrouth et a accompli son mastère suivi d'un doctorat en architecture à l'université de Tokyo (1989). Il a fondé Hapsitus, « agence pluridisciplinaire se consacrant à la création d'un vocabulaire urbain original », en 1996 à Beyrouth. Hapsitus a conçu de vastes projets d'art urbain pour des villes comme Beyrouth, Kwangju, Prague, Londres, Tokyo, Nara et Melbourne. Nadim Karam a exposé son travail artistique dans différentes biennales et a été commissaire de la participation libanaise à la première Biennale d'architecture de Rotterdam. Il a enseigné la conception à l'Institut de technologie Shibaura à Tokyo, à l'Université américaine de Beyrouth, au SCI-Arc Vico Morcote et a été doyen de la faculté d'architecture, d'art et de design de l'université Notre-Dame du Liban de 2000 à 2003. Ses réalisations comprennent la villa Sehnaoui (Mansourieh, Liban, 2008) ; le Nuage de Dubaï (Dubaï, EAU, 2007–) ; le Dialogue des collines (Amman, Jordanie, 2010–) ; le showroom Cadillac (Monza, Italie, 2011–) ; la chaîne de restaurants Casper & Gambini (Amman, Damas, Djeddah et Khartoum, 2011–) et le projet de siège de la BLC Bank (Beyrouth, 2011–, publié ici).

BLC BANK HEADQUARTERS

Beirut, Lebanon, 2011–

Address: Adlieh, Beirut 01 42 96 66, Lebanon
Area: 18 238 m². Client: BLC Bank Beirut. Cost: $35 million

In busy, earthquake-prone Beirut, the new BLC Bank Headquarters building will stand out as a bold statement of the audacity of the directors of the institution.

Die neue Zentrale der BLC Bank in Beirut, einer geschäftigen aber auch erdbebengefährdeten Metropole, wird zweifellos als gewagtes Statement des Bankdirektors verstanden werden.

Dans une ville encombrée, menacée par des mouvements sismiques, le nouveau siège de la BLC Bank se détache du panorama urbain en une affirmation de l'audace de la politique de cette institution.

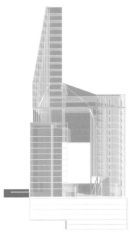

Because the Bank wished to keep an existing building on the site, the architects have cantilevered the new tower over the older more conventional structure, which will be integrated into the full complex on completion of the new tower.

Weil die Bank ein älteres Gebäude auf dem Grundstück erhalten wollte, ließen die Architekten den neuen Turm über dem älteren, konventionelleren Bau auskragen. Dieser wird nach Fertigstellung des neuen Turms in den Gesamtkomplex integriert sein.

La banque souhaitant conserver un immeuble existant déjà sur la parcelle, les architectes ont dressé la nouvelle tour en porte-à-faux au-dessus de ce bâtiment conventionnel qui sera intégré au complexe une fois la tour achevée.

BLC BANK BEIRUT changed its administration in 2007, engaging in rapid growth that imposed the need for a new headquarters building. The competition design brief required a building that would be a "landmark" in the urban texture of Beirut. The presence of the existing bank building at the corner of the prominent site was "an enigma" according to Nadim Karam. It occupied a key corner position, and was required by the client to be incorporated into any new design. With the "landmark" concept as a driving force, Hapsitus "proposed a solution created by the cantilevering of a new structure above the existing building to make an urban gate addressing the city," according to the architects.

Nach einem Verwaltungswechsel 2007 bei der **BLC BANK BEIRUT** wuchs das Unternehmen so rasch, dass ein neues Gebäude für den Hauptsitz dringend gebraucht wurde. Laut Briefing war ein Entwurf gefordert, der sich als „Wahrzeichen" im urbanen Kontext Beiruts behaupten würde. Ein bestehendes Gebäude, gelegen in der Ecke des prominent gelegenen Grundstücks, war Nadim Karam „ein Rätsel". Es besetzte die Schlüssel-Ecklage und sollte auf Wunsch des Auftraggebers in den neuen Entwurf integriert werden. Angesichts der Forderung nach einem „Wahrzeichen" als zentralem Element des Auftrags entwickelte Hapsitus „eine Lösung, indem man den Neubau über dem älteren Gebäude auskragen ließ und damit zugleich ein urbanes Tor schuf, das sich der Stadt zuwendet", so die Architekten.

La **BLC BANK DE BEYROUTH**, qui a changé de direction en 2007, a connu une croissance rapide qui a nécessité la construction d'un nouveau siège. L'appel d'offre demandait de réfléchir à un immeuble qui soit un « monument » intégré au tissu urbain de Beyrouth. La présence d'un premier bâtiment bancaire existant à l'angle de ce terrain très en vue représentait une « énigme » pour Nadim Karam. Il occupait en effet une position clé et, selon les désirs du client, devait être intégré au nouveau projet. À partir de cette idée de « monument », Hapsitus a « proposé une solution à partir de la mise en porte-à-faux du nouvel immeuble au-dessus du bâtiment existant, pour créer une sorte de porte face à la ville », explique l'architecte.

Conceived with the assistance of Arup London for the structural studies, the daring BLC Bank Headquarters tower will have such features as this staircase in the interstitial space between the old and new buildings.

Die Statik für den gewagten Turm der BLC Bank-Zentrale wurde mit Unterstützung von Arup London geplant. Highlights sind unter anderem diese Treppenanlage zwischen altem und neuen Gebäude.

Conçu avec l'assistance d'Arup London pour les études structurelles, l'audacieuse tour du siège de la BLC Bank présentera d'intéressantes caractéristiques comme cet escalier glissé dans l'espace interstitiel entre l'ancien immeuble et le nouveau.

Below, a drawing of the ground floor showing the wrapping mass of the new tower, and another drawing showing the floor that unites the two structures (right). Above, computer-generated perspectives of the public space and entrance beneath the new tower.

Unten eine Zeichnung vom Erdgeschoss mit dem ausgreifenden Baukörper des neuen Turms sowie ein Geschossplan der Etage, in der die beiden Bauten zusammengeführt werden (rechts). Oben Renderings der öffentlichen Zonen und des Eingangsbereichs unter dem neuen Turm.

Ci-dessous, plan du rez-de-chaussée montrant la masse enveloppante de la nouvelle tour et le plan du niveau auquel les deux structures se rejoignent (à droite). Ci-dessus, perspectives en images de synthèse de l'entrée et de l'espace public qui sera ouvert sous la tour.

HPLUSF

Hodgetts + Fung
5837 Adams Boulevard
Culver City, CA 90232
USA

Tel: +1 323 937 2150
Fax: +1 323 937 2151
E-mail: mailbox@hplusf.com
Web: www.hplusf.com

CRAIG HODGETTS studied architecture at the University of California (Berkeley, 1962–64) and received his M.Arch degree at Yale (1964–66). He is principal and cofounder, as well as Creative Director of Hodgetts + Fung. His partner, **HSINMING FUNG**, is Director of Design for the firm, which was created in 1985. She was born in China, raised in Vietnam, and received her M.Arch degree from UCLA in 1980. She has been Director of Graduate Programs at SCI-Arc since 2002. Recent projects include the Yamano Gakuen Mixed-Use Tower and Classroom Wing (Shinjuku, Tokyo, Japan, 2006); the Downtown Independent Theater (Los Angeles, California, 2007); Menlo Atherton Performing Arts Center (MAPAC, Menlo Park, California, 2009); Wild Beast Pavilion (Valencia, California, 2008–10, published here); Ralph J. Scott Museum (Los Angeles, California, 2010); the Jesuit Chapel of the North American Martyrs (Sacramento, California, 2010); and the Donna Rio Bravo Port of Entry Border Station (Donna, Texas, 2010). Current work includes the Hans Zimmer Mobile Theater (California), all in the USA unless stated otherwise.

CRAIG HODGETTS studierte Architektur an der University of California (Berkeley, 1962–64) und absolvierte seinen M.Arch in Yale (1964–66). Er ist Direktor und Mitbegründer sowie Kreativdirektor von Hodgetts + Fung. Seine Partnerin **HSINMING FUNG** ist Direktorin und verantwortet die Entwürfe des Büros, das 1985 gegründet wurde. Sie wurde in China geboren, wuchs in Vietnam auf und schloss ihr Studium an der UCLA 1980 mit einem M.Arch ab. Seit 2002 ist sie Direktorin der Graduierten-programme am SCI-Arc. Neuere Projekte des Teams sind u.a. ein Hochhaus mit gemischter Nutzung und ein Flügel mit Seminarräumen für Yamano Gakuen (Shinjuku, Tokio, Japan, 2006), das Downtown Independent Theater (Los Angeles, Kalifornien, 2007), das Menlo-Atherton-Center für darstellende Künste (MAPAC, Menlo Park, Kalifornien, 2009), der Wild-Beast-Pavillon (Valencia, Kalifornien, 2008–10, hier vorgestellt), das Ralph J. Scott Museum (Los Angeles, Kalifornien, 2010), eine Kapelle für die Jesuiten der North American Martyrs (Sacramento, Kalifornien, 2010) und die Grenzstation in Donna Rio Bravo (Donna, Texas, 2010). Zu ihren aktuelleren Projekten zählen das Hans Zimmer Mobile Theater (Kalifornien), all in den USA, sofern nicht anders angegeben.

CRAIG HODGETTS a étudié l'architecture à l'université de Californie (Berkeley, 1962–64) et a passé son diplôme de M. Arch. à Yale (1964–66). Il est cofonda-teur, dirigeant et directeur de la création de Hodgetts + Fung. Son associée, **HSINMING FUNG**, est directrice de la conception de l'agence fondée en 1985. Née en Chine, élevée au Vietnam, elle a obtenu son diplôme M. Arch. à l'UCLA en 1980. Elle dirige le programme d'études supérieures du SCI-Arc depuis 2002. Parmi leurs projets récents figurent la tour mixte et l'aile des classes de cours de Yamano Gakuen (Shinjuku, Tokyo, 2006) ; le Downtown Independent Theater (Los Angeles, 2007) ; le Centre des arts du spectacle Menlo Atherton (MAPAC, Menlo Park, Californie, 2009) ; le Wild Beast Pavilion (Valencia, Californie, 2008–10, publié ici) ; le musée Ralph J. Scott (Los Angeles, 2010) ; la chapelle jésuite des martyrs d'Amérique du Nord (Sacramento, Californie, 2010) et le poste de douane du Rio Bravo (Donna, Texas, 2010). Actuelle-ment, l'agence travaille au projet du Théâtre mobile Hans Zimmer (Californie).

I AM
INTERESTED
IN HOW
THE WILD BEAST
LIVES IN
THE JUNGLE.
NOT IN
THE ZOO.

MORTON FELDMAN

WILD BEAST PAVILION

Valencia, California, USA, 2008–10

Address: California Institute of the Arts, 24700 McBean Parkway, Valencia, CA 91355–2340,
USA, +1 661 255 1050, www.calarts.edu
Area: 228 m². Client: California Institute of the Arts. Cost: $2.35 million

The **WILD BEAST PAVILION** is a multipurpose performance space that can be quickly transformed from an enclosed classroom and recital hall to an open-air orchestra shell. The structure is dedicated to the avant-garde composer Morton Feldman, whose thoughts about "elegant but minimal musical strategies" has influenced the architecture. The name of the pavilion is related to Feldman's interest in "how this wild beast lives in the jungle and not in the zoo." The pavilion seats 120 people in a recital configuration and is intended to accommodate two instrumental recitals per day and two to four performances per week during the school year. It has a monocoque roof structure that cantilevers over the floor in a single sweep, providing a carefully studied acoustic volume. It represents a willful contrast with surrounding buildings at the entrance to the 1970s campus of the California Institute of the Arts. A spiral ramp facilitates access on the sloping site.

Der **WILD-BEAST-PAVILLON** ist eine Mehrzweckbühne, die sich rasch von einem geschlossenen Unterrichtsraum oder Konzertsaal in eine Freilicht-Konzertmuschel verwandeln lässt. Gewidmet ist der Bau dem avangardistischen Komponisten Morton Feldman, dessen Überlegungen zu „eleganten aber minimalistischen musikalischen Strategien" die Architektur beeinflusst haben. Der Name des Pavillons ist eine Anspielung auf Feldmans Äußerung, dass „ein wildes Tier im Dschungel lebt und nicht im Zoo". Bei Konzerten finden 120 Zuhörer im Pavillon Platz. Hier sollen während des Semesters zwei Instrumentalkonzerte täglich und zwei bis vier Aufführungen pro Woche stattfinden. Die Monocoque-Dachkonstruktion schwingt sich hoch über den Boden auf, so entsteht ein Raum mit sorgsam berechneten akkustischen Eigenschaften. Der Pavillon sucht bewusst den Kontrast zur angrenzenden Bebauung am Eingangsbereich zum Campus des California Institute of the Arts, der in den 1970er-Jahren erbaut wurde. Eine spiralförmige Rampe erleichtert den Zugang zum Hanggrundstück.

Ce **WILD BEAST PAVILION** (Pavillon de la bête sauvage) est un lieu de spectacle polyvalent qui peut se transformer rapidement en salle de classe, salon de récital ou auvent pour orchestre de plein air. Il est dédié au compositeur d'avant-garde Morton Feldman dont la réflexion sur « des stratégies musicales élégantes mais minimalistes » a influencé l'architecture. Le nom du pavillon renvoie d'ailleurs à une citation de Feldman inscrite sur sa façade : « La bête sauvage vit dans la jungle et non pas dans un zoo. » Le pavillon peut recevoir 120 spectateurs assis en configuration pour récital et devrait accueillir deux concerts instrumentaux par jour et deux à quatre spectacles par semaine pendant l'année scolaire. Il possède une structure de toiture monocoque qui s'élance en porte-à-faux au-dessus du sol en un seul mouvement, et offre un volume de qualité acoustique soigneusement étudiée. Le pavillon contraste fortement avec les bâtiments d'entrée du campus de l'Institut des arts de Californie, datant des années 1970. Une rampe en spirale en facilite l'accès.

The shape of the pavilion, as seen in these images and in the elevation drawing below, is quite simple, yet the dramatic effect of the curvature of the roof gives it an undeniable presence.

Die Grundform des Pavillons ist eher schlicht, wie auf den Ansichten und dem Aufriss unten zu sehen. Dennoch gewinnt er durch die Krümmung des Dachs dramatische Wirkung und unverkennbare Präsenz.

La forme du pavillon (photographies et élévation ci-dessous) est assez simple, mais l'effet spectaculaire de la courbe du toit lui confère une présence indéniable.

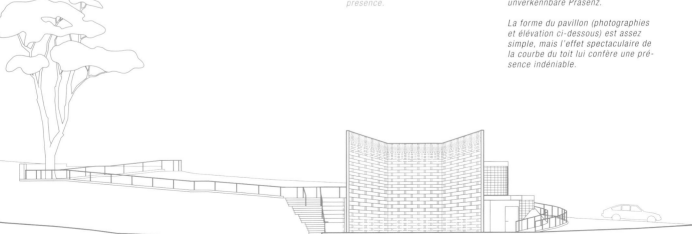

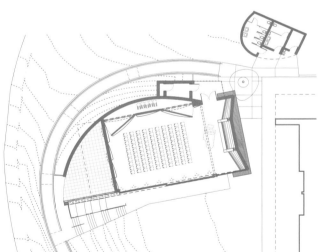

The curving, column-free interior space can be opened to the exterior for concerts. Acoustic panels give a scaled appearance to the walls that rise up to form the ceiling.

Der geschwungene, stützenfreie Innenraum lässt sich bei Open-Air-Konzerten öffnen. Akustiktafeln sorgen für einen schuppenartigen Effekt an den Wänden, die nach oben zur Decke werden.

Sans colonnes, le volume intérieur incurvé peut s'ouvrir sur l'extérieur à l'occasion de concerts. Des panneaux acoustiques posés en écailles habillent les murs qui se recourbent pour constituer le plafond.

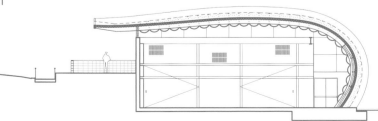

IA+B

IA+B
Plaza Pedro Eguileor 2, 1º Izda.
48008 Bilbao
Spain

Tel: +34 94 479 22 30
Fax: +34 94 479 28 59
E-mail: iab@iab-arkitek.com
Web: www.iab-arkitek.com

IÑAKI AURREKOETXEA AURRE was born in 1953 in Zamudio, Bizkaia, Spain. He graduated from the ETSA in San Sebastián in 1979. He has alternated work for public administrations with private architectural practice throughout his career, serving, for example, as Director General of Housing and Architecture for the Basque Government (1994–96). Since 1997, he has managed the architecture studio I.Aurrekoetxea eta Bazkideak, S.L. (IA+B). Born in 1973 in Bilbao, Spain, **ALEX LASKURAIN** graduated from the ETSA in San Sebastián in 2002. He joined IA+B in 1998, and has been an Associated Architect with the firm since 2003. **MONICA GAZTELU**, also an Associate Architect with the firm, which she joined in 2001, was born in 1969 in Bilbao and graduated from the ETSA in San Sebastián in 2001, having also studied at the Belleville Architecture School in Paris. Their work includes the Hesperia Bilbao Hotel (Bilbao, 2005); Urdaibai Museum (Busturia, Bizkaia, 2008); Isozaki Atea (in collaboration with Arata Isozaki, Bilbao, 2008); Estepona Theater (with David Chipperfield Architects, competition won in 2005, Estepona, Málaga); Hurtago Amezaga Residential Building (Bilbao, 2008); and Olarra Winery Visitor Center (Logroño, 2009–10, published here), all in Spain.

IÑAKI AURREKOETXEA AURRE wurde 1953 in Zamudio, Bizkaia, Spanien, geboren. Sein Studium schloss er 1979 an der ETSA in San Sebastián ab. Im Laufe der Zeit arbeitete er sowohl für die öffentliche Verwaltung als auch privat für sein eigenes Büro. So war er unter anderem als Direktor für Wohnbau und Architektur für die baski-sche Regierung tätig (1994–96). Seit 1997 leitet er das Architekturstudio I.Aurrekoetxea eta Bazkideak, S.L. (IA+B). **ALEX LASKURAIN**, geboren 1973 in Bilbao, Spanien, schloss sein Studium 2002 an der ETSA in San Sebastián ab. Er arbeitet seit 1998 bei IA+B und ist seit 2003 assoziierter Architekt des Büros. **MONICA GAZ-TELU**, ebenfalls assoziierte Architektin des Büros, für das sie seit 2001 arbeitet, wurde 1969 in Bilbao geboren und machte ihren Abschluss 2001 an der ETSA in San Sebastián. Sie studierte außerdem an der Architekturfakultät der Universität Paris-Belleville. Zu ihren Projekten zählen das Hotel Hesperia Bilbao (Bilbao, 2005), ein Museum in Urdaibai (Busturia, Bizkaia, 2008), das Isozaki-Atea-Hochhaus (in Zusammenarbeit mit Arata Isozaki, Bilbao, 2008), das Estepona-Theater (mit David Chipperfield Architects, Siegerbeitrag zum Wettbewerb 2005, Estepona, Málaga), ein Wohnhaus an der Hurtago Amezaga (Bilbao, 2008) sowie das Besucherzentrum des Weinguts Olarra (Logroño, 2009–10, hier vorgestellt), alle in Spanien.

IÑAKI AURREKOETXEA AURRE, né en 1953 à Zamudio (Biscaye, Espagne), est diplômé de l'ETSA de Saint-Sébastien (1979). Tout au long de sa carrière, il a alterné des passages dans l'administration publique avec des projets pour des clients privés. Il a été, par exemple, directeur général du logement et de l'architecture du gouvernement de la région basque (1994–96). Depuis 1997, il dirige l'agence d'architecture I. Aurrekoetxea eta Bazkideak, S.L. (IA+B). Né en 1973 à Bilbao, **ALEX LASKURAIN** est diplômé de l'ETSA de Saint-Sébastien (2002). Il rejoint l'agence IA+B en 1998, dont il est architecte associé depuis 2003. **MONICA GAZTELU**, née en 1969 à Bilbao, également architecte associée de l'agence où elle est entrée en 2001, est diplômée de l'ETSA de Saint-Sébastien (2001). Elle a également étudié à l'École d'architecture de Belleville à Paris. Parmi leurs réalisations, toutes en Espagne : l'hôtel Hesperia Bilbao (Bilbao, 2005) ; le musée Urdaibai (Busturia, Biscaye, 2008) ; Iso-zaki Atea (en collaboration avec Arata Isozaki, Bilbao, 2008) ; le Théâtre Estepona (avec David Chipperfield Architects, concours remporté en 2005, Estepona, Málaga) ; l'immeuble d'appartements Hurtago Amezaga (Bilbao, 2008) et le centre d'accueil des visiteurs des chais Olarra (Logroño, 2009–10, publié ici).

OLARRA WINERY VISITOR CENTER

Logroño, Spain, 2009–10

Address: Avenida Mendavia 30, Logroño, Spain
Area: 1066 m². Client: Bodegas Olarra S.A. Cost: €930 700
Collaboration: Ming and Bilbao (Structure), Luís Díaz (Mechanical)

The architects were called on to design a visitors center within the ample atrium of an existing concrete industrial-style building. "Far from establishing any rivalry with its powerful setting," say the architects, "our proposal seeks to engage in a playful relationship with the existing structure while adding the smells and tastes of the world of Olarra's excellent wines." The program includes a shopping area, and wine-tasting and exhibition spaces, with a stairway linking the volumes. IA+B made ample use of colored glass intended to evoke the colors of wine. The wine-tasting area, offices, and a conference room are set below the hexagonal atrium and above the colored glass composition.

Die Architekten erhielten den Auftrag, ein Besucherzentrum im großzügigen Atrium eines bestehenden Industriebaus aus Beton zu realisieren. „Statt irgendwie in Konkurrenz zum eindrucksvollen Umfeld zu treten", so die Architekten, „ging es uns bei unserem Entwurf vielmehr darum, sich auf ein spielerisches Verhältnis mit dem bestehenden Gebäude einzulassen und außerdem die Dimensionen ‚Duft' und ‚Geschmack' der exzellenten Weine von Olarra mit einzubinden." Zum Programm gehören ein Verkaufsbereich und ein Bereich für Weinverkostung und Präsentation; eine Treppe fungiert als Bindeglied zwischen den baulichen Zonen. IA+B arbeitete auffällig mit farbigem Glas, das die Farbigkeit des Weins aufgreift. Weinverkostung, Büros sowie ein Konferenzraum liegen unterhalb des hexagonalen Atriums bzw. über dem Arrangement aus farbigem Glas.

Il s'agissait d'aménager un centre d'accueil des visiteurs à l'intérieur du vaste atrium d'un bâtiment industriel en béton. « Loin de créer une rivalité quelconque avec ce cadre puissant », expliquent les architectes, « notre proposition a cherché à susciter une relation ludique avec la structure existante en l'enrichissant des senteurs et des saveurs de l'univers des grands vins Olarra. » Le programme comprenait une boutique, des espaces de dégustation et d'exposition, et un escalier reliant les divers volumes. IA+B a abondamment utilisé le verre de couleur pour évoquer les nuances des vins. La salle de dégustation, les bureaux et une salle de conférence sont implantés dans l'atrium hexagonal, au-dessus de la vaste composition de verre coloré.

By using a steel frame and colored glass panes, the architects create a joyful and dramatic space inside the existing building for this visitor center.

Mithilfe von Stahlrahmenkonstruktionen und farbigen Glaspaneelen gestalteten die Architekten heitere und zugleich dramatische Räume für das Besucherzentrum in dem alten Industriebau.

En insérant une structure en acier et des panneaux de verre coloré, les architectes ont fait de ce centre d'accueil des visiteurs un espace spectaculaire d'atmosphère ludique, à l'intérieur d'un bâtiment existant.

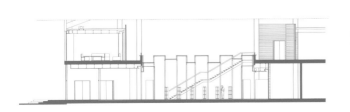

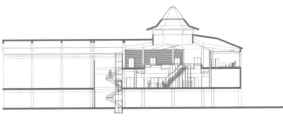

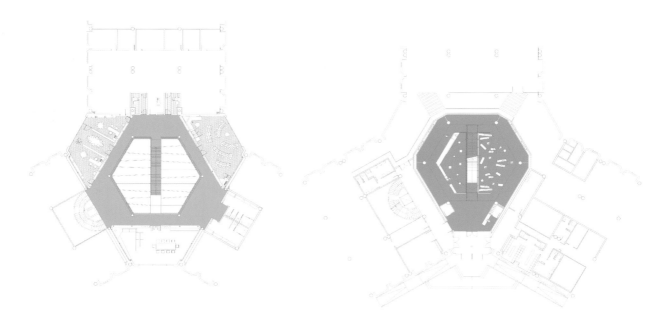

The colored glass gives way on the upper level to the original concrete and glass structure of the old industrial building. Plans (below) show the relationship of the visitor center to the rest of the building.

Im Obergeschoss löst die ursprüngliche Beton- und Glaskonstruktion des alten Industriebaus das farbige Glas ab. Grundrisse (unten) veranschaulichen das Verhältnis des Besucherzentrums zum übrigen Komplex.

Au niveau supérieur, le verre de couleur laisse place à la structure d'origine en béton et verre de l'ancien bâtiment industriel. Les plans ci-dessous montrent la relation entre le centre et le reste du bâtiment.

ARATA ISOZAKI

Arata Isozaki & Associates
Nogizaka Atelier
9–6–17 Akasaka, Minato-ku
Tokyo 107–0052
Japan

Tel: +81 3 3405 1526
Fax: +81 3 3475 5265
E-mail: info@isozaki.co.jp
Web: www.isozaki.co.jp

Born in Oita City on the island of Kyushu, Japan, in 1931, **ARATA ISOZAKI** graduated from the Architectural Faculty of the University of Tokyo in 1954 and established Arata Isozaki & Associates in 1963, having worked in the office of Kenzo Tange. Winner of the 1986 RIBA Gold Medal, his notable buildings include the Museum of Modern Art, Gunma (Gunma, 1971–74); the Tsukuba Center Building (Tsukuba, 1978–83); the Museum of Contemporary Art (Los Angeles, California, USA, 1981–86); Art Tower Mito (Mito, 1986–90); Higashi Shizuoka Convention and Arts Center (Shizuoka, 1993–98); and Ohio's Center of Science and Industry (COSI, Columbus, Ohio, USA, 1994–99), all in Japan unless stated otherwise. Recent work includes the Shenzhen Cultural Center (Shenzhen, China, 1997–2008); Central Academy of Fine Art, Museum of Art (Beijing, China, 2003–08); Obscured Horizon, Pioneertown (California, USA, 2008–10, published here); Himalayas Center (Shanghai, China, 2003–11); Qatar National Convention Center (Doha, Qatar, 2004–11); and the ongoing Milano Fiera (Milan, Italy, 2003–).

ARATA ISOZAKI, 1931 in Oita auf der Insel Kyushu geboren, schloss sein Studium 1954 an der Architekturfakultät der Universität Tokio ab. Anschließend arbeitete er im Büro von Kenzo Tange und gründete 1963 Arata Isozaki & Associates. 1986 wurde er mit der RIBA-Goldmedaille ausgezeichnet. Zu seinen wichtigsten Bauten zählen das Museum für moderne Kunst in Gunma (Gunma, 1971–74), das Tsukuba Center (Tsukuba, 1978–83), das Museum of Contemporary Art in (Los Angeles, Kalifornien, USA, 1981–86), der Art Tower Mito (Mito, 1986–90), das Messe- und Kunstzentrum Higashi Shizuoka (Shizuoka, 1993–98) und das Zentrum für Wissenschaft und Industrie von Ohio (COSI, Columbus, Ohio, USA, 1994–99), alle in Japan, sofern nicht anders angegeben. Neuere Projekte sind u.a. das Kulturzentrum Shenzhen (Shenzhen, China, 1997–2008), das Kunstmuseum der Central Academy of Fine Art (CAFA) in Peking (China, 2003–08), Obscured Horizon, Pioneertown (Kalifornien, USA, 2008–10, hier vorgestellt), das Himalaya-Zentrum (Shanghai, China, 2003–11), das nationale Kongresszentrum von Qatar (Doha, Qatar, 2004–11) sowie der noch im Bau befindliche Entwurf für die Fiera Milano (Mailand, Italien, 2003–).

Né à Oita sur l'île de Kyushu au Japon en 1931, **ARATA ISOZAKI** est diplômé de la faculté d'architecture de l'université de Tokyo (1954) et a créé son agence, Arata Isozaki & Associates, en 1963 après avoir travaillé auprès de Kenzo Tange. Récipiendaire de la médaille d'or du RIBA en 1986, ses réalisations les plus connues, essentiellement au Japon, comprennent : le Musée d'art moderne de Gunma (Gunma, 1971–74) ; l'immeuble du Tsukuba Center (Tsukuba, 1978–83) ; le Musée d'art contemporain (Los Angeles, Californie, 1981–86) ; la tour d'Art de Mito (Mito, 1986–90) ; le Centre de congrès et d'expositions d'Higashi Shizuoka (Shizuoka, 1993–98) et le Centre des sciences et de l'industrie COSI (Columbus, Ohio, 1994–99). Plus récemment, il a réalisé le Centre culturel de Shenzhen (Shenzhen, Chine, 1997–2008) ; l'Académie centrale des Beaux-Arts, musée d'art (Pékin, 2003–08) ; Obscured Horizon, Pioneertown (Californie, 2008–10, publié ici) ; le Centre des Himalayas (Shanghaï, 2003–11) ; le Centre national de congrès du Qatar (Doha, Qatar, 2004–11) et des bâtiments pour la Foire de Milan (Milan, 2003–).

OBSCURED HORIZON

Pioneertown, California, USA, 2008–10

Address: Mojave Desert, California, USA
Area: 9 m². Client: Eba and Jerry Sohn. Cost: not disclosed

Located in the Mojave Desert where rain is very rare, this project consists of a series of freestanding pavilions that have neither electricity nor water. The project was carried out in collaboration with the artist Lawrence Weiner. The owner and the architect agreed to make three beds reflecting the different seasons in different areas of the property. "The Summer bed is a concrete platform set 1.8 meters off the ground to avoid the danger of snakes. The Spring and Fall bed has a ceiling to avoid morning dew, and Winter is surrounded by walls." All the same size, these "bed rooms" have "the desert as a floor, the sky as a ceiling, and no walls but unframed landscape" in the words of Arata Isozaki. The architect, like some of his younger Japanese colleagues such as Sou Fujimoto, has sought, with such a "fundamental" series of small structures, to address issues that concern the very nature of architecture. "Here," he says, "we should be referring to the property size as 'as far as you can see' or the height of the building as 'the height of the sky.'"

Das mitten in der regenarmen Mojave-Wüste gelegene Projekt besteht aus einer Reihe freistehender Pavillons, die weder über Strom noch Wasser verfügen. Realisiert wurde das Projekt in Zusammenarbeit mit dem Künstler Lawrence Weiner. Auftraggeber und Architekt kamen überein, drei „Betten" zu entwerfen, die an verschiedenen Standorten auf dem Grundstück symbolisch für die Jahreszeiten stehen. „Das Sommer-Bett ist eine Plattform aus Beton, die 1,8 m über dem Boden aufgeständert ist, um Schutz vor Schlangen zu bieten. Das Frühling- und Herbst-Bett hat ein Dach, um vor Morgentau zu schützen, der Winter ist von Wänden umschlossen." Diese „Bett-Räume" sind jeweils gleich groß und „haben die Wüste zum Boden, den Himmel als Decke und keine Wände, sondern ungerahmte Landschaft", so Arata Isozaki. Wie andere japanische Kollegen, darunter auch der jüngere Sou Foujimoto, beschäftigt sich Isozaki, besonders bei einer Reihe „fundamentaler" Kleinbauten, mit Definitionen von Architektur schlechthin. „Hier", erklärt Isozaki, „lässt sich die Größe des Grundstücks mit den Worten ‚so weit das Auge reicht' beschreiben, die Höhe der Bauten als ‚himmelhoch'."

Mise en œuvre en plein désert de Mojave où les pluies sont rares, ce projet conçu en collaboration avec l'artiste conceptuel Lawrence Weiner se compose d'une série de pavillons indépendants qui ne possèdent ni eau ni électricité. Le propriétaire et l'architecte se sont accordé sur la construction de trois « lits » rappelant les différentes saisons et implantés à différents endroits de la propriété. « Le lit d'été est une plate-forme de béton suspendue à 1,8 mètre du sol pour se protéger des serpents. Le lit du printemps et de l'automne possède un plafond qui abrite de la rosée matinale et celui d'hiver est entouré de murs. » Toutes des mêmes dimensions ces « chambres à coucher » ont « le désert pour sol, le ciel pour plafond, aucun mur et s'ouvrent sur un paysage sans limite », selon Arata Isozaki. Comme certains de ses plus jeunes confrères dont Sou Fujimoto, l'architecte cherche par des séries « fondatrices » de petites structures à aborder les problèmes qui concernent la nature même de l'architecture. « Ici », dit-il, « les expressions "aussi loin que l'on peut voir" et "aussi haut que le ciel" définissent les dimensions de la propriété. »

Isozaki's work in this instance is closer to sculpture or installation art than it is to architecture in the traditional sense—or rather, it is an effort to define what represents the minimalist limit of any building.

Isozakis Entwurf ist hier eher Skulptur oder Installationskunst als Architektur im klassischen Sinne – bzw. vielmehr der Versuch zu entdecken, was die Minimalgrenzen eines Gebäudes sein könnten.

Ici, l'intervention d'Isozaki est plus proche de la sculpture ou de l'installation que de l'architecture au sens traditionnel. Plus précisément, elle représente un effort de définition des limites minimales de toute construction.

Placed in a voluntary way in the vast western landscape, Isozaki's interventions can also be likened to the garden follies of another era, albeit on a willfully reduced scale.

Man könnte die willkürlich in der weiten Landschaft des Westens platzierten Interventionen mit Follies vergleichen, Fantasiebauten der Gartenkunst früherer Zeiten. Allerdings fallen Isozakis Arbeiten bewusst kleiner aus.

Positionnées de manière très précise dans cet immense paysage, les interventions d'Isozaki peuvent aussi se comparer aux « folies » de jardins d'autres époques, mais à une échelle volontairement réduite.

JAKOB + MACFARLANE

Jakob + MacFarlane SARL d'Architecture
13 Rue des Petites Écuries
75010 Paris
France

Tel: +33 1 44 79 05 72
Fax: +33 1 48 00 97 93
E-mail: info@jakobmacfarlane.com
Web: www.jakobmacfarlane.com

DOMINIQUE JAKOB was born in 1966 and holds a degree in Art History from the Université de Paris I (1990) and a degree in Architecture from the École d'Architecture Paris-Villemin (1991). Born in New Zealand in 1961, **BRENDAN MACFARLANE** received his B.Arch at SCI-Arc, Los Angeles (1984), and his M.Arch degree at the Harvard Graduate School of Design (1990). From 1995 to 1997, MacFarlane was an architecture critic at the Architectural Association (AA) in London. They founded their own agency in 1992 in Paris, and were also cofounders with E. Marin-Trottin and D. Trottin of the exhibition and conference organizer Periphériques (1996–98). Their main projects include the T House (La-Garenne-Colombes, 1994, 1998); the Georges Restaurant (Pompidou Center, Paris, 1999–2000); the restructuring of the Maxim Gorky Theater (Petit-Quevilly, 1999–2000); and the Renault International Communication Center (Boulogne, 2004). Recent and current work includes the City of Fashion and Design (Paris, 2007–08); another dock project, the Orange Cube (Lyon, 2010, published here); the FRAC Contemporary Art Center in Orléans (2006–11); and the Saint-Nazaire Theater (Saint-Nazaire, ongoing), all in France.

DOMINIQUE JAKOB wurde 1966 geboren und schloss ihr Studium der Kunstgeschichte an der Université de Paris I (1990) sowie der Architektur an der École d'Architecture Paris-Villemin (1991) ab. **BRENDAN MACFARLANE**, geboren 1961 in Neuseeland, absolvierte seinen B.Arch am SCI-Arc, Los Angeles (1984), und seinen M.Arch an der Harvard Graduate School of Design (1990). Von 1995 bis 1997 war MacFarlane Architekturkritiker an der Architectural Association (AA) in London. 1992 gründeten die beiden ihre eigene Agentur in Paris. Gemeinsam mit E. Marin-Trottin und D. Trottin waren sie Mitbegründer der Ausstellungs- und Messeagentur Periphé-riques (1996–98). Ihre wichtigsten Projekte sind u.a. das Maison T (La-Garenne-Colombes, 1994, 1998), das Restaurant Georges (Centre Pompidou, Paris, 1999–2000), der Umbau des Maxim-Gorki-Theaters (Petit-Quevilly, 1999–2000) sowie das Internationale Kommunikationszentrum von Renault (Boulogne, 2004). Zu ihren jüngeren und aktuellen Arbeiten zählen die Cité de la Mode et du Design (Paris, 2007–08), der Orange Cube, ein weiteres Hafenprojekt (Lyon, 2010, hier vorgestellt), das Zentrum für zeitgenössische Kunst FRAC in Orléans (2006–11) sowie das Theater Saint-Nazaire (Saint-Nazaire, in Planung), alle in Frankreich.

DOMINIQUE JAKOB, née en 1966, est diplômée en histoire de l'art de l'université de Paris I (1990) et en architecture de l'École d'architecture Paris-Villemin (1991). Né en Nouvelle-Zélande en 1961, **BRENDAN MACFARLANE** a obtenu son B. Arch. au SCI-Arc (Los Angeles, 1984), et son M. Arch. à Harvard GSD (1990). De 1995 à 1997, il a été critique de projets à l'Architectural Association de Londres. Ils ont fondé leur agence à Paris en 1992 à Paris et ont aussi été cofondateurs, avec E. Marin-Trottin et D. Trottin, de l'agence Périphériques (1996–98). Parmi leurs principaux projets, tous en France : la maison T (La-Garenne-Colombes, 1994, 1998) ; le restaurant Georges (Centre Pompidou, Paris, 1999–2000) ; la restructuration du Théâtre Maxime Gorki (Petit-Quevilly, 1999–2000) et le Centre international de communication Renault (Boulogne-Billancourt, 2004). Plus récemment, ils ont réalisé la Cité de la mode et du design (Paris, 2007–08) ; un projet immobilier sur un quai de la Saône, le Cube Orange (Lyon, 2010, publié ici) ; le FRAC d'Orléans (2006–11) et le Théâtre de Saint-Nazaire (en cours).

ORANGE CUBE

Lyon, France, 2010

Address: 45 Quai Rambaud, Lyon, France
Area: 6300 m². Client: Rhone Saône Développement/Cardinal. Cost: not disclosed
Collaboration: Raffaela Schmied

This project is part of a larger urban planning effort in the old harbor zone of Lyon intended to reinvest the docks on the river side with architecture and a cultural and commercial program. The architects explain the **ORANGE CUBE** "as a simple orthogonal 'cube' into which a giant hole is carved, responding to necessities of light, air movement, and views. This hole creates a void, piercing the building horizontally from the riverside inwards and upwards through the roof terrace." The five-level structure is designed around a 29 x 33-meter framework. It is painted orange in reference to an "industrial color often used for harbor zones." The void in the cube is conceived as a "perturbation" of the original, strict geometry. Sustainable development strategies, such as heat pumps, are employed. A top-floor terrace offers a view of Lyon, La Fourvière, and the Lyon Confluence area. The Orange Cube contains the headquarters of the Cardinal Group real estate developers and a design showroom.

Das Projekt ist Teil einer umfassenden Erschließung des alten Hafens von Lyon, in deren Zuge an den Kaianlagen Architektur, Kultur- und Gewerbeeinrichtungen angesiedelt werden sollen. Die Architekten beschreiben den **ORANGE CUBE** „als einen schlichten, rechtwinkligen ‚Würfel', der von einer monumentalen Lochaussparung durchschnitten wird, der den Bau mit Licht, Luft und Aussicht versorgt. Das Loch schafft ein räumliches Vakuum, das den gesamten Bau horizontal vom Fluss aus nach innen und oben durchschneidet, bis hinauf zur Dachterrasse." Der fünfstöckige Bau basiert auf einer 29 x 33 m großen Rahmenkonstruktion. Die Farbwahl Orange ist eine Referenz an „eine Industriefarbe, die oft in Hafenbereichen zu sehen ist". Die Aussparung im Kubus ist als „Störung" der ursprünglich strengen Geometrie geplant. Zum Einsatz kamen außerdem nachhaltige Bauentwicklungsstrategien wie Wärmepumpen. Die Dachterrasse bietet Ausblick über Lyon, La Fourvière und das Stadtviertel Lyon Confluence. Untergebracht im Orange Cube ist unter anderem die Zentrale der Immobilienentwickler Cardinal Group sowie ein Showroom für Design.

Ce projet a été réalisé dans le cadre d'une importante opération d'urbanisme sur les terrains de l'ancien port fluvial de Lyon, qui multiplie les programmes immobiliers, commerciaux et culturels sur les rives du Rhône et de la Saône. Les architectes présentent ce **CUBE ORANGE** comme « un simple cube orthogonal dans lequel a été foré un gigantesque trou qui répond à des besoins d'éclairage naturel, d'aération et de perspectives. Ce vide transperce horizontalement l'immeuble du quai vers l'intérieur et de bas en haut jusqu'au toit en terrasse », expliquent les architectes. De cinq niveaux, le bâtiment repose sur une ossature de 29 x 33 mètres. Il est peint en orange en référence à « une couleur industrielle souvent utilisée dans les zones portuaires ». Le vide pratiqué est une « perturbation » de la stricte géométrie d'origine du projet. Des éléments de développement durable tels que des pompes thermiques ont été intégrés. En toiture, une terrasse offre une vue sur Lyon, la colline de Fourvière et le quartier de Lyon Confluence. Le Cube Orange abrite le siège social du groupe de promoteurs immobiliers Cardinal et un showroom de design.

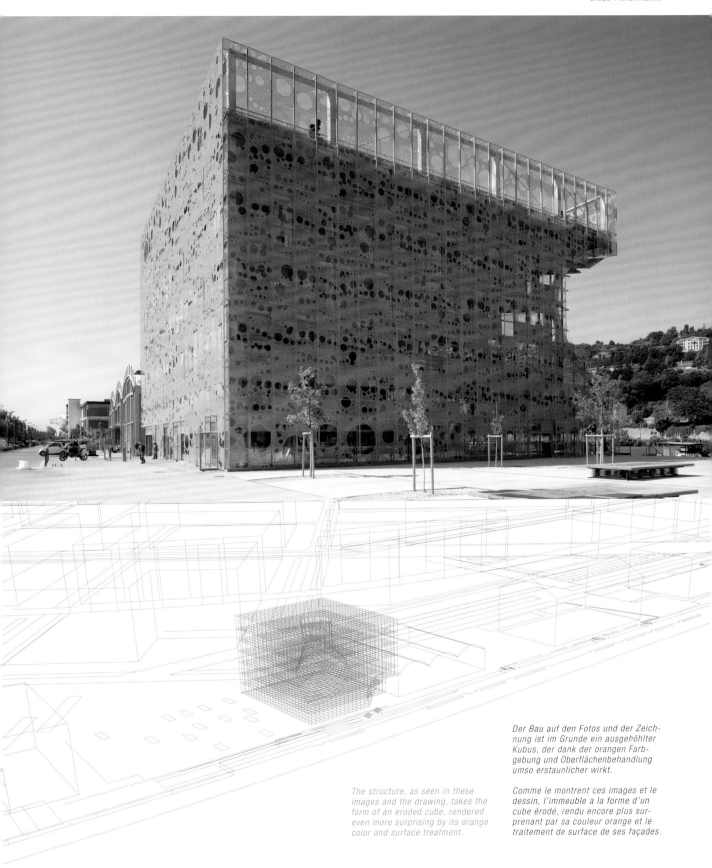

Der Bau auf den Fotos und der Zeichnung ist im Grunde ein ausgehöhlter
Kubus, der dank der orangen Farb-
gebung und Oberflächenbehandlung
umso erstaunlicher wirkt.

Comme le montrent ces images et le
dessin, l'immeuble a la forme d'un
cube érodé, rendu encore plus surprenant par sa couleur orange et le
traitement de surface de ses façades.

The structure, as seen in these
images and the drawing, takes the
form of an eroded cube, rendered
even more surprising by its orange
color and surface treatment.

Visible in elevation drawings (above) but even more spectacularly in the photo opposite and above, the building is actually pierced by a large opening, bringing natural light into interior areas.

Wie auf den Aufrissen (oben) zu sehen und umso spektakulärer auf den Aufnahmen rechts und oben, wird der Bau von einer gewaltigen Öffnung durchbohrt, die Tageslicht ins Innere einfallen lässt.

Vu en élévation (plan ci-dessus) et de manière plus spectaculaire encore sur les photos ci-dessus et à droite, l'immeuble est percé d'une énorme ouverture qui introduit l'éclairage naturel au cœur du bâtiment.

Interior design continues on the
theme of grated surfaces and openings that pierce the solid volumes in
the design showroom space, visible
on these pages.

Auch in der Innenarchitektur findet
sich das Motiv der perforierten Oberflächen und Öffnungen, die feste
Baukörper durchdringen, wie die Ausstellungsräume für Design auf diesen
Seiten zeigen.

L'architecture intérieure joue également sur le thème des surfaces
perforées et des ouvertures percées
dans des volumes pleins, comme
dans ce showroom de mobilier
contemporain.

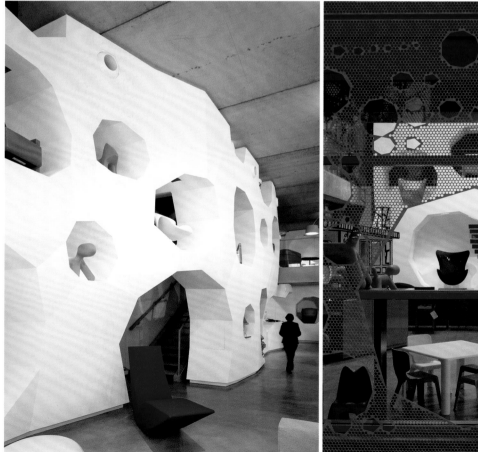

Floor plans show the basic strict square as it is pierced or "perturbed" by the openings imagined by the architects. The innovation here consists in basing the overall design on typical geometry and then disturbing the obvious solidity of the form.

Etagengrundrisse zeigen ein strenges Quadrat als Grundform, das mit Öffnungen durchsetzt oder „gestört" wird. Besonders innovativ ist hier, dass die Architekten zunächst eine typische Geometrie wählen, um die vermeintliche Solidität dieser Form dann wieder aufzubrechen.

Les plans au sol montrent comment la forme strictement carrée est percée ou « perturbée » par les ouvertures imaginées par les architectes. L'innovation consiste ici à mettre en œuvre une géométrie globalement basique, qui est ensuite bousculée par des interventions volontaires.

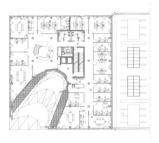

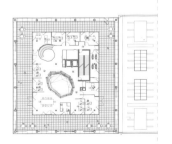

DIÉBÉDO FRANCIS KÉRÉ

Kéré Architecture
Arndtstr. 34
10965 Berlin
Germany

Tel: +49 30 78 95 23 91
Fax: +49 30 78 95 23 98
E-mail: mail@kere-architecture.com
Web: www.kere-architecture.com

DIÉBÉDO FRANCIS KÉRÉ, born in Burkina Faso, studied at the Technische Universität Berlin. He puts an emphasis on education about architecture in his own country. He states: "The community needs to be educated about how to monitor the climatic circumstances and to use local materials. Only people who take part in the building process can maintain and spread the word about these architectural projects." His first project, a primary school in his native village (Gando, Burkina Faso, 2001), won a 2004 Aga Khan Award for Architecture because of its exemplarity as well as its concise and elegant architecture. As well as this primary school, his work includes the National Park of Mali (Bamako, Mali, 2010, published here); the Earthen Architecture Center (Mopti, Mali, 2010); and the permanent exhibition for the Red Cross Museum (Geneva, Switzerland, 2010–11). Ongoing work includes the Women's Community Center (Gando, 2009–); a library (Gando, 2010); a training center (in collaboration with DAZ e.V., Dapaong, Togo, 2010–); and Zhoushan Harbor Development (Zhoushan, China, 2010–).

DIÉBÉDO FRANCIS KÉRÉ, geboren in Burkina Faso, studierte an der Technischen Universität Berlin. Ein besonderes Anliegen ist ihm die Vermittlung von Architektur in seinem Heimatland. Er erklärt: „Es muss den Menschen vermittelt werden, wie man mit den klimatischen Gegebenheiten umgeht und lokale Materialien nutzt. Nur Menschen, die am Bauprozess teilhaben, können diese Architekturprojekte erhalten und weitervermitteln." Für sein erstes Projekt, eine Grundschule in seinem Heimatdorf (Gando, Burkina Faso, 2001) erhielt er 2004 den Aga-Khan-Preis für Architektur, der sowohl den Vorbildcharakter als auch die Präzision und Eleganz seiner Architektur würdigte. Neben der Grundschule umfasst sein Werk den Nationalpark von Mali (Bamako, Mali, 2010, hier vorgestellt), das Zentrum für Lehmbau (Mopti, Mali, 2010) sowie die Dauerausstellung für das Museum des Roten Kreuzes (Genf, Schweiz, 2010–11). Laufende Projekte sind u.a. ein Frauengemeindezentrum (Gando, 2009–), eine Bibliothek (Gando, 2010), ein Ausbildungszentrum (in Zusammenarbeit mit DAZ e.V., Dapaong, Togo, 2010–) sowie eine Bauerschließung im Hafen von Zhoushan (Zhoushan, China, 2010–).

Né au Burkina Faso, **DIÉBÉDO FRANCIS KÉRÉ** a étudié à l'Université technique de Berlin. Il s'intéresse beaucoup à la formation à l'architecture dans son pays et a déclaré : « Notre communauté doit être éduquée sur les façons de contrôler les conditions climatiques et sur l'utilisation des matériaux locaux. Seuls ceux qui participent au processus de construction sont en mesure de maintenir et de diffuser ces idées. » Son premier projet, une école primaire pour son village natal (Gando, Burkina Faso, 2001), a remporté le prix Aga Khan d'architecture 2004 pour son exemplarité, sa concision et son élégance. Ses réalisations comprennent le parc national du Mali (Bamako, Mali, 2010, publié ici) ; le Centre d'architecture en terre (Mopti, Mali, 2010) et le Centre permanent d'exposition du musée de la Croix-Rouge (Genève, 2010–11). Il travaille actuellement sur des projets comme un Centre communautaire pour les femmes (Gando, 2009–) ; une bibliothèque (Gando, 2010) ; un centre de formation (en collaboration avec DAZ e.V., Dapaong, Togo, 2010–) et l'urbanisation du port de Zhoushan (Zhoushan, Chine, 2010–).

NATIONAL PARK OF MALI

Bamako, Mali, 2010

Address: Avenue de la Liberté, Bamako, Mali
Area: 103 ha (park); 3000 m² (structures). Client: Aga Khan Trust for Culture. Cost: not disclosed
Collaboration: Pichler Engineers

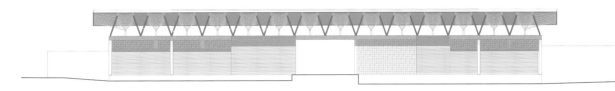

Working for the Aga Khan Trust for Culture, based in Geneva, the architect has carefully inserted modest buildings into the park setting. Above, the principal entrance and an elevation drawing.

Für den in Genf ansässigen Aga Khan Trust for Culture integrierte der Architekt einfühlsam bescheidene Bauten in das Parkgelände. Oben der Haupteingang sowie ein Aufriss.

Dans le cadre d'un projet du Trust Aga Khan pour la culture, basé à Genève, l'architecte a inséré avec soin de discrètes constructions dans l'environnement du parc. Ci-dessus, l'entrée principale et une élévation.

The gentle landscaping of the park and its colors combine well with the architecture that is open and inviting without any hint of modern aggression.

Die unaufdringliche Landschaftsgestaltung des Parks und dessen Farben harmonieren ideal mit der offenen, einladenden Architektur, die nie auch nur ansatzweise aggressiv modern wirkt.

Le délicat aménagement paysager du parc et ses couleurs se combinent harmonieusement avec l'architecture ouverte et accueillante, sans aucune agressivité contemporaine.

The government of Mali defined the outlines of the **NATIONAL PARK OF MALI**, an area of 103 hectares within a larger protected forest reserve of 2100 hectares. Under the terms of a public-private partnership, the government asked the Aga Khan Trust for Culture to work on the park's 103 hectares, a large, semicircular canyon of protected forest that lies beneath the terraced outcrops of the Koulouba plateau, between the National Museum and the Presidential Palace Complex. The park was designed to offer large open spaces for leisure and educational activities for the general public, school groups, and tourists. Phase 1 also included the redevelopment and integration of eight existing facilities. Diébédo Francis Kéré was commissioned to design the primary entrance and two secondary north and east entrances, a sports center, and a restaurant.

Die Geländegrenzen des **NATIONALPARKS VON MALI** wurden von der Regierung des Landes festgesetzt, die hierfür eine Fläche von 103 ha innerhalb eines größeren, 2100 ha großen, geschützten Waldgebiets vorgesehen hatte. Im Rahmen einer öffentlich-privaten Partnerschaft beauftragte die Regierung den Aga Khan Trust for Culture mit der Arbeit am 103 ha großen Gelände. Der Park, eine halbkreisförmige Schlucht in einem Waldschutzgebiet, liegt unterhalb der Felsterrassen des Koulouba-Plateaus, zwischen dem Nationalmuseum und dem Komplex des Präsidentenpalasts. Der Park sollte unter freiem Himmel großflächige Freizeit- und Bildungsangebote für die Öffentlichkeit, Schulklassen und Touristen bieten. Zur ersten Bauphase gehörte auch die Umgestaltung und Einbindung von acht bestehenden Einrichtungen. Diébédo Francis Kéré erhielt den Auftrag zur Gestaltung des Haupteingangsbereichs und zweier Eingänge im Norden und Osten sowie eines Sportzentrums und eines Restaurants.

C'est à l'intérieur d'une réserve protégée de 2100 hectares que le gouvernement malien a créé le **PARC NATIONAL DU MALI**, zone de 103 hectares située dans un vaste canyon semi-circulaire de forêts protégées au pied des terrasses qui bordent le plateau de Koulouba, entre le Musée national et le complexe du palais présidentiel. Dans le cadre d'un partenariat public-privé, il a demandé au Trust Aga Khan pour la culture de proposer un projet. Le parc offre de vastes espaces ouverts et couverts pour des loisirs et des activités éducatives destinées au grand public, aux classes d'écoliers et aux touristes. La phase 1 comprenait également la restructuration et l'intégration de huit équipements existants. L'architecte a reçu commande de l'entrée principale et de deux entrées secondaires au nord et à l'est, d'un centre sportif et d'un restaurant.

Above, a view of the restaurant taken from the park. Both the lightness of the architecture and its integration into the site are remarkable.

Oben, ein Blick aus dem Park auf das Restaurant. Sowohl die Leichtigkeit der Architektur als auch deren Integration in ihr Umfeld sind bemerkenswert.

Ci-dessus, une vue du restaurant prise du parc. La légèreté de cette architecture et son intégration dans le site sont remarquables.

Two elevation drawings show the sports center. Above, the architect uses a base of earthen materials that blends with the walkways of the park and, indeed, with the color scheme of the natural setting.

Zwei Aufrisse zeigen das Sportzentrum. Ausgangspunkt des Architekten sind erdige Materialien, die nahtlos an die Pfade im Park anknüpfen und ebenso nahtlos mit der Palette des natürlichen Umfelds verschmelzen.

Les deux élévations ci-dessous représentent le centre sportif. Ci-dessus, l'architecte a choisi des matériaux simples et d'aspect irrégulier qui se fondent dans les allées du parc et les couleurs de la nature.

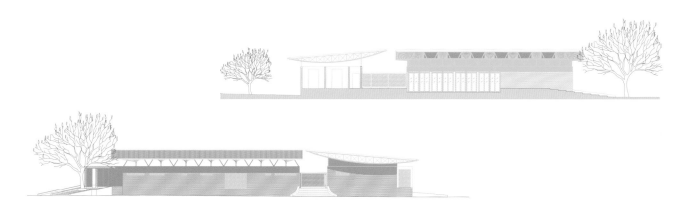

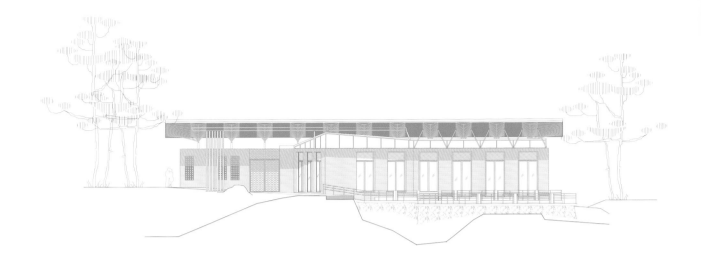

On this page, a nighttime view of the restaurant and an elevation of the structure that is built on a platform above the natural rocks in the park.

Auf dieser Seite: eine nächtliche Ansicht des Restaurants sowie ein Aufriss des Gebäudes, das auf einer Plattform über den natürlichen Fels-formationen im Park errichtet wurde.

Sur cette page, vue de nuit du restau-rant et élévation de la structure construite sur une plate-forme de rochers.

Elevation drawings of the restaurant seen from two sides and the photo above show the way it is integrated into the natural setting, or rather sits lightly on it.

Aufrisse des Restaurants von zwei verschiedenen Seiten und das Foto oben veranschaulichen, wie der Bau sich in seine natürliche Umgebung integriert.

La photographie ci-dessus et les élévations des deux façades du restaurant qui semble à peine reposer sur un rocher, montrent la façon dont il s'intègre dans son cadre naturel.

KENGO KUMA

Kengo Kuma & Associates
2–24–8 Minami Aoyama
Minato-ku
Tokyo 107–0062
Japan

Tel: +81 3 3401 7721
Fax: +81 3 3401 7778
E-mail: kuma@ba2.so-net.ne.jp
Web: www.kkaa.co.jp

Born in 1954 in Kanagawa, Japan, **KENGO KUMA** graduated in 1979 from the University of Tokyo with an M.Arch degree. In 1985–86 he received an Asian Cultural Council Fellowship Grant and was a Visiting Scholar at Columbia University. In 1987 he established the Spatial Design Studio, and in 1991 he created Kengo Kuma & Associates. His work includes the Karuizawa Resort Hotel (Karuizawa, 1993); Kiro-san Observatory (Ehime, 1994); Atami Guesthouse, a guesthouse for Bandai Corp (Atami, 1992–95); the Japanese Pavilion for the Venice Biennale (Venice, Italy, 1995); Tomioka Lakewood Golf Club Clubhouse (Tomioka, 1993–96); and Toyoma Noh-Theater (Miyagi, 1995–96). He has also completed the Great (Bamboo) Wall Guesthouse (Beijing, China, 2002); One Omotesando (Tokyo, 2003); LVMH Osaka (2004); the Nagasaki Prefecture Art Museum (2005); and the Zhongtai Box, Z58 building (Shanghai, China, 2003–06). Recent work includes the Steel House (Bunkyo-ku, Tokyo, 2005–07); Sakenohana (London, UK, 2007); Tiffany Ginza (Tokyo, 2008); Nezu Museum (Tokyo, 2007–09); Museum of Kanayama (Ota City, Gunma, 2009); Glass Wood House (New Canaan, Connecticut, USA, 2007–10, published here); Yusuhara Marché (Yusuhara, Kochi, 2009–10, also published here); and the GC Prostho Museum Research Center, Torii Matsu Machi (Aichi, 2009–10, also published here), all in Japan unless stated otherwise.

KENGO KUMA wurde 1954 in Kanagawa, Japan, geboren und schloss sein Studium an der Universität Tokio 1979 mit einem M.Arch ab. 1985–86 erhielt er ein Stipendium des Asian Cultural Council und war Gastdozent an der Columbia University. 1987 gründete er das Büro Spatial Design Studio, 1991 folgte die Gründung von Kengo Kuma & Associates. Sein Werk umfasst das Hotel Karuizawa (Karuizawa, 1993), das Planetarium Kiro-san (Ehime, 1994), das Atami-Gästehaus für Bandai (Atami, 1992–95), den japanischen Pavillon für die Biennale in Venedig (1995), das Tomioka Lakewood Golfclubhaus (Tomioka, 1993–96) und das No-Theater in Toyoma (Miyagi, 1995–96). Darüber hinaus realisierte er das Great (Bamboo) Wall Guest House (Peking, China, 2002), One Omotesando (Tokio, 2003), LVMH Osaka (2004), das Kunstmuseum der Präfektur Nagasaki (2005) sowie die Zhongtai Box, Z58 (Shanghai, China, 2003–06). Jüngere Projekte sind u.a. das Steel House (Bunkyo-ku, Tokio, 2005–07), Sakenohana (London, GB, 2007), Tiffany Ginza (Tokio, 2008), das Nezu Museum (Tokio, 2007–09), das Museum von Kanayama (Ota City, Gunma, 2009), das Glass Wood House (New Canaan, Connecticut, USA, 2007–10, hier vorgestellt), Yusuhara Marché (Yusuhara, Kochi, 2009–10, ebenfalls hier vorgestellt) sowie das Forschungszentrum des GC Prostho Museum, Torii Matsu Machi (Aichi, 2009–10, ebenfalls hier vorgestellt), alle in Japan, sofern nicht anders angegeben.

Né en 1954 à Kanagawa (Japon), **KENGO KUMA** est diplômé d'architecture de l'université de Tokyo (1979). En 1985–86, il bénéficie d'une bourse de l'Asian Cultural Council et devient chercheur invité à l'université Columbia. En 1987, il crée le Spatial Design Studio et, en 1991, Kengo Kuma & Associates. Parmi ses réalisations : l'hôtel de vacances Karuizawa (Karuizawa, 1993) ; l'observatoire Kiro-san (Ehime, 1994) ; la maison d'hôtes d'Atami pour Bandai Corp (Atami, 1992–95) ; le Pavillon japonais pour la Biennale de Venise 1995 ; le club-house du golf du lac de Tomioka (Tomioka, 1993–96) et le Théâtre de nô Toyoma (Miyagi, 1995–96). Il a également réalisé la maison d'hôte de la Grande Muraille de bambou (Pékin, 2002) ; l'immeuble One Omotesando (Tokyo, 2003) ; l'immeuble LVMH Osaka (2004) ; le Musée d'art de la préfecture de Nagasaki (2005) et l'immeuble Zhongtai Box, Z58 (Shanghaï, 2003–06). Plus récemment, il a construit la Maison en acier (Bunkyo-ku, Tokyo, 2005–07) ; le restaurant Sakenohana (Londres, 2007) ; l'immeuble Tiffany Ginza (Tokyo, 2008) ; le musée Nezu (Tokyo, 2007–09) ; le musée de Kanayama (Ota, Gunma, 2009) ; la Maison en bois et verre (New Canaan, Connecticut, 2007–10, publiée ici) ; le marché de Yusuhara (Yusuhara, Kochi, 2009–10, également publié ici) et le centre de recherches du musée GC Prostho, Torii Matsu Machi (Aichi, 2009–10, également publié ici).

GLASS WOOD HOUSE

New Canaan, Connecticut, USA, 2007–10

Area: 830 m². Client: not disclosed. Cost: not disclosed
Collaboration: Yuki Ikeguchi, Satoshi Sano

This project involved the renovation of a house designed by Philip Johnson in 1956 and the construction of a new house on the site. The original structure is described by Kengo Kuma as a "symmetric glass box standing alone in a forest." "Philip Johnson's house stands alone," says Kuma, "so we proposed the L-shaped plan in which the new building hitched onto the old one, in order to present a new relation between nature and the architecture." The new structure has 7.6 x 15.2-centimeter flat steel bar pillars and a wooden roof. "We created a major change in the existing house," says the architect, "by getting rid of the symmetry and covering the exterior with wooden louvers, so that the architecture would gain more 'intimacy.'" In Kengo Kuma's terms the result is to create a sort of "intimate" or "mild" transparency that supercedes the "isolated" transparency conceived in the 1950s.

Das Projekt umfasste die Sanierung eines 1956 von Philip Johnson entworfenen Hauses sowie den Neubau eines Wohnhauses auf demselben Grundstück. Den ursprünglichen Bau beschreibt Kengo Kuma als „symmetrische Glasbox, die allein in einem Wald steht". Kuma erklärt: „Philip Johnsons Haus steht allein, deshalb entwickelten wir einen L-förmigen Grundriss, bei dem der Neubau an den älteren Bau anschließt, sodass ein neues Verhältnis zwischen Natur und Architektur entsteht." Der Neubau hat ein Holzdach und Stützen aus 7,6 x 15,2 cm starken Stahlträgern. „Beim Altbau nahmen wir eine wesentliche Veränderung vor", berichtet der Architekt, „indem wir uns von der Symmetrie verabschiedeten und den Bau außen mit hölzernen Sonnenschutzblenden versahen, sodass die Architektur mehr ‚Intimität' gewann." Kengo Kuma zufolge ist das Ergebnis eine „intime" bzw. „mildere" Transparenz, die die „isolierte" Transparenz der 1950er-Jahre ablöst.

Ce projet comprenait la rénovation d'une maison conçue par Philip Johnson en 1956 et la construction d'une nouvelle résidence sur le même terrain. La construction d'origine est présentée par Kengo Kuma comme « une boîte de verre symétrique isolée dans la forêt. La maison de Philip Johnson est isolée », explique-t-il, « ainsi avons-nous proposé un plan en L dans lequel la construction nouvelle s'accroche à l'ancienne pour créer une relation nouvelle entre la nature et l'architecture. » La nouvelle construction qui repose sur des piliers en acier de 7,6 x 15,2 centimètres de section est recouverte d'une toiture en bois. « Nous avons apporté un changement majeur à la maison existante en supprimant la symétrie et en recouvrant les façades de volets de bois pour que l'architecture gagne en "intimité" ». Kengo Kuma explique également avoir créé une sorte de transparence « intime » ou « douce » qui remplace la transparence « isolée » des années 1950.

Kengo Kuma is a master of lightness
and integration of modern architecture into a natural setting, as is evident here, far from his native Japan.

Kengo Kuma ist ein Meister der
Leichtigkeit und der Einbindung
moderner Architektur in eine Landschaft. Das wird auch hier deutlich,
fernab seines Heimatlands Japan.

Kengo Kuma est un orfèvre en matière de légèreté et d'intégration
de formes contemporaines dans un
cadre naturel, comme il le montre ici,
loin de son Japon natal.

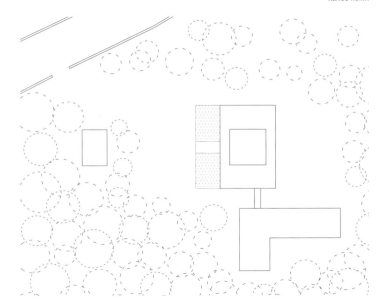

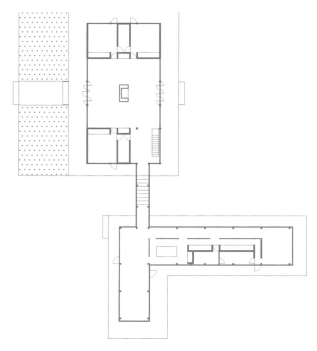

Plans show the strictly geometric design, but images demonstrate the extreme lightness of the structure—a fact that allows it to sit in the natural setting without disturbing it.

Während Grundrisse die strenge Geometrie des Entwurfs belegen, zeugen Aufnahmen von der auffälligen Leichtigkeit des Baus – ihr ist zu verdanken, dass das Haus in der Landschaft liegt, ohne sie zu stören.

Ces plans illustrent la géométrie rigoureuse du projet dont les images expriment l'extrême légèreté qui lui permet de s'intégrer avec délicatesse dans son cadre naturel sans le perturber.

In the image above, or in the one on the right, the forest penetrates the house in a visual sense, and the building floats above the sloping site.

Auf der Ansicht oben und auch rechts scheint der Wald das Haus ganz zu durchdringen. Es schwebt geradezu über dem Hanggrundstück.

Dans l'image ci-dessus ou celle de droite, la forêt semble pénétrer visuellement dans la maison en suspension au-dessus de la pente du terrain.

YUSUHARA MARCHÉ

Yusuhara, Kochi, Japan, 2009–10

Address: 1196–1 Yusuhara, Takaoka-gun, Kochi, Japan
Area: 1132 m². Cost: not disclosed. Client: Tomio Yano, Mayor of Yusuhara
Collaboration: Kazuhiko Miyazawa, Suguru Watanabe

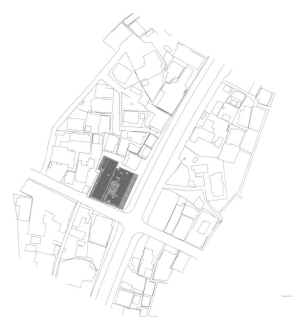

Though this building is rather substantial in its apparent mass, the architect alleviates the feeling of weight with full glazing on the ground floor. A site plan (left) shows how the building fits into the dense town pattern.

Obwohl der Bau von der Masse her substanziell wirkt, gelingt es dem Architekten, diesen Eindruck durch geschosshohe Verglasung im Parterre aufzulockern. Ein Lageplan (links) illustriert, wie sich das Gebäude in die dichte städtische Bebauung fügt.

Bien que ce bâtiment soit de dimensions assez importantes, l'architecte a allégé le sentiment éventuel de massivité en vitrant entièrement le rez-de-chaussée. Un plan (à gauche) montre comment le projet s'est adapté à la densité de son environnement urbain.

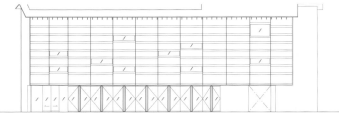

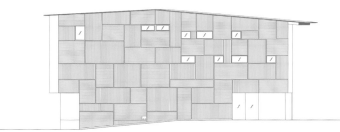

This is a market selling local products coupled with a small 15-room hotel. Yusuhara is a town of 3900 people located in the mountains. The architect employed thatching in deference to regional traditions. Glass marks the front entrance, with straw modules in the "unprecedented" form of a curtain wall bound to the structure. Cedar logs are used inside with irregular bark peeling. Kengo Kuma states: "Using rough-textured materials, such as thatch and logs, we tried to create new characteristics for Yusuhara."

In diesem Marktgebäude zum Verkauf lokaler Produkte ist auch ein kleines Hotel mit 15 Zimmern untergebracht. Yusuhara ist eine Kleinstadt mit 3900 Einwohnern und liegt in den Bergen. In Anlehnung an regionale Bautraditionen arbeitete der Architekt mit einer Reetdachtechnik. Der Haupteingang wird von Glas dominiert, während Strohmodule in Form einer „nie dagewesenen" Curtain Wall vor der Fassade angebracht wurden. Im Innern des Baus kamen Zedernholzstämme mit teilweise entfernter Rinde zum Einsatz. Kengo Kuma erklärt: „Indem wir Materialien mit rauen Oberflächen nutzten, wie etwa Reet und Holzstämme, versuchten wir, neue Besonderheiten in Yusuhara einzuführen."

Ce petit marché de produits locaux couplé à un hôtel de 15 chambres été construit à Yusuhara, ville de 3900 habitants située dans une région montagneuse. L'architecte a utilisé le chaume par respect des traditions régionales. La façade d'entrée est néanmoins en verre surmontée de panneaux modulaires en chaume qui forment un mur-rideau « sans précédent ». À l'intérieur, on remarque des grumes de cèdre grossièrement équarries. Pour Kengo Kuma : « En utilisant des matériaux de texture brute, comme le chaume et les grumes, nous avons voulu donner à Yusuhara un nouveau caractère architectural. »

By using flattened blocks of thatched straw, the architect both calls on local materials and yet makes his materials modern through their form and accumulation.

Durch den Einsatz von gepressten Reetballen nimmt der Architekt Bezug auf lokale Baumaterialien, gibt diesen jedoch durch formale Gestaltung und Bündelung ein modernes Gesicht.

L'architecte utilise des panneaux de chaume, matériau local qu'il modernise aussi bien dans sa façon de l'utiliser que par son accumulation.

Wood is used inside the building, including these treelike columns and the rough wood ceiling. Modernity is thus firmly balanced with a natural or rural ambiance. To the right, one of the 15 hotel rooms in the building.

Im Innern des Gebäudes wurde Holz verarbeitet, etwa in Form von baumähnlichen Stützen und unbehandeltem Holz an der Decke. So entsteht ein gelungenes Gleichgewicht zwischen Moderne und natürlichem bzw. ländlichem Ambiente. Rechts eines der 15 Hotelzimmer.

Le bois brut est très présent à l'intérieur, comme dans les colonnes en forme d'arbre ou le plafond. La modernité du projet n'empêche pas une ambiance de nature ou de ruralité. À droite, l'une des 15 chambres de l'hôtel.

The image above and the section drawing showing the building's structure both emphasize the intelligent mixture of very contemporary materials and the rougher presence of numerous wooden elements.

Das Bild oben und der Querschnitt der Gebäudekonstruktion rechts unterstreichen die ausgesprochen intelligente Kombination zeitgenössischer Materialien und zahlreicher Elemente aus Holz.

La photographie ci-dessus et le dessin de coupe montrant la structure du bâtiment mettent en évidence l'intelligent mélange de matériaux contemporains et de multiples éléments en bois.

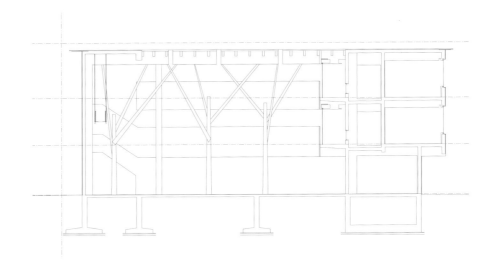

GC PROSTHO MUSEUM RESEARCH CENTER

Torii Matsu Machi, Aichi, Japan, 2009–10

Area: 626 m². Client: GC Corporation. Cost: not disclosed
Collaboration: Shin Ohba, Sayaka Mizuno

Kengo Kuma speaks of "forgetting about ready-made details in order to carve and cook materials in new and different ways." He has certainly done that in this building for a dental care company located in central Japan.

Kengo Kuma spricht davon, „Fertigbauelemente zu vergessen, um Materialien auf neue, andere Weise zu erfinden und zu erarbeiten." Bei diesem Gebäude für eine Zahnpflegefirma in Zentral-Japan ist ihm das zweifellos gelungen.

Kengo Kuma parle « d'oublier le préfabriqué pour travailler les matériaux de façon nouvelle et différente ». C'est ce qu'il a fait pour ce petit siège d'une entreprise de matériel dentaire située dans le centre du Japon.

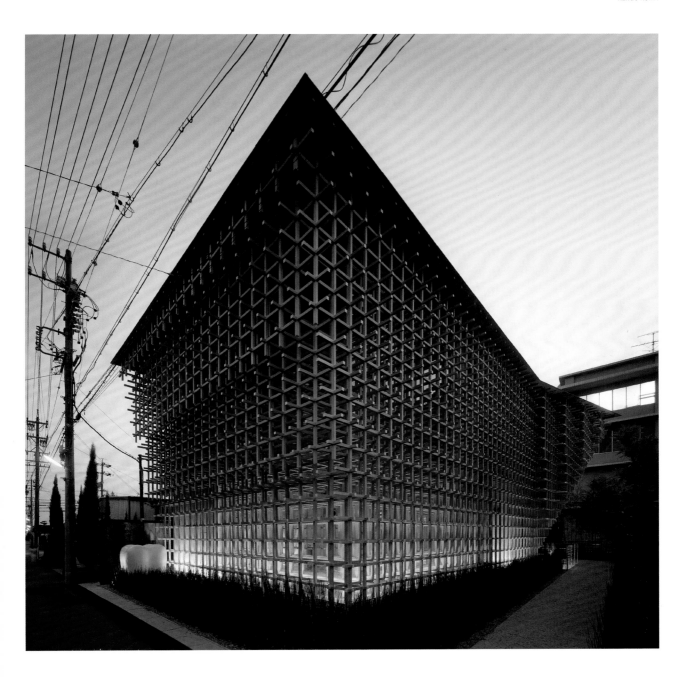

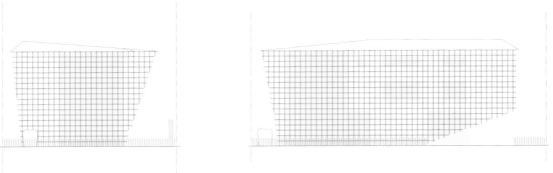

The architect used an old Japanese toy, the Cidori, a flexible assembly of wooden sticks with very particular joints, to inspire the design of this museum research center. The extendable nature of the original toy was tested by the structural engineer Jun Sato at the larger scale required for a building. He confirmed that the mechanism of the toy could indeed be used for architecture. The 10-meter-high structure has three stories above grade and one below. Kengo Kuma states: "We worked on the project in the hope that the era of machine-made architecture would be over, and that human beings would build again by themselves." The concept is certainly original.

Beim Entwurf dieses Forschungszentrums eines Museums ließ sich der Architekt von einem alten japanischen Spielzeug, dem Cidori inspirieren, einem Baukasten mit Holzstäben, die sich durch spezielle Gelenkverbindungen auszeichnen. Dass sich das Spielzeug in der Tat auf einen soviel größeren Maßstab übertragen ließ, der für den Bau eines Gebäudes erforderlich war, wurde eigens vom Statiker Jun Sato geprüft. Er bestätigte, dass sich das Prinzip des Baukasten tatsächlich architektonisch nutzen ließ. Der 10 m hohe Bau hat drei oberirdische Ebenen sowie ein Untergeschoss. Kengo Kuma erklärt: „Wir arbeiteten an diesem Projekt in der Hoffnung, dass die Ära der maschinengefertigten Architektur beendet ist und Menschen wieder selbst bauen." Zweifellos ein unverwechselbares Konzept.

Le cidori, ancien jeu de construction japonais fait de bâtonnets de bois reliés par des joints d'un type très particulier, a inspiré la conception de ce centre de recherche d'un musée. Extensible par sa nature même, ce principe de construction a été testé par l'ingénieur structurel Jun Sato à l'échelle du bâtiment, qui a confirmé sa validité en architecture. La construction de 10 mètres de haut s'étage sur quatre niveaux dont un en sous-sol. Pour Kengo Kuma : « Nous avons travaillé sur ce projet dans l'espoir que la fin de l'ère de l'architecture mécaniste approche et que les êtres humains recommencent à construire par eux-mêmes. » Ce concept ne manque pas d'originalité.

Using a children's wooden stick assembly toy as his source of inspiration, the architect develops a gridded web of wood that attains an unusual and haunting presence.

Inspiriert von einem Holzsteckkasten für Kinder entwickelte der Architekt ein Gitterwerk aus Holz, das von ungewöhnlicher und faszinierender Präsenz ist.

S'inspirant d'un jeu d'assemblage de pièces de bois pour enfants, l'architecte a mis au point une structure de tasseaux de bois d'une fascinante présence.

As the drawing below and the photos show, the wooden grid has a varying presence and density, but, in the case of the image to the right, there is a distinct impression that temple architecture has influenced Kuma.

Wie Zeichnung und Aufnahmen belegen, ist das Gitterwerk von unterschiedlich starker Präsenz und Dichte. Besonders rechts im Bild scheint es, als wäre Kuma von Tempelarchitektur beeinflusst worden.

Comme le montre le plan ci-dessous et les photographies, la densité et la force de la présence de la trame de bois varient. Dans l'image de droite, il semble que Kuma se soit inspiré de l'architecture des temples japonais.

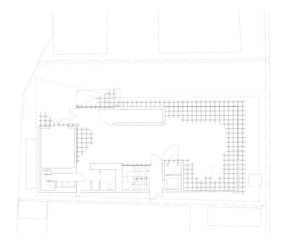

LI XIAODONG

Li Xiaodong Atelier
School of Architecture 224
Beijing 100084
China

Tel: +86 139 0100 9654
Fax: +86 10 6277 0314
E-mail: xd-li@tsinghua.edu.cn
Web: www.lixiaodong.net

LI XIAODONG graduated from the School of Architecture at Tsinghua University in Beijing in 1984 and received his Ph.D. at the School of Architecture, Delft University of Technology (1989–93). He is currently the Chair Professor of the Architecture program at the School of Architecture, Tsinghua University. He is a practicing architect, educator, and researcher on architecture. Li Xiaodong's design ranges from interior architecture to urban spaces. His Yuhu Elementary School and Community Center (Lijiang, China, 2004) was widely praised and published and his Bridge School in Xiashi (Fujian, China, 2008–09, published here) was the winner of the 2009 AR Emerging Architecture Award and winner of a 2010 Aga Khan Award for Architecture.

LI XIAODONG schloss sein Architekturstudium 1984 an der Universität Tsinghua in Peking ab und promovierte an der Architekturfakultät der Technischen Universität Delft (1989–93). Gegenwärtig ist er leitender Professor der Studiengangs Architektur an der Universität Tsinghua. Er ist praktizierender Architekt, Lehrer und Wissenschaftler. Li Xiaodongs Entwürfe reichen von Innenarchitektur bis hin zu urbanen Räumen. Großes Lob erntete seine Grundschule mit Gemeindezentrum in Yuhu (Lijiang, China, 2004), die weithin publiziert wurde. Seine Brückenschule in Xiashi (Fujian, China, 2008–09, hier vorgestellt) wurde 2009 mit dem AR Award für neue Architektur und 2010 mit einem Aga Khan Award für Architektur ausgezeichnet.

LI XIAODONG, diplômé de l'École d'architecture de l'université Tsinghua à Pékin en 1984 et docteur de l'École d'architecture de l'Université de technologie de Delft (1989–93), est actuellement professeur titulaire du programme d'architecture de l'université Tsinghua. Il est architecte praticien, enseignant et chercheur en architecture. Il intervient aussi bien en architecture intérieure qu'en urbanisme. Son école élémentaire et centre communal de Yuhu (Lijiang, Chine, 2004) a été saluée et largement publiée et son école-pont à Xiashi (Fujian, Chine, 2008–09, publiée ici) a remporté le prix 2009 de l'architecture émergeante de l'Architectural Review et un prix Aga Khan pour l'architecture en 2010.

BRIDGE SCHOOL

Xiashi, Fujian, China, 2008–09

Address: Xiashi, Fujian, China. Area: 200 m²
Client: Xiashi Village. Cost: $100 000

This structure connects the two parts of a small village that are divided by a creek. Two steel trusses span the creek with the space between them housing a school. A pedestrian bridge for the people of the village is suspended beneath the school. Stages can be created for performances at either end of the bridge, and a public library is located between classrooms. Though its style is not specifically related to the region, the **BRIDGE SCHOOL** serves evident public functions for the village. The jury of the Aga Khan Award stated: "The Bridge School achieves unity at many levels: temporal unity between past and present, formal unity between traditional and modern, spatial unity between the two riverbanks, social unity between one-time rival communities, as well as unity with the future."

Der Bau verbindet zwei Teile eines Dorfes, das durch einen kleinen Fluss geteilt ist. Zwei Stahlträger überspannen den Fluss, zwischen ihnen befindet sich das Schulgebäude. Unter dem Schulgebäude verläuft eine Fußgängerbrücke für die Dorfbewohner. An beiden Seiten der Brücke lassen sich Bühnen für Theateraufführungen nutzen; zwischen den Klassenräumen liegt eine öffentliche Bibliothek. Zwar knüpft die **BRÜCKENSCHULE** nicht spezifisch an regionale Baustile an, ist jedoch offensichtlich von öffentlichem Nutzen für das Dorf. Die Jury des Aga Khan Award schrieb: „Die Bridge School schafft Einheit auf zahlreichen Ebenen: zeitliche Einheit zwischen Vergangenheit und Gegenwart, formale Einheit zwischen Tradition und Moderne, räumliche Einheit zwischen den beiden Flussufern, soziale Einheit zwischen den einst rivalisierenden [Dorf-]Gruppen und schließlich Einheit mit der Zukunft."

Cette construction relie les deux parties d'un petit village séparées par un ruisseau. Deux poutres d'acier ont été jetées entre les deux rives, sur lesquelles a été construite l'école. Une passerelle piétonnière pour les villageois a été suspendue en dessous. Deux scènes ont été aménagées en plein air de chaque côté du pont tandis qu'une bibliothèque publique était installée entre les salles de classe. Si son style n'est pas vraiment proche de celui des bâtiments de la région, l'**ÉCOLE-PONT** répond à des fonctions qui sont utiles pour le village. Le jury du prix Aga Khan a écrit : « L'école-pont réussit à atteindre à l'unité à de nombreux niveaux : unité temporelle entre le passé et le présent, unité formelle entre la tradition et la modernité, unité spatiale entre les deux rives, unité sociale entre des communautés jadis rivales, ainsi qu'unité avec le futur. »

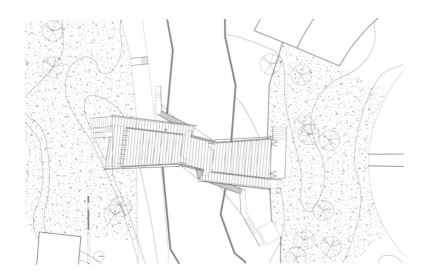

This bridge-like structure spans not only a creek but also two distinct parts of a village. Despite its location in China, it was singled out for one of the 2010 Aga Khan Awards for Architecture.

Die brückenähnliche Konstruktion überspannt nicht nur einen kleinen Fluss, sondern auch zwei separate Teile eines Dorfs. Obwohl der Bau in China liegt, wurde er 2010 für einen Aga Khan Award für Architektur ausgewählt.

La construction conçue comme un pont franchit un ruisseau et réunit les deux parties d'un village. Projet réalisé en Chine, il n'en a pas moins reçu un des prix Aga Khan d'architecture 2010.

Drawings show the simple, elegant
design of the Bridge School. In the
photo below, the light, airy architecture is seen in the context of a classroom space.

Zeichnungen veranschaulichen die
schlichte elegante Gestaltung der
Brückenschule. Auf der Ansicht unten
ist ein Klassenraum zu sehen, Teil der
leichten, luftigen Architektur.

Plans illustrant le dessin simple et
élégant de l'école en forme de pont.
Dans la photo ci-dessous, une classe
a naturellement trouvé sa place dans
cette architecture légère et aérienne.

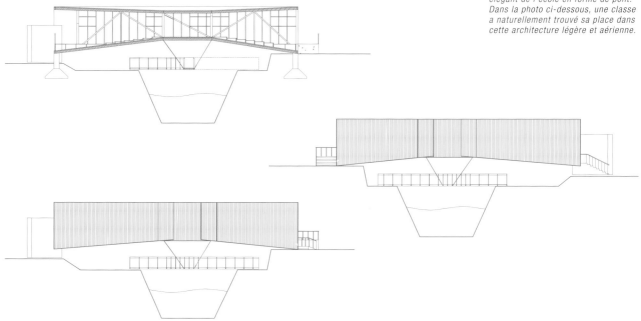

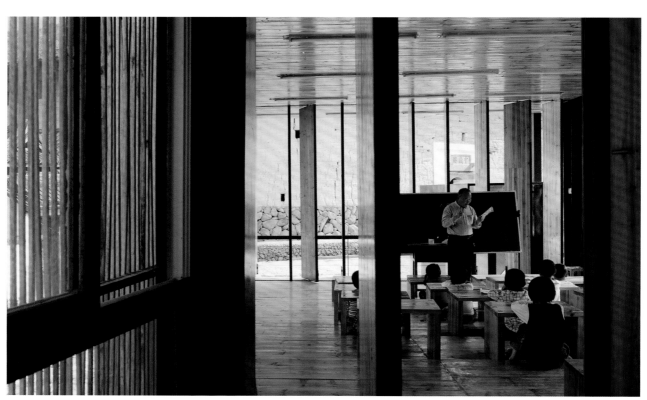

The light wooden cladding is mounted on a more solid steel structure, but the whole seems almost to float above the site and the creek.

Die leichte Holzverkleidung wurde auf eine stabilere Stahlkonstruktion aufgebracht. Nichtsdestotrotz scheint der Bau über dem Grundstück und dem Fluss zu schweben.

Le bardage léger en bois est fixé sur une structure en acier. L'ensemble paraît flotter au-dessus du sol et du ruisseau.

LIN FINN GEIPEL GIULIA ANDI

LIN
Finn Geipel Giulia Andi Architects Urbanists
Helmholtzstr. 2–9
10587 Berlin
Germany

Tel: +49 30 39 80 09 00
Fax: +49 30 39 80 09 09
E-mail: office@lin-a.com
Web: www.lin-a.com

FINN GEIPEL was born in 1958 in Stuttgart, Germany. He received his Diploma in Architecture in his native city in 1984. He worked with Bernd Hoge and Jochen Hunger in the firm Labfac Stuttgart from 1983 to 1987, and in the period 1987–2001 with Nicholas Michelin in Labfac Paris. Since 2000 he has been the head of the Laboratory for Integrative Architecture LIA at the Technische Universität Berlin. He established LIN in Berlin and Paris with Giulia Andi in 2001. **GIULIA ANDI** was born in 1972 in Rome, Italy, where she studied architecture, obtaining her diploma in 2001. She has been the manager of LIN offices in Berlin and Paris since 2001. Their work includes a house for the Kleyer family (Oldenburg, Germany, 2002–03); and the recently completed Cité du Design, a center for the exhibition and study of design in Saint-Étienne (France, 2006–09, published here). Current work includes the architectural design of four metro stations, extension of lines 4 and 12 (Paris, France, 2010–); and Quai Henri IV, Collective Housing (Paris, France, 2011–).

FINN GEIPEL wurde 1958 in Stuttgart geboren. 1984 schloss er sein Architekturstudium als Diplomingenieur in seiner Heimatstadt ab. Von 1983 bis 1987 arbeitete Finn Geipel mit Bernd Hoge und Jochen Hunger im Büro Labfac in Stuttgart, von 1987 bis 2001 mit Nicholas Michelin bei Labfac in Paris. Seit 2000 ist er Professor an der Technischen Universität Berlin. 2001 gründete er gemeinsam mit Giulia Andi das Labor für Integrative Architektur (LIA) in Berlin und Paris. **GIULIA ANDI** wurde 1972 in Rom geboren, wo sie Architektur studierte und 2001 ihr Diplom machte. Seit 2001 ist sie Geschäftsführerin der LIN-Büros in Berlin und Paris. Zu ihren Projekten zählen das Haus Kleyer (Oldenburg, 2002–03) sowie die unlängst fertig gestellte Cité du Design, ein Ausstellungs- und Studienort für Design in Saint-Étienne (Frankreich, 2006–09, hier vorgestellt). Aktuelle Projekte sind u.a. die architektonische Gestaltung von vier Metrostationen entlang der Streckenerweiterung der Linien 4 und 12 (Paris, 2010–) sowie eine genossenschaftliche Wohnanlage am Quai Henri IV (Paris, 2011–).

FINN GEIPEL, né en 1958 à Stuttgart (Allemagne), a fait ses études d'architecture dans sa ville natale (diplômé en 1984). Il travaille avec Bernd Hoge et Jochen Hunger de l'agence Labfac Stuttgart de 1983 à 1987 et, en 1987–2001, avec Nicholas Michelin à Labfac Paris. Depuis 2000, il dirige le Labor für Integrative Architektur (LIA) à l'Université technique de Berlin. Il fonde l'agence LIN à Berlin et Paris avec Giulia Andi en 2001. **GIULIA ANDI** est née en 1972 à Rome, où elle a étudié l'architecture (diplômée en 2001). Elle dirige les bureaux de LIN à Berlin et Paris depuis 2001. Parmi leurs réalisations : la maison pour la famille Kleyer (Oldenburg, Allemagne, 2002–03) ; la Cité du design, centre d'études et d'expositions sur le design à Saint-Étienne (France, 2006–09, publiée ici) ; la conception architecturale de quatre stations de métro pour l'extension des lignes 4 et 12 (Paris, 2010–) et Quai Henri IV, un immeuble de logements sociaux (Paris, 2011–).

CITÉ DU DESIGN
Saint-Étienne, France, 2006–09

Address: 3 Rue Javelin Pagnon, 42000 Saint-Étienne, France, +33 477 33 53 88, www.citedudesign.com
Area: 17 340 m². Client: Saint-Étienne Métropole. Cost: €41.5 million

Though its exterior appearance might appear monolithic during the day, the Cité du Design has a light, almost ethereal presence in these nighttime views.

Auch wenn die Cité du Design tagsüber geradezu wie ein Monolith wirkt – auf diesen nächtlichen Ansichten gibt sie sich fast durchscheinend.

Malgré une présence extérieure un peu monolithique en vision de jour, la Cité du design prend un aspect léger, presque éthéré, la nuit venue.

The **CITÉ DU DESIGN** is a new institution dedicated to design, located on the historic but formerly disused site of the national arms manufacture in Saint-Étienne. Since the functions of the building are not fully defined, the architects imagined it as an "open network, of which buildings, gardens, courtyards, and squares are the nodes." The Cité du Design is made up of several renovated historical buildings, two gardens, a large public esplanade (the Place d'Armes), and a 31-meter-high observation tower; a long, low building (200 x 32 meters), the Platine (a French word used to designate a record turntable), designed as a "place of merging and irrigation for the site," acts as a connecting switchboard articulating the different activities in the Cité du Design. The building's outer sheath is an open envelope made up of 14 000 equilateral triangles, either opaque or clear, and including photovoltaic surfaces.

DIE CITÉ DU DESIGN, eine neue Institution für Design, liegt auf dem historischen jedoch lange Zeit nicht genutzten Gelände der staatlichen Rüstungsfabriken in Saint-Étienne. Da die Funktionen des Komplexes nicht zwingend festgelegt sind, entwickelten die Architekten ein „offenes Netzwerk, dessen Gebäude, Gärten, Höfe und Plätze als Knotenpunkte dienen". Die Cité du Design umfasst mehrere historische Bauten, zwei Gärten, eine große öffentliche Esplanade (die Place d'Armes), einen 31 m hohen Aussichtsturm und ein schmales (200 x 32 m langes) Gebäude, die sogenannte Platine (frz. für Plattenspieler). Das Gebäude wurde als ein „Ort des Zusammenflie-ßens und der Befruchtung des Geländes" geplant, als verbindende Schaltzentrale, in der die verschiedenen Angebote der Cité du Design einen Ausdruck finden. Die Gebäudehülle besteht aus 14 000 gleichschenkligen Dreiecken, manche opak, manche transparent sowie aus Photovoltaiksegmenten.

LA CITÉ DU DESIGN est une nouvelle institution consacrée au design et installée sur l'ancien site de la fameuse Manufacture d'armes et cycles de Saint-Étienne. Comme les fonctions du bâtiment n'étaient pas encore complètement définies au départ, les architectes ont imaginé « un réseau ouvert dont les bâtiments, les jardins, les cours et les places constituent les points nodaux ». La Cité du design se compose de plusieurs bâtiments historiques rénovés, de deux jardins, d'une vaste esplanade publique (la place d'Armes), d'une tour d'observation de 31 mètres de haut et d'un bâtiment long de 200 x 32 mètres, la Platine, « lieu de fusion et d'irrigation du site », sorte de plate-forme de connexion articulant les diverses activités de la Cité. C'est une enveloppe ouverte construite à l'aide de 14 000 triangles équilatéraux opaques ou transparents dont certain intègrent des panneaux photovoltaïques.

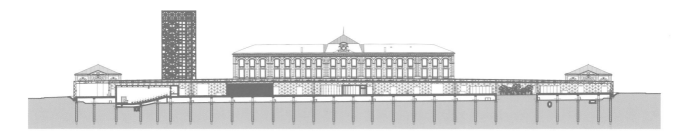

The architects play on a triangular cladding pattern that is open or closed according to interior requirements. This mixture of irregularity with basic geometric forms gives the structure an unexpected variety according to points of view.

Bei der Gebäudehaut spielen die Architekten mit einem Muster aus Dreiecken, die je nach funktionalen Anforderungen offen oder geschlossen sind. Die Mischung aus Asymmetrie und geometrischen Grundformen lässt den Bau je nach Blickwinkel überraschend facettenreich wirken.

Les architectes ont joué sur un habillage triangulaire composé de triangles ouverts et fermés selon les besoins. L'association de formes géométriques de base et de l'irrégularité de la composition apporte une variété d'aspects inattendue selon les points de vue.

Renovated historic buildings are part of the complex in which the Cité du Design is located, forming what the architects call an "open network."

Auch sanierte historische Bauten gehören zum Komplex der Cité du Design, wo den Architekten zufolge ein „offenes Netzwerk" entsteht.

Certains bâtiments anciens ont été rénovés et conservés dans le complexe qui accueille la Cité du design, pour former ce que les architectes appellent « un réseau ouvert ».

Vast column-free spaces are housed in the basic rectangular form of the Cité, seen in the plan below and in the images on this double page.

In der rechteckigen Grundform der Cité sind weitläufige stützenfreie Räume untergebracht, zu sehen im Grundriss unten und auf den Abbildungen dieser Seite.

De vastes espaces sans colonnes ont été créés à l'intérieur de l'enveloppe de forme rectangulaire, comme le montrent le plan ci-dessous et les images de cette double page.

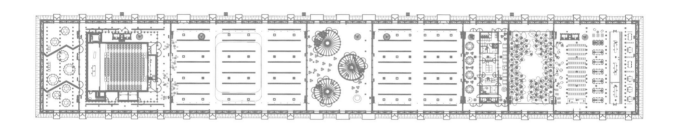

LUIS LONGHI

Longhi Architects
Calle 14 # 169, Corpac
San Isidro
Lima 27
Peru

Tel: +51 1 224 2695
E-mail: llonghi@longhiarchitect.com
Web: www.longhiarchitect.com

Born in Puno, Peru, in 1954, **LUIS LONGHI** received his B.Arch degree at the Universidad Ricardo Pama in Lima. He simultaneously obtained an M.Arch degree and a Master of Fine Arts with a major in Sculpture in 1984 at the University of Pennsylvania. As a student he met B. V. Doshi, a collaborator of both Le Corbusier and Louis Kahn, who invited him to work at his studio in Ahmedabad, India, where he designed housing systems. He then worked with a number of firms in the United States, including Gruen Associates in Los Angeles, where he began to use computers for design work in 1991. He returned to Peru in 1994 and used his experience in both sculpture and architecture to design buildings, exhibitions, and stage sets. His work includes guest housing and a spa for Eco Tourism, commissioned by the native community of Taquile Island at Lake Titicaca (Puno, 2007); Lefevre Beach House at Punta Misterio (Lima, 2009); Pachacamac House (Pachacamac, Lima, 2006–10, published here); House Q, "Floating at the desert" (Asia, 2010); House AB, Misterio Beach (Lima, 2010); and House C2, Misterio Beach (Lima, 2010). Current work includes the Club House at Misterio Beach (Lima, 2012); and the Chucuito Ecolodge, Lake Titicaca (Puno, 2013), all in Peru.

LUIS LONGHI, geboren 1954 in Puno, Peru, absolvierte seinen B.Arch an der Universidad Ricardo Pama in Lima. Parallel hierzu schloss er 1984 ein Studium an der Universität Pennsylvania mit einem M.Arch sowie einem Master of Fine Arts (Hauptfach Bildhauerei) ab. Während seines Studiums begegnete er B. V. Doshi, der sowohl mit Le Corbusier als auch mit Louis Kahn gearbeitet hatte und ihn in sein Studio in Ahmedabad in Indien, einlud, wo er Wohnanlagen entwickelte. Danach arbeitete Longhi für verschiedene Büros in den USA, darunter für Gruen Associates in Los Angeles, wo er 1991 erstmals Computer zum Entwerfen einsetzte. 1994 kehrte er nach Peru zurück und nutzte seine Erfahrung in Bildhauerei und Architektur, um Gebäude, Ausstellungen und Bühnenbilder zu entwerfen. Zu seinen Projekten zählen ein Gästehaus und Spa für nachhaltigen Tourismus, ein Auftrag der indigenen Bevölkerung auf der Insel Taquile im Titicacasee (Puno, 2007), die Casa Lefevre am Strand von Punta Misterio (Lima, 2009), die Casa Pachacamac (Pachacamac, Lima, 2006–10, hier vorgestellt), das „in der Wüste schwebende" House Q (Asia, 2010), die Casa AB, Playa Misterio (Lima, 2010) sowie die Casa C2, Playa Misterio (Lima, 2010). Laufende Projekte sind u.a. ein Clubhaus in Playa Misterio (Lima, 2012) sowie das ökologische Ferienhaus Chucuito im Titicacasee (Puno, 2013), alle in Peru.

Né à Puno (Pérou) en 1954, **LUIS LONGHI** a obtenu son B. Arch. à l'université Ricardo Pama à Lima. Dans le même temps, il a obtenu un diplôme de M. Arch. et un Master of Fine Arts spécialisé en sculpture en 1984 à l'université de Pennsylvanie. Encore étudiant, il a rencontré B. V. Doshi, collaborateur à la fois de Le Corbusier et de Louis Kahn, qui l'a invité à travailler dans son agence à Ahmedabad (Inde), où il conçoit de multiples systèmes d'habitations. Il travaille ensuite pour diverses agences américaines dont Gruen Associates à Los Angeles, où il commence à utiliser l'ordinateur en conception en 1991. Il revient au Pérou en 1994 et met son expérience d'architecte et de sculpteur à profit pour créer des bâtiments, des expositions et des décors de scène. Son œuvre, entièrement réalisée au Pérou, comprend : des chambres d'hôtes et spa pour l'écotourisme, commande de la communauté de l'île de Taquile sur le lac Titicaca (Puno, 2007) ; la maison de plage Lefevre à Punta Misterio (Lima, 2009) ; la maison Pachacamac (Pachacamac, Lima, 2006–10, publiée ici) ; la maison Q « flottant sur le désert », (Asia, 2010) ; la maison AB, plage de Misterio (Lima, 2010), et la maison C2, plage de Misterio (Lima, 2010). Actuellement, il travaille sur un projet de club-house pour la plage de Misterio (Lima, 2012) et l'écogîte Chucuito (lac Titicaca, Puno, 2013).

PACHACAMAC HOUSE

Pachacamac, Lima, Peru, 2006–10

Address: Lomas de Jatosisa I, Pachacamac, Lima, Peru
Area: 480 m². Client: not disclosed. Cost: $3.8 million
Collaboration: Hector Suasnabar, Christian Bottger, Carla Tamariz

The house emerges from its brown hillside setting as though it were a "transformation" of nature, as the architect states. Its stone cladding makes it almost indistinguishable from the background from certain angles.

Dem Architekten zufolge steigt das Haus aus dem braunen Hügelgrundstück empor wie eine „Transformation" der Natur. Dank der Steinverblendung ist es aus bestimmten Blickwinkeln fast nicht von seinem Hintergrund zu unterscheiden.

La maison émerge du flanc de la colline dont elle emprunte les couleurs ocre dans une effet de « transformation » de la nature, explique l'architecte. Vue sous certains angles, son parement de pierre la fait presque disparaître dans le paysage.

The architect describes this project as "a retirement home for a couple of philosophers." Luis Longhi goes on to set his own thoughts about the house in philosophical terms—positing that "nature is a divine creation, and is therefore perfect," and that as a consequence "any kind of intervention in nature becomes an attempt to transform perfection." From this basis he goes on to suggest that design (defined as "the act of making divine decisions") can nonetheless transform nature. For Luis Longhi: "The understanding is that architects' great responsibility is that of transforming nature, which means transforming perfection with and to perfection. In other words, the understanding of architecture as the nature of nature." All of this, of course, does not really explain the **PACHACAMAC HOUSE**, which is perhaps better understood through the drawings and photos published here.

Der Architekt beschreibt das Projekt als „Ruhesitz für ein Philosophenpaar". Seine eigenen Überlegungen zum Haus führt Luis Longhi dann auch in philosophischen Begriffen aus. So postuliert er etwa: „Die Natur ist eine göttliche Schöpfung und deshalb vollkommen", folglich sei „jede Art von Eingriff in die Natur ein Versuch, diese Vollkommenheit zu verändern". Trotz dieser Prämisse ist er dennoch der Ansicht, dass Gestaltung (die er definiert als „Akt, göttliche Entscheidungen zu treffen") die Natur verändern kann. Luis Longhi zufolge: „Es gilt die Annahme, dass es die große Verantwortung des Architekten ist, die Natur zu verändern, was bedeutet, Vollkommenheit mit und auf Vollkommenheit hin zu verändern. Anders gesagt: Architektur als die Natur der Natur zu begreifen." All dies ist natürlich nicht wirklich eine Erläuterung der **CASA PACHACAMAC**, die sich vielleicht besser anhand der hier vorgestellten Zeichnungen und Aufnahmen erschließt.

L'architecte présente son projet comme « une retraite pour un couple de philosophes ». Luis Longhi réfléchit sur la maison en termes quasi religieux : « La nature est une création divine, elle est donc parfaite », ce qui a pour conséquence que « toute sorte d'intervention sur la nature est une tentative de modifier la perfection ». À partir de là, il suggère que la conception (définie comme « l'acte de prendre des décisions divines ») peut néanmoins transformer la nature : « Il faut savoir que la grande responsabilité de l'architecte est de transformer la nature, ce qui signifie transformer la perfection par et vers la perfection. En d'autres termes, l'architecture est donc la nature de la nature. » Dessins et photos permettent peut-être une appréciation plus concrète de la **MAISON PACHACAMAC**.

The topographic site drawing corresponds to the aerial view of the house seen below, albeit from a different angle. Elements are notched into the hillside, and it is only at its extremity that the house appears as a fully geometric "entity."

Der topografische Lageplan korrespondiert mit der Luftaufnahme des Hauses unten, wenn auch aus einer etwas anderen Perspektive. Teile des Gebäudes wurden in den Hügel eingelassen, nur an dessen äußersten Ende zeichnet sich das Haus vollständig als geometrische „Einheit" ab.

La topographie du lieu correspond à la vue aérienne de la maison telle que présentée ci-dessous, sous un angle différent. Certains éléments sont traités comme des encoches découpées dans le flanc de la colline et ce n'est qu'à sa pointe que la maison devient une véritable « entité » architecturale.

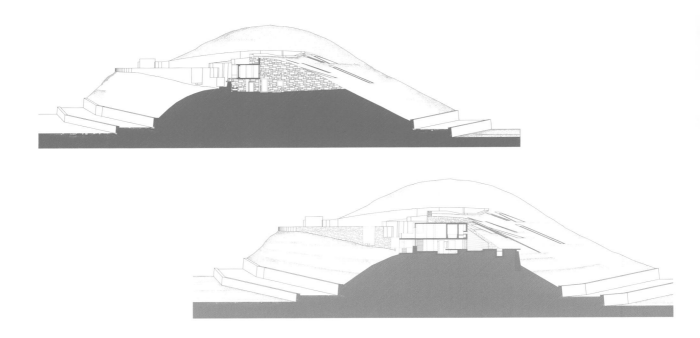

With its passages and walls angled
and notched into the hillside, the
house takes on the appearance of a
fortification from some points of view,
following the forms of the land itself.

Durch die in den Hügel eingelassenen
Korridore und Mauern wirkt das Haus
aus bestimmten Blickwinkeln wie eine
Festung und folgt den Konturen der
Erdoberfläche.

La maison, ses passages et ses murs
inclinés pris dans le flanc de la colline donne, sous certains angles,
l'impression de fortifications suivant
le profil du terrain.

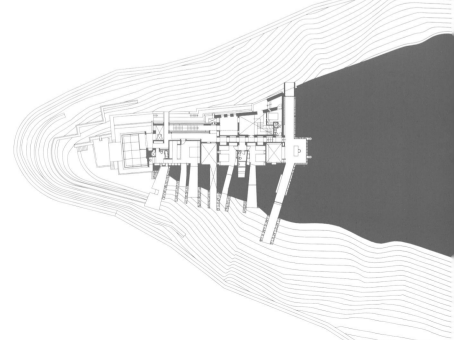

Interior images taken before the house was fully occupied have a strong, mineral appearance, with light and views mitigating the rather massive, built-in elements that form the essential internal landscape.

Innenaufnahmen zeigen das Haus vor dem endgültigen Bezug und vermitteln einen strengen, mineralischen Raumeindruck. Licht und Ausblicke mildern die Wirkung der recht massiven Einbauten ab, die die innere Landschaft des Hauses prägen.

Photos de l'intérieur prises avant que cette maison à forte présence minérale ne soit définitivement occupée. Des percements et des jeux de lumière atténuent l'effet massif des éléments intégrés constitutifs du paysage intérieur.

LOT-EK

LOT-EK
55 Little West 12th Street
New York, NY 10014
USA

Tel: +1 212 255 9326
Fax: +1 212 255 2988
E-mail: info@lot-ek.com
Web: www.lot-ek.com

ADA TOLLA was born in 1964 in Potenza, Italy. She received her M.Arch from the Architecture Faculty of the "Federico II" University (Naples, 1982–89) and did postgraduate studies at Columbia University (New York, 1990–91). She is one of the two founding partners of LOT-EK, created in New York in 1993. She is currently an Associate Professor at Columbia University in the Graduate School of Architecture, Planning, and Preservation. **GIUSEPPE LIGNANO** was born in Naples, Italy, in 1963. He also received his M.Arch degree from the "Federico II" University (1982–89) and did postgraduate studies at Columbia at the same time as Ada Tolla. He is the other founding partner of LOT-EK and is currently an Associate Professor at Columbia University in the Graduate School of Architecture, Planning, and Preservation. Their temporary work includes "X-Static Process" (Deitch Projects, New York, 2003); Uniqlo Container Stores (New York, 2006); the Theater for One (Princeton University, Princeton, New Jersey, 2007); PUMACity (Alicante, Spain, and Boston, Massachusetts, 2008); and PUMA DDSM (South Street Seaport, New York, 2010); together with the permanent APAP OpenSchool (Anyang, South Korea, 2010, published here), all in the USA unless stated otherwise.

ADA TOLLA wurde 1964 in Potenza, Italien, geboren. Sie absolvierte ihren M.Arch an der Fakultät für Architektur der Universität Federico II (Neapel, 1982–89) sowie ein Aufbaustudium an der Columbia University (New York, 1990–91). Sie ist eine der zwei Gründungspartner von LOT-EK, gegründet 1993 in New York. Aktuell lehrt Ada Tolla als außerordentliche Professorin am Graduiertenprogramm für Architektur, Stadtplanung und Denkmalschutz der Columbia University. **GIUSEPPE LIGNANO** wurde 1963 in Neapel geboren. Auch er absolvierte seinen M.Arch an der Universität Federico II (1982–89) sowie ein Aufbaustudium an der Columbia, zeitgleich mit Ada Tolla. Er ist der zweite Gründungspartner von LOT-EK und aktuell außerordentlicher Professor am Graduiertenprogramm für Architektur, Stadtplanung und Denkmalschutz der Columbia University. Zu den temporären Projekten des Teams zählen *X-Static Process* (Deitch Projects, New York, 2003), Uniqlo Container Stores (New York, 2006), das Theater for One (Princeton University, Princeton, New Jersey, 2007), PUMACity (Alicante, Spanien, und Boston, Massachusetts, 2008) und PUMA DDSM (South Street Seaport, New York, 2010) sowie der permanente Bau der APAP OpenSchool (Anyang, Südkorea, 2010, hier vorgestellt), alle in den USA, sofern nicht anders angegeben.

ADA TOLLA, née en 1964 à Potenza (Italie), a obtenu son M. Arch. à la faculté d'architecture de l'université Federico II de Naples (1982–89) et a effectué des études supérieures à l'université Columbia (New York, 1990–91). Elle est l'une des deux associés fondateurs de l'agence LOT-EK créée à New York en 1993. Elle est actuellement professeure associée à l'université Columbia (Graduate School of Architecture, Planning and Preservation). **GIUSEPPE LIGNANO**, né à Naples en 1963, a également obtenu son M. Arch. à l'université Federico II (1982–89) et étudié à Columbia en même temps qu'Ada Tolla, avec laquelle il a fondé LOT-EK. Il est lui aussi professeur associé à Columbia (Graduate School of Architecture, Planning and Preservation). Parmi leurs projets d'architecture temporaire, tous aux États-Unis sauf mention contraire : *X-Static Process* (Deitch Projects, New York, 2003) ; Uniqlo Container Stores (New York, 2006) ; le Theater for One (université de Princeton, New Jersey, 2007) ; PUMACity (Alicante, Espagne, et Boston, Massachusetts, 2008) ; PUMA DDSM (South Street Seaport, New York, 2010) et le bâtiment permanent de l'OpenSchool APAP (Anyang, Corée du Sud, 2010, publiée ici).

APAP OPENSCHOOL

Anyang, South Korea, 2010

Address: Hakwoon Park, Anyang, South Korea
Area: 241 m² (121 m² inside). Client: Kyong Park, Artistic Director of APAP 2010, Anyang Public Art Program
Cost: not disclosed. Collaboration: Tommy Manual (Project Architect)

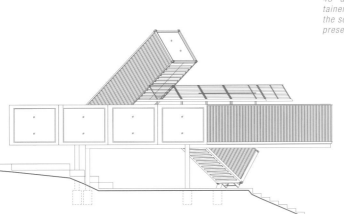

Lifted off the ground or perched at a 45° angle, the eight shipping containers that form the basic body of the school form a strong, graphic presence in their green setting.

Die über dem Boden aufgeständerten bzw. im 45°-Winkel schrägstehenden acht Schiffscontainer, die den zentralen Baukörper der Schule bilden, behaupten sich als ausdrucksstarke, grafische Präsenz in ihrem grünen Umfeld.

Surélevés par rapport au sol ou inclinés à 45°, les huit conteneurs qui constituent l'essentiel de la structure affirment une forte présence graphique dans leur cadre de verdure.

As they have in earlier work, LOT-EK conceived this **OPENSCHOOL** structure on the basis of shipping containers. The architects explain: "Eight shipping containers are skewed at a 45-degree angle and combined in a fishbone pattern to generate a large arrow-like volume that hovers three meters over the landscape. The structure is strategically placed over Hakwoon Park pedestrian walkway at the city level, right on the edge of the drop to the river bank. This marks the territory as a focal place of gathering, resting, and viewing." A public amphitheater is formed by the footprint of the structure at ground level, while a large multipurpose space occupies part of the second level. Peep holes offer views out to the surrounding landscape, while an interior stairway leads to the top-level deck overlooking the Anyang River. The client for this project, Kyong Park, is the former Director of the Storefront for Art and Architecture in New York.

Wie schon bei früheren Projekten, entwickelte LOT-EK den Bau für die **OPENSCHOOL** auf Basis von Frachtcontainern. Die Architekten erklären: „Acht Container wurden schräg in einem 45°-Winkel zu einem Fischgrätmuster angeordnet und bilden einen pfeilartigen Baukörper, der 3 m über dem Boden schwebt. Das Bauwerk wurde strategisch über einem Fußweg im Hakwoon Park, auf Augenhöhe mit der Stadt platziert, unmittelbar am Abhang zum Flussufer. Dies macht den Standort zum zentralen Ort der Begegnung, der Ruhe und der Aussicht." Zu ebener Erde entsteht durch den Umriss des Gebäudes ein Amphitheater, die zweite Ebene wird als Mehrzweckraum genutzt. Kleine Fassadenöffnungen ermöglichen den Blick in die Landschaft. Eine Treppe im Gebäude führt zur Dachterrasse mit Blick über den Anyang. Auftraggeber des Projekts ist Kyong Park, der ehemalige Direktor der Storefront for Art and Architecture in New York.

Comme pour de précédents projets, LOT-EK a conçu pour son **OPENSCHOOL** une structure en conteneurs maritimes. « Huit conteneurs d'expédition inclinés à 45° et montés en chevrons créent un vaste volume en forme de flèche à trois mètres au-dessus du sol. La construction est stratégiquement suspendue au-dessus d'une allée piétonnière du parc de Hakwoon, en haut de la pente menant à la rivière, au même niveau que la ville. Elle s'impose ainsi sur le site comme un lieu de rencontre, de repos et de contemplation. » L'emprise de la structure au niveau du sol a été aménagée en amphithéâtre et un vaste volume polyvalent occupe une partie de l'étage. De petites ouvertures offrent des perspectives sur le paysage environnant. À l'intérieur, un escalier conduit à la terrasse en toiture qui domine la rivière Anyang. Le client de ce projet, Kyong Park, est l'ancien directeur de la galerie new-yorkaise Storefront for Art and Architecture.

Bright and cheerful, the interiors make use of the basic industrial vocabulary of the shipping containers, but render the spaces open and easy to use.

Die fröhlichen hellen Innenräume spielen mit der industriellen Formensprache der Frachtcontainer. Dennoch wirken die Räume offen und nutzerfreundlich.

Lumineux, l'engageant intérieur renvoie au vocabulaire industriel des conteneurs d'expédition, mais dans un cadre d'espaces ouverts et d'utilisation aisée.

Aside from the sharp angle of parts of the structure, its bright yellow color and powerful graphics give an exciting dynamic appearance, which is carried over into the interiors seen on the right.

Abgesehen von der Spitzwinkligkeit einzelner Gebäudeteile tragen auch das leuchtende Gelb und die auffälligen grafischen Elemente zur faszinierenden Dynamik des Gebäudes bei. Sie spiegelt sich auch in den Innenräumen rechts.

En dehors de la forte inclinaison de certains éléments, le jaune vif et les interventions graphiques marquées confèrent à l'ensemble un aspect dynamique, qui se retrouve dans les aménagements intérieurs (à droite).

GURJIT SINGH MATHAROO

Matharoo Associates
24-E Capital Commercial Centre, Ashram Road
Ahmedabad
380 009 Gujarat
India

Tel: + 91 79 2657 7757
Mobile: +91 98 7954 3505
E-mail: studio@matharooassociates.com
Web: www.matharooassociates.com

GURJIT SINGH MATHAROO was born in Ajmer, Rajasthan, India, in 1966. He received a Diploma in Architecture from the Center for Environmental Planning and Technology (CEPT, Ahmedabad, India, 1989). He worked for one year in the office of Michele Arnaboldi and Giorgio Guschetti in Ticino, Switzerland, before creating his own firm, Matharoo Associates in Ahmedabad in 1991. The firm, which has a staff of 15 persons has projects in the area of architecture, interior design, product design, and structural design. His work includes the Prathama Blood Centre (Ahmedabad. 2000); the Parag Shah Residence (Surat, 2005); the Parents' House (Ajmer, Rajasthan, 2010); as well as the Net House (Ahmedabad, 2009–10, published here), all in India.

GURJIT SINGH MATHAROO wurde 1966 in Ajmer (Rajasthan, Indien) geboren. Er erwarb sein Architekturdiplom am Center for Environmental Planning and Technology (CEPT, Ahmedabad, 1989). Nachdem er ein Jahr lang im Büro von Michele Arnaboldi und Giorgio Guscetti im Tessin (Schweiz) gearbeitet hatte, gründete er 1991 sein eigenes Büro, Matharoo Associates, in Ahmedabad. Das Büro beschäftigt derzeit 15 Mitarbeiter und realisiert Projekte in den Bereichen Architektur, Innenarchitektur, Produktdesign und Baustatik. Zu Marathoos Arbeiten zählen u.a. das Prathama Blood Centre (Ahmedabad, 2000); das Parag Shah Anwesen (Surat, 2005); das Parents' House (Ajmer, Rajasthan, 2010) sowie das Net House (Ahmedabad, 2009–10, hier vorgestellt), alle in Indien.

GURJIT SINGH MATHAROO, né à Ajmer (Rajasthan, Inde) en 1966, est diplômé d'architecture du Centre de planification et de technologies environnementales (CEPT, Ahmedabad, 1989). Il a travaillé un an dans l'agence de Michele Arnaboldi et Giorgio Guscetti à Ticino (Suisse), avant de créer sa propre structure, Matharoo Associates, à Ahmedabad en 1991. L'agence qui compte 15 collaborateurs intervient dans les domaines de l'architecture, de l'architecture intérieure, du design produit et de la conception structurelle. Parmi ses réalisations, toutes en Inde : le Centre du sang Prathama (Ahmedabad, 2000) ; la résidence Parag Shah (Surat, 2005) ; la maison des Parents (Ajmer, Rajasthan, 2010) et la maison Net (Ahmedabad, 2009–10, publiée ici).

NET HOUSE

Ahmedabad, India, 2009–10

Area: 200 m². Client: Dr. Urmish Chudgar
Cost: $560 400

The architect uses the word "Net" in the sense of "clear of all else, subject to no further deductions." The **NET HOUSE** provides a square twelve-meter space without columns and has a monolithic 90-ton concrete slab set on an elaborate steel frame. The skin of the house is made up of net shutters, providing a play on the different meanings of the name of the house. The sliding mosquito nets, roll-up blinds, and folding glass panels allow residents to adjust their level of privacy or the openness to nature of each space. A thin (15-centimeter) pipe surrounded by a glass stairway draws monsoon rainwater from the roof into a fountain that empties into a 1.4-million-liter underground storage tank. The net-enclosed space on the upper floor has a gazebo, and allows for sunbathing or the practice of yoga. Aside from the house there is a 200-square-meter car park and a 50-square-meter storage block.

Der Architekt verwendet das englische Wort „net" im Sinne von „ohne alles andere, nicht weiter reduzierbar". Das **NET HOUSE** besteht aus einem 12 m langen, quadratischen, stützenfreien Raum mit einer monolitischen, 90 t schweren Betonplatte, die auf ein sorgfältig ausgearbeitetes Stahlskelett gesetzt wurde. Die Außenhaut besteht aus netzbespannten Rahmen, die ein Spiel mit den verschiedenen Bedeutungen des Hausnamens bilden. Die verschiebbaren Moskitonetze sowie aufrollbare Jalousien und aufklappbare Glastafeln ermöglichen es den Bewohnern, in jedem Raum selbst das gewünschte Maß an Abschirmung oder Öffnung zur Natur zu regeln. Ein enges Rohr von 15 cm Durchmesser leitet im verglasten Treppenhaus das Wasser der Monsunregen vom Dach in einen Brunnen, der sich in einen unterirdischen, 1,4 Mio. l fassenden Tank entleert. In dem von Netzen umgebenen Bereich im Obergeschoss befindet sich auch eine Laube, wo man Sonnenbäder nehmen oder sich seinen Yogaübungen widmen kann. Neben dem Wohnbau gehören auch ein 200 m² großer Parkplatz und ein 50 m² großer Lagerraum zum Komplex.

L'architecte utilise le terme anglais de « net » dans le sens non pas de filet, mais de « dégagé de toute autre chose, échappant à toute déduction ». La **MAISON NET** offre un espace carré de douze mètres de côté sans colonnes, reposant sur une dalle monolithique de béton de 90 tonnes appuyée sur une structure en acier. La peau de la maison est faite de grands volets tendus d'un maillage fin, un filet (double jeu sur le nom de la maison). Des moustiquaires coulissantes, des stores enroulables et des panneaux de verre repliables permettent aux habitants de régler, pour chaque volume, le niveau d'intimité ou d'ouverture sur la nature souhaité. Au centre de l'escalier de verre, un petit tuyau de 15 centimètres de diamètre récupère l'eau de la mousson de la toiture qu'il dirige vers une fontaine se déversant dans un réservoir souterrain de 1400 mètres cubes. Entouré de filets, l'espace avec belvédère situé au niveau supérieur permet de prendre des bains de soleil ou de pratiquer le yoga. Une annexe de stockage de 50 mètres carrés et un parking de 200 mètres carrés sont situés à proximité.

At a certain remove, as in the photo above, the Net House might be taken for an elegant industrial building, with its carefully measured square and rectangular elements.

Aus gewisser Distanz, wie auf der Ansicht oben, könnte man das Net House mit seinen quadratischen und rechteckigen Stilelementen für einen eleganten Industriebau halten.

Vue d'une certaine distance, comme sur la photo ci-dessus, cette maison faite de modules carrés et rectangulaires pourrait se confondre avec un bâtiment industriel élégant.

The Net House is made with a concrete slab and steel-and-concrete
space frame structure. The mosquito
net seen below served as inspiration
for the house.

*Konstruktiv gesehen besteht das Net
House aus Betonplatten in einem
Stahl- und Beton-Raumfachwerk. Das
Moskitonetz unten im Bild inspirierte
den Bau.*

*La maison Net est constituée d'une
ossature à entretoises d'écartement
en acier et béton reposant sur une
dalle de béton. La moustiquaire ci-
dessous a servi d'inspiration au projet.*

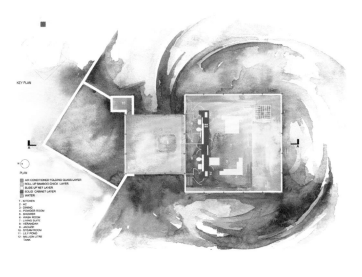

MAURER UNITED

Maurer United Architects (MUA)
PO Box 3038
6202 NA Maastricht
The Netherlands

Tel: +31 43 409 81 20
Fax: +31 43 325 53 07
E-mail: office@maurerunited.com
Web: www.maurerunited.com

MARC MAURER was born in Eindhoven, the Netherlands, in 1969. He studied architecture at Eindhoven University of Technology, obtaining an M.Sc degree in Architecture and Urbanism in 1995. **NICOLE MAURER-LEMMENS** was born in 1969 in Slenaken, the Netherlands. She studied architecture at the Antwerp Academie voor de Schone Kunsten (Belgium) for one year. In 1998 she received her Master's in Architecture and Urbanism at the Eindhoven University of Technology and created Maurer United with Marc Maurer the same year. Their work includes the Witch House (Heerlen, The Netherlands, 2009); Coolhouse (Heerlen, The Netherlands, 2009); Indemann Watchtower (Inden, Germany, 2009, published here); the Medular Pavilion, an outdoor "social space" (Shenzhen, China, 2009); and the Dutch Pavilion for Guangzhou Design Week (Guangzhou, China, 2010).

MARC MAURER wurde 1969 in Eindhoven, Niederlande, geboren. Sein Architekturstudium an der Technischen Universität Eindhoven schloss er 1995 mit einem M.Sc in Architektur und Städteplanung ab. **NICOLE MAURER-LEMMENS** wurde 1969 in Slenaken, Niederlande, geboren. Sie studierte ein Jahr lang Architektur an der Academie voor de Schone Kunsten in Antwerpen (Belgien). 1998 absolvierte sie ihren Master in Architektur und Städtebau an der TU Eindhoven und gründete im selben Jahr mit Marc Maurer das Büro Maurer United. Zu ihren Projekten zählen das Witch House (Heerlen, Niederlande, 2009), das Coolhouse (Heerlen, Niederlande, 2009), der Aussichtsturm Indemann (Inden, Deutschland, 2009, hier vorgestellt), der Medular-Pavillon, ein „Gemeinschaftsort" unter freiem Himmel (Shenzhen, China, 2009) und der niederländische Pavillon für die Design Week in Guangzhou (Guangzhou, China, 2010).

MARC MAURER, né à Eindhoven (Pays-Bas) en 1969, a étudié l'architecture à l'Université de technologie de cette ville et obtenu son M. Sc. en architecture et urbanisme en 1995. **NICOLE MAURER-LEMMENS**, née en 1969 à Slenaken (Pays-Bas), a étudié à l'académie des beaux-arts d'Anvers (Belgique) pendant un an. Elle a obtenu un mastère en architecture et urbanisme de l'Université de technologie d'Eindhoven en 1998 et a fondé Maurer United avec Marc Maurer la même année. Parmi leurs réalisations : la maison de la Sorcière (Heerlen, Pays-Bas, 2009) ; la Coolhouse (Heerlen, Pays-Bas, 2009) ; la tour d'observation Indemann (Inden, Allemagne, 2009, publiée ici) ; le pavillon Medular, « espace social » en plein air (Shenzhen, Chine, 2009) et le Pavillon néerlandais pour la semaine du design de Guangzhou (Guangzhou, Chine, 2010).

INDEMANN WATCHTOWER

Inden, Germany, 2009

Address: Goltsteinkuppe, Inden, Germany, +49 2465/39–0, www.inden.de
Area: 860 m². Client: Gemeinde Inden / G.I.S. Gesellschaft für Industrieservice GmbH, Düren
Cost: €2.5 million

The **INDEMANN WATCHTOWER** offers a broad view on a 4500-hectare mining area in Germany. It is located near the A4 highway that links Aachen and Cologne. The area is slated to be transformed into a water sports and recreation area by 2030. The 36-meter-high steel tower "has the shape of an enormous robot" according to the architects. Its façade carries 40 000 LED lights that play uploaded animations during the night. This is the first such large-scale LED installation completed in Europe. Described as a piece of "social media architecture" this work can also be assimilated to large-scale public sculpture. It is also intended to mark the transition from an industrial to an electronic society.

Der **AUSSICHTSTURM INDEMANN** bietet weiten Ausblick über eine 4500 ha große Tagebau-Region in Deutschland. Der Turm liegt unweit der A4 zwischen Aachen und Köln. Bis 2030 ist die Umgestaltung der Region in ein Wassersport- und Naherholungsgebiet vorgesehen. Der 36 m hohe Stahlturm „hat die Form eines gigantischen Roboters", so die Architekten. Seine Fassade ist mit 40 000 LEDs ausgestattet, die nachts programmierte Animationen abspielen. Es ist die erste LED-Großinstallation dieser Art in Europa. Das Projekt will als „soziale Medienarchitektur" verstanden sein und lässt sich zur öffentlichen Großskulptur umfunktionieren. Darüber hinaus signalisiert der Bau den Übergang der Industrie- zur elektronischen Gesellschaft.

La **TOUR D'OBSERVATION INDEMANN** offre une vue panoramique sur une ancienne zone d'exploitation minière de 4500 hectares, à proximité de l'autoroute Aix-la-Chapelle-Cologne. La zone devrait être nettoyée et transformée en base de sports nautiques et de loisirs en 2030. La tour en acier de 36 mètres de haut « a la forme d'un gigantesque robot », expliquent ses architectes. Sa façade est équipée de 40 000 DEL qui produisent en nocturne des animations lumineuses. C'est la première installation de DEL de cette envergure en Europe. Présentée comme une œuvre d'« architecture médiasociale », elle fait également figure de sculpture publique monumentale marquant la transition entre la société industrielle et la société électronique.

With its imposing and yet relatively open metallic structure, the Watch tower has an industrial feel that is appropriate for its position near a former mining area.

Mit seiner beeindruckenden und doch relativ offenen Metallkonstruktion wirkt der Aussichtsturm industriell. Recht passend, angesichts seines Standorts unweit eines ehemaligen Tagebaugebiets.

Constituée d'une structure métallique imposante et relativement ouverte, la tour d'observation affiche son inspiration industrielle, adaptée à sa situation à proximité d'anciennes exploitations minières.

Colored lighting and the LED banks of the tower give an animated appearance at night (above and right page). Drawings show the robot-like appearance of the structure and its assembly.

Durch das farbige Licht der LED-Leuchten ist der Turm nachts eine dynamisch Erscheinung (oben und rechte Seite). Auf den Zeichnungen wird die roboterähnliche Anmutung der Konstruktion und deren Montage ersichtlich.

La nuit, de puissants éclairages de couleur et des batteries de DEL animent la présence de la tour (ci-dessus et page de droite). Les plans illustrent son aspect de « robot » et son assemblage.

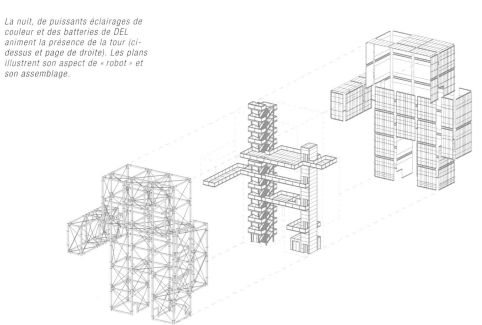

GIANCARLO MAZZANTI

Mazzanti & Arquitectos
Calle 29 #6-94
Bogotá 110311
Colombia

Tel: +57 1 340 6564
E-mail: mazzanti.arquitectos@gmail.com
Web: www.giancarlomazzanti.com

GIANCARLO MAZZANTI SIERRA was born in 1963 in Barranquilla, Colombia. He received a Diploma in Architecture from the Javeriana University (Bogotá, 1989) and completed postgraduate studies in the history and theory of architecture at the University of Florence (Italy, 1999). Built work includes the International Convention Center (Medellín, 2002); Santo Domingo Library Park (Medellín, 2006–07); and the Ordoñez House (Bogotá, 2007). His recent and current work includes Four Sports Coliseums for the South American Games (Medellín, 2009–10, published here); El Porvenir Social Kindergarten (Bogotá, 2008–09, also published here); Tulio Ospina Park (Medellín, 2008, under development); and the Museum of Modern Art of Barranquilla (Barranquilla, 2008, also under development), all in Colombia. Juan Felipe Mesa Rico, with whom Mazzanti was associated for the Four Sports Coliseums project, was born in 1975 in Medellín, Colombia. He studied architecture at the Universidad Pontificia Bolivariana (Medellín, 1993–98) and received his M.Arch degree from the Universidad Politécnica de Cataluña (UPC Barcelona, 1999–2000). He founded Plan B Arquitectos in 2000.

GIANCARLO MAZZANTI SIERRA wurde 1963 in Barranquilla, Kolumbien, geboren. Seinen Diplomabschluss in Architektur absolvierte er an der Javeriana-Universität (Bogotá, 1989); er schloss einen Aufbaustudiengang in Architekturgeschichte und -theorie an der Universität Florenz ab (Italien, 1999). Zu seinen realisierten Projekten zählen das Internationale Messezentrum (Medellín, 2002), der Santo Domingo Library Park (Medellín, 2006–07) sowie das Haus Ordoñez (Bogotá, 2007). Jüngere und aktuelle Projekte sind u.a. Vier Arenen für die Südamerikaspiele (Medellín, 2009–10, hier vorgestellt), Sozialkindergarten El Porvenir (Bogotá, 2008–09, ebenfalls hier vorgestellt), Tulio Ospina Park (Medellín, 2008, in Arbeit) sowie das Museum für Moderne Kunst in Barranquilla (2008, ebenfalls in Arbeit), alle in Kolumbien. Juan Felipe Mesa Rico, mit dem Mazzanti an den Vier Arenen zusammenarbeitete, wurde 1975 in Medellín, Kolumbien, geboren. Er studierte Architektur an der Universidad Pontificia Bolivariana (Medellín, 1993–98) und absolvierte seinen M.Arch an der Universidad Politécnica de Cataluña (UPC Barcelona, 1999–2000). 2000 gründete er Plan B Arquitectos.

GIANCARLO MAZZANTI SIERRA, né en 1963 à Barranquilla (Colombie), est diplômé en architecture de l'Université Javeriana (Bogotá, 1989) et a achevé ses études supérieures en histoire et théorie de l'architecture à l'université de Florence (Italie, 1999). Parmi ses réalisations : le Centre international de congrès (Medellín, 2002) ; le parc de la bibliothèque de Santo Domingo (Medellín, 2006–07) et la maison Ordoñez (Bogotá, 2007). Plus récemment, il a réalisé les Colisées des quatre sports pour les Jeux sud-américains (Medellín, 2009–10, publiés ici) ; le jardin d'enfants El Porvenir Social (Bogotá, 2008–09, également publié ici) ; le parc Tulio Ospina (Medellín, 2008, en cours) et le Musée d'art moderne de Barranquilla (Barranquilla, 2008, en cours). Juan Felipe Mesa Rico, avec lequel Mazzanti était associé pour le projet des Colisées, est né en 1975 à Medellín (Colombie). Il a étudié l'architecture à l'Universidad Pontificia Bolivariana (Medellín, 1993–98) et a passé son M. Arch. à l'Université polytechnique de Catalogne (UPC Barcelona, 1999–2000). Il a fondé l'agence Plan B Arquitectos en 2000.

FOUR SPORTS COLISEUMS FOR THE SOUTH AMERICAN GAMES

Medellín, Colombia, 2009–10

Address: Cr. 70, Colombia Avenue, Medellín, Colombia
Area: 45 760 m². Client: INDER. Cost: $55 million
Collaboration: Felipe Mesa

According to the architects, this project was conceived as a "new geography in the elongated Aburrá Valley, midway between Cerro Nutibara and Cerro El Volador. It is a building that seems to be another mountain in the city." The undulating steel structure allows filtered sunlight into its interior. Outdoor public space and sporting venues are conceived in a continuous manner, although each of the four facilities can function separately. The architects speak of a "skeleton" as being the organizational system of a complex that they describe in terms of physiognomy: "columns, bases, beams, roofs, strips, canals, interior space." With this project and earlier work, Mazzanti and Mesa demonstrate clearly that there is an inventive school of contemporary architecture at work in Colombia today.

Die Architekten planten das Projekt als „neue Geografie im langgestreckten Aburrá-Tal, auf halbem Weg zwischen Cerro Nutibara und Cerro El Volador. Es ist ein Bauwerk, das wie ein weiterer Berg mitten in der Stadt wirkt." Die wellenförmige Stahlkonstruktion lässt gefiltertes Sonnenlicht ins Innere fallen. Obwohl Außenbereiche und Sportanlagen organisch ineinander übergehen, können alle vier Anlagen separat genutzt werden. Die Architekten sprechen von einem „Skelett" als organisierendes System des Komplexes, den sie als Physiognomie beschreiben: „Säulen, Basen, Träger, Dächer, Streifen, Kanäle, Innenräume". Mit diesem und früheren Entwürfen beweisen Mazzanti und Mesa ohne Frage, dass es heute eine Schule zeitgenössischer Architekten in Kolumbien gibt, die höchst erfinderisch arbeitet.

Ce projet est « une nouvelle géographie insérée dans l'étroite vallée d'Aburra, à mi-chemin entre Cerro Nutibara et Cerro El Volador. Le bâtiment semble être une montagne supplémentaire intégrée au panorama urbain », expliquent les architectes. Sa structure en acier de forme ondulée permet de filtrer le soleil vers l'intérieur. Les espaces publics extérieurs et les salles de compétitions sportives sont traités en continu, bien que chaque installation puisse fonctionner séparément. Les architectes évoquent une organisation en « squelette » qu'ils décrivent en termes architecturaux de « colonnes, socles, poutres, toits, bandeaux, canaux, espaces intérieurs ». Dans ce projet et d'autres réalisations antérieures, Mazzanti et Mesa montrent qu'il existe aujourd'hui en Colombie une école d'architecture contemporaine créative.

As the drawings below show, together with photos of the complex, there is a relation between the hills and mountains around Medellín and the forms of the roofs.

Wie Zeichnungen (unten) und Aufnahmen des Komplexes belegen, ergeben sich Korrespondenzen zwischen den Bergen um Medellín und der Form der Dächer.

L'illustration ci-dessous et les photographies du complexe montrent la relation formelle qui existe entre les toitures et les montagnes entourant Medellín.

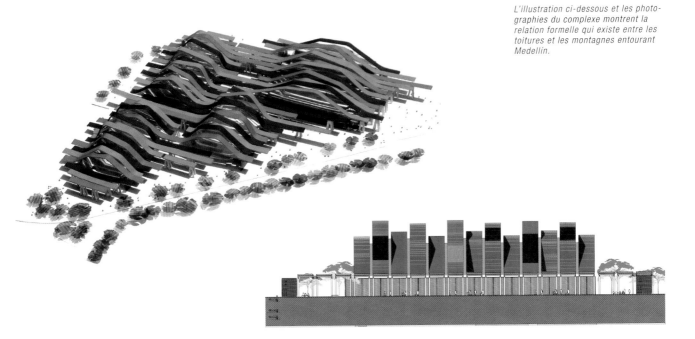

The irregularity of the roof profiles, as seen in the image above and the drawings below, confirms the mountain metaphor used by the architect, in this scheme that generates vast covered spaces (right page).

Die unregelmäßigen Dachprofile, zu sehen auf Foto (oben) und Zeichnungen (unten), unterstreichen das vom Architekten gewählte Bergmotiv. Der Komplex umfasst auch riesige überdachte Bereiche wie rechts im Bild.

Comme le montre la photo ci-dessus ou les dessins ci-dessous, l'irrégularité voulue du profil des toits est une métaphore des montagnes avoisinantes, qui permet de dégager de vastes espaces couverts (à droite).

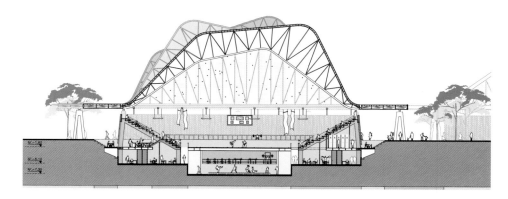

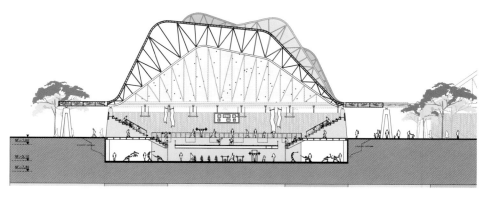

The arching, articulated roofs of the facilities are the clear result of the "mountain" or geological profile adapted for the exterior. Drawings show the Volleyball Coliseum.

Die gewölbte, ausdrucksstarke Dachkonstruktion des Komplexes ergibt sich offenkundig aus dem geologischen „Bergprofil" des Außenbaus. Zeichnungen zeigen die Volleyballhalle.

À l'intérieur, les arcs des toits et leur articulation résultent du profil géologique « montagneux » de l'aspect extérieur. Les plans sont ceux de la salle de volley-ball.

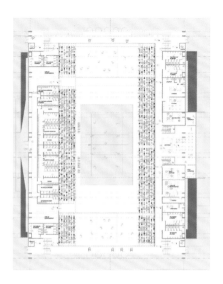
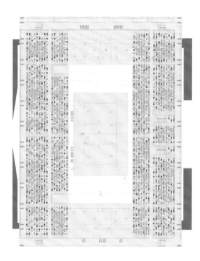

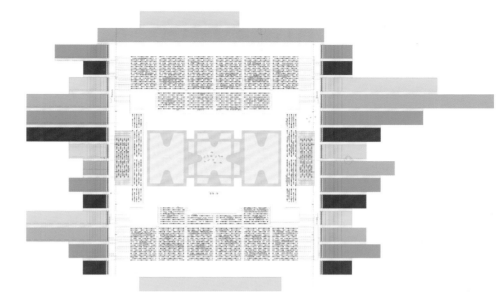

The Basketball Coliseum allows for a large number of spectators, as can be seen in the image below. A drawing of the first floor of the facility is seen above.

Die Basketballhalle bietet zahlreichen Besuchern Platz, wie auf dem Foto unten zu sehen ist. Oben ein Grundriss des Erdgeschosses.

La salle de basket-ball peut accueillir un très grand nombre de spectateurs comme le montre l'image ci-dessous. Ci-dessus, plan du rez-de-chaussée de la salle.

EL PORVENIR SOCIAL KINDERGARTEN

Bogotá, Colombia, 2008–09

Address: Calle 49 s – Kr. 92, Bogotá, Colombia
Area: 2100 m². Client: Secretaria de Integración Social. Cost: not disclosed

The architect describes this school as being based on a modular system that can be repeated with "multiple options." Rotatable classroom modules are "planned like a chain construction and each module is related to the next, generating spaces that enrich the journey and the uses of the school, forming yards, streets, and subspaces." The system also provides for ways to adapt the edges of the project to different sites and lot forms. "Public" modules are situated at the periphery of the school in order to allow other public uses—these include areas for administration, general services, a kitchen, and a dining room. In this instance, the structure, defined as a curtain-walled, laser-cut lattice metal container on a base that serves as a balcony, faces the city in a generous and open way.

Den Architekten zufolge basiert der Entwurf des Kindergartens auf einem modularen System, das sich in einer „Vielzahl von Varianten" wiederholen lässt. Rotierbare Raummodule lassen sich „wie eine Kettenkonstruktion planen. Jedes Modul nimmt Bezug auf das nächste, sodass Räume entstehen, die den Kindergarten bereichern – als Reise ebenso wie funktional –, indem sie Höfe, Straßen und Nebenbereiche bilden." Das System lässt sich an die Abmessungen unterschiedlicher Baugrundstücke anpassen. „Öffentliche" Module liegen in den äußeren Zonen der Komplexes, um auch anderweitige öffentliche Nutzungen zu ermöglichen – hierzu gehören Bereiche für die Verwaltung, Haustechnik, eine Küche und ein Speisesaal. Hier wurde der Bau als Curtain-Wall-Konstruktion aus lasergeschnittenem Metall realisiert; der Sockel dient zugleich als Terrasse und öffnet sich großzügig zur Stadt.

Ce jardin d'enfants a été réalisé à partir d'un principe modulaire qui peut se répéter sous la forme de « multiples options ». Les modules de salles de classe pivotent et « s'organisent comme un jeu de construction, chacun se reliant au suivant pour créer des espaces qui enrichissent les usages et les fonctions de l'établissement par la création de cours, de rues et de sous-espaces ». Ce système s'adapte aisément aux limites d'un terrain et aux différents types de sites et de parcelles. Les modules « publics » – bureaux administratifs, services généraux, cuisine, réfectoire – sont implantés en périphérie pour permettre un usage public diversifié. La structure, qui pourrait se définir comme un conteneur en lattis de métal découpé au laser sur une base qui fait office de balcon, s'ouvre généreusement sur la ville.

Within its circular heart, the school is formed from individually placed rectangular units, a new departure from typical school design, or, indeed, from the neighboring structures seen in the aerial view above.

Der Kindergarten besteht aus individuell platzierten rechteckigen Baukörpern, eingeschrieben in sein kreisrundes „Herz". Es ist eine pauschale Abkehr von typischer Schularchitektur oder etwa den Nachbargebäuden auf der Luftaufnahme oben.

Le jardin d'enfants est constitué d'unités rectangulaires indépendantes disposées à l'intérieur d'une structure circulaire, qui fait rupture avec les plans classiques des lieux d'enseignement et la typologie architecturale du quartier environnant.

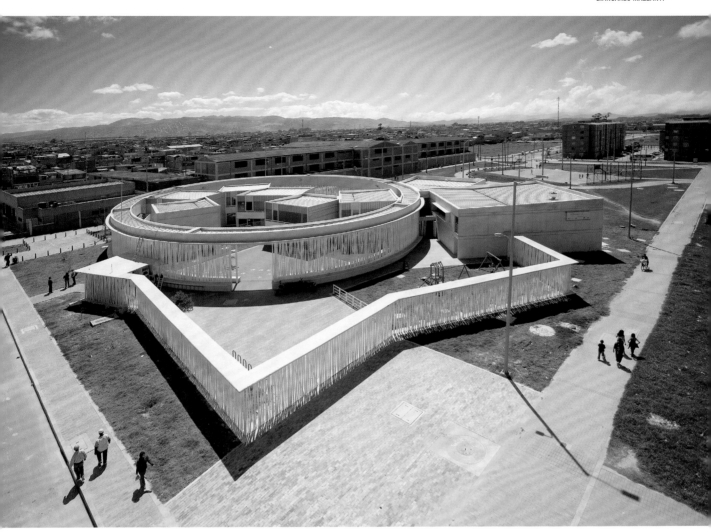

Right, a plan of the school and above,
another image taken closer to ground
level. Bright and open in appearance,
the school nonetheless encloses and
protects children.

Rechts ein Grundriss des Kindergartens und oben eine weitere Ansicht,
aufgenommen aus geringerer Höhe.
Der Komplex wirkt hell und offen und
bietet den Kindern zugleich ein
geschütztes Umfeld.

Plan et photographie du jardin d'enfants en vue rapprochée. D'aspect
ouvert et lumineux, l'établissement
n'en est pas moins un lieu fermé où
les enfants sont protégés.

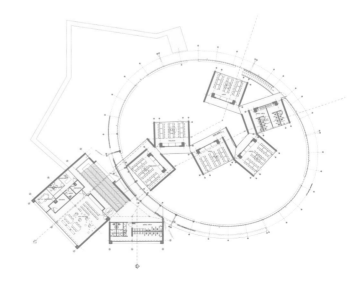

Bright colors are used for floor cladding, and the outer wall of the complex provides a safe, controlled environment for classes. Below, elevations show the simple, repetitive nature of the actual classroom units.

Für den Bodenbelag wurden leuchtende Farben gewählt. Die Außenmauer des Komplexes schafft ein sicheres, überschaubares Umfeld. Unten Aufrisse, die die schlichte Reihung der Räume in einem sich wiederholenden Muster zeigen.

Les sols ont reçu un revêtement de couleur vive. Le mur extérieur garantit un environnement sûr et contrôlé. Ci-dessous, élévations illustrant le principe simple et répétitif des blocs des salles de classe.

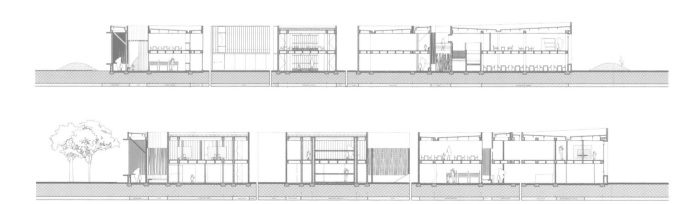

Bright colors and ample natural light are the rule within the school walls, as can be seen in the courtyard view above and the play space below.

Kräftige Farben und viel Tageslicht sind hier die Regel, wie der Blick in den Hof (oben) oder einen Spielbereich (unten) zeigt.

Ici, les couleurs vives et un éclairage naturel généreux sont de mise, comme le montrent la cour ci-dessus et l'aire de jeux ci-dessous.

MORPHOSIS

Morphosis
3440 Wesley Street
Culver City, CA 90232
USA

Tel: +1 424 258 6200
Fax: +1 424 258 6299
E-mail: studio@morphosis.net
Web: www.morphosis.com

Morphosis principal **THOM MAYNE**, born in Connecticut in 1944, received his B.Arch in 1968 from the University of Southern California, Los Angeles, and his M.Arch degree from Harvard in 1978. He created Morphosis in 1979. He has taught at UCLA, Harvard, Yale, and SCI-Arc, of which he was a founding Board Member. Thom Mayne was the winner of the 2005 Pritzker Prize. Some of the main buildings by Morphosis are the Kate Mantilini Restaurant (Beverly Hills, California, 1986); Cedars-Sinai Comprehensive Cancer Care Center (Beverly Hills, California, 1987); Crawford Residence (Montecito, 1987–92); the Blades Residence (Santa Barbara, California, 1992–97); and International Elementary School (Long Beach, California, 1997–99). More recent work includes the NOAA Satellite Operation Facility in Suitland (Maryland, 2001–05); San Francisco Federal Building (San Francisco, California, 2003–07); 41 Cooper Square (New York, New York, 2006–09); and the Giant Interactive Group Corporate Headquarters (Shanghai, China, 2006–10, published here).They are working on the Museum of Nature and Science (Dallas, Texas) and the Alexandria Bay Port of Entry (Alexandria Bay, New York), all in the USA unless stated otherwise.

THOM MAYNE, Direktor von Morphosis, wurde 1944 in Connecticut geboren. Seine Studien schloss er 1968 mit einem B.Arch an der University of Southern California, Los Angeles, sowie 1978 mit einem M.Arch in Harvard ab. 1979 gründete er Morphosis. Mayne lehrte an der UCLA, in Harvard, in Yale und am Sci-Arc, zu dessen Gründungsmitgliedern er zählt. 2005 wurde Mayne mit dem Pritzker-Preis ausgezeichnet. Ausgewählte Bauten von Morphosis sind u.a. Kate Mantilini Restaurant (Beverly Hills, Kalifornien, 1986), Cedars-Sinai Krebsklinik (Beverly Hills, Kalifornien, 1987), Crawford Residence (Montecito, 1987–92), Blades Residence (Santa Barbara, Kalifornien, 1992–97), sowie die International Elementary School (Long Beach, Kalifornien, 1997–99). Jüngere Arbeiten sind u.a. das NOAA-Satellitenzentrum in Suitland (Maryland, 2001–05), das San Francisco Federal Building (San Francisco, Kalifornien, 2003–07), 41 Cooper Square (New York, 2006–09) und der Hauptsitz der Giant Interactive Group (Shanghai, China, 2006–10, hier vorgestellt). Das Büro arbeitet derzeit an einem Museum für Naturkunde (Dallas, Texas) sowie am Importhafen Alexandria Bay (Alexandria Bay, New York), alle in den USA, sofern nicht anders angegeben.

Directeur de l'agence Morphosis, **THOM MAYNE**, né dans le Connecticut en 1944, est diplômé B. Arch. de l'université de Californie du Sud-Los Angeles (1968) et M. Arch. d'Harvard (1978), et a fondé l'agence en 1979. Il a enseigné à l'UCLA, Harvard, Yale et SCI-Arc dont il est l'un des fondateurs. Il a reçu le Prix Pritzker en 2005. Parmi ses principales réalisations : le restaurant Kate Mantilini (Beverly Hills, Californie, 1986) ; le Centre anticancéreux de Cedars-Sinai (Beverly Hills, Californie, 1987) ; la résidence Crawford (Montecito, Californie, 1987–92) ; la résidence Blades (Santa Barbara, Californie, 1992–97) et l'école élémentaire internationale de Long Beach (Californie, 1997–99). Plus récemment, il a construit le Centre opérationnel de communication par satellites NOAA (Suitland, Maryland, 2001–05) ; le San Francisco Federal Building (San Francisco, 2003–07) ; l'immeuble 41 Cooper Square (New York, 2006–09) et le siège social du Giant Interactive Group (Shanghai, Chine, 2006–10, publié ici). L'agence travaille sur un projet de Musée de la nature et de la science (Dallas, Texas) et le bâtiment de l'Alexandria Bay Port of Entry (Alexandria Bay, New York).

GIANT INTERACTIVE GROUP CORPORATE HEADQUARTERS

Shanghai, China, 2006–10

Area: 23 996 m². Client: Giant Interactive Group
Cost: not disclosed

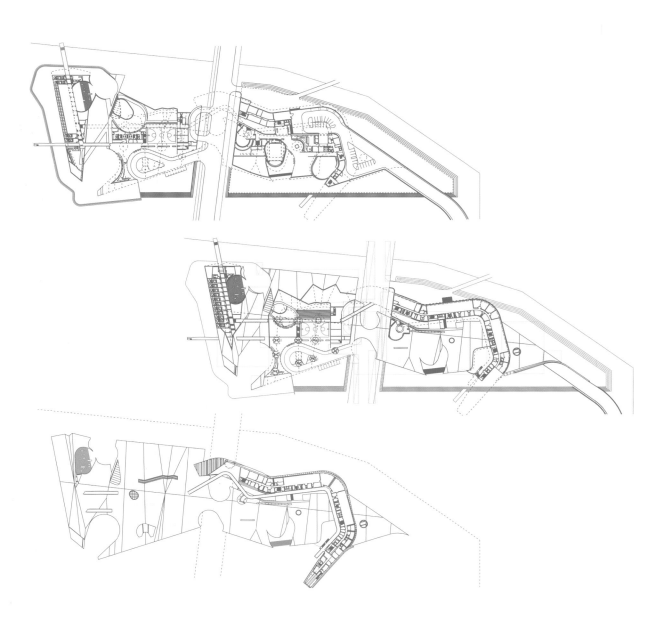

As the plans above and the photos on the right show, the large complex has an intricate form that appears to emerge from the landscaping, creating a natural, flowing feeling of continuity.

Wie Grundrisse (oben) und Aufnahmen (rechts) belegen, scheint die hochkomplexe Anlage geradezu aus der Landschaft herauszuwachsen. Es entsteht der Eindruck eines natürlichen, fließenden Kontinuums.

Comme le montrent les plans ci-dessus et les photos de la page de droite, cette vaste structure à la composition complexe semble émerger du sol dans un mouvement de flux continu.

Built on a 3.2-hectare site, this very large structure includes offices, an exhibition hall, conference rooms, auditorium, library, gymnasium, hotel, clubhouse, and pool. The site includes existing canals and a new man-made lake. According to the architects, the project seeks to join "architecture to landscape and environment to site. The forms of the architecture move in and out of a folded landscape plane." The East Campus building contains open, non-hierarchical office space, private offices, and executive suites, which cantilever over the lake. The landscape is used to house the auditorium, exhibition space, and a café in this area. The West Campus uses the same strategy to insert a pool, sports court, and relaxation and fitness spaces for employees beneath a green roof. The green roof, of course, also has energy-efficiency benefits. A hotel for company guests completes the installation to the west. Outdoor pedestrian walkways and plazas further connect users to the site. The office building has a narrow profile which maximizes the entry of natural light where it is beneficial to users.

Zu dem ungewöhnlich großen Komplex auf einem 3,2 ha großen Grundstück gehören Büroräume, eine Messehalle, Konferenzräume, ein Auditorium, eine Bibliothek, eine Sporthalle, ein Hotel, ein Clubhaus und ein Pool. Zum Gelände gehören außerdem einige ältere Kanäle sowie ein neuer künstlicher See. Den Architekten zufolge soll das Projekt „die Architektur an die Landschaft und das Umfeld an das Grundstück" anbinden. „Die Formen der Architektur schlängeln sich durch die gefaltete Landschaftsebene." Im Ostcampus sind offene, hierarchiefreie Büroflächen untergebracht, private Büros sowie Räume für das gehobene Management, die über den See hinausragen. In diesem Bereich der Landschaft sind auch das Auditorium, die Messehalle und ein Café angesiedelt. Auf dem Westcampus befinden sich auf strategisch ähnliche Weise ein Schwimmbad, Sporthallen und Entspannungs- sowie Fitnessräume für die Angestellten – alles unter einem begrünten Dach, das zur Energieeffizienz beiträgt. Abgerundet wird der Komplex im Westen durch ein Firmenhotel für Gäste. Fußwege und Plätze in den Außenanlagen schaffen zusätzliche Bindung zwischen Nutzern und Gelände. Das Bürogebäude hat ein schmales Profil, was den Einfall von Tageslicht dort maximiert, wo die Nutzer von ihm profitieren.

Édifié sur un terrain de 3,2 hectares, comprenant des canaux et un lac artificiel, ce vaste complexe regroupe des bureaux, une salle d'exposition, des salles de conférence, un auditorium, une bibliothèque, un gymnase, un hôtel, un club-house et une piscine. Le projet cherche à « lier l'architecture au paysage et l'environnement au site », expliquent les architectes. Les formes architecturales se meuvent comme les plis du sol dans un paysage. Le bâtiment du Campus Est contient des bureaux de plan ouvert non hiérarchisé, des bureaux fermés et des appartements pour la direction en surplomb au-dessus du lac. Dans la même zone se trouvent un auditorium privé, un espace d'exposition et un café. Le Campus Ouest applique une stratégie identique en intégrant une piscine, des terrains de sport et des espaces de relaxation et de remise en forme pour les employés, le tout réuni sous un toit végétalisé qui permet par ailleurs des économies d'énergie. À l'ouest, un hôtel pour les hôtes de l'entreprise complète ces installations. Des allées piétonnières et diverses places offrent des connexions supplémentaires avec le site. Le bâtiment des bureaux est étroit pour optimiser l'éclairage naturel des postes de travail.

The powerful cantilever of the building seen above contrasts with the insertion of other parts of the complex into the earth. The whole assumes the appearance of a kind of quasi-mechanical entity that is nonetheless earthbound.

Die beeindruckende Auskragung des Gebäudeflügels oben ist ein deutlicher Kontrast zu den teilweise in den Boden versenkten Teilen des Komplexes. Die Anlage wirkt fast maschinenhaft, aber dennoch erdverbunden.

Cet imposant porte-à-faux (ci-dessus) contraste avec l'enfoncement dans le sol d'autres bâtiments du complexe. L'ensemble présente un aspect quasi mécanique qui n'en reste pas moins étroitement lié à la terre.

An elevation and photos of the green roofs of the buildings emphasize the way in which it appears to emerge from the site, with its spaces formed at the interstitial point between the natural and the artificial.

Aufriss und Ansichten der begrünten Dächer machen deutlich, wie stark die Bauten aus dem Boden herauszuwachsen scheinen. Es entstehen Räume zwischen Natur und Technik.

Une élévation et des photos des toitures végétalisées font ressortir l'aspect « émergeant » de ce projet dont les volumes se déploient aux intersections du naturel et de l'artificiel.

Spectacular curves and unexpected forms characterize both interior and exterior, as seen in these images. Thom Mayne and Morphosis continue to innovate and challenge architectural assumptions.

Innen- wie Außenbau überraschen mit dramatischen Kurven und Formen, wie diese Ansichten belegen. Thom Mayne und Morphosis verstehen es nach wie vor, architektonische Grundannahmen zu hinterfragen und innovativ zu erneuern.

Comme le montrent ces images, l'intérieur et l'extérieur se caractérisent par des courbes aussi spectaculaires qu'inattendues. Thom Mayne et Morphosis poursuivent leur veine innovante et leur remise en question des idées architecturales reçues.

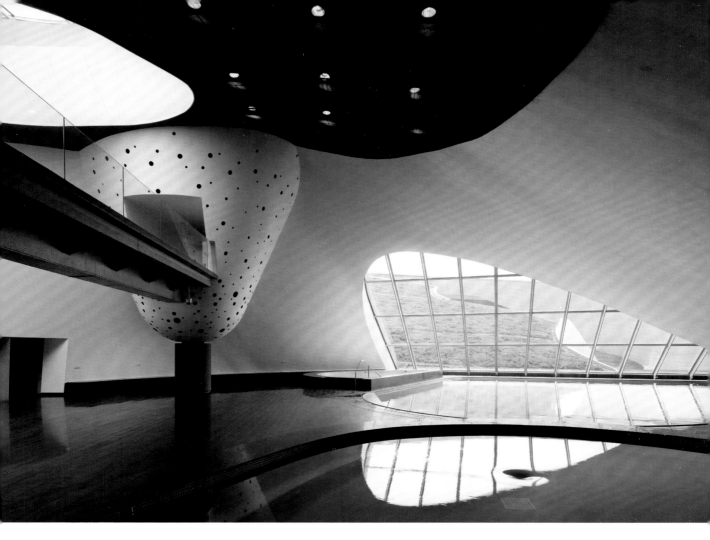

A pool with a large curving window that opens out to the landscaped exterior from which the buildings emerge is visible here, together with elevations showing how the roof in some places dips down to the earth.

Ein Schwimmbad mit großem geschwungenen Fenster bietet Ausblick in die Grünanlagen, aus denen die Bauten aufzusteigen scheinen. Aufrisse lassen erkennen, dass das Dach teilweise bis zum Boden hinuntergezogen ist.

Ci-dessus : piscine face à une grande baie de forme libre qui ouvre sur l'environnement paysager d'où émergent les bâtiments. Ci-dessous : élévations montrant la façon dont le toit plonge dans le sol à certains endroits.

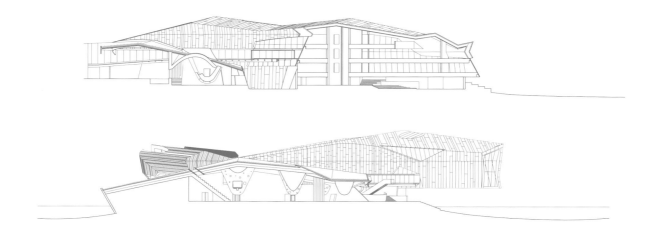

NERI & HU

Neri & Hu Design and Research Office
88 Yuqing Road
Shanghai 200030
China

Tel: +86 21 6082 3777
Fax: +86 21 6082 3778
E-mail: info@nhdro.com
Web: www.nhdro.com

LYNDON NERI received his B.Arch degree from the University of California (Berkeley, 1987) and his M.Arch degree from Harvard (1992). He worked in the offices of Steven Harris (New York, 1992) and Michael Graves (Princeton, 1993–2003), before founding Design Republic (Shanghai, 2006) and Neri & Hu (Shanghai, 2004). **ROSSANA HU** also studied at the University of California (Berkeley, B.Arch, 1990) and then received a Master of Architecture and Urban Planning at Princeton (1995). After working with Skidmore, Owings & Merrill (New York, 1993) and Michael Graves (1996–99), she cofounded Design Republic and Neri & Hu with Lyndon Neri. The Waterhouse at South Bund (Shanghai, China, 2010, published here) is a recent project.

LYNDON NERI absolvierte seinen B.Arch an der University of California (Berkeley, 1987) und seinen M.Arch in Harvard (1992). Er arbeitete in den Büros von Steven Harris (New York, 1992) und Michael Graves (Princeton, 1993–2003), bevor er Design Republic (Shanghai, 2006) und Neri & Hu (Shanghai, 2004) gründete. Auch **ROSSANA HU** studierte an der University of California (Berkeley, B.Arch 1990) und absolvierte ihren Master in Architektur und Stadtplanung in Princeton (1995). Nachdem sie für Skidmore, Owings & Merrill (New York, 1993) und Michael Graves (1996–99) gearbeitet hatte, gründete sie mit Lyndon Neri die Büros Design Republic und Neri & Hu. Das Waterhouse in South Bund (Shanghai, China, 2010, hier vorgestellt) ist ein aktuelles Projekt.

LYNDON NERI a obtenu son B. Arch. à l'université de Californie (Berkeley, 1987) et son M. Arch. à Harvard (1992). Il a travaillé dans les agences de Steven Harris (New York, 1992) et de Michael Graves (Princeton, 1993–2003) avant de fonder Design Republic (Shanghaï, 2006) et Neri & Hu (Shanghaï, 2004). **ROSSANA HU**, qui a également fait ses études à l'université de Californie (Berkeley, B. Arch. 1990), a passé son mastère en architecture et urbanisme à Princeton (1995). Après avoir travaillé pour Skidmore, Owings & Merrill (New York, 1993) et Michael Graves (1996–99), elle a fondé Design Republic et Neri & Hu avec Lyndon Neri. Ils ont récemment réalisé l'hôtel Waterhouse at South Bund (Shanghaï, 2010, publié ici).

THE WATERHOUSE AT SOUTH BUND

Shanghai, China, 2010

Address: Maojiayuan Road No. 1–3, Zhongshan Road South, Huangpu District, Shanghai 200011,
China, +86 21 6080 2988, www.waterhouseshanghai.com
Area: 2800 m². Client: Cameron Holdings Hotel Management Limited. Cost: not disclosed
Collaboration: Debby Haepers, Cai Chun Yan, Markus Stoecklein, Jane Wang

This unusual four-story 19-room boutique hotel was created in the remains of a three-story Japanese Army headquarters building dating from the 1930s. It is part of the Cool Docks development area in the South Bund District. Additions built over the old concrete building were made using Cor-ten steel, a homage on the part of the architects to the industrial nature of the shipping activity on the neighboring Huangpu River. Inside, their design relies on "a blurring and inversion of the interior and exterior, as well as between the public and private realms." Peeks into private rooms from the public spaces or from rooms to the public areas are amongst the surprises created by Neri & Hu. Furnishings, also selected by the designers, include custom pieces, antiques, and items from Moooi, Magis, and Emeco, as well as Tom Dixon lights.

Das ungewöhnliche „Boutique"-Hotel mit vier Stockwerken und 19 Zimmern wurde in die baulichen Überreste eines dreistöckigen Hauptquartiers der japanischen Armee aus den 1930er-Jahren integriert. Das Hotel entstand im Zuge der Erschließung der sogenannten Cool Docks im Stadtteil South Bund. Anbauten an den Altbau aus Beton wurden aus Corten-Stahl realisiert: Eine Hommage der Architekten an den Schiffsverkehr auf dem nahe gelegenen Huangpu Jiang. Im Innern entfaltet das Design besonders durch „das Verschwimmen und die Umkehrung der Grenzen von Innen und Außen, sowie von öffentlichen und privaten Bereichen" seine Wirkung. Einige der Überraschungen, mit denen Neri & Hu aufwarten, sind Einblicke in private Räume aus den öffentlichen Bereichen bzw. aus den Zimmern in die öffentlichen Bereiche. Die ebenfalls von den Architekten ausgewählte Innenausstattung umfasst sowohl Maßeinbauten, als auch Antiquitäten und Objekte von Moooi, Magis und Emeco sowie Leuchten von Tom Dixon.

Ce curieux « hôtel-boutique » de 19 chambres sur quatre niveaux occupe les anciens locaux de l'état-major de l'armée japonaise dans les années 1930, inclus dans l'opération de rénovation urbaine des Cool Docks du quartier sud du Bund. Des extensions en acier Corten ont été ajoutées à l'ancien bâtiment en béton, en rappel des chantiers de construction navale du fleuve Huangpu tout proche. À l'intérieur, le projet repose sur « une confusion et une inversion de l'intérieur et de l'extérieur, des parties privatives et parties publiques ». On y découvre des surprises comme des perspectives sur l'intérieur des chambres à partir des circulations, ou le contraire. Le mobilier, choisi par les architectes, comprend des meubles spécialement réalisés pour le projet, des meubles anciens et des créations de Moooi, Magis, Emeco et Tom Dixon pour les luminaires.

Visitors to Shanghai know that next to its sleek modern towers a good number of older buildings, with a kind of patina of the past, do remain in some areas. The architects here have played on this presence of the relatively recent past.

Wer Shanghai kennt, weiß, dass neben den glatten modernen Hochhausbauten in manchen Gegenden auch eine Reihe alter Gebäude erhalten sind, an denen noch die Patina früherer Zeiten haftet. Die Architekten spielen mit diesem Aspekt der vergleichsweise jungen Vergangenheit.

Les visiteurs de Shanghaï savent qu'au pied de ses innombrables tours subsiste dans certains quartiers un grand nombre de bâtiments anciens marqués par la patine du temps. Les architectes ont joué ici de la présence d'un passé relativement récent.

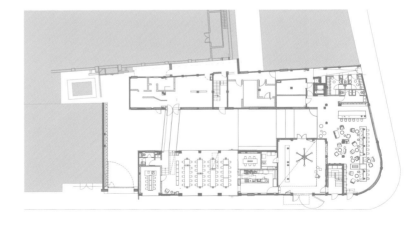

Rough, almost untreated surfaces are contrasted with a decided sense of trendy elegance in these images. To the right, the reception area (seen from the opposite side, above), and below, a section drawing of the hotel.

Raue, fast unbehandelte Oberflächen wirken auf diesen Aufnahmen wie ein Kontrastprogramm zur trendbewussten Eleganz des Baus. Rechts der Empfangsbereich (oben links aus einer anderen Perspektive), unten ein Querschnitt des Hotels.

Les surfaces non traitées, quasiment brutes, contrastent avec l'élégance tendance voulue de certains aménagements. À droite, la réception (vue ci-dessus de la perspective opposée) et ci-dessous, une coupe de l'hôtel.

Rough wood tables recall the atmosphere of the exterior of the hotel or its entrance lobby area, but the décor here tends toward more overt sophistication.

Tische aus grobem Holz knüpfen an die Atmosphäre des Außenbaus und den Eingangsbereich bzw. die Lobby an. Insgesamt ist die Ausstattung jedoch deutlich gehoben.

Les tables en bois brut rappellent l'atmosphère de l'extérieur de l'hôtel et de sa réception, même si le décor fait ici preuve d'une plus grande sophistication.

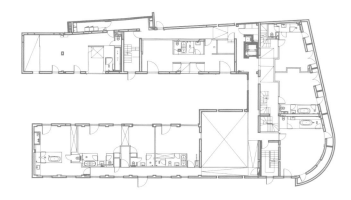

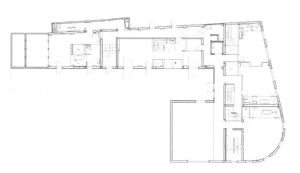

Guest rooms offer all of the comforts to which visitors to this type of hotel are accustomed. Surfaces alternate between opacity and transparency, or roughness and smoothness.

Die Zimmer bieten jeden Komfort, den Gäste von Hotels dieser Klasse erwarten. Oberflächen sind wechselweise opak oder transparent, rau oder glatt.

Les chambres offrent le confort auquel la clientèle de ce type d'hôtel est habituée. On observe l'alternance de plans opaques et transparents, lisses ou bruts.

NEUTELINGS RIEDIJK

Neutelings Riedijk Architects
PO Box 527
3000 AM Rotterdam
The Netherlands

Tel: +31 10 404 66 77
Fax: +31 10 414 27 12
E-mail: info@neutelings-riedijk.com
Web: www.neutelings-riedijk.com

WILLEM JAN NEUTELINGS was born in 1959 in Bergen op Zoom, the Netherlands. He studied at the Technical University in Delft (1977–86), and worked for OMA with Rem Koolhaas (1981–86). He has taught at the Academy of Architecture in Rotterdam and at the Berlage Institute in Rotterdam (1990–99). **MICHIEL RIEDIJK** was born in Geldrop, the Netherlands, in 1964. He attended the Technical University in Delft (1983–89) before working with J. D. Bekkering in Amsterdam. He has taught at the Technical University in Eindhoven and at the Academies of Architecture in Amsterdam, Rotterdam, and Maastricht, and is still a Professor at the Technical University in Delft. Their built work includes Lakeshore Housing, first phase (Huizen, 1994–96); Borneo Sporenburg Housing (Amsterdam, 1994–97); and the Minnaert Building (Utrecht, 1994–98), all in the Netherlands. More recent work includes the Netherlands Institute for Sound and Vision (Hilversum, The Netherlands, 2006); and the city museum MAS Museum aan de Stroom (Antwerp, Belgium, 2006–10, published here). Current work includes an extension of the Cincinnati Art Museum (Cincinnati, Ohio, USA, 2007–); Opera and Hotel (Ljubljana, Slovenia, 2004–) and the Culturehouse (Arnhem, The Netherlands, 2011–).

WILLEM JAN NEUTELINGS wurde 1959 in Bergen op Zoom, Niederlande, geboren. Er studierte an der Technischen Universität Delft (1977–86) und arbeitete bei OMA mit Rem Koolhaas (1981–86). Er lehrte an der Academie van Bouwkunst in Rotterdam und dem Berlage Instituut in Rotterdam (1990–99). **MICHIEL RIEDIJK** wurde 1964 in Geldrop, Niederlande, geboren. Er studierte an der TU Delft (1983–89) und arbeitete anschließend bei J. D. Bekkering in Amsterdam. Er lehrte an der TU Eindhoven und den Architekturhochschulen in Amsterdam, Rotterdam und Maastricht und ist Professor an der TU Delft. Zu ihren realisierten Entwürfen zählen die Wohnanlage Lakeshore, erster Bauabschnitt (Huizen, 1994–96), die Wohnanlage Borneo Sporenburg (Amsterdam, 1994–97) sowie das Minnaert-Gebäude (Utrecht, 1994–98), alle in den Niederlanden. Jüngere Projekte sind das Niederländische Institut für Bild und Klang (Hilversum, Niederlande, 2006) sowie das städtische Museum MAS Museum aan de Stroom (Antwerpen, Belgien, 2006–10, hier vorgestellt). Derzeit in Arbeit sind u.a. eine Erweiterung des Cincinnati Art Museum (Cincinnati, Ohio, USA, 2007–), ein Opernhaus und Hotel (Ljubljana, Slowenien, 2004–) sowie ein Kulturzentrum (Arnhem, Niederlande, 2011–).

WILLEM JAN NEUTELINGS, né en 1959 à Bergen op Zoom (Pays-Bas), a étudié à l'Université technique de Delft (1977–86) et travaillé pour OMA, l'agence de Rem Koolhaas (1981–86). Il a enseigné à l'académie d'architecture à Rotterdam et à l'institut Berlage à Rotterdam (1990–99). **MICHIEL RIEDIJK**, né à Geldrop (Pays-Bas) en 1964, a étudié à l'Université technique de Delft (1983–89) avant de travailler pour J. D. Bekkering à Amsterdam. Il a enseigné à l'Université technique d'Eindhoven et aux académies d'architecture d'Amsterdam, Rotterdam et Maastricht. Il enseigne toujours à l'Université technique de Delft. Parmi leurs réalisations, toutes aux Pays-Bas : des logements à Lakeshore, phase I (Huizen, 1994–96) ; les logements de Borneo Sporenburg (Amsterdam, 1994–97) ; l'immeuble Minnaert (Utrecht, 1994–98). Plus récemment, ils ont réalisé l'Institut néerlandais pour l'audiovisuel (Hilversum, Pays-Bas, 2006) et le musée municipal MAS (Museum aan de Stroom, Anvers, Belgique, 2006–10, publié ici). Actuellement, ils travaillent sur l'extension du Musée d'art de Cincinnati (Cincinnati, Ohio, 2007–) ; un opéra et un hôtel (Ljubljana, Slovénie, 2004–) et une maison de la culture (Arnhem, Pays-Bas, 2011–).

MAS MUSEUM AAN DE STROOM

Antwerp, Belgium, 2006–10

Address: Hanzestedenplaats 1, 2000 Antwerp, Belgium, www.mas.be
Area: 19 500 m². Client: City of Antwerp. Cost: €33 million

This 60-meter-high tower is located in the old port area of Antwerp that is currently being redeveloped. As the architects describe it: "Ten gigantic natural stone boxes are piled up as a physical demonstration of the gravity of history, full of historical objects that our ancestors left behind. It is a storehouse of history in the heart of the old docks." Each of these blocks is twisted by a quarter turn, whence the unusual stacked appearance of the building. The museum concerns the history of the port and the city. Hand-cleaved red Indian sandstone was used for the exterior cladding. Four different stone shades were applied using a computer-generated pattern. A large spiral gallery has a corrugated glass curtain wall, while a pattern of metal ornaments (inspired by the logo of the city) was applied to the façade and interior spaces. The square in front of the museum is also part of the design.

Der 60 m hohe Turm liegt im alten Hafen von Antwerpen, der derzeit neu erschlossen wird. Die Architekten erklären: „Hier wurden zehn gewaltige Boxen aus Naturstein übereinander gestapelt: ein physisches Symbol für die Schwerkraft und das Gewicht der Geschichte, [ein Bau] voller historischer Objekte, die unsere Vorfahren uns hinterlassen haben. Es ist ein Lagerhaus der Geschichte im Herzen der alten Hafenanlagen." Jeder Quader wurde um eine Vierteldrehung versetzt, wodurch die ungewöhnliche Optik des Baus entsteht. Das Museum ist der Stadt- und Hafengeschichte gewidmet. Der Außenbau wurde mit handgespaltenem roten indischen Sandstein verblendet. Mithilfe eines computergenerierten Schemas wurden vier verschiedene Farbschattierungen des Steins verarbeitet. Den großzügigen, spiralförmig umlaufenden Ausstellungsräumen ist eine Curtain Wall aus wellblechartig gewölbtem Glas vorgehängt. Ein Muster aus Metallornamenten (inspiriert vom Wappen der Stadt) ziert Fassade und Innenräume. Auch der Platz vor dem Museum ist integraler Bestandteil des Entwurfs.

Cette tour de 60 mètres de haut est située dans un quartier du vieux port d'Anvers en cours de rénovation. « Dix boîtes gigantesques en pierre naturelle s'empilent dans une illustration physique du poids de l'histoire, remplies d'objets historiques que nos ancêtres ont laissés derrière eux. C'est un entrepôt de l'histoire au cœur des anciens docks », expliquent les architectes. Chacun de ces blocs pivote d'un quart de tour, d'où la forme curieuse de l'immeuble. Le musée est consacré à l'histoire du port et de la ville. Son habillage externe est en grès indien rouge clivé à la main. Quatre nuances différentes de pierre ont été choisies et sont réparties selon un rythme calculé par ordinateur. Une importante galerie en spirale protégée par un mur-rideau en verre ondulé sépare ces blocs minéraux. Des ornements métalliques (inspirés du logo de la ville) décorent la façade et l'intérieur. La place qui fait face au musée relève également du projet.

The unusual stacked and notched appearance of the building makes it stand out in the port environment where low buildings dominate.

Dank der ungewöhnlichen gestapelten, gekerbten Optik fällt das Gebäude in seinem Hafenumfeld auf, in dem sonst eher niedrigere Bauten dominieren.

L'aspect inhabituel créé par l'effet d'empilement et de décalages des niveaux singularise cet immeuble qui se dresse dans un environnement portuaire de bâtiments bas.

A young woman stands before the fully glazed double-height wall that offers a view of the port of Antwerp. With its rounded forms, the glazing gives a note of unexpected variety to the structure.

Eine junge Frau steht vor einer doppelgeschossigen Glaswand mit Blick auf den Hafen von Antwerpen. Mit ihrer geschwungenen Form gibt die Glasfront dem Bau eine überraschende Note.

Jeune fille devant un mur de verre ondulé sur toute sa hauteur, contemplant la vue sur le port d'Anvers. Cette ondulation apporte au projet une note de variété inattendue.

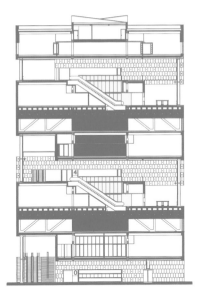
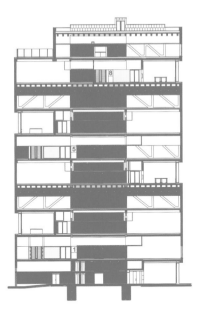
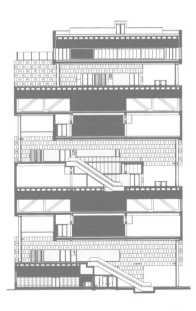

The same high, glazed space seen on the left page is viewed here from another angle. Above, section drawings of the building show that it is essentially a fairly "normal" rectangular block.

Hier ein Blick in denselben hohen, verglasten Bereich wie links, jedoch aus einem anderen Blickwinkel. Querschnitte (oben) zeigen das Gebäude als vergleichsweise „gewöhnlichen" linearen Baukörper.

Pris sous un angle différent, le même espace que page de gauche. Ci-dessus, coupes du bâtiment montrant sa composition rectangulaire assez « classique ».

RYUE NISHIZAWA

Office of Ryue Nishizawa
1–5–27 Tatsumi
Koto-ku
Tokyo 135–0053
Japan

Tel: +81 3 5534 0117
Fax: +81 3 5534 1757
E-mail: office@ryuenishizawa.com
Web: www.ryuenishizawa.com

RYUE NISHIZAWA was born in Tokyo, Japan, in 1966. He graduated from Yokohama National University with an M.Arch in 1990, and joined the office of Kazuyo Sejima & Associates in Tokyo the same year. In 1995, he established SANAA with Kazuyo Sejima, and two years later his own practice, the Office of Ryue Nishizawa. He has worked on all the significant projects of SANAA and has been a Visiting Professor at Yokohama National University (2001–), the University of Singapore (2003), Princeton (2006), and the Harvard GSD (2007). His work outside SANAA includes a Weekend House (Gunma, 1998); the N Museum (Kagawa, 2005); the Moriyama House (Tokyo, 2006); House A (East Japan, 2006); Towada Art Center (Aomori, 2006–08); and the Teshima Art Museum (Teshima Island, Kagawa, 2009–10, published here), all in Japan.

RYUE NISHIZAWA wurde 1966 in Tokio geboren und schloss sein Studium 1990 mit einem M.Arch an der Nationaluniversität in Yokohama ab. Noch im selben Jahr schloss er sich dem Büro von Kazuyo Sejima & Associates in Tokio an. Gemeinsam mit Kazuyo Sejima gründete er 1995 SANAA, zwei Jahre später sei eigenes Büro Ryue Nishizawa. Er war an sämtlichen Schlüsselprojekten von SANAA beteiligt und hatte Gastprofessuren an der Nationaluniversität Yokohama (2001–), der Universität von Singapur (2003), in Princeton (2006) sowie am Harvard GSD (2007). Zu seinen Projekten unabhängig von SANAA zählen ein Wochenendhaus (Gunma, 1998), das N Museum (Kagawa, 2005), das Haus Moriyama (Tokyo, 2006), Haus A (Ostjapan, 2006), das Towada Art Center (Aomori, 2006–08) und das Kunstmuseum auf Teshima (Teshima Island, Kagawa, 2009–10, hier vorgestellt), alle in Japan.

RYUE NISHIZAWA, né à Tokyo en 1966, a obtenu son M. Arch. à l'Université nationale de Yokohama (1990). Il a commencé à travailler dans l'agence de Kazuyo Sejima & Associates à Tokyo la même année, avant qu'ils ne fondent ensemble SANAA en 1995 et sa propre agence Office of Ryue Nishizawa deux ans plus tard. Il a été professeur invité à l'Université nationale de Yokohama (2001–), aux universités de Singapour (2003), Princeton (2006) et la Harvard GSD (2007). Il est intervenu sur tous les grands projets de SANAA. Son œuvre personnelle comprend une maison de week-end (Gunma, 1998) ; le musée N (Kagawa, 2005) ; la maison Moriyama (Tokyo, 2006) ; la maison A (Japon oriental, 2006) ; le Centre d'art Towada (Aomori, 2006–08) et le Musée d'art de Teshima (île de Teshima, Kagawa, 2009–10, publié ici), le tout au Japon.

TESHIMA ART MUSEUM

Teshima Island, Kagawa, Japan, 2009–10

Address: 607 Karato, Teshima, Tonosho-cho, Shozu-gun, Kagawa 7614662, Japan, +81 879 68 3555,
www.benesse-artsite.jp/en/teshima-artmuseum/index.html
Area: 2335 m². Client: Naoshima Fukutake Art Museum Foundation. Cost: not disclosed
Collaboration: Rei Naito (Artist)

Teshima is a small island located in Japan's Inland Sea, not far from Naoshima, where Tadao Ando has worked for over 20 years on various projects. The same client commissioned Ryue Nishizawa to build this museum. "We proposed an architectural design composed of free curves, echoing the shape of a water drop," says the architect. "Our idea was that the curved drop-like form would create a powerful architectural space in harmony with the undulating landforms around it." The remarkable thin concrete shell of the structure reaches over four meters at its maximum ceiling height, "creating a large, organic interior space," but remains very horizontal inside. Openings in the shell let light, air, and rain inside. Rei Naito's subtle work is based on water, and Nishizawa concludes: "Our goal is to generate a fusion of the environment, art, and architecture, and we hope these three elements work together as a single entity."

Teshima ist eine kleine Insel in der Seto-Inlandsee, unweit von Naoshima, wo Tadao Ando seit über 20 Jahren an einer Reihe von Projekten arbeitet. Derselbe Bauherr beauftragte Ryue Nishizawa mit dem Bau dieses Museums. „Wir entwickelten einen Entwurf aus frei geformten Kurven, die der Form eines Wassertropfens nachempfunden sind", erklärt der Architekt. „Unsere Idee war es, durch die geschwungene, tropfenartige Form einen eindringlichen architektonischen Raum zu schaffen, der mit der Hügellandschaft harmoniert." Die erstaunlich dünnwandige Betonschale des Baus erreicht an ihrem höchsten Punkt eine Höhe von über 4 m, wodurch „ein großer, organischer Innenraum entsteht". Im Innern dominieren jedoch horizontale Formen. Öffnungen in der Gebäudeschale lassen Licht, Luft und Regen in den Bau. Die feinsinnige Kunst der Bildhauerin Rei Naito kreist um Wasser, und Nishizawa fasst zusammen: „Unser Ziel ist eine Verschmelzung von Umwelt, Kunst und Architektur; wir hoffen, diese drei Elemente zu einer Einheit zusammenzuführen."

Teshima est une petite île de la mer intérieure du Japon, non loin de Naoshima où Tadao Ando a travaillé pendant plus de 20 ans sur divers projets. Le même client a demandé à Ryue Nishizawa de construire ce petit musée. « Nous avons proposé un projet en courbes libres qui rappelle la forme d'une goutte d'eau », explique l'architecte. « Notre idée était que cette forme en goutte crée un espace architectural fort en harmonie avec les formes du terrain tout autour. » L'étonnante coque mince en béton s'élève à plus de quatre mètres, « déterminant un vaste volume organique intérieur » au-dessus d'un plan horizontal. Des ouvertures pratiquées dans la coque laissent passer la lumière, l'air et la pluie. Le subtil travail de l'artiste présentée, Rei Naito, s'inspire de l'eau. « Notre objectif est de fusionner l'environnement, l'art et l'architecture pour que ces trois éléments fonctionnent en une entité unique », conclut l'architecte.

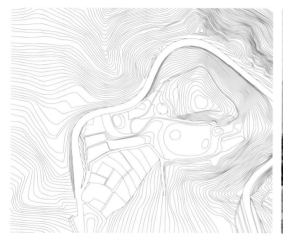

The Teshima Art Museum is in many senses set into its environment, as can be seen in the topographical site plan (above) and the photos on both of these pages.

Das Teshima Art Museum ist in vielerlei Hinsicht in sein Umfeld eingebunden, wie der topografische Lageplan zeigt (oben bzw. Aufnahmen auf beiden Seiten).

Le Musée d'art de Teshima est à de nombreux égards totalement intégré à son environnement, comme le montrent le plan topographique ci-dessus ainsi que les photos.

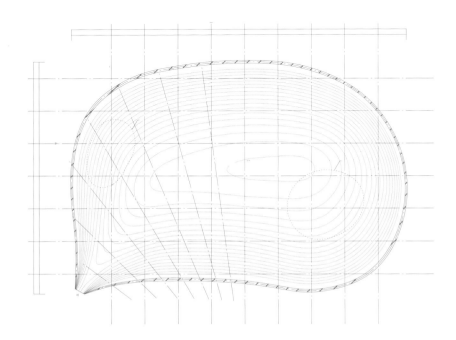

Shaped like a drop of water (plan, left), the structure has several large, round openings that allow natural light to enter it, and, indeed, for rain to come in as well.

Der wie ein Wassertropfen geformte Bau (Zeichnung links) hat mehrere runde Öffnungen, durch die Tageslicht einfällt – ebenso wie Regen.

En forme de goutte d'eau (plan de gauche), le musée est percé de plusieurs ouvertures rondes qui laissent pénétrer le soleil… et la pluie.

JEAN NOUVEL

Ateliers Jean Nouvel
10 Cité d'Angoulème
75011 Paris
France

Tel: +33 1 49 23 83 83 / Fax: +33 1 43 14 81 10
E-mail: info@jeannouvel.fr / Web: www.jeannouvel.com

Born in 1945 in Fumel, France, **JEAN NOUVEL** studied in Bordeaux and then at the Paris École des Beaux-Arts (1964–72). From 1967 to 1970, he was an assistant of Claude Parent and Paul Virilio. In 1970, he created his first office with François Seigneur. Jean Nouvel received the RIBA Gold Medal in 2001. His first widely noticed project was the Institut du Monde Arabe (with Architecture Studio, Paris, 1981–87). Other works include his Nemausus Housing (Nîmes, 1985–87); Lyon Opera House (1986–93); Vinci Conference Center (Tours, 1989–93); Euralille Shopping Center (Lille, 1991–94); and Fondation Cartier (Paris, 1991–94), all in France. His major completed projects since 2000 are the Music and Conference Center (Lucerne, Switzerland, 1998–2000); the Agbar Tower (Barcelona, Spain, 2001–03); social housing at the Cité Manifeste (Mulhouse, France, 2004); the extension of the Reina Sofia Museum (Madrid, Spain, 1999–2005); the Quai Branly Museum (Paris, France, 2001–06); an apartment building in SoHo (New York, New York, USA, 2006); and the Guthrie Theater (Minneapolis, Minnesota, USA, 2006). Recent projects include Les Bains des Docks (Le Havre, France, 2006–08); the city hall in Montpellier (France, 2002–09); Concert House, Danish Radio (Copenhagen, Denmark, 2003–09); Sofitel Vienna Stephansdom-Stilwerk (Vienna, Austria, 2006–10, published here); Chelsea Apartment Building (New York, 2006–10, also published here); and the Serpentine Pavilion (London, UK, 2010). Ongoing projects are the new Philharmonic Hall in Paris (France, 2014); the Louvre Abu Dhabi (UAE, 2010–13); and the National Museum of Qatar (Doha, 2014).

JEAN NOUVEL, geboren 1945 in Fumel, Frankreich, studierte zunächst in Bordeaux und schließlich an der Pariser École des Beaux-Arts (1964–72). Von 1967 bis 1970 war er Assistent bei Claude Parent und Paul Virilio. 1970 gründete er mit François Seigneur sein erstes Büro in Paris. 2001 wurde Jean Nouvel mit der RIBA-Goldmedaille ausgezeichnet. Sein erstes weithin bekannt gewordenes Projekt ist das Institut du Monde Arabe (mit Architecture Studio, Paris, 1981–87). Weitere Projekte sind u.a. das Wohnbauprojekt Nemausus (Nîmes, 1985–87), die Oper in Lyon (1986–93), das Konferenzzentrum Vinci (Tours, 1989–93), das Einkaufszentrum Euralille (Lille, 1991–94) und die Fondation Cartier (Paris, 1991–94), alle in Frankreich. Seine bedeutendsten realisierten Projekte seit 2000 sind das Kultur- und Kongresszentrum Luzern (Schweiz, 1998–2000), der Agbar-Turm (Barcelona, Spanien, 2001–03), Sozialwohnungen in der Cité Manifeste (Mulhouse, Frankreich, 2004), die Erweiterung der Reina Sofia (Madrid, Spanien, 1999–2005), das Museum am Quai Branly (Paris, Frankreich, 2001–06), ein Apartmenthaus in SoHo (New York, USA, 2006) und das Guthrie-Theater (Minneapolis, USA, 2006). Jüngere Projekte sind u.a. Les Bains des Docks (Le Havre, Frankreich, 2006–08), das Rathaus in Montpellier (Frankreich, 2002–09), das Konzerthaus für den Dänischen Rundfunk (Kopenhagen, 2003–09), das Sofitel Vienna Stephansdom-Stilwerk (Wien, Österreich, 2006–10, hier vorgestellt), ein Apartmenthaus in Chelsea (New York, 2006–10, ebenfalls hier vorgestellt) sowie der Pavillon für die Serpentine Gallery (London, GB, 2010). Laufende Projekte sind u.a. die Philharmonie in Paris (Frankreich, 2014), der Louvre Abu Dhabi (VAE, 2010–13) und das Nationalmuseum von Qatar (Doha, 2014).

Né en 1945 à Fumel, **JEAN NOUVEL** étudie à l'école des beaux-arts de Bordeaux, puis de Paris (1964–72). De 1967 à 1970, il est assistant de Claude Parent et de Paul Virilio. En 1970, il crée une première agence avec François Seigneur. Il reçoit la médaille d'or du RIBA en 2001. Son premier projet largement salué par la presse est l'Institut du monde arabe (Paris, 1981–87), en collaboration avec Architecture Studio. Parmi ses autres réalisations : les immeubles de logements Nemausus (Nîmes, 1985–87) ; l'Opéra de Lyon (1986–93) ; le Centre de congrès Vinci (Tours, 1989–93) ; le centre commercial Euralille (Lille, 1991–94) et la Fondation Cartier (Paris, 1991–94). Parmi ses principaux projets depuis 2000 figurent : le Centre de congrès et de musique de Lucerne (Suisse, 1998–2000) ; la tour Agbar (Barcelone, 2001–03) ; des logements sociaux (Cité Manifeste, Mulhouse, 2004) ; l'extension du musée Reina Sofia (Madrid, 1999–2005) ; le musée du quai Branly (Paris, 2001–06) ; un immeuble d'appartements à SoHo (New York, 2006) et le Guthrie Theater (Minneapolis, Minnesota, 2006). Plus récemment, il a réalisé Les Bains des Docks (Le Havre, 2006–08) ; l'hôtel de ville de Montpellier (2002–09) ; la salle de concert de la radio danoise (Copenhague, 2003–09) ; le Sofitel Vienne Stephansdom-Stilwerk (Vienne, 2006–10, publié ici) ; l'immeuble d'appartements Chelsea (New York, 2006–10, également publié ici) et le Pavillon de la Serpentine Gallery (Londres, 2010). Des projets en cours sont la nouvelle salle philharmonique de la Cité de la musique à Paris (2014) ; le Louvre Abou Dhabi (EAU, 2010–13) et le Musée national du Qatar (Doha, 2014).

SOFITEL VIENNA STEPHANSDOM-STILWERK

Vienna, Austria, 2006–10

*Address: Praterstr. 1, 1020 Vienna, Austria, +43 1 90 61 60 / +43 1 906 16 20 00,
www.sofitel.com/gb/hotel-6599-sofitel-vienna-stephansdom/index.shtml
Area: 46 000 m². Client: UNIQA Praterstraße Projekterrichtungs GmbH, Vienna, Austria
Cost: €140 million*

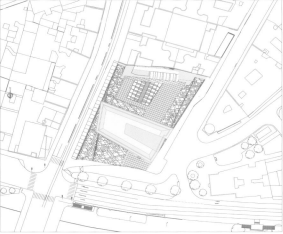

Making use of the unusual trapezoidal site, Nouvel places a fairly "normal" rectangular block on a sloping, patterned base.

Nouvel nutzt das ungewöhnliche, trapezförmige Grundstück, indem er einen vergleichsweise „konventionellen" rechteckigen Baukörper auf einen schiefen, gemusterten Sockel setzt.

Tirant parti de la forme en trapèze de la parcelle, Nouvel y implante une tour rectangulaire « normale », dressée sur un socle incliné orné d'un motif géométrique.

This 18-story building located near the Stephansdom includes convention and banquet spaces, 182 hotel rooms, and a panoramic restaurant on the top level. Energy-saving measures concerning the heating and electrical systems cost approximately €2.6 million but are due to generate €500 000 per year in savings. The building includes spectacular back-lit ceiling works by the noted Swiss artist Pipilotti Rist. "Architecture," says Jean Nouvel, "is the art of taming constraints; of poetizing contradictions; of looking differently at common and trivial things in order to reveal their singularity. Architecture is an opportunity, in a city marked by history, to continue games begun by others… an occasion to modify, to deepen, or to change the meaning of a context." Referring specifically to this building he says: "At the limit between building and sky there is another flat plane that reveals the appearance-disappearance of changing faces, an evocation of the multiple faces forever linked to the depth of imagery born of this city."

Im 18-stöckigen Bau unweit des Stephansdoms befinden sich Konferenz- und Bankettsäle, 182 Hotelzimmer sowie ein Panoramarestaurant im Dachgeschoss. Rund 2,6 Millionen Euro wurden in eine energiesparende Wärme- und Stromversorgung investiert, die jährlich Ersparnisse von 500 000 Euro bringen soll. Im Bau befinden sich darüber hinaus spektakuläre hinterleuchtete Deckenarbeiten der renommierten Schweizer Künstlerin Pipilotti Rist. „Architektur", so Jean Nouvel, „ist die Kunst, Zwänge zu überwinden, Widersprüche zu poetisieren, gewöhnliche, ja triviale Dinge auf andere Weise zu betrachten und so ihre Unverwechselbarkeit aufzuzeigen. In einer von Geschichte geprägten Stadt ist Architektur eine Chance, die von anderen begonnenen Spiele fortzuführen … eine Chance, Kontexte inhaltlich zu modifizieren, zu vertiefen oder zu verändern." Spezifisch im Hinblick auf dieses Projekt erklärt Nouvel: „An der Grenze zwischen Bauwerk und Himmel präsentiert eine weitere, flache Ebene einen Wechsel aufscheinender und wieder schwindender Gesichter, eine Anspielung auf die zahlreichen Gesichter, die für immer mit der vielschichtigen Bildsprache verknüpft sein werden, die diese Stadt hervorgebracht hat."

Cet immeuble de 18 étages situé non loin de la cathédrale de Vienne compte 182 chambres, des installations pour congrès et banquets et un restaurant panoramique à son sommet. Les dispositifs d'économies d'énergie mis en place (chauffage et électricité) qui ont coûté environ 2, 6 millions d'euros devraient générer des économies annuelles de 500 000 euros. L'immeuble se remarque pour ses spectaculaires plafonds rétroéclairés signés de la célèbre artiste suisse Pipilotti Rist. « L'architecture », explique Jean Nouvel, « est l'art d'apprivoiser les contraintes. De poétiser les contradictions. De poser un autre regard sur les banalités et les trivialités pour les singulariser. L'architecture est l'occasion, dans une ville marquée par l'histoire, de continuer des jeux commencés par d'autres… l'occasion de modifier, d'approfondir ou de changer le sens d'un contexte… » Sur l'hôtel même, il ajoute : « À la limite du ciel un plan plane pour révéler l'apparition-disparition de visages mutants, évocation de multiples visages à jamais attachés à la profondeur des images nées de cette ville. »

The strong, gray lines of the building are set off by the patterned, sloped base that marks the intervention of this talented architect.

Die markanten grauen Linien des Gebäudes heben sich vom gemusterten schiefen Sockel ab, der den Entwurf dieses renommierten Architekten auszeichnet.

La forme massive et sombre de la tour est rendue moins agressive par le profil incliné de son socle, intervention talentueuse de l'architecte.

The architect collaborated with the noted Swiss artist Pipilotti Rist where the back-lit décor of roof surfaces was concerned. This is an unusual element that sets the architecture apart from its environment.

Bei den hinterleuchteten Flächen der Dachkonstruktion kollaborierte Nouvel mit der bekannten Schweizer Künstlerin Pipilotti Rist. Das ungewöhnliche Element hebt den Entwurf aus seinem baulichen Umfeld heraus.

Jean Nouvel a collaboré avec la célèbre artiste suisse Pipilotti Rist pour les décors rétroéclairés des plafonds, éléments originaux qui signalent la présence de l'hôtel dans son environnement.

As section drawings of the tower show, and as the image above confirms, the form of the tower is quite simply geometric with the sloped surface beneath the main block being the most unexpected element.

Wie Querschnitte des Hochhauses belegen und die Ansicht oben bestätigt, ist die Form des Turms geometrisch äußerst schlicht; die schiefe Ebene unterhalb des Hauptbaukörpers ist sein überraschendstes Element.

Comme le montrent les plans de coupe et le confirme l'image ci-dessus, le profil de la tour est assez classique, l'élément le plus surprenant étant la partie inclinée sous le bloc principal.

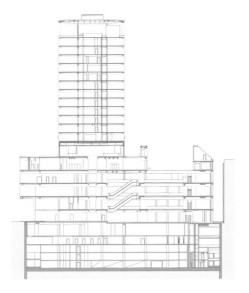
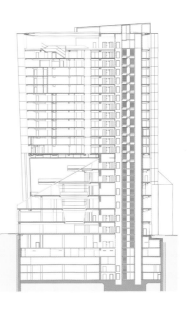

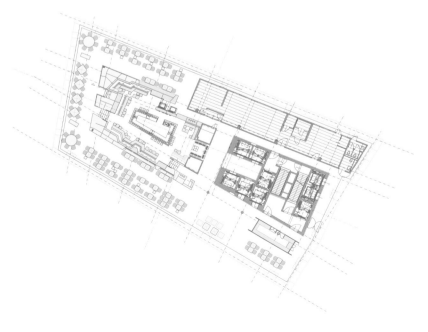

Works by Pipilotti Rist form the ceiling of the upper level lounge and dining area. A floor plan (left) shows the trapezoidal form of the entire building.

Die Decken von Bar und Restaurant im Dachgeschoss sind mit Arbeiten von Pipilotti Rist gestaltet. Ein Grundriss (links) zeigt die Trapezform des Gebäudes.

Des créations de Pipilotti Rist ornent le plafond du salon et de la salle à manger du dernier étage. Le plan au sol (à gauche) montre la forme trapézoïdale du projet.

Rist's ceiling designs are back-lit and colorful, which makes them stand out in a particularly forceful way at night.

Die Deckengestaltung von Pipilotti Rist ist hinterleuchtet und farbintensiv, was nachts besonders eindrücklich wirkt.

Les couleurs des plafonds rétroéclairés de Pipilotti Rist leur assurent une présence particulièrement forte la nuit.

CHELSEA APARTMENT BUILDING

New York, New York, USA, 2006–10

Address: West 19th Street, New York, NY, USA
Area: 13 400 m². Client: Alf Naman Real Estate Cape Advisors, Inc.
Cost: not disclosed

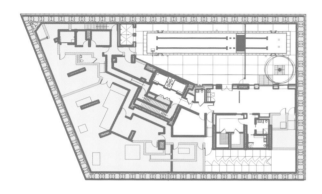
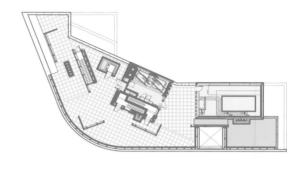

Nouvel's apartment building has an unusual, irregular window pattern, seen from different angles in these two photos. The building occupies a corner at West 19th Street near the Hudson River.

Nouvels Apartmenthochhaus zeichnet sich durch die unregelmäßige Anordnung der Fensteröffnungen aus, hier aus zwei verschiedenen Blickwinkeln zu sehen. Der Bau steht auf einem Eckgrundstück an der Ecke der West 19th Street, unweit des Hudson River.

Situé à l'angle de la 19e Rue Ouest près de l'Hudson, l'immeuble d'appartements de Jean Nouvel, vu sous différents angles ici, se remarque par son fenêtrage de composition irrégulière.

This tall, thin apartment building is located at the extremity of West 19th Street, just across from buildings by Frank Gehry and Shigeru Ban. In describing his own building, Nouvel asks the rhetorical question: "Is it possible to have a neighbor more prestigious, more white and luminous than Frank Gehry?" As is often the case, the architect wrote a rather poetic text about this building before it was built: "On a curved angle, like the eye of an insect, differently oriented facets capture reflections and send out their own shafts of light. The apartments are in the 'eye,' they decompose and recompose the complex cityscape: one frames the horizon, another the white curve in the sky, yet another the boats on the Hudson, and finally the skyline of Midtown." With its unusual articulated façade, the building, containing 72 apartments and a restaurant, stands out and clearly offers its residents unprecedented views on the city and the river.

Das hohe, schlanke Apartmentgebäude am äußersten Ende der West 19th Street liegt in unmittelbarer Nachbarschaft zu Bauten von Frank Gehry und Shigeru Ban. Bei der Beschreibung seines Gebäudes stellt Nouvel die rhetorische Frage: „Kann man einen renommierteren Nachbarn haben, etwas Strahlenderes und Weißeres als Frank Gehry?" Wie so oft verfasste der Architekt einen ausgesprochen poetischen Text, bevor der Bau realisiert wurde: „Unterschiedlich, in einem geschwungenen Winkel ausgerichtete Facetten – wie das Auge eines Insekts – fangen Spiegelungen ein und senden ihrerseits Lichtfanale aus. Die Apartments liegen im ‚Auge' selbst, fragmentieren die komplexe Stadtlandschaft und setzen sie neu wieder zusammen: Eins rahmt den Horizont, ein anderes die geschwungenen weißen Linien am Himmel, wieder andere die Schiffe auf dem Hudson und schließlich die Skyline von Midtown." Im Gebäude mit der ungewöhnlich artikulierten Fassade befinden sich 72 Apartments und ein Restaurant; der Bau fällt auf und bietet den Bewohnern beispiellose Aussicht über den Fluss und die Stadt.

Ce mince immeuble de grande hauteur se trouve à l'extrémité de la 19e Rue Ouest, juste en face de ceux construits par Frank Gehry et Shigeru Ban. Décrivant son projet, Nouvel pose la question rhétorique suivante : « Peut-on avoir à l'angle de la rue un voisin plus prestigieux que Frank Gehry, plus blanc, plus lumineux ? » Comme souvent, l'architecte a rédigé un texte assez poétique sur cet immeuble avant qu'il ne soit construit : « Sur un angle courbe, tel l'œil d'un insecte, des facettes différemment orientées saisissent tous les reflets et lancent des éclats. Les appartements sont dans "l'œil", ils décomposent et recomposent ce paysage complexe : un cadre sur l'horizon… un autre sur la courbe blanche dans le ciel… un autre sur les bateaux de l'Hudson River et, de l'autre coté, un sur le skyline de Midtown. » Grâce à son étonnante façade articulée, cet immeuble de 72 appartements et un restaurant se distingue de son environnement et offre à ses résidents une vue incomparable sur la ville et le fleuve.

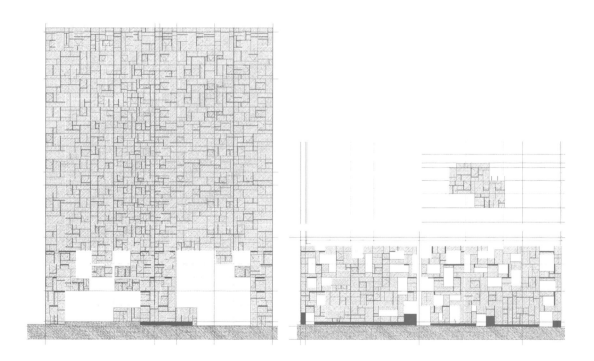

An elevation drawing shows the complex, irregular pattern of the windows and frames that occupy the façades that face south and toward the river.

Ein Aufriss zeigt die komplexe asymmetrische Anordnung der Fenster und Rahmenelemente an den Fassaden nach Süden und zum Fluss.

Un plan d'élévation montre la composition complexe et irrégulière des façades et de leurs ouvertures face au sud et au fleuve.

The articulated surface of the building, located in the Chelsea area of Manhattan, stands out from other buildings, including Frank Gehry's IAC building seen to the right of Nouvel's structure above.

Die stark gegliederte Oberfläche des Gebäudes im Stadtviertel Chelsea in Manhattan ist ein Kontrast zur übrigen Bebauung, einschließlich des IAC Building von Frank Gehry, das auf der Ansicht (oben) rechts von Nouvels Entwurf zu sehen ist.

La façade articulée de la tour, située dans Chelsea à Manhattan, se singularise par rapport à ses voisins, dont l'immeuble ICA de Frank Gehry vu ci-dessus, à droite du projet de l'architecte français.

In an area formerly dominated by older buildings, Nouvel's tower offers luxury apartments on a street where Frank Gehry and Shigeru Ban have also built recently.

In einer ehemals von Altbauten dominierten Gegend hat Nouvels Turm Luxusapartments zu bieten. Auf derselben Straße haben auch Frank Gehry und Shigeru Ban gebaut.

Dans un quartier naguère dominé par des constructions anciennes, la tour de Nouvel propose des appartements de luxe à proximité de réalisations de Frank Gehry et de Shigeru Ban.

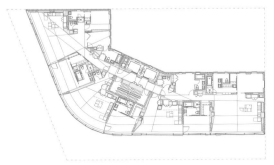

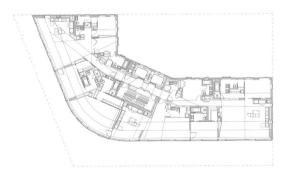
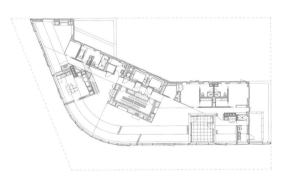

BASSAM EL OKEILY

Bassam El Okeily Architect
25 Greepstraat
Brussels 1000
Belgium

Tel: +32 498 48 23 52
E-mail: bassam@elokeily.com
Web: www.bassamelokeily.com

BASSAM EL OKEILY was born in Alexandria, Egypt, in 1974. He attended French secondary school in Casablanca, Morocco, and worked in the office of Christian de Portzamparc in Paris from 1998 to 1999. In 2001, he graduated from the École Spéciale d'Architecture located on the Boulevard Raspail in Paris and created his own office, Atelier Bassam El Okeily, in Brussels in 2006. He has worked on the Cultural Center of Samiri (Samiri, Niger, 2001); SOS Médecins (Strasbourg, France, 2006); Roterman Opticians (Ghent, Belgium, 2008); the Narrow House (Bilzen, Belgium, 2008–09, published here); and the ECFY&KUBES Blind Art Gallery (Maastricht, The Netherlands, 2010).

BASSAM EL OKEILY wurde 1974 in Alexandria, Ägypten, geboren. Er besuchte die französischsprachige Oberschule in Casablanca, Marokko, und arbeitet von 1998 bis 1999 im Büro von Christian de Portzamparc in Paris. 2001 schloss er sein Studium an der École Spéciale d'Architecture am Boulevard Raspail in Paris ab und gründete sein eigenes Büro, Atelier Bassam El Okeily, 2006 in Brüssel. Er arbeitete u.a. am Kulturzentrum von Samiri (Samiri, Niger, 2001), am SOS Médecins (Straßburg, Frankreich, 2006), dem Augenoptiker Roterman (Gent, Belgien, 2008), dem Narrow House (Bilzen, Belgien, 2008–09, hier vorgestellt) sowie der Blind Art Gallery ECFY&KUBES (Maastricht, Niederlande, 2010).

BASSAM EL OKEILY, né à Alexandrie (Égypte) en 1974, a fait ses études secondaires au lycée français de Casablanca et travaillé à Paris chez Christian de Portzamparc de 1998 à 1999. Il est diplômé de l'École spéciale d'architecture (Paris, 2001) et a fondé son agence, Atelier Bassam El Okeily, à Bruxelles en 2006. Parmi ses réalisations : le Centre culturel de Samiri (Samiri, Niger, 2001) ; le siège de SOS Médecins (Strasbourg, France, 2006) ; le magasin d'optique Roterman (Gand, Belgique, 2008) ; la Maison étroite (Bilzen, Belgique, 2008–09, publiée ici) et la ECFY&KUBES Blind Art Gallery (Maastricht, Pays-Bas, 2010).

THE NARROW HOUSE

Bilzen, Belgium, 2008–09

Area: 215 m². Client: Mr Menten and Ms Bienkens. Cost: not disclosed
Collaboration: Architect Karla Menten

This house is just 5.3 meters wide and is located in the small town of Bilzen near the border with the Netherlands. This is the first house designed by the architect. The clients are an art historian and his wife, an artist. The exterior of the ground floor is closed, containing the entrance area and the garage. The upper part of the house is, by contrast, fully glazed. Two balconies project from the façade into the house. The lower one contains a library and offers a sheltered view of the street. The upper balcony accommodates the artist's studio. Blue light "turns the façade into a light sculpture after dark. It's a narrow house in a narrow street," says the architect, "which tells the tale of a man, a woman, and their passion. Architecture becomes a pretext where a wall is something like a will. A house is a space to live; it could also be a place to remain."

Das nur 5,3 m breite Haus liegt in Bilzen, einer Kleinstadt unweit der niederländischen Grenze. Es ist der erste Wohnbau des Architekten. Bauherren sind ein Kunsthistoriker und seine Frau, eine Künstlerin. Im Erdgeschoss zeigt sich die Fassade geschlossen, hier befinden sich Eingangsbereich und Garage. Der obere Teil des Hauses hingegen ist voll verglast. Hinter der Fassade kragen zwei Balkone aus. Hinter dem unteren Balkon liegt eine Bibliothek, von hier aus bietet sich ein geschützter Blick auf die Straße. Hinter dem oberen Balkon verbirgt sich das Atelier der Künstlerin. Durch blaues Licht „wird die Fassade nachts zu einer Lichtskulptur. Es ist ein schmales Haus auf einer schmalen Straße", erklärt der Architekt, „das die Geschichte von einem Mann, einer Frau und ihrer Leidenschaft erzählt. Architektur wird zum Vorwand, wo eine Wand so etwas wie ein Wille ist. Ein Haus ist ein Ort zum Wohnen, es könnte ein Ort zum Bleiben sein."

Cette maison de tout juste 5,30 mètres de large, la première conçue par l'architecte, se trouve dans la petite ville de Bilzen près de la frontière néerlandaise. Ses clients sont un historien d'art et son épouse, elle-même artiste. La façade du rez-de-chaussée qui contient l'entrée et un garage semble totalement close, en revanche, les deux niveaux supérieurs sont entièrement vitrés. Deux balcons se projettent de l'intérieur vers la face interne de cette façade de verre. Le balcon inférieur contient une bibliothèque et offre une vue filtrée sur la rue. Le balcon supérieur accueille l'atelier de l'artiste. Un éclairage bleu « transforme la façade en sculpture lumineuse, la nuit venue. C'est une maison étroite dans une rue étroite », explique l'architecte, « qui raconte l'histoire d'un homme, d'une femme et de leur passion. L'architecture devient ici un prétexte où un mur s'apparente à une volonté. Une maison est un espace où vivre, et pourrait aussi être un lieu où demeurer ».

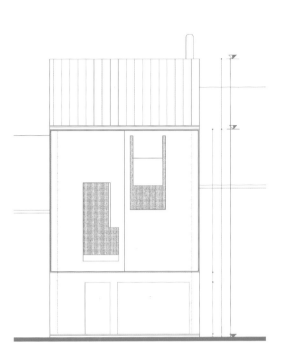

The simple forms of the house seen in the drawing above are rendered more complex by a series of sculptural interior openings and the unusual street-side window.

Die schlichte Grundform des Hauses (Zeichnung oben) gewinnt an Komplexität durch eine Reihe skulpturaler Öffnungen im Innern des Baus und seine ungewöhnliche Glasfront zur Straße hin.

La simplicité des formes de la maison (voir dessin ci-dessus) est rendue plus complexe par une série d'ouvertures sculpturales à l'intérieur et l'étonnante façade-fenêtre donnant sur la rue.

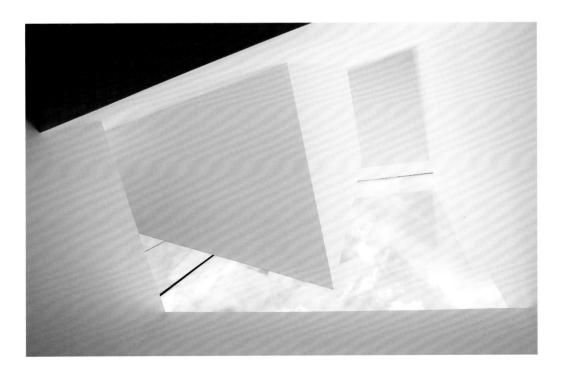

Long and narrow, the house nonetheless admits ample quantities of daylight, whose effect is augmented by the entirely white walls and ceilings.

Das lange schmale Haus wird dennoch reichlich mit Tageslicht versorgt, dessen Wirkung durch die ausschließlich weißen Wände und Decken verstärkt wird.

Bien que longue et étroite, la maison n'en bénéficie pas moins d'un généreux éclairage naturel dont l'effet est accru par la couleur blanche des murs et des plafonds.

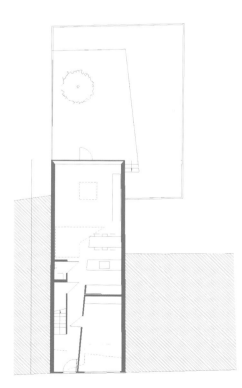
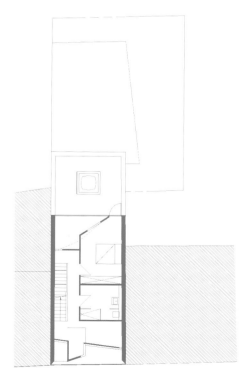

OLSON KUNDIG

Olson Kundig Architects
159 South Jackson Street, Suite 600
Seattle, WA 98104
USA

Tel: +1 206 624 5670
Fax: +1 206 624 3730
E-mail: newinquiry@olsonkundigarchitects.com
Web: www.olsonkundigarchitects.com

TOM KUNDIG received his B.A. in Environmental Design (1977) and his M.Arch (1981) degrees from the University of Washington. He was a principal of Jochman/ Kundig (1983–84) before becoming a principal of Olson Kundig Architects (since 1986). Tom Kundig is the recipient of the 2008 National Design Award in Architecture Design, awarded by the Smithsonian's Cooper-Hewitt National Design Museum. As Olson Sundberg Kundig Allen Architects the firm received the 2009 National AIA Architecture Firm Award. The firm's work includes Chicken Point Cabin (Northern Idaho, 2002); the widely published Delta Shelter (Mazama, Washington, 2005); the Rolling Huts (Mazama, Washington, 2007); Montecito Residence (Montecito, California, 2008); and Hong Kong Villa (lead architect Jim Olson, Shek-O, China, 2008); 1111 E. Pike (Seattle, Washington, 2008); The Pierre (San Juan Islands, Washington, 2008–10, published here); and Art Stable (Seattle, Washington, 2010), all in the USA unless stated otherwise.

TOM KUNDIG absolvierte seinen B.A. in Umweltplanung (1977) und seinen M.Arch (1981) an der Universität von Washington. Er war leitender Architekt bei Joch- man/Kundig (1983–84) und ist seit 1986 Direktor bei Olson Kundig Architects. Tom Kundig wurde 2008 mit dem Nationalpreis für architektonisches Entwerfen ausge- zeichnet, der vom Cooper-Hewitt National Design Museum der Smithsonian Institution verliehen wird. 2009 wurde das Team unter der Firmierung Olson Sundberg Kundig Allen Architects mit dem Nationalpreis für Architekturbüros der AIA ausgezeichnet. Projekte des Büros sind u.a. Chicken Point Cabin (Nord-Idaho, 2002), die vielfach publizierte Delta Shelter (Mazama, Washington, 2005), die Rolling Huts (Mazama, Washington, 2007), die Montecito Residence (Montecito, Kalifornien, 2008) sowie die Hong Kong Villa (leitender Architekt Jim Olson, Shek-O, China, 2008), das Apartmenthaus 1111 E. Pike (Seattle, Washington, 2008), The Pierre (San Juan Islands, Washington, 2008–10, hier vorgestellt) und der Art Stable (Seattle, Washington, 2010), alle in den USA, sofern nicht anders angegeben.

TOM KUNDIG a obtenu son B. A. en conception environnementale (1977) et son M. Arch. (1981) à l'université de Washington. Il a été associé et dirigeant de Jochman/Kundig (1983–84) avant de diriger Olson Kundig Architects depuis 1986. Il a reçu le prix national de Conception architecturale 2008 du Smithsonian's Cooper- Hewitt National Design Museum. Sous la dénomination d'Olson Sundberg Kundig Allen Architects, l'agence a reçu en 2009 le prix national de l'Agence d'architecture de l'année de l'AIA. Parmi les réalisations de l'agence : le chalet de Chicken Point (nord de l'Idaho, 2002) ; le refuge Delta, abondamment publié (Mazama, Washington, 2005) ; les Huttes à roulettes (Rolling Huts, Mazama, Washington, 2007) ; la résidence de Montecito (Montecito, Californie, 2008) ; la villa Hong Kong (architecte principal Jim Olson, Shek-O, Chine, 2008) ; l'immeuble 1111 E. Pike (Seattle, Washington, 2008) ; la maison The Pierre (San Juan Islands, Washington, 2008–10, publié ici) et l'Art Stable (Seattle, Washington, 2010).

THE PIERRE

San Juan Islands, Washington, USA, 2008–10

Area: 232 m². Client: not disclosed. Cost: not disclosed

With its high concrete side walls, generous glazing, and green roof, the house is inserted into its rocky site, providing open views of the water.

Mit hohen Sichtbetonmauern, großzügiger Verglasung und begrüntem Dach wurde das Haus in das felsige Grundstück eingelassen und bietet so unverstellte Aussicht aufs Wasser.

Délimitée par deux hauts murs en béton, une façade de verre et une toiture végétalisée, la maison s'est insérée dans un terrain rocheux en se ménageant des vues sur la baie.

Conceived as a retreat nestled into the rock, according to the architects "**THE PIERRE** (the French word for stone) celebrates the materiality of the site. From certain angles, the house—with its rough materials, encompassing stone, a green roof, and surrounding foliage—almost disappears into nature." Parts of the original rock were excavated with the marks of the work left in place, and the same rock was used as crushed aggregate for the concrete floors. Large blocks of stone from the excavation served for the carport structure. A main level includes an open kitchen and dining and living areas. A wooden storage box links inside and outside, while the master suite is situated at a right angle to these main spaces. Rock "extrudes into the space" in numerous locations, "contrasting with the luxurious textures of the furnishings." Even a powder room is carved out from the rock. Contemporary works of art by Cameron Martin, Jesse Paul Miller, Andres Serrano, Franz West, and Claude Zervas are mounted inside and outside the house.

Das Haus, geplant als in den Fels geschmiegtes Feriendomizil, beschreiben die Architekten wie folgt: „**THE PIERRE** (von frz. Stein) lässt sich voll und ganz auf die Stofflichkeit des Geländes ein. Aus bestimmten Blickwinkeln scheint das Haus – mit seinen rauen Materialien, darunter Stein, mit seinem begrünten Dach und dem Baumbestand – fast in der Natur zu verschwinden." Ein Teil des ursprünglichen Felsgrunds wurde abgetragen (die Spuren wurden belassen) und als zermahlener Zuschlag für die Betonböden verwendet. Große Steinblöcke, die bei der Abtragung gewonnen wurden, kamen beim Bau des Carports zum Einsatz. Im Hauptgeschoss liegen eine offene Küche, Ess- und Wohnbereiche. Ein holzummantelter Abstellraum ist Bindeglied zwischen Innen- und Außenraum. Das Hauptschlafzimmer liegt im rechten Winkel zu den Hauptwohnbereichen. An mehreren Stellen „dringt" der Fels „in den Raum hinein" und „bildet einen Kontrast zu den Texturen der luxuriösen Einrichtung". Selbst ein Badezimmer wurde aus dem Fels geschlagen. Werke zeitgenössischer Künstler, darunter Arbeiten von Cameron Martin, Jesse Paul Miller, Andres Serrano, Franz West und Claude Zervas, finden sich im wie außerhalb des Hauses.

Retraite nichée dans les rochers « **THE PIERRE** (au sens de rocher) célèbre la matérialité de son site. Sous certains angles, la maison – matériaux bruts, dont la roche, toiture végétalisée et arbres environnants – disparaît presque dans la nature », expliquent les architectes. Des parties du rocher d'origine ont été creusées en laissant les marques du travail d'excavation. La même pierre a été récupérée et broyée pour servir d'agrégat dans la composition du béton des sols. D'autres gros blocs de pierre du site forment la structure de l'auvent à voitures. Au niveau principal se trouve une cuisine ouverte, un coin salle à manger et un séjour. Un réduit en bois fait le lien entre l'intérieur et l'extérieur. La suite principale est perpendiculaire aux espaces de vie. La roche « infiltre l'espace » en de nombreux endroits, « contrastant avec les riches textures du mobilier ». Des toilettes ont même été creusées dans la roche. Des œuvres d'art contemporain de Cameron Martin, Jesse Paul Miller, Andres Serrano, Franz West et Claude Zervas sont présentées à l'intérieur et à l'extérieur de la maison.

A concrete wall encounters and penetrates a rock formation, emphasizing the mineral aspect of both the architecture and the site.

Eine Mauer aus Beton läuft auf einen Felsen zu und durchdringt ihn: Eine Geste, die den mineralischen Charakter von Architektur und Grundstück unterstreicht.

Un mur de béton pénètre littéralement dans la formation rocheuse, ce qui renforce l'aspect minéral de l'architecture et du site.

An outdoor seating area and a fireplace that also opens to the exterior create an ordered corner on the edge of the rough, rocky site.

Durch eine Sitzecke im Freien und einen Außenkamin entsteht eine klar gegliederte Eckzone am Rande des rauen, felsigen Grundstücks.

Un coin salon et une cheminée à l'extérieur créent un espace ordonné, délimité par les rochers qui entourent la maison.

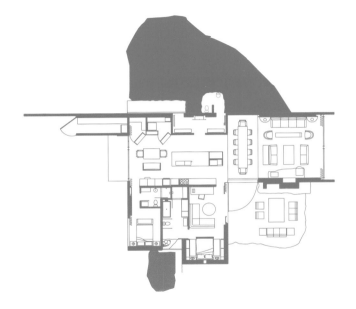

The rocks that the house is built on "intrude" frequently inside, contrasting with the smoother surfaces of the architecture itself.

An vielen Stellen „erobern" die Felsen, auf denen das Haus gebaut ist, den Innenraum und kontrastieren mit den glatteren Oberflächen der Architektur.

Les rochers sur lesquels la maison a été édifiée s'invitent fréquemment à l'intérieur, contrastant avec l'aspect lisse du bâti.

In the living and dining area concrete walls give way to a large opening provided by a folding window system.

Im Wohn- und Essbereich werden die Sichtbetonmauern durch eine großzügige Öffnung mit einer seitlich öffnenden Glastür aufgelockert.

Dans le séjour-salle à manger, les murs en béton sont interrompus par une vaste baie fermée par des panneaux de verre en accordéon.

CARLOS OTT

Carlos Ott Architect
Zonamerica Business and Technology Park
Ruta 8 Km 17.5, Edificio Beta 4 of. 103, Montevideo 91600, Uruguay
Tel: +598 2 518 2235 / Fax: +598 2 518 2234
E-mail: info@carlosott.com / Web: www.carlosott.com

Edgar Baruzze
Cebollati 1698 apto. 203, Montevideo 11200, Uruguay
Tel: +598 2 410 8893 / E-mail: edbar@adinet.com.uy

CARLOS OTT was born in Montevideo, Uruguay, in 1946. He received his M.Arch degrees from the Washington University School of Architecture (Saint Louis, Missouri) and Hawaii University (Honolulu) in 1972. Carlos Ott became an international figure when he won the open, anonymous international competition for the Opera Bastille in Paris (1989). Ott created his current firm in 1992 with a head office in Montevideo, Uruguay, and branches in Shanghai, Abu Dhabi, Toronto, Paris, and Montréal. The firm employs about 60 architects. Completed projects include the National Bank of Dubai (Dubai, 1998); Dubai Hilton Hotel (Dubai, 2001); National Bank of Abu Dhabi (Abu Dhabi, 2003); Etisalat Headquarters (Abu Dhabi, 2003), all in the UAE; and the Hangzhou Grand Theater (Zhejiang, China, 2004). Other current work includes Calgary Federal Court House (Alberta, Canada, 2005–07); Seasons Tower (Punta del Este, Uruguay, 2005–08); Artech Residential Building (Aventura, Florida, USA, 2006–08); the AAM Tower (Dubai, UAE, 2008); Rambla Rep. Del Perú Residencial Building (Montevideo, Uruguay, 2005–09); Jade Ocean Residential Tower (North Miami Beach, Florida, USA, 2005–09); and Ushuaia International Airport Extension (Tierra del Fuego, Argentina, 2007–09). He was associated with Edgar Baruzze for the Playa Vik (Faro José Ignacio, Maldonado, Uruguay, 2007–10, published here).

CARLOS OTT wurde 1946 in Montevideo, Uruguay, geboren. Er schloss sein Architekturstudium an der Washington University (Saint Louis, Missouri) und der Hawaii University (Honolulu) 1972 jeweils mit einem M.Arch ab. Carlos Ott wurde international bekannt, als er den offenen anonymen Wettbewerb für die Opéra Bastille in Paris (1989) gewann. Ott gründete sein aktuelles Büro 1992 mit Hauptsitz in Montevideo, und Niederlassungen in Shanghai, Abu Dhabi, Toronto, Paris und Montréal. Das Büro beschäftigt 60 Architekten. Realisierte Projekte sind u.a. die Nationalbank von Dubai (Dubai, 1998), das Dubai Hilton (Dubai, 2001), die Nationalbank von Abu Dhabi (Abu Dhabi, 2003), die Zentrale von Etisalat (Abu Dhabi, 2003), alle in den VAE, sowie das Hangzhou-Grand-Theater (Zhejiang, China, 2004). Zu Otts weiteren Projekten zählen das Bundesgerichtsgebäude in Calgary (Alberta, Canada, 2005–07), der Seasons Tower (Punta del Este, Uruguay, 2005–08), die Wohnanlage Artech (Aventura, Florida, USA, 2006–08), der AAM Tower (Dubai, VAE, 2008), die Wohnanlage an der Rambla Rep. Del Perú (Montevideo, Uruguay, 2005–09), das Apartmenthochhaus Jade Ocean (North Miami Beach, Florida, USA, 2005–09) sowie die Erweiterung des internationalen Flughafens von Ushuaia (Tierra del Fuego, Argentinien, 2007–09). Gemeinsam mit Edgar Baruzze entwarf er die Ferienanlage in Playa Vik (Faro José Ignacio, Maldonado, Uruguay, 2007–10, hier vorgestellt).

CARLOS OTT, né à Montevideo (Uruguay) en 1946 a obtenu ses diplômes M. Arch. à l'École d'architecture de l'université de Washington (Saint Louis, Missouri) et à l'université d'Hawaii (Honolulu, 1972). Il a acquis une notoriété internationale en remportant le concours ouvert et anonyme lancé pour la construction de l'Opéra Bastille à Paris (1989). Son agence actuelle, qui compte une soixantaine d'architectes, possède son siège à Montevideo et des bureaux à Shanghaï, Abou Dhabi, Toronto, Paris et Montréal. Parmi ses projets réalisés figurent la Banque nationale de Dubaï (Dubaï, 1998) ; l'hôtel Hilton Dubaï (Dubaï, 2001) ; la Banque nationale d'Abou Dhabi (Abou Dhabi, 2003) ; le siège d'Etisalat (Abou Dhabi, 2003) et le Grand Théâtre d'Hangzhou (Zhejiang, Chine, 2004). Il a également réalisé le bâtiment de la Cour fédérale de Calgary (Alberta, Canada, 2005–07) ; la Seasons Tower (Punta del Este, Uruguay, 2005–08) ; l'immeuble résidentiel Artech (Aventura, Floride, 2006–08) ; la tour AAM (Dubaï, EAU, 2008) ; l'immeuble résidentiel Rambla Rep. Del Perú (Montevideo, Uruguay, 2005–09) ; la tour d'appartements Jade Ocean (North Miami Beach, Floride, 2005–09) et l'extension de l'aéroport international d'Ushuaia (Terre de Feu, Argentine, 2007–09). Il s'est associé avec Edgar Baruzze pour le projet de complexe de vacances de Playa Vik (Faro José Ignacio, Maldonado, Uruguay, 2007–10, publié ici).

PLAYA VIK

Faro José Ignacio, Maldonado, Uruguay, 2007–10

Address: Calle Los Cisnes y Los Horneros, Faro José Ignacio, Maldonado, Uruguay, +598 94 60 5212, www.playavik.com
Area: 2022 m². Client: Bermick S.A.. Cost: $14 million
Collaboration: Edgar Baruzze (Associated Architect)

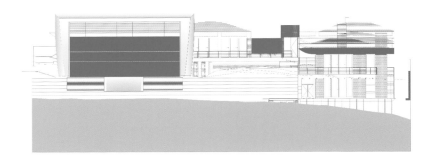

This beach resort is on the south Atlantic coast of Uruguay. Its central feature is called the "Sculpture" by the owners and is a double-curved titanium and glass building with a 16.8-meter-wide sliding glass wall. An L-shaped pavilion made of six houses that can serve as individual residences is arrayed around the Sculpture. A collection of contemporary art, including works by such figures as Anselm Kiefer and James Turrell, is part of the complex. A 23-meter-long black granite pool and wooden deck cantilever over the beach, located ten meters below. Green roofs, water recycling, radiant heat, natural ventilation, and an "intelligent" system to control energy usage are part of the overall "environmentally friendly" strategy of the architect and owners.

Die Ferienanlage liegt am Strand der Südatlantikküste von Uruguay. Zentrales Merkmal ist das Hauptgebäude, von den Eigentümern „Skulptur" genannt, mit seiner zweifach geschwungenen Fassade aus Glas und Titan mit einer 16,8 m breiten Glasschiebetür. Ein L-förmiger Pavillon aus sechs Wohnbauten, die individuell genutzt werden können, gruppiert sich um die „Skulptur". Zum Komplex gehört auch eine Sammlung zeitgenössischer Kunst mit Werken von u.a. Anselm Kiefer und James Turrell. Ein 23 m langer Pool aus schwarzem Granit und ein Holzdeck kragen in 10 m Höhe über dem Strand aus. Als Teil der „umweltfreundlichen" Strategie von Architekt und Eigentümern entschied man sich für begrünte Dächer, Fußbodenheizung, natürliche Belüftung und ein „intelligentes" System zur Steuerung des Energieverbrauchs.

Ce complexe de vacances situé sur la côte uruguayenne de l'Atlantique Sud se signale par ce que ses propriétaires appellent « la sculpture », un bâtiment de verre à murs inclinés en titane, dont une façade est une paroi vitrée coulissante de 16,80 mètres de large. Il est entouré d'une composition en L de six résidences utilisables en maisons individuelles. Le petit complexe possède une collection d'œuvres d'art contemporain, dont des pièces d'Anselm Kiefer et James Turrell. Une piscine de 23 mètres de long en granit noir et entourée d'un platelage en bois se projette en porte-à-faux au-dessus de la plage, située à dix mètres en contrebas. Des toitures végétalisées, un système de recyclage des eaux, des chauffages radiants, la ventilation naturelle et un système intelligent de contrôle de l'utilisation de l'énergie font partie de la stratégie « écologique » voulue par l'architecte et les propriétaires.

The spectacular oceanside setting of the hotel is emphasized by the long narrow pool that projects beyond the outside deck. As the elevation drawings above and these photos show, Playa Vik is built on a sloping site.

Durch den langen schmalen Pool, der über das Terrassendeck hinaus auskragt, kommt die dramatische Lage des Hauses am Meer besonders zur Geltung. Wie auf Aufrissen und Ansichten zu sehen, liegt die Playa Vik auf einem Hanggrundstück.

Le cadre spectaculaire de l'hôtel face à l'océan est sublimé par un long couloir de nage qui se poursuit au-delà de sa bordure. Les élévations et les photographies montrent que Playa Vik a été construite sur un terrain incliné.

Bungalow-type structures offer clients private decks and uninterrupted views of the ocean. The architect mixes wooden exterior elements with a more mineral aspect in the actual buildings.

Die Bungalow-ähnlichen Häuser bieten Besuchern private Terrassen und unverstellten Blick aufs Meer. Holzelemente am Außenbau kombiniert der Architekt mit eher mineralischen Elementen in den Innenbereichen.

Les bâtiments de type pavillon offrent à leurs hôtes des terrasses et des vues panoramiques sur l'océan. L'architecte a tempéré l'aspect minéral des constructions par des composants extérieurs en bois.

The pool leads to the main building of the Playa Vik in an axial arrangement that emphasizes the continuity from the land to the ocean.

Der Pool läuft auf das Hauptgebäude von Playa Vik zu. Die axiale Komposition verknüpft Land und Meer zu einem Kontinuum.

La piscine part du bâtiment principal de Playa Vik, orientée sur un axe qui souligne la continuité entre la terre et l'océan.

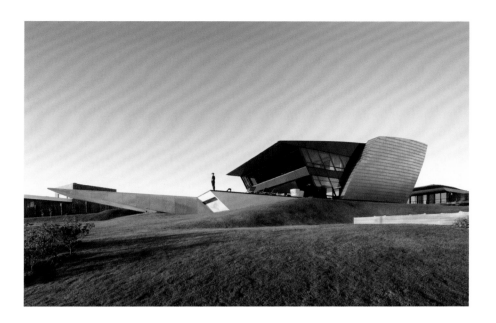

MUTI RANDOLPH

Muti Randolph
Praia de Botafogo, 68/601
22250–040 Rio de Janeiro, RJ
Brazil

Tel: +55 21 9179 6290
E-mail: info@mutirandolph.com
Web: www.mutirandolph.com

MUTI RANDOLPH is an illustrator, graphic art designer, set maker, and creator of a number of noted interiors. His clubs like D-Edge or U-Turn (both in São Paulo) are inspired by "computers and electronic equipment" as well as the "unique freedom and playfulness" of the 1960s. "My main concern is to design space that changes over time, reacting to music through the use of digital technology," he says. Born in 1967 in Rio de Janeiro, Muti Randolph studied Visual Communications and Industrial Design at the Pontificia Universidade Católica do Rio de Janeiro. He started his career as a graphic designer and illustrator in the late 1980s. One of the pioneers in computer art, 3D illustration, and animation in Brazil, he began shifting from virtual 3D to real 3D spaces. His interest in music and technology is very apparent in his projects, where he explores the relation between music and space. He has been developing a software to synch live music and video used in some current permanent and temporary projects. Some of his noted projects are U-Turn Nightclub (São Paulo, 1997); D-Edge Nightclub (Campo Grande, 2001); D-Edge Nightclub (São Paulo, 2003); Galeria Melissa (São Paulo, 2005); São Paulo Fashion Week (2005); "I Capuleti e i Montecchi" Opera at the Theatro Municipal do Rio de Janiero (2006); "Tube," The Creators Project, Galeria Baró (São Paulo, 2010, published here); and "Deep Screen," The Creators Project (Beijing, China, 2010, also published here), all in Brazil unless stated otherwise.

MUTI RANDOLPH ist Illustrator, Grafikdesigner und Bühnenbildner und wurde durch seine Gestaltung zahlreicher Interieurs bekannt. Seine Clubs wie D-Edge oder U-Turn (beide in São Paulo) sind inspiriert von „Computern und elektronischen Geräten", aber auch von der „einzigartigen Freiheit und Spielfreude" der 1960er-Jahre. „Mein Ziel ist in erster Linie, einen Raum zu gestalten, der durch digitale Technik auf Musik reagiert und sich mit der Zeit verändert", erklärt Randolph. 1967 in Rio de Janeiro geboren, studierte er Visuelle Kommunikation und Industriedesign an der Pontificia Universidade Católica do Rio de Janeiro. Seine Laufbahn begann in den späten 1980er-Jahren als Grafikdesigner und Illustrator. Randolph ist einer der Pioniere der digitalen Kunst, 3D-Illustration und Animation in Brasilien und begann schließlich, den Schritt von virtuellen zu realen 3D-Räumen zu machen. Sein Interesse an Musik und Technik spiegelt sich deutlich in seinen Projekten, bei denen er sich mit der Beziehung von Musik und Raum befasst. Er entwickelte eine Software zu Synchronisierung von Live-Musik und Videos, die bei verschiedenen temporären und permanenten Installationen zum Einsatz kommt. Zu seinen bekannten Projekten zählen: U-Turn Club (São Paulo, 1997), D-Edge Club (Campo Grande, 2001), D-Edge Club (São Paulo, 2003), Galeria Melissa (São Paulo, 2005), São Paulo Fashion Week (2005), die Oper *I Capuleti e i Montecchi* am Theatro Municipal do Rio de Janiero (2006), *Tube*, The Creators Project, Galeria Baró (São Paulo, 2010, hier vorgestellt) und *Deep Screen*, The Creators Project (Beijing, China, 2010, ebenfalls hier vorgestellt), alle in Brasilien, sofern nicht anders angegeben.

MUTI RANDOLPH est illustrateur, graphiste, typographe et auteur de nombreux projets d'aménagements intérieurs remarqués. Les clubs qu'il a réalisés, dont le D-Edge ou le U-Turn à São Paulo, lui ont été inspirés par « des équipements informatiques et électroniques » et « la liberté et le sens du jeu » caractéristiques des années 1960. « Mon principal objectif est de concevoir des espaces qui se modifient dans le temps, réagissent à la musique grâce aux technologies numériques », explique-t-il. Né en 1967 à Rio de Janeiro, il a étudié la communication visuelle et le design industriel à la Pontificia Universidade Católica de Rio de Janeiro et a débuté sa carrière comme graphiste et illustrateur à la fin des années 1980. Un des pionniers de l'art numérique, de l'illustration en 3D et de l'animation au Brésil, il a commencé à évoluer de la 3D virtuelle vers de vrais espaces tridimensionnels. Son intérêt pour la musique et la technologie se manifeste fortement dans des projets où il explore les relations entre la musique et l'espace. Il a développé un logiciel de synchronisation en temps réel de musiques et de vidéos qu'il utilise dans certains projets permanents ou temporaires. Parmi ses réalisations remarquées : le night-club U-Turn (São Paulo, 1997) ; le night-club D-Edge (Campo Grande, 2001) ; le night-club D-Edge (São Paulo, 2003) ; la Galeria Melissa (São Paulo, 2005) ; la Semaine de la mode de São Paulo (2005) ; les décors de l'opéra *I Capuleti e i Montecchi* au Théâtre municipal de Rio de Janeiro (2006) ; l'installation *Tube*, The Creators Project, Galeria Baró (São Paulo, 2010, publiée ici) et l'installation *Deep Screen*, The Creators Project (Pékin, Chine, 2010, également publié ici).

"TUBE"

The Creators Project, Galeria Baró, São Paulo, Brazil, 2010

Address: Galeria Baró, Barra Funda 216, São Paulo, Brazil, www.thecreatorsproject.com/events/the-creators-project-são-paulo-2010
Area: 18 m². Client: Intel, Vice. Cost: not disclosed. Collaboration: Dimitre Lima (Programming)

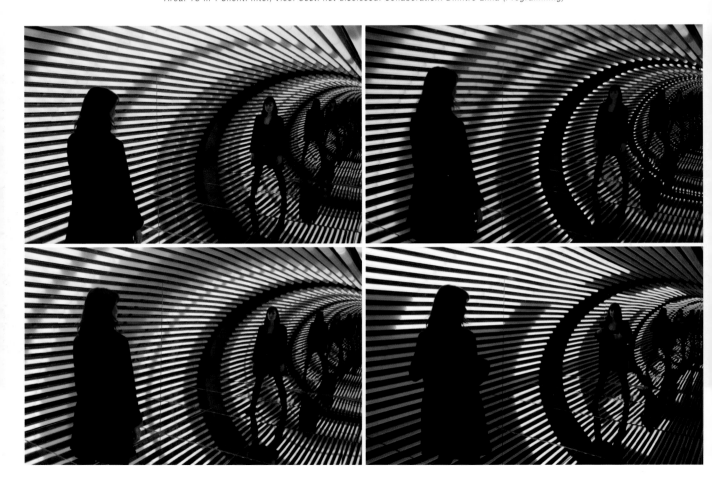

Muti Randolph explains that this installation is "a tube made of tubes." Its actual shape is a half cylinder, echoing the hangar-shaped building of the gallery. Mirrors multiply the 141 LED tubes into what appears to be an infinitely long, five-meter-wide light tube. Software generates animations that relate to the form, simulating speed and rotational movement. Sound is also generated by the software in real time and reacts to the speed, color, and position of the pixels. The designer calls this the "next best thing to big wave tube riding."

Wie Muti Randolph erklärt, ist seine Installation „eine Röhre aus Röhren". Tatsächlich handelt es sich um einen Halbzylinder, der die hangarähnlichen Galerie-räume formal aufgreift. Spiegel vervielfältigen die 141 LED-Röhren zu einem scheinbar endlosen, 5 m breiten Lichttunnel. Eine Software steuert Animationen, die auf die Röhrenform der Installation Bezug nehmen und Geschwindigkeit und Drehbewegungen simulieren. Die Software generiert außerdem einen Soundtrack in Echtzeit, der auf Geschwindigkeit, Farbe und Position der Pixel abgestimmt ist: dem Designer zufolge „das Nächstbeste nach dem Surfen im Tunnel einer großen Welle".

Muti Randolph présente cette installation comme « un tube fait de tubes ». Concrètement, la forme est un demi-cylindre qui rappelle le profil du hangar dans lequel est installée la galerie. Des miroirs multiplient les 141 tubes de DEL pour créer ce qui semble être un tube de cinq mètres de large se prolongeant à l'infini. Un logiciel pilote des animations liées à la forme tubulaire, qui simulent des effets d'accélération et de rotation. Il contrôle également le son en temps réel en réagissant à la vitesse, à la couleur et à la position des pixels. Pour le designer, c'est « ce qui se fait de mieux après la vague creuse pour un surfeur ».

Known for his light installations in nightclubs, Muti Randolph has branched out here into a work destined for a gallery.

Muti Randolph, bekannt für seine Lichtinstallationen für Clubs, reali-siert hier eine Arbeit für eine Galerie.

Connu pour ses installations d'éclai-rage de night-clubs, Muti Randolph s'est ici diversifié en créant une œuvre destinée à une galerie.

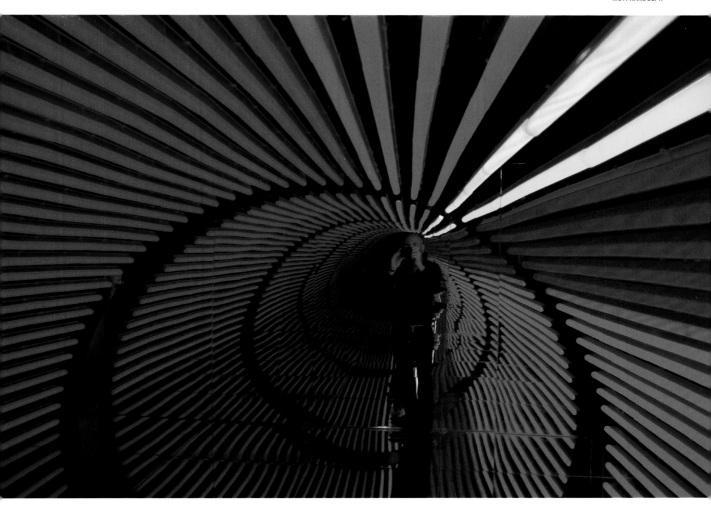

The effect is one of an infinite variety of light patterns and, indeed, a seemingly endless progression of neon tubes.

Es entsteht der Eindruck einer unendlichen Variationsbreite von Lichtmustern und einer scheinbar endlosen Folge von Neonröhren.

L'effet obtenu par Randolph est celui d'une multiplicité de motifs lumineux et la prolongation quasi infinie des tubes au néon.

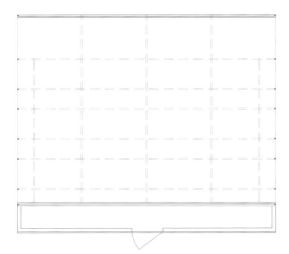

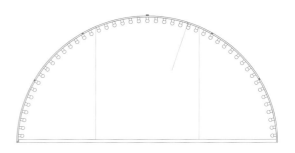

"DEEP SCREEN"

The Creators Project, Beijing, China, 2010

Address: No. 4 Jiuxian Bridge Road, 798 Art District, Beijing, China,
www.thecreatorsproject.com/events/the-creators-project-beijing-2010
Area: 16 m². Client: Intel, Vice. Cost: not disclosed. Collaboration: Coddart (Programming)

DEEP SCREEN is a 3D cubic video display made of 6144 RGB LED clusters. Software generated animations appear to occur in space and participants can move around the display as well as go inside it. The content consists of eight different scenes called "Rain," "RGB Solids," "Cubic Transit," "Cubic Explosion," "Spherical Explosion," "Flags," "Barnett," and "Presence." Some of these react to the movements of visitors and others are random. The same program that generates the images also synthesizes sound that is directly related to the image, varying in frequency, volume, and tone according to the position and color of the pixels. Muti Randolph states: "'Deep Screen' proposes a new relation with video, placing the spectator inside the display."

DEEP SCREEN ist eine Videoinstallation aus 6144 RGB-LED-Clustern in Form eines dreidimensionalen Würfels. Die softwaregenerierten Animationen wirken räumlich, die Besucher können um die Installation herumgehen, sie aber auch betreten. Programmiert sind acht verschiedene Szenen: „Regen", „RGB-Festkörper", „kubischer Transit", „kubische Explosion", „sphärische Explosion", „Flaggen", „Barnett" und „Präsenz". Manche reagieren auf die Bewegungen der Besucher, andere sind zufällig. Dasselbe Programm, dass die Visuals generiert, erzeugt auch synthetische Sounds, die unmittelbar an die Bilder gekoppelt sind, und variieren dabei in Frequenz, Lautstärke und Tonhöhe, je nach Position und Farbe der Pixel. Muti Randolph erklärt: „*Deep Screen* schafft eine neue Beziehung zur Video[kunst], indem es den Betrachter in die Installation hineinversetzt."

DEEP SCREEN est une installation vidéo en 3D de forme cubique composée de 6144 ensembles de DEL RVB. Un logiciel programme des animations qui donnent l'impression de se produire dans l'espace. Les spectateurs peuvent regarder le cube ou y pénétrer. Le programme propose huit scènes différentes intitulées : Pluie, Solides RVB, Transit cubique, Explosion cubique, Explosion sphérique, Drapeaux, Barnett et Présence. Certaines animations réagissent aux mouvements des spectateurs, d'autres fonctionnent de façon aléatoire. Le même programme synthétise également le son directement en lien avec l'image. Le volume, la fréquence et la tonalité varient en fonction de la position et de la couleur des pixels. « *Deep Screen* propose une relation nouvelle avec la vidéo en plaçant le spectateur au centre du dispositif », précise Muti Randolph.

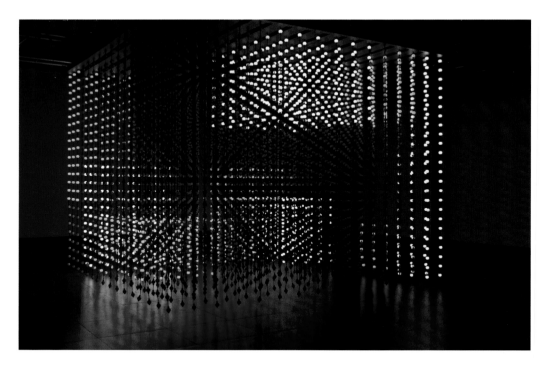

The possibility of LEDs to change color in complex patterns directed by a computer allows the designer to create an almost infinite variety of moods and impressions with this installation.

Die Möglichkeit, per Computer Farbwechsel und komplexe Muster für seine LED-Installation zu programmieren, erlaubt dem Designer, eine schier unendliche Bandbreite von Stimmungen und Eindrücken zu erzeugen.

Les changements de couleurs commandés par ordinateur selon des motifs et des rythmes complexes que permettent les DEL, ont offert au designer la liberté de créer une variété infinie d'ambiances et d'impressions.

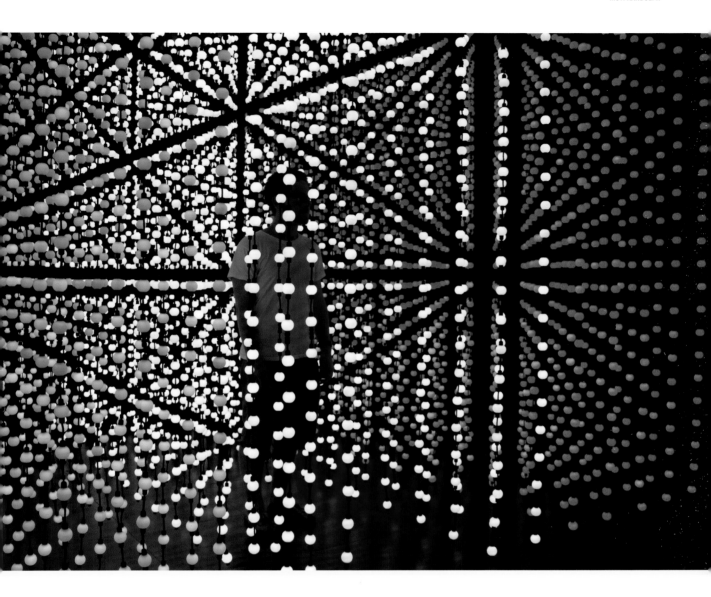

Although it measures just 16 square meters in floor area, "Deep Screen" calls on combinations of light and color to give an impression of nearly endless space. In this sense, the work enters the realm of architecture.

Trotz eine Fläche von lediglich 16 m² erzeugt Deep Screen mit Licht- und Farbkombinationen einen fast unendlichen Raumeindruck. In dieser Hinsicht ist die Installation zweifellos ein architektonisches Werk.

Bien que de 16 m² de surface seulement, Deep Screen utilise des combinaisons de lumière et de couleur qui donnent un sentiment d'espace presque infini. En ce sens, l'œuvre rejoint la création architecturale.

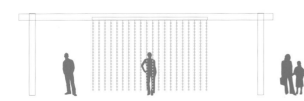

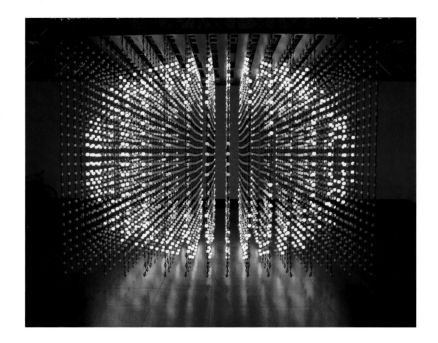

The LED system allows for the creation of forms other than that of the basic cube—such as the rounded volume above, or the layered progression seen to the right.

Mithilfe des LED-Systems lassen sich auch andere Formen als die eines schlichten Würfels erzeugen – etwa der sphärische Körper oben oder die schichtartige Progression rechts im Bild.

Les DEL permettent de créer des formes autres que le cube de base, comme le volume ovoïde ci-dessus, ou des effets de progression par strates (à droite).

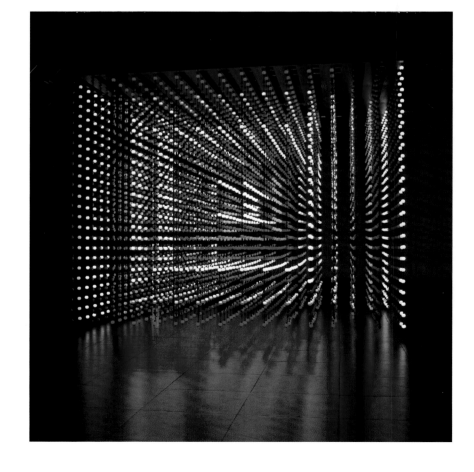

RARE ARCHITECTURE

rare architecture
Studio 110
10 Great Russell Street
London WC1B 3BQ
UK

Tel: +44 20 32 39 93 32
E-mail: info@r-are.net
Web: www.r-are.net

MICHEL DA COSTA CONÇALVES was born in 1973 in Lille, France. He received his DPLG from the École National Supérieure d'Architecture et de Paysage (Lille, 1999). He also obtained an Emergent Technologies + Design M.A. (Architectural Association [AA], London, 2005). He worked in the office of Shigeru Ban (2003–04). He is a cofounder (2005) and Director of rare architecture. **NATHALIE ROZENCWAJG** was born in 1975 in Luxembourg. She studied architecture at the University of Tel Aviv (1994–96) before obtaining an AA Diploma, RIBA Part II (2001). She is also a cofounder and Director of rare. Their work includes Town Hall Hotel (London, UK, 2008–10, published here), and they are currently working on a master plan for a hotel complex (Lapland, Finland, ongoing); a Housing development (Boulogne, France, ongoing); social housing (Beuvrages, France, in design development); and the refurbishment of the Domaine du Château de Pleurs (Pleurs, France, ongoing).

MICHEL DA COSTA CONÇALVES wurde 1973 in Lille, Frankreich, geboren. Er machte sein Diplom (DPLG) an der École National Supérieure d'Architecture et de Paysage (Lille, 1999). Außerdem absolvierte er einen M.A. in Neuen Technologien + Design (Architectural Association [AA], London, 2005). Er arbeitete im Büro von Shigeru Ban (2003–04) und ist Mitbegründer (2005) und Direktor von rare architecture. **NATHALIE ROZENCWAJG** wurde 1975 in Luxemburg geboren. Sie studierte Architektur an der Universität Tel Aviv (1994–96) und absolvierte anschließend ein Diplom (RIBA Part II) an der AA (2001). Sie ist Mitbegründerin und Direktorin von rare. Arbeiten des Teams sind u.a. das Town Hall Hotel (London, 2008–10, hier vorgestellt). Derzeit in Planung sind der Masterplan für einen Hotelcomplex (Lappland, Finnland, in Arbeit), eine Wohnanlage (Boulogne, Frankreich, in Arbeit), Sozialwohnungen (Beuvrages, Frankreich, im Entwurf) sowie die Sanierung der Domaine du Château de Pleurs (Pleurs, Frankreich, in Arbeit).

MICHEL DA COSTA CONÇALVES, né en 1973 à Lille (France) est architecte DPLG, diplômé de l'École nationale supérieure d'architecture et de paysage (Lille, 1999). Il a également obtenu un M. A. en technologies émergentes et design à l'Architectural Association (AA) à Londres en 2005. Il a travaillé chez Shigeru Ban (2003–04) et a fondé en 2005 l'agence rare architecture qu'il dirige avec sa cofondatrice **NATHALIE ROZENCWAJG**. Celle-ci, née en 1975 à Luxembourg, a étudié l'architecture à l'université de Tel-Aviv (1994–96) avant d'obtenir le diplôme RIBA Part II de l'AA (2001). Leurs projets incluent le Town Hall Hotel (Londres, 2008–10, publié ici), et ils travaillent actuellement sur le plan directeur d'un complexe hôtelier (Laponie, Finlande, en cours) ; un immeuble de logements (Boulogne, France, en cours) ; des logements sociaux (Beuvrages, France, en cours de conception) et la rénovation du domaine du Château de Pleurs (Pleurs, France, en cours).

TOWN HALL HOTEL

London, UK, 2008–10

Address: Patriot Square, London E2 9NP, UK, + 44 20 78 71 04 60, www.townhallhotel.com/index.html
Area: 8900 m². Client: not disclosed. Cost: not disclosed

The volume added by the architects to the old town hall takes on a decidedly different, almost kinetic appearance. An old smokestack provides further contrast with the aluminum-skinned hotel block.

Der von den Architekten entworfene neue Anbau für das ehemalige Rathaus unterscheidet sich optisch stark vom Altbau, wirkt geradezu kinetisch-bewegt. Ein weiterer Kontrast zur Aluminiumhaut des Hotelbaus entsteht durch den alten Schornstein.

Le volume greffé par les architectes sur l'ancien hôtel de ville est d'aspect surprenant, presque cinétique. Une ancienne cheminée offre un contraste supplémentaire avec le bloc de l'hôtel habillé d'aluminium.

This project involves a new 98-room luxury hotel, restaurant, and bar located in the old Bethnal Green Town Hall in London's East End. A contemporary wing and a top-floor space (1500 m²) were added at the same time as the Grade II listed 1910 Edwardian building and its 1937 extension were restored. The approval of English Heritage for the rather daring project followed by planning permission were obtained in 2008. The new spaces are wrapped in a patterned, laser-cut aluminum skin with no windows or doors visible. The pattern, designed by the architects, is repeated in the entrance reception space of the hotel, and on the interior courtyard façades in the extension. Each of the 98 rooms has different dimensions. Rare designed the interiors with "pods of discrete beds, desks, storage space, kitchens, and bathroom suites rendered in materials ranging from CNC-milled MDF, Corian, Green Lime marble, glass, oak, and Cardoso and Vals stone." A 14-meter titanium-tiled lap pool in the basement is also part of the scheme, as well as a separately developed bar and restaurant called Viajante.

Das Projekt, ein Luxushotel mit 98 Zimmern, einem Restaurant und einer Bar wurde im ehemaligen Rathaus von Bethnal Green im Londoner East End realisiert. Hier wurde nicht nur der denkmalgeschützte Edwardianische Altbau von 1910 und sein Anbau von 1937 saniert, sondern auch ein moderner Flügel und ein neues Obergeschoss (1500 m²) aufgestockt. Die Zustimmung der Denkmalschutzbehörde English Heritage für das recht gewagte Projekt und schließlich die Baugenehmigung erfolgten 2008. Die Neubaubereiche sind von einer Haut aus lasergeschnittenem Aluminium umfangen und lassen von außen weder Fenster noch Türen erkennen. Das von den Architekten entworfene Muster taucht auch im Empfangsbereich des Hotels und auf den Innenhoffassaden des Anbaus auf. Alle 98 Zimmer sind unterschiedlich groß. Rare gestaltete auch die Interieurs als „Kapseln mit diskreten Betteinbauten, Schreibtischen, Stauraum, Küchen und Bädern, die in Materialien wie CNC-gefrästem MDF, Corian, grünem Marmor, Glas, Eiche und Stein aus Cardoso und Vals gefertigt wurden". Ein 14 m langes Schwimmbecken mit Titanfliesen im Untergeschoss gehört ebenso zur Ausstattung wie die separate Bar und das Restaurant Viajante.

Cet hôtel de luxe comprenant 98 chambres, un restaurant et un bar a été aménagé dans l'ancien hôtel de ville de Bethnal Green dans l'East End de Londres. Le nouveau projet a ajouté une aile contemporaine et un volume de 1500 mètres carrés au dernier étage de ce bâtiment classé de style édouardien datant de 1910, et déjà agrandi en 1937. L'accord de l'administration des monuments historiques et le permis de construire ont été obtenus en 2008. Le bâti nouveau est enveloppé d'une peau d'aluminium découpée au laser qui masque les fenêtres et les portes. Son motif, dessiné par les architectes, se retrouve dans la réception de l'hôtel et sur les façades de la cour intérieure de l'extension. Chacune des 98 chambres est de dimension différente. Rare a conçu les aménagements intérieurs autour de « *pods* de lits, bureaux, rangements, cuisines et salles de bains de style discret, exécutés dans divers matériaux allant du médium fraisé par CNC au Corian, en passant par un marbre citron vert, le verre, le chêne et la pierre de Cardoso ou de Vals ». La piscine de 14 mètres de long au liner de titane en sous-sol ainsi qu'un bar restaurant indépendant, le Viajante, font également partie de ce projet.

The differing materials of elements in the composition seen in the photo on the left might be said to innovate with respect to what is to be expected of modern architecture. The key here is variety and contextualism juxtaposed with an enveloping, contemporary concept.

Der Einsatz verschiedener Materialien bei dieser architektonischen Komposition (links) ist zweifellos innovativ im Vergleich zu anderen modernen Bauten. Schlüssel sind hier Vielfältigkeit sowie ein Gespür für den Kontext, integriert in ein zeitgenössisches Gesamtkonzept.

Les différences dans le choix des matériaux (photo de gauche) constituent en soi une recherche architecturale innovante. L'objectif est ici d'apporter une variété et d'utiliser l'idée de contextualisation dans un concept d'enveloppe d'esprit très contemporain.

Inside, the hotel also combines
modern elements with preexisting
volumes adapted to the new use of
the space.

Auch im Innern des Hotels findet sich
das Zusammenspiel von modernen
Elementen und alten Räumen, die für
die neue Nutzung umgebaut wurden.

À l'intérieur, l'hôtel intègre des éléments contemporains dans les volumes préexistants adaptés à de nouvelles utilisations de l'espace.

Unusual spatial arrangements, introduced in the exterior appearance of the hotel, are continued throughout, as in the bathrooms that are shielded from the bed area only by a low glass wall.

Ungewöhnliche Formen der Raumgestaltung, wie sie sich am Außenbau ankündigen, ziehen sich durch das gesamte Hotel, etwa bei den Bädern, die von der Schlafzone nur durch eine niedrige Glaswand getrennt sind.

Des aménagements spatiaux originaux déjà annoncés par les façades de l'hôtel se retrouvent à l'intérieur comme dans les salles de bains uniquement séparées du lit par une petite paroi de verre.

REX

REX
42 North Moore Street
New York, NY 10013
USA

Tel: +1 646 230 6557
E-mail: office@rex-ny.com
Web: www.rex-ny.com

JOSHUA PRINCE-RAMUS received a B.A. in Philosophy from Yale in 1991 and an M.Arch from Harvard University in 1996. He was the founding partner of OMA New York, the American affiliate of the Office for Metropolitan Architecture (OMA) / Rem Koolhaas in the Netherlands, and served as its principal until he renamed the firm REX in 2006. He was partner in charge of the Guggenheim-Hermitage Museum in Las Vegas and the Seattle Central Library by OMA. He is now the principal of REX. Recently completed projects include the AT&T Performing Arts Center Dee and Charles Wyly Theatre in Dallas (Texas, USA, 2006–09, published here) and the Vakko Fashion Center and Power Media Center in Istanbul (Turkey, 2008–10, also published here). Current work includes Museum Plaza, a 62-story mixed-use skyscraper housing a contemporary art center in Louisville (Kentucky, USA, 2007–); the new headquarters for Activision/Blizzard in Santa Monica (California, USA, 2011/12–); the new Central Library and Music Conservatory for the city of Kortrijk (Belgium, 2012/13–); and a 350 000-square-meter luxury residential development in Songdo Landmark City (South Korea, 2012/13–).

JOSHUA PRINCE-RAMUS schloss sein Studium 1991 mit einem B.A. in Philosophie an der Universität Yale sowie 1996 mit einem M.Arch an der Universität Harvard ab. Er war einer der Gründungspartner von OMA New York, der amerikanischen Niederlassung des Office for Metropolitan Architecture (OMA)/Rem Koolhaas in den Niederlanden, und war dort leitender Architekt, bis er das Büro 2006 unter dem Namen REX fortführte. Bei OMA war er verantwortlich für Projekte wie das Guggenheim-Hermitage Museum in Las Vegas oder die Seattle Central Library. Inzwischen ist er Direktor von REX. In letzter Zeit fertiggestellt wurden u.a. das Dee & Charles Wyly Theatre des AT&T Performing Arts Centers in Dallas (Texas, USA, 2006–09, hier vorgestellt) sowie das Vakko Fashion Center und Power Media Center in Istanbul (Türkei, 2008–10, ebenfalls hier vorgestellt). Laufende Projekte sind u.a. das Museum Plaza, ein 62-stöckiger Wolkenkratzer mit gemischter Nutzung und einem Zentrum für zeitgenössische Kunst in Louisville (Kentucky, USA, 2007–), die neue Zentrale für Activision/Blizzard in Santa Monica (Kalifornien, USA, 2011/12–), der Neubau für die Zentralbibliothek und das Konservatorium in Kortrijk (Belgien, 2012/13–) sowie eine 350 000 m² große Luxuswohnanlage in Songdo Landmark City (Südkorea, 2012/13–).

JOSHUA PRINCE-RAMUS a obtenu son B. A. en philosophie à l'université Yale (1991) et son M. Arch. à l'université Harvard (1996). Il a été l'un des fondateurs de l'agence OMA New York, branche américaine de l'Office for Metropolitan Architecture (OMA)/Rem Koolhaas aux Pays-Bas, et l'a dirigée avant de la renommer REX en 2006 et d'en prendre la direction. Il a été partenaire en charge du musée Guggenheim-Hermitage à Las Vegas et de la bibliothèque centrale de Seattle signée OMA. Parmi ses projets récemment achevés figurent : le Centre des arts du spectacle AT&T – Théâtre Dee and Charles Wyly à Dallas (Texas, 2006–09, publié ici) et le Centre de la mode de Vakko et siège de Power Media à Istanbul (Turquie, 2008–10, publié ici). Actuellement, il travaille sur les projets suivants : le Museum Plaza, gratte-ciel mixte de 62 étages incluant un centre d'art contemporain à Louisville (Kentucky, 2007–) ; le nouveau siège d'Activision/Blizzard à Santa Monica (Californie, 2011/12–) ; la nouvelle bibliothèque centrale et le conservatoire de musique de Courtrai (Belgique, 2012/13–) et un ensemble d'appartements de luxe de 350 000 m² à Songdo Landmark City (Corée du Sud, 2012/13–).

DEE AND CHARLES WYLY THEATRE

Dallas, Texas, USA, 2006–09

Address: 2400 Flora Street, Dallas, TX 75201, USA, +1 214 978 2800,
www.dallastheatercenter.org / www.attpac.org
Area: 7460 m². Client: AT&T Performing Arts Center. Cost: $62.5 million. Collaboration: Rem Koolhaas

This project was designed by REX, a company formerly known as OMA New York. The Dallas Theater Center (DTC) was housed in the Arts District Theater, a dilapidated metal shed known as the most flexible theater in America. The costs of constantly reconfiguring its stage, however, became a financial burden and they decided to seek a new venue that would give them just as much freedom on a controlled budget. The design achieves this by stacking front and back-of-house functions above and below. REX explains: "At the push of a button, the theater can be transformed into a wide array of configurations—including proscenium, thrust, and flat floor—freeing directors and scenic designers to choose the stage-audience configuration that fulfills their artistic desires." The performance chamber is intentionally made of materials that are not precious in order to encourage alterations. Thus: "On consecutive days, the Wyly Theatre can produce Shakespeare on a proscenium stage or Beckett in a flat-floor configuration silhouetted against the Dallas cityscape."

Das Projekt ist ein Entwurf von REX, vormals OMA New York. Das Dallas Theater Center (DTC) war zuvor im Arts District Theater untergebracht, einem baufälligen Metallbau, der den Ruf hatte, Amerikas flexibelstes Theater zu sein. Doch die Kosten für die ständigen Bühnenumbauten wurden zur finanziellen Belastung und man begann nach einem neuen Quartier zu suchen, das im Rahmen eines begrenzten Budgets ebenso viel Freiheit bot. Diesem Anspruch konnten die Architekten gerecht werden, indem sie Publikums- und Backstagefunktionen übereinanderstapelten. REX führt aus: „Die Bühne lässt sich per Knopfdruck in eine ganze Bandbreite verschiedener Konfigurationen verwandeln – ob Proszenium, in den Zuschauerraum ragende Podestbühne oder Black Box –, er gibt Regisseuren und Bühnenbildern damit die Freiheit zu entscheiden, welche Bühnen-Publikums-Konfiguration ihren künstlerischen Vorstellungen am ehesten gerecht wird." Der Zuschauerraum wurde bewusst in Materialien gehalten, die eher industriell wirken, um Umbauten anzuregen. Das bedeutet: „An aufeinanderfolgenden Tagen kann das Wyly also Shakespeare auf einer Proszeniumsbühne geben oder Beckett in einer Black Box mit der Skyline von Dallas als Kulisse."

Ce projet a été conçu par Rex, agence new-yorkaise précédemment connue sous le nom d'OMA New York. Le Dallas Theater Center (DTC) était jusqu'alors logé dans l'Arts District Theater, un entrepôt métallique réputé être la salle de théâtre la plus polyvalente d'Amérique. Le coût de la reconfiguration permanente de la scène s'étant alourdi au fil des années, il a été décidé de chercher un nouveau lieu qui autorise la même liberté mais pour un budget limité. Le projet a tenu le pari en recourant à l'empilement des fonctions de la salle, de la scène et des coulisses. « En appuyant sur un bouton, le théâtre peut prendre de multiples configurations – y compris scène et avant-scène, scène en avancée et scène-plateau entièrement plate – ce qui permet aux metteurs en scène et décorateurs de choisir la configuration scénique qui répond à leurs souhaits artistiques », explique REX. La salle elle-même a été volontairement réalisée en matériaux simples pour faciliter les modifications. Ainsi, « d'un jour à l'autre, le Wyly Theatre peut produire une pièce de Shakespeare sur scène classique ou de Beckett en plateau dont la mise en scène se détache en silhouette sur le panorama de Dallas ».

The somewhat unexpected vertical form of the theater emerges from a sloping entrance, as seen in the image above. Drawings reveal the inner workings of the structure.

Der eher ungewöhnliche vertikale Theaterbau erhebt sich über einer abschüssigen Zugangsrampe, wie oben im Bild zu sehen. Zeichnungen illustrieren den mechanischen Aufbau des Gebäudes.

La forme verticale quelque peu insolite du théâtre se dresse au-dessus d'une entrée en pente, comme le montre la photo ci-dessus. Les dessins révèlent les mécanismes internes du bâtiment.

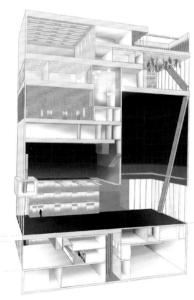
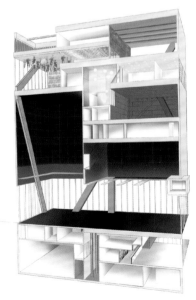

Materials, forms, colors, and even lighting participate in the creation of spaces that are rigorous in their conception and efficient in their function.

Materialien, Formen, Farben und Beleuchtung tragen zur Gestaltung von Räumen bei, die ebenso konsequent in der Konzeption wie effizient in ihrer Funktionalität sind.

Les matériaux, les formes, les couleurs et même l'éclairage participent à la mise en forme d'espaces de conception rigoureuse et de fonctionnement efficace.

The architects play on the ideas of
opacity and weight (above), and on
metallic transparency in the staircase
to the right.

*Die Architekten spielen mit Effekten
wie Opazität und Schwere (oben) oder
mit metallischer Transparenz, etwa im
Treppenhaus rechts.*

*Les architectes ont joué sur des idées
d'opacité et de gravité (ci-dessus), ou
de transparence, comme dans l'escalier à droite.*

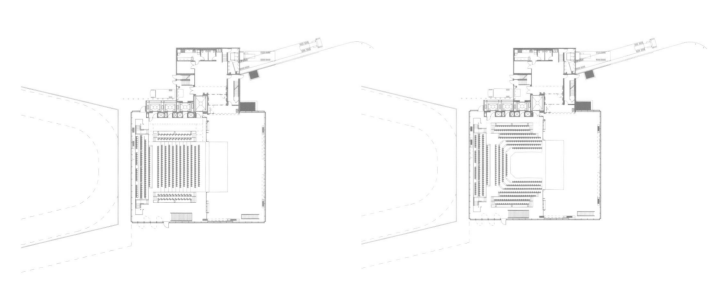

The metallic and technical appearance of the theater ceiling is cheerfully balanced with the use of bright green seats. Green returns in technical areas or foyer spaces, offsetting the gray or black elements of the actual architecture.

Die von Metall dominierte, technisch anmutende Deckenkonstruktion findet ihr Gegengewicht in den fröhlich grünen Sitzen. Grün taucht außerdem bei den technischen Einbauten und im Foyer auf, als Kontrast zu den grauen und schwarzen Elementen der Bausubstanz.

L'aspect technique et métallique du plafond du théâtre est contrebalancé par la présence de sièges d'un vert éclatant. Ce vert se retrouve dans les zones techniques ou le foyer, où il adoucit la forte présence architecturale du gris et du noir.

VAKKO FASHION CENTER

Istanbul, Turkey, 2008–10

*Address: Kuşbakışı Caddesi 35, Istanbul, Turkey, +90 216 554 0700, www.vakko.com
Area: 9104 m². Client: Vakko. Cost: $24 million*

The Director of Vakko (a fashion house) and Power Media (Turkey's equivalent of MTV) approached REX with plans to design and construct a new headquarters building by the year's end using an unfinished, abandoned hotel. By a stroke of luck construction documents that the firm had prepared for an abandoned project (Annenberg Center, Caltech) could be adapted to the concrete skeleton of the hotel in Turkey. Construction on a perimeter office block actually began just four days after Vakko approached REX. The interior was designed so as not to disturb the seismic design of the skeleton. Television and radio studios were placed in the upper level of the existing underground parking area. Given the short time schedule, REX designed steel boxes that could be assembled in different configurations for the "Showcase" interiors. A circulation path winds from the top to the bottom of this mirror-clad element. With a structural solution, the architects managed to create a very thin sheath of glass that envelopes the original bulky skeleton.

Der Direktor von Vakko (einem Modehaus) und Power Media (dem türkischen Pendant zu MTV) wandte sich mit der Bitte an REX, bis Ende des Jahres eine neue Firmenzentrale zu entwerfen und zu bauen. Diese sollte in einer verlassenen Hotelbaustelle realisiert werden. Durch einen glücklichen Zufall konnte das Büro Pläne für ein abgesagtes Projekt (Annenberg Center, Caltech) nutzen und für das Betonskelett des Hotels in der Türkei adaptieren. Tatsächlich begannen die Bauarbeiten an einem Bürogebäude am Rande des Grundstücks nur vier Tage nachdem Vakko REX kontaktiert hatte. Das Interieur des Baus wurde so gestaltet, dass die erdbebensichere Grundkonstruktion des Skeletts nicht beeinträchtigt wurde. Fernseh- und Rundfunkstudios wurden auf der oberen Ebene der bestehenden Tiefgarage untergebracht. Angesichts des engen Zeitrahmens entwarf REX Stahlboxen, die sich unterschiedlich konfigurieren ließen; so entstand ein „Showcase"-Interieur. Verkehrsflächen erstrecken sich umlaufend von oben nach unten um das verspiegelte Element. Durch eine konstruktive Lösung konnten die Architekten das ursprünglich massige Skelett mit einer ausgesprochen dünnwandigen Glashaut überziehen.

Le directeur de Vakko (une maison de mode) et de Power Media (l'équivalent turc de MTV) avait demandé à REX de concevoir et de construire un nouveau siège social avant la fin de l'année dans un ancien hôtel dont le chantier n'avait jamais été terminé. Par chance, les plans préparés par l'agence pour un de ses projets abandonnés (Annenberg Center, Caltech) étaient adaptables au squelette de béton de l'hôtel projeté. La construction débuta quatre jours seulement après le premier contact. L'intérieur fut conçu de façon à ne pas affaiblir le caractère antisismique de la structure. Les studios de radio et de télévision ont été aménagés au niveau supérieur du parking souterrain existant. Devant l'extrême brièveté des délais, REX a dessiné des boîtes en acier assemblables selon diverses configurations pour le showroom. Un parcours s'étend du haut vers le bas de cet élément habillé de miroirs. Les architectes ont réussi à masquer la structure qui leur était imposée d'un fourreau de verre mince qui enveloppe entièrement la masse du bâti d'origine.

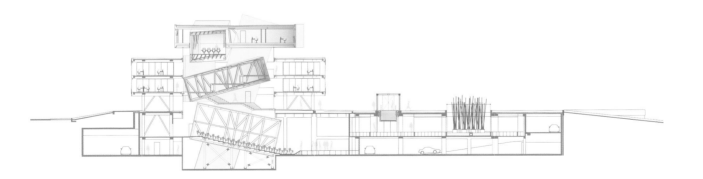

Although the Vakko Center appears to be a relatively simple, and surprisingly transparent block, the section drawing above reveals the real complexity of the structure.

Während das Vakko Center zunächst wie ein eher schlichter, überraschend transparenter Baukörper wirkt, verrät der Schnitt oben die tatsächliche Komplexität des Gebäudes.

Si l'immeuble du Centre Vakko semble relativement simple et étonnement transparent, le plan de coupe ci-dessus témoigne de la complexité réelle de sa structure.

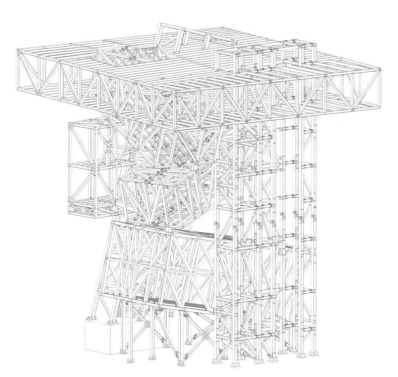

The Vakko Center is a surprising mixture of almost ethereal lightness, as seen in the image above, and technical complexity, as evidenced in this drawing of the metal "box" structure inserted by the architect into the existing building.

Das Vakko Center ist eine überraschende Kombination aus fast ätherischer Leichtigkeit (Foto oben) und technischer Komplexität, wie die Zeichnung der Metall-„Box" belegt, die der Architekt in das vorhandene bauliche Gerüst einfügte.

Le Centre Vakko présente un surprenant mélange de légèreté presque éthérée, comme le montre l'image ci-dessus, et de complexité technique, dont le plan de l'ossature de la « boîte » de métal insérée dans le bâtiment existant donne une idée.

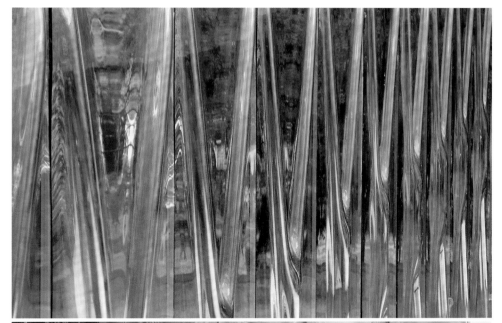

Transparency, taken to its logical extreme, alternates with the density of some elements of the design. The preexisting building structure is completely transformed by the architect.

Auf die Spitze getriebene Transparenz und die hermetische Geschlossenheit einzelner baulicher Elemente wechseln einander ab. Dem Architekten gelang die völlige Transformation des vorhandenen baulichen Gerüsts.

Une transparence poussée alterne avec des éléments plus denses. La construction préexistante a été entièrement transformée par l'architecte.

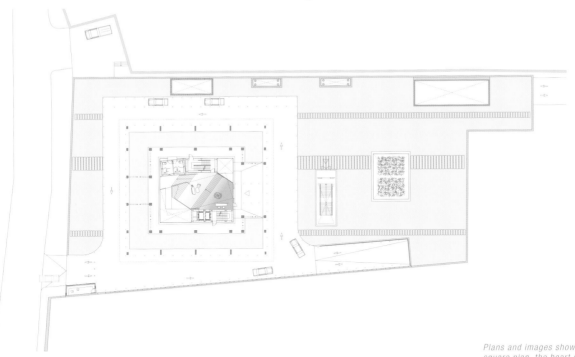

Plans and images show that within a square plan, the heart of the building has taken on a surprising complexity while leaving the floor plates free for the client's use.

Wie auf Plänen und Aufnahmen zu sehen, wurde der Kern des Baus überraschend komplex umgestaltet, während die Etagenflächen frei blieben und vom Auftraggeber beliebig genutzt werden können.

Plans et images montrent comment, dans le cadre d'un plan de forme carrée, le cœur du bâtiment présente une étonnante complexité tout en créant des plateaux entièrement dégagés.

In the lobby of the building, the sculptural profusion of forms is the most visible aspect of the complex box system installed by REX.

Am auffälligsten zeigt sich das komplexe, von REX realisierte „Box"-System in der Lobby, wo die skulpturalen Formen geradezu überborden.

Au niveau de l'entrée, la profusion de formes sculpturales est l'aspect le plus visible du principe de boîte complexe mise en place par REX.

FERNANDO ROMERO

FREE / Fernando Romero
511 West 25th St. 911
New York, NY 10001
USA

Tel: +1 212 242 3104
E-mail: ny@fr-ee.org
Web: www.fr-ee.org

FERNANDO ROMERO was born in 1971. He received his degree in Architecture from the Universidad Iberomaericana (Mexico City). Prior to creating his own firm, FREE, in Mexico City, Romero worked in the office of OMA in Rotterdam. His rising influence was noted in 2002 when he was amongst the recipients of the Global Leader of Tomorrow Award at the World Economic Forum (Davos). His work includes the Bicentennial Moebius Ring (Mexico City, 2009); Chapel in Central de Abastos (Mexico City, 2009); Casa Toluca (Toluca, 2009–10); The Pyramid (Merida, 2009–10); Mercedes-Benz Business Center (Yerevan, Armenia, 2010); Soumaya Museum (Mexico City, 2005–11, published here); Reforma Tower (Mexico City, 2011); New York Tower (New York, USA, 2011); a Museum in Panama (Panama, 2011); a Museum in Tulum (Quintana Roo, 2011); and La Villa, a mixed-use project in front of the Basilica of Guadalupe (Mexico City, 2011), all in Mexico unless stated otherwise.

FERNANDO ROMERO wurde 1971 geboren. Sein Architekturstudium schloss er an der Universidad Iberomaericana (Mexico City) ab. Bevor er sein eigenes Büro FREE in Mexico City gründete, hatte Romero bei OMA in Rotterdam gearbeitet. 2002 war er unter den Preisträgern des Global Leader of Tomorrow Award auf dem Weltwirtschaftsforum in Davos, ein deutliches Zeichen für seinen wachsenden Einfluss. Zu seinen Entwürfen zählen der Bicentennial Moebius Ring (Mexico City, 2009), eine Kapelle in Central de Abastos (Mexico City, 2009), die Casa Toluca (Toluca, 2009–10), die Pyramide (Merida, 2009–10), das Mercedes-Benz Business Center (Jerewan, Armenien, 2010), das Soumaya Museum (Mexico City, 2005–11, hier vorgestellt), der Reforma Tower (Mexico City, 2011), der New York Tower (New York, USA, 2011), ein Museum in Panama (Panama, 2011), ein Museum in Tulum (Quintana Roo, 2011) und La Villa, ein Komplex mit gemischter Nutzung unweit der Basilika der Jungfrau von Guadalupe (Mexico City, 2011), alle in Mexiko, sofern nicht anders angegeben.

FERNANDO ROMERO, né en 1971, est diplômé en architecture de l'Université ibéroaméricaine (Mexico). Avant de fonder son agence FREE à Mexico, il avait travaillé chez OMA à Rotterdam. Son influence grandissante a été saluée en 2002 par le prix du « Global Leader of Tomorrow » au Forum économique mondial de Davos. Parmi ses réalisations : l'anneau de Moebius du Bicentenaire (Mexico, 2009) ; la chapelle de Central de Abastos (Mexico, 2009) ; la maison Toluca (Toluca, 2009–10) ; La Pyramide (Merida, 2009–10) ; le Centre Mercedes-Benz (Erevan, Arménie, 2010) ; le musée Soumaya (Mexico, 2005–11, publié ici) ; la tour Reforma (Mexico, 2011) ; la tour New York (New York, 2011) ; un musée à Panama (Panama, 2011) ; un musée à Tulum (Quintana Roo, 2011) et La Villa, projet immobilier face à la basilique de Guadalupe (Mexico, 2011).

SOUMAYA MUSEUM

Mexico City, Mexico, 2005–11

Address: Museo Soumaya, Miguel de Cervantes Saavedra, Granada, Miguel Hidalgo,
11529 Mexico City, Mexico, +52 55 4976 0179, www.museosoumaya.org
Area: 17 000 m² (6000 m² of exhibition space)
Client: Museo Soumaya "Fundación Carlos Slim". Cost: not disclosed

The unusual shape of the Soumaya Museum makes it a local landmark. Whether seen from the air (below) or from the ground (right page), it stands out and intrigues passersby.

Dank seiner ungewöhnlichen Form wurde das Soumaya Museum zum Wahrzeichen des Viertels. Ob auf Luftaufnahmen (unten) oder vom Boden aus gesehen (rechte Seite): Es fällt auf und fasziniert.

La forme originale du musée Soumaya en fait un des grands monuments de la capitale qui, vu du ciel (ci-dessous), ou du sol (page de droite), surprend et intrigue.

In both plan and section, the Soumaya Museum has an unexpected configuration where curves dominate.

Grundriss wie Querschnitt belegen die erstaunliche Konfiguration des Soumaya Museums, bei der geschwungene Formen dominieren.

En plan comme en coupe, le musée présente une configuration surprenante dominée par des courbes.

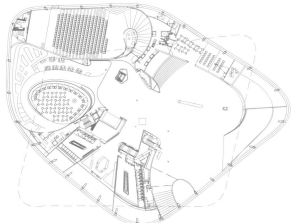

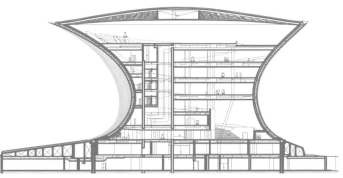

The **SOUMAYA MUSEUM** is part of a large-scale mixed-use urban development located at the edge of the Polanco district, one of the most exclusive areas of Mexico City. Built on a 1940s industrial site it is viewed as the preeminent cultural program in the area. From the outset, the goal was "to create a strong urban and iconic presence." Thus, according to the architect: "The Soumaya Museum was conceived as a rotating sculptural block that creates an organic and asymmetrical shape that is both an object and a part of the city." The opaque façade is made of hexagonal aluminum modules that minimize exterior openings while optimizing the strength of the entire building. The museum houses a heterogeneous group of works including the world's second largest collection of Rodin sculptures, a wing of medieval and Renaissance art, and a gallery devoted to Impressionism. The 6000-square-meter exhibition space is spread over six levels. The building also includes a number of public and private programs, including a 350-seat auditorium, library, restaurant, gift shop, a multipurpose lounge, and administrative offices. A "non-linear circulation zone" connects the programs. The shell of the building was built with 28 unique curved steel columns of varying thicknesses, geometry, and form. A system of seven rings located on each floor stabilizes the structure.

Das **SOUMAYA MUSEUM** ist Teil einer großanlegten Stadterneuerung mit Wohn- und Gewerbeflächen am Rande des Stadtteils Polanco, eines der exklusivsten Viertel von Mexico City. Das Museum, erbaut auf einem Industriegrundstück aus den 1940er-Jahren, gilt als herausragende Kulturstätte des Viertels. Ziel war von Anfang an, „ein eindrucksvolles urbanes Wahrzeichen zu schaffen". „Das Soumaya Museum", so der Architekt, „wurde als rotierender skulpturaler Block entworfen, der mit seiner organischen, asymmetrischen Form zugleich Objekt und Teil der Stadt ist." Die opake Fassade besteht aus sechseckigen Aluminiumsegmenten, die einerseits zur Stabilität des Baus beitragen, anderseits die Anzahl von Öffnungen am Außenbau minimieren. Das Museum beherbergt eine heterogene Gruppe von Werken, darunter die weltweit zweitgrößte Sammlung von Rodin-Skulpturen, einen Flügel mit Kunst des Mittelalters und der Renaissance sowie eine Galerie der Impressionisten. Die 6000 m² großen Ausstellungsflächen verteilen sich über sechs Ebenen. Im Gebäude untergebracht sind außerdem verschiedene öffentliche und private Funktionen, darunter ein Auditorium mit 350 Plätzen, eine Bibliothek, ein Restaurant, ein Museumsshop, eine Mehrzwecklounge und Verwaltungsbüros. „Non-lineare Verkehrsflächen" verbinden die verschiedenen Programme. Die Gebäudeschale wurde mithilfe von 28 individuell gebogenen Stahlträgern unterschiedlicher Stärke, Geometrie und Form realisiert. Ein System aus sieben Ringen, verteilt über die Etagen, stabilisiert den Bau.

Le **MUSÉE SOUMAYA** fait partie d'une vaste opération de rénovation urbaine mixte en limite de Polanco, l'un des quartiers les plus élégants de Mexico. Construit sur une ancienne zone industrielle datant des années 1940, il est le plus important projet culturel de ce projet. Dès le départ, l'objectif était de « créer une présence urbaine forte et iconique ». Ainsi, comme l'explique l'architecte : « Le musée Soumaya a été conçu comme un bloc sculptural en rotation qui génère une forme organique asymétrique à la fois objet et composante de Mexico. » La façade d'apparence aveugle est habillée de modules hexagonaux en aluminium qui renforcent la solidité du bâtiment tout en réduisant le nombre des ouvertures. Le musée abrite un ensemble d'œuvres hétérogènes, dont la seconde collection au monde de pièces de Rodin, une galerie d'art médiéval et de la Renaissance et une autre consacrée à l'impressionnisme. L'espace d'exposition de 6000 mètres carrés se répartit sur six niveaux. Le musée comprend également un certain nombre d'équipements publics et administratifs comme un auditorium de 350 places, une bibliothèque, un restaurant, une boutique, un salon polyvalent et des bureaux, réunis par une « zone de circulation non linéaire ». La structure repose sur 28 colonnes en acier d'épaisseurs, de profil et d'incurvations diverses. Elle est stabilisée par sept anneaux, un à chaque niveau.

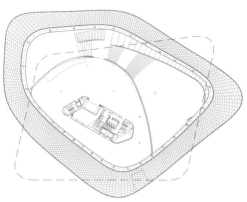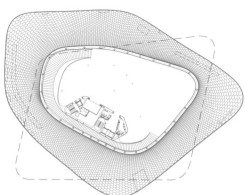

The skin of the structure has a scaled appearance and shows very few obvious openings. Even the entrance (left) is discreet, especially as compared to the size of the building. The plans above show exhibition levels.

Die Hülle des Baus wirkt wie die Schuppenhaut eines Fischs und hat sehr wenige erkennbare Öffnungen. Selbst der Eingang (links) ist diskret, gerade im Verhältnis zur Größe des Gebäudes. Die Etagengrundrisse oben zeigen zwei Ausstellungsebenen.

La peau de la structure à l'aspect d'écailles ne laisse entrevoir que de rares ouvertures. Même l'entrée (à gauche) se fait discrète, surtout en comparaison de la taille du bâtiment. Ci-dessus, les plans des niveaux d'exposition.

Drawings showing the uppermost
exhibition levels with the curving
ramp—visible in the image below,
and in the drawing on the left.

Zeichnungen zeigen die obersten
Ausstellungsebenen. Die geschwungene Rampe auf dem Foto unten ist
auf der linken Zeichnung erkennbar.

Plans des étages d'exposition supérieurs et de la rampe en courbe visible sur la photographie ci-dessous
(dessin de gauche).

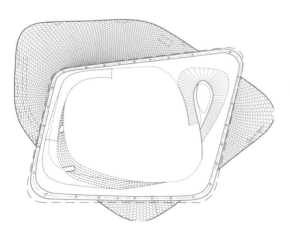

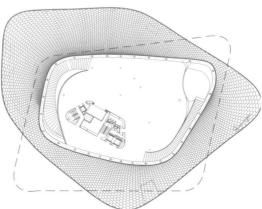

Despite its closed appearance from the exterior, the museum benefits from overhead natural lighting at the topmost level. Other exhibition areas are intentionally shielded from outdoor light.

Obwohl das Museum von außen völlig geschlossen wirkt, wird die oberste Etage mit Tageslicht versorgt. Die übrigen Ausstellungsbereiche sind bewusst vor Tageslicht geschützt.

Malgré son aspect extérieur très fermé, le musée bénéficie d'un éclairage naturel zénithal en partie supérieure. Les autres étages réservés aux collections sont volontairement protégés de la lumière naturelle.

TODD SAUNDERS

Saunders Architecture
Vestretorggaten 22
5015 Bergen
Norway

Tel: +47 97 52 57 61
E-mail: post@saunders.no
Web: www.saunders.no

TODD SAUNDERS was born in 1969 in Gander, Newfoundland, Canada. He obtained his M.Arch from McGill University (Montréal, Canada, 1993–95) and a Bachelor of Environmental Planning from the Nova Scotia College of Art and Design (1988–92). He has worked in Austria, Germany, Russia, Latvia, and Norway (since 1997). He teaches part-time at the Bergen School of Architecture. His work includes the Aurland Lookout (with Tommie Wilhelmsen, Aurland, 2006); Villa Storingavika (Bergen, 2004–07); Villa G (Hjellestad, Bergen, 2007–09); the Long Studio (Fogo Island, Newfoundland, Canada, 2010, published here); and Solberg Tower and Park (Sarpsborg, Øsfold, 2010, also published here), all in Norway unless stated otherwise.

TODD SAUNDERS wurde 1969 in Gander, Neufundland, Kanada, geboren. Er absolvierte seinen M.Arch an der McGill University (Montreal, Kanada, 1993–95) sowie einen Bachelor in Umweltplanung am Nova Scotia College of Art and Design (1988–92). Er hat in Österreich, Deutschland, Russland, Lettland und Norwegen gearbeitet (seit 1997). Er lehrt in Teilzeit an der Bergen School of Architecture. Zu seinen Projekten zählen der Aurland Aussichtspunkt (mit Tommie Wilhelmsen, Aurland, 2006), die Villa Storingavika (Bergen, 2004–07), die Villa G (Hjellestad, Bergen, 2007–09), das Long Studio (Fogo Island, Neufundland, Kanada, 2010, hier vorgestellt) sowie der Solberg-Turm und -Park (Sarpsborg, Øsfold, 2010, ebenfalls hier vorgestellt), alle in Norwegen, sofern nicht anders angegeben.

Né en 1969 à Gander (Terre-Neuve, Canada), **TODD SAUNDERS** a obtenu son M. Arch. à l'université McGill (Montréal, 1993–95) et son B. A. en planification environnementale au Collège d'art et de design de la Nouvelle-Écosse (1988–92). Il a travaillé en Autriche, Allemagne, Russie, Lituanie et Norvège (depuis 1997). Il enseigne à temps partiel à l'École d'architecture de Bergen. Parmi ses réalisations, toutes en Norvège : le belvédère d'Aurland (avec Tommie Wilhelmsen, Aurland, 2006) ; la villa Storingavika (Bergen, 2004–07) ; la villa G (Hjellestad, Bergen, 2007–09) ; l'Atelier en longueur (île de Fogo, Terre-Neuve, Canada, 2010, publié ici) et la tour et le parc Solberg (Sarpsborg, Øsfold, Norvège, 2010, également publié ici).

THE LONG STUDIO

Fogo Island, Newfoundland, Canada, 2010

Area: 120 m². Client: Shorefast Foundation and The Fogo Island Arts Corporation
Cost: not disclosed

The simple trapezoidal form of the building is seen in the drawing on the left page. The structure opens and juts out on pilotis over the rough seaside.

Auf der Zeichnung links ist die schlichte Trapezform des Gebäudes zu erkennen. Der Bau schwebt auf pilotis, öffnet sich zur rauen See und kragt dorthin aus.

La forme trapézoïdale du bâtiment est illustrée sur le plan de la page de gauche. Reposant sur des pilotis, la structure s'ouvre et se projette en direction de la mer déchaînée.

This studio is intended for an artist residency program created by the Shorefast Foundation and The Fogo Island Arts Corporation. The organizers are committed to preserving local traditions, but seek to rejuvenate the island through arts and culture. The architect sought to create strong geometric shapes that contrast with their natural setting but do not compete with it. Six of the studios are slated to be built in remote locations on the island. **THE LONG STUDIO** is a linear volume that has three rooms combining open and closed areas.

Das Atelierhaus wurde für ein Stipendiatenprogramm der Shorefast Foundation und der Fogo Island Arts Corporation entworfen. Den Organisatoren ist es ein besonderes Anliegen, lokale Traditionen zu pflegen und gleichzeitig zur Verjüngung der Insel durch Kunst und Kultur beizutragen. Der Architekt wählte ausdrucksstarke, geometrische Formen, die einen bewussten Kontrast zur Küstenlandschaft bilden, jedoch nicht mit ihr rivalisieren. Sechs weitere Ateliers sollen an entlegenen Standorten auf der Insel realisiert werden. **DAS LONG STUDIO** ist ein linearer Baukörper mit drei Zimmern und einer Mischung aus offenen und geschlossenen Räumen.

Cet atelier d'artiste fait partie d'un programme pour artistes en résidence initié par la Fondation Shorefast et la Société des arts de l'île de Fogo. Les commanditaires veulent préserver les traditions locales et cherchent à redonner vie à l'île par le biais de l'art et de la culture. L'architecte a créé de puissantes formes géométriques qui contrastent avec leur cadre naturel sans pour autant entrer en concurrence avec lui. Six ateliers devraient être construits dans des lieux déserts. **LE LONG STUDIO,** un « atelier en longueur », est un volume linéaire de trois pièces qui combine des espaces clos et ouverts.

Black on its outer surfaces, the studio is white where the architect has notched out a partially covered exterior space (below). Views of the setting are framed, as in the image on the lower right page. Elevations show the structure with one side more open than the other.

Das Studio mit seinen schwarzen Außenwänden ist weiß, wo der Architekt einen teilweise überdachten Freisitz angelegt hat (unten). Ausblicke in die Landschaft sind gerahmt (rechte Seite unten), Aufrisse zeigen, dass der Bau auf einer Seite deutlich offener ist als auf der anderen.

De couleur noire pour l'extérieur, l'atelier et les espaces extérieurs en partie couverts (ci-dessous) sont traités en blanc. Les ouvertures cadrent des vues sur la nature, comme l'illustre la photographie de droite. Les coupes montrent qu'une des façades longues est beaucoup plus ouverte que l'autre.

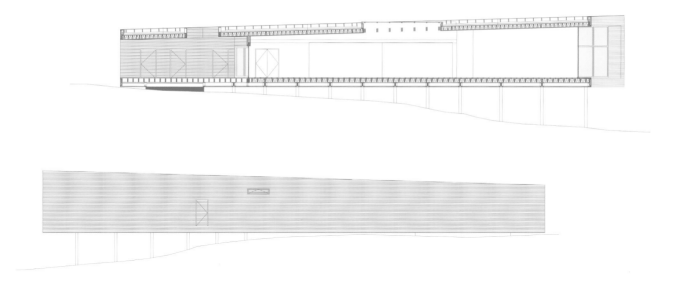

Despite its relatively small (120 m²) area, the Long Studio does boast a long, high empty space, to be used by artists according to their wishes.

Trotz der eher geringen Nutzfläche (120 m²) verfügt das Long Studio über einen langen hohen, leeren Raum, der von den Künstlern beliebig genutzt werden kann.

Malgré sa surface relativement faible (120 m²), l'atelier offre un vaste espace vide et allongé, utilisable par les artistes en fonction de leurs besoins.

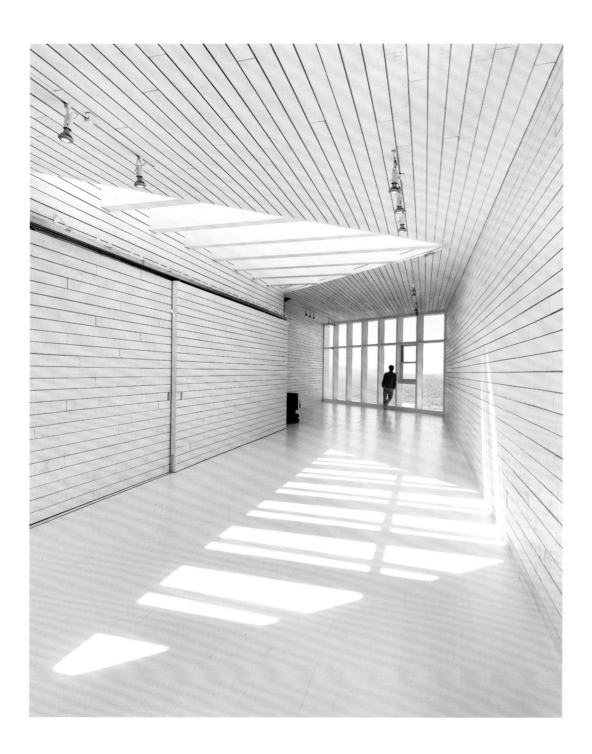

Above, a kitchen space, also seen in the plan below, is notched into the wall volume of the studio, providing a good deal of autonomy for artists who use the structure.

Oben der Küchenbereich (siehe auch Grundriss unten). Die in die Wand des Studios eingelassene Küchenzeile bietet den hier arbeitenden Künstlern einige Unabhängigkeit.

Ci-dessus, le coin cuisine (vu également sur le plan ci-dessous) creusé dans l'épaisseur du mur, pour laisser davantage d'espace utile aux occupants.

SOLBERG TOWER AND PARK

Sarpsborg, Øsfold, Norway, 2010

*Area: 2000 m². Client: Statens Vegvesen, Østfold fylkeskommune,
Sarpsborg kommune og Fredrikstad kommune. Cost: $9 million*

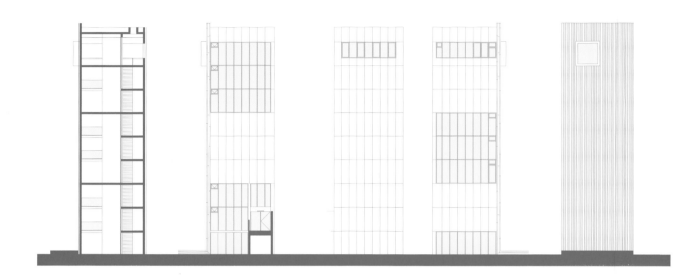

Located in south Norway, Sarpsborg is a traditional stopover for travelers on the route to and from Sweden. In 2004, the Norwegian highway department together with the regional government approached the architect for a new project in the area, surprisingly without having predetermined the commission's particular needs. Saunders designed seven small pavilions working with graphic designer Camilla Holcroft, showcasing information on the local rock carvings from the Bronze Age, an exhibition that continues on ramp walls. The surrounding forest is full of rock carvings. The structures also offer space for temporary artist exhibitions. The ramp's asymmetrical walls rise to form a 30-meter, nine-story-tall tower on the site's northern edge that contains only a staircase and an elevator. Named Solberg (which means "sun mountain"), the tower offers views toward the nearby coastline and Oslo fjord. The main materials used were Cor-ten steel for the exterior walls and oiled hardwood for the courtyard's design elements and information points. Local slate and fine gravel pave the ground level.

Die Stadt Sarpsborg in Südnorwegen ist ein typischer Zwischenstopp für Reisende auf dem Weg von und nach Schweden. 2004 wurde der Architekt von der norwegischen Behörde für Schnellstraßen und der Regionalregierung kontaktiert, um ein Projekt in der Gegend zu realisieren – erstaunlicherweise ohne dass konkrete Vorgaben für den Auftrag festgesetzt worden wären. Gemeinsam mit der Grafikdesignerin Camilla Holcroft entwarf Saunders sieben kleine Pavillons, die Informationen zu Felszeichnungen der Bronzezeit präsentieren. Die Ausstellung zieht sich außerdem über die Wände der Rampe der Anlage. Die Felszeichnungen finden sich im gesamten Waldgebiet der Umgebung. In den Bauten ist außerdem Platz für künstlerische Sonderausstellungen. Die asymmetrischen Wandsegmente der Rampe werden zunehmend höher und führen zum 30 m hohen, neunstöckigen Turm am Nordende der Anlage, in dem sich nichts als eine Treppe und ein Aufzug befinden. Der Turm Solberg („Sonnenberg") bietet Ausblick bis zur nahe gelegenen Küstenlinie und dem Oslofjord. Hauptbaumaterialien sind Corten-Stahl für die Fassaden und geöltes Hartholz für die baulichen Elemente im Innenhof und die Informationsstationen. Auf dem Boden wurde lokaler Schiefer verlegt oder feiner Kies aufgebracht.

En Norvège méridionale, Sarpsborg est une halte traditionnelle pour les voyageurs en route vers ou de la Suède. En 2004, le Département des autoroutes norvégien et l'administration régionale ont demandé à l'architecte de réfléchir à un aménagement des lieux sans préciser leurs attentes. Saunders, en collaboration avec la graphiste Camilla Holcroft, a conçu sept petits pavillons qui informent sur les rochers sculptés datant de l'âge de bronze qui abondent dans les forêts avoisinantes, exposition qui se poursuit sur les murs de la rampe d'accès. Ces petites constructions servent également de lieux pour des expositions d'art temporaires. Les murs asymétriques de la rampe s'élèvent jusqu'à une tour de 30 mètres de haut et neuf niveaux implantée à l'extrémité nord du site, qui ne contient qu'un escalier et un ascenseur. Appelée Solberg (qui signifie « montagne du soleil » en norvégien), la tour offre un panorama sur la côte voisine et le fjord d'Oslo. Les matériaux principaux sont l'acier Corten pour les murs extérieurs et un bois huilé pour les bancs et les points d'information. Le sol est en ardoise locale et gravier fin.

The nine-story tower is partially clad in Cor-ten steel, making it stand out in a rather enigmatic fashion from its background in the image on the right.

Der neunstöckige Turm ist teilweise mit Corten-Stahl verblendet, wodurch er auf der Aufnahme (rechts) fast mysteriös vor seinem Hintergrund erscheint.

De neuf étages de hauteur, la tour est en partie habillée d'acier Corten, ce qui lui confère un aspect assez énigmatique par rapport à son environnement (page de droite).

A long curving wood and steel wall reaches out and embraces a park area, leading up to the unusual look-out tower.

Eine lange, geschwungene Mauer aus Holz und Stahl greift aus und umfängt die Parklandschaft. Die Rampe führt zum ungewöhnlichen Aussichtsturm.

Une longue rampe prise entre un mur de bois et un mur d'acier se déploie pour entourer la zone du parc et conduire à la tour insolite.

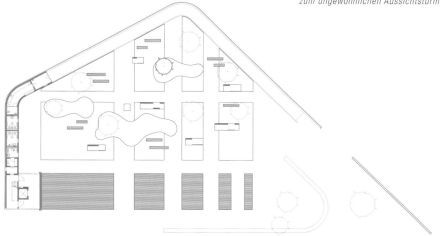

The whole complex is seen in the drawing to the right, while the park area, partially covered in wood and embraced by the ramp walls, is visible in the image below.

Auf der Zeichnung rechts die Gesamtanlage, auf der Aufnahme unten ein Blick auf den Park mit seinen Holzböden, der von den Wänden der Rampe eingefasst wird.

Image de droite : vue d'ensemble du complexe. Ci-dessous : la zone du parc, au sol en partie équipé de plates-formes en bois, est délimitée par la rampe d'accès.

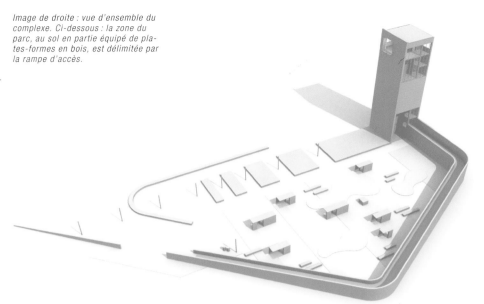

SAVIOZ FABRIZZI

Savioz Fabrizzi Architectes
Rue de l'Industrie 23
1950 Sion
Switzerland

Tel: +41 27 322 68 81
Fax: +41 27 322 68 83
E-mail: info@sf-ar.ch
Web: www.sf-ar.ch

LAURENT SAVIOZ was born in 1976 and received his degree in Architecture from the Haute École Spécialisée (HES) of Fribourg (1998). He worked in the office of Bonnard and Woeffray in Monthey, Switzerland (1999–2003), before cofounding Savioz Meyer Fabrizzi in Sion with François Meyer and Claude Fabrizzi in 2004. The current firm, created in 2005, is an association between Savioz and **CLAUDE FABRIZZI**, born in 1975 in Sierre, and also a graduate of the HES in Fribourg (1995–98). Savioz carried forward the Roduit House (Chamoson, 2003–05) on his own. Projects he worked on with Savioz Meyer Fabrizzi include the Hôtel de la Poste (Sierre, 2006–07); the Iseli House (Venthône, 2007); a primary school (Vollèges, 2009–10, published here); and Val d'Entremont House (Val d'Entremont, 2009–10, also published here). Current work includes a mountain refuge (Cabane de Tracuit, Zinal, 2011–); another primary school (Sierre, 2011–); and a triple sports hall (Viège, 2011–), all in Switzerland.

LAURENT SAVIOZ wurde 1976 geboren und schloss sein Architekturstudium an der Haute École Spécialisée (HES) in Fribourg ab (1998). Er arbeitete für Bonnard & Woeffray in Monthey, Schweiz (1999–2003), bevor er 2004 mit François Meyer und Claude Fabrizzi in Sion das Büro Savioz Meyer Fabrizzi gründete. Im 2005 gegründeten, aktuellen Büro ist Savioz mit **CLAUDE FABRIZZI** assoziiert. Fabrizzi, geboren 1975 in Sierre, schloss sein Studium ebenfalls an der HES in Fribourg ab (1995–98). Das Haus Roduit (Chamoson, 2003–05) realisierte Savioz allein. Zu den gemeinsamen Projekten mit Savioz Meyer Fabrizzi zählen das Hôtel de la Poste (Sierre, 2006–07), das Haus Iseli (Venthône, 2007), eine Grundschule (Vollèges, 2009–10, hier vorgestellt) sowie ein Haus in Val d'Entremont (Val d'Entremont, 2009–10, ebenfalls hier vorgestellt) Aktuelle Projekte sind u.a. eine Berghütte (Cabane de Tracuit, Zinal, 2011–), eine weitere Grundschule (Sierre, 2011–) und eine Dreifachsporthalle (Viège, 2011–), alle in der Schweiz.

LAURENT SAVIOZ, né en 1976, est diplômé en architecture de la Haute École Spécialisée (HES) de Fribourg (1998). Il a travaillé chez Bonnard & Woeffray à Monthey (Suisse, 1999–2003) avant de fonder Savioz Meyer Fabrizzi à Sion avec François Meyer et **CLAUDE FABRIZZI** en 2004. L'agence actuelle a été créée en 2005 par L. Savioz et C. Fabrizzi, né en 1975 à Sierre, également diplômé de l'HES de Fribourg (1995–98). Savioz a réalisé seul la maison Roduit (Chamoson, 2003–05). Parmi les projets réalisés sous le nom de Savioz Meyer Fabrizzi figurent l'hôtel de la Poste (Sierre, 2006–07) ; la maison Iseli (Venthône, 2007) ; une école primaire (Vollèges, 2009–10, publiée ici) et la maison Val d'Entremont (Val d'Entremont, 2009–10, également publiée ici). L'agence travaille actuellement, en Suisse, sur les projets d'un refuge de haute montagne (cabane de Tracuit, Zinal, 2011–) ; d'une autre école primaire (Sierre, 2011–) et d'une triple salle de sports (Viège, 2011–).

PRIMARY SCHOOL
Vollèges, Switzerland, 2009–10

Area: 1100 m². Client: Town of Vollèges. Cost: €3.2 million
Collaboration: Cédric Felley

The architects essentially employed cast-in-place concrete, generous glazing, and wooden floors to create a solid, and unexpectedly inviting, **PRIMARY SCHOOL** environment in a town that has relatively little modern architecture. The three-story school, which contains nine classrooms, a library, and teachers' rooms, was built as a result of a 2007 competition, won by the architects. In a delicate but well-handled transition, the architects connected the new school to an existing multipurpose hall, creating an open courtyard for play. An unusual feature of the building is its gently angled concrete exterior surfaces that appear to give it a different appearance from almost every angle. Careful attention to insulation and energy usage allowed the building to carry the Minergie environmental sustainability label.

Die Architekten arbeiteten vorwiegen mit Ortbeton, großzügiger Verglasung und Holzböden und schufen so ein massiv anmutendes aber auch überraschend einladendes Umfeld für die **GRUNDSCHULE** in einer Kleinstadt, in der es kaum moderne Architektur gibt. Die dreistöckige Schule mit neun Klassenzimmern, einer Bibliothek und Lehrerzimmern wurde erbaut, nachdem die Architekten 2007 einen entsprechenden Wettbewerb gewonnen hatten. Auf feinfühlige Weise gelang es den Architekten, die neue Schule an eine ältere Mehrzweckhalle anzubinden, sodass zudem ein offener Hof zum Spielen entstand. Ungewöhnliches Merkmal des Baus sind seine leicht winklig versetzten Fassadenflächen, durch die sich aus fast jeder Perspektive neue Ansichten ergeben. Dank sorgfältiger Dämmung und Energieeffizienz trägt das Bauwerk ein Minergie-Label für Umweltfreundlichkeit und Nachhaltigkeit.

Dans une ville où l'architecture moderne est rare, les architectes ont réalisé cette **ÉCOLE PRIMAIRE** massive, mais accueillante, en n'utilisant que du béton coulé sur place, des vitrages généreux et du bois naturel pour les sols. Le projet de ce bâtiment de deux étages qui contient neuf salles de classe, une bibliothèque et des salles des professeurs, avait remporté un concours organisé en 2007. Dans une connexion délicate mais bien maîtrisée, les architectes ont relié l'école à une salle polyvalente adjacente en créant une cour de jeux ouverte. Le bâtiment se remarque par ses murs extérieurs curieusement facettés qui lui donnent un aspect changeant selon l'angle sous lequel on le regarde. Une attention méticuleuse à l'isolation thermique et à la maîtrise de la consommation énergétique a permis à ce projet d'obtenir le label environnemental suisse Minergie.

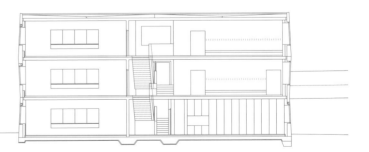

The school is located in the small town of Vollèges in the valley leading up to Verbier in the Valais region of Switzerland. As the elevation and the images show, the structure is basically a trapezoidal concrete box with large windows.

Die Schule liegt in der Ortschaft Vollèges im Tal von Verbier im Schweizer Kanton Wallis. Wie der Aufriss und die Ansichten zeigen, ist der Bau im Grunde eine trapezförmige Beton-„Box" mit großen Fensteröffnungen.

L'école se trouve à Vollèges, petite ville de la vallée menant à Verbier (canton du Valais, Suisse). Comme le montrent l'élévation et les photographies, le bâtiment est une boîte en béton de forme trapézoïdale, percée de grandes baies.

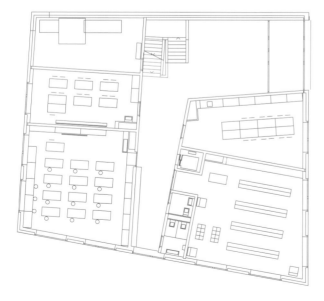

The use of wood inside the school somewhat lightens the impression given by the overall concrete composition, seen clearly in the stairway on the right page.

Der Einsatz von Holz in den Klassenzimmern lockert den Gesamteindruck der Betonkomposition etwas auf, der besonders im Treppenhaus auf der rechten Seite augenfällig ist.

Les boiseries des aménagements intérieurs atténuent un peu l'impression sévère donnée par la forte présence du béton, comme dans cette image de l'escalier (page de droite).

VAL D'ENTREMONT HOUSE

Val d'Entremont, Switzerland, 2009–10

Area: 240 m². Client: not disclosed
Cost: not disclosed

Located in a small rural mountain village, this house sits in the upper part of the town, at the lower limit of grazing pastures. It is very much apart in an environment where there appears to be no other contemporary architecture. The architects have employed cast-in-place concrete, glass and stainless steel, and wood façade coverings as the main materials. The house has three levels, with the middle one containing the living and dining space together with a kitchen, all of which open amply to the mountain scenery and the village below. The house makes use of geothermal energy and rooftop solar panels that permitted it to earn a Minergie label, the Swiss certification of ecological sustainability.

Das in einem kleines Bergdorf gelegene Wohnhaus befindet sich im oberen Teil des Dorfs am Rande der Weiden. Es liegt inmitten eines Umfelds, in dem es augenscheinlich keine weiteren zeitgenössischen Bauten gibt. Als Hauptmaterial entschieden sich die Architekten für Ortbeton, Glas, Edelstahl und eine Holzverschalung. Das Haus hat drei Ebenen, deren mittlere von Wohn- und Essbereichen sowie der Küche eingenommen wird, die sich großzügig zum Alpenpanorama und dem darunter liegenden Dorf öffnen. Das Haus ist mit einer Erdwärmeanlage und Solarpaneelen auf dem Dach ausgestattet, was ihm ein Minergie-Label einbrachte, das Schweizer Zertifikat für ökologische Nachhaltigkeit.

Cette maison construite dans la partie supérieure d'un petit village de montagne, en limite des pâturages, se singularise dans son environnement dépourvu de toute construction contemporaine. Les architectes ont choisi comme matériaux le béton coulé sur place, le verre, l'acier inoxydable et un bardage extérieur en bois. La maison se répartit sur trois niveaux, l'intermédiaire contenant le séjour, la cuisine et la zone des repas, tous généreusement ouverts sur le paysage des montagnes et du village en contrebas. Une installation géothermique et des panneaux solaires en toiture ont permis à ce projet de se voir attribuer le label environnemental suisse Minergie.

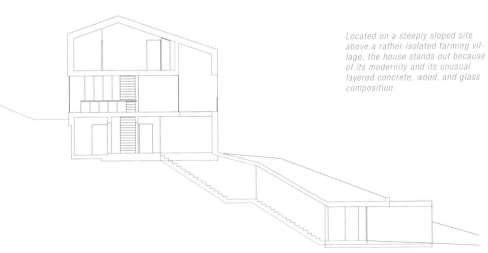

Located on a steeply sloped site above a rather isolated farming village, the house stands out because of its modernity and its unusual layered concrete, wood, and glass composition.

Das auf einem steilen Hanggrundstück über einem isolierten Bauerndorf gelegene Haus fällt durch seine moderne Formensprache und die ungewöhnliche Schichtoptik aus Beton, Holz und Glas auf.

Positionnée sur un terrain en forte pente au-dessus d'un village agricole assez isolé, la maison se distingue par sa modernité et sa surprenante composition en béton, bois et verre.

The main living space, see in the image on the left, is located in the fully glazed middle portion of the house. These photos were taken shortly after construction—the house is now surrounded by grass.

Der zentrale Wohnraum links im Bild liegt in der voll verglasten mittleren Ebene des Hauses. Die Aufnahmen entstanden kurz nach dem Bau, inzwischen umschließt eine Rasenfläche das Haus.

L'espace de séjour principal (à gauche) se trouve dans la partie centrale entièrement vitrée de la maison. Contrairement à ce que montrent ces photos prises peu après l'achèvement du chantier, la maison est aujourd'hui entourée de pelouses.

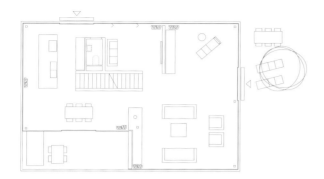

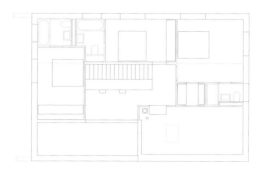

The interiors of the house offer unimpeded views of the countryside and neighboring mountains. Plans (above) and the photo below render explicit the strict geometric composition imagined by the architects.

Aus dem Inneren des Hauses bietet sich unverstellter Ausblick in die Landschaft und auf die nahen Berge. Grundrisse (oben) und Fotografie (unten) zeigen den streng geometrischen Entwurf der Architekten.

La maison bénéficie de vues magnifiques sur les alpages et les montagnes. Les plans (ci-dessus) et la photo (ci-dessous) explicitent la composition strictement géométrique voulue par les architectes.

Sparse furnishing emphasizes the rather "hard" aspect of the architecture, alleviated here by views of the exterior environment. Below, bedrooms are located essentially on the topmost level.

Die sparsame Möblierung unterstreicht die eher „harte" Architektur, was hier durch Ausblicke in die Umgebung gemildert wird. Die Schlafzimmer liegen zumeist im Obergeschoss (unten).

Le mobilier réduit fait ressortir l'aspect « dur » de cette architecture, en partie allégé par les perspectives sur l'environnement. Ci-dessous, les chambres, pour la plupart situées au dernier niveau.

Mirrored surfaces multiply the
impression of views of the scenery,
but furnishings echo the mainly hard
surfaces of the house.

Spiegelflächen vervielfältigen den
Blick in die Landschaft, während das
Mobiliar die überwiegend harten
Oberflächen des Hauses aufgreift.

Des surfaces recouvertes de panneaux en miroir multiplient les vues
sur le paysage. Le mobilier est en
accord avec le traitement assez sec
des surfaces en verre et béton.

KAZUYO SEJIMA & ASSOCIATES

Kazuyo Sejima & Associates
1–5–27, Tatsumi, Koto-ku
Tokyo 135–0053
Japan

Tel: +81 3 3450 1754
Fax: +81 3 345 0757
E-mail: press@sanaa.co.jp

Born in Ibaraki Prefecture, Japan, in 1956, **KAZUYO SEJIMA** received her M.Arch degree from the Japan Women's University in 1981 and went on to work in the office of Toyo Ito the same year. She established Kazuyo Sejima & Associates in Tokyo in 1987. Ryue Nishizawa was born in Tokyo in 1966, and graduated from the National University (Yokohama, 1990). He began working with Sejima the same year, and the pair created the new firm Kazuyo Sejima + Ryue Nishizawa / SANAA in 1995. SANAA was awarded the 2010 Pritzker Prize. The work of SANAA includes the 21st Century Museum of Contemporary Art (Kanazawa, Ishikawa, 2002–04); and abroad for the first time, the Glass Pavilion of the Toledo Museum of Art (Ohio, USA, 2003–06), and a theater and cultural center in Almere (De Kunstlinie, The Netherlands, 2007). In terms of media exposure, they reached still higher with the New Museum of Contemporary Art, located on the Bowery in New York (USA, 2007), and the vast open spaces of the Rolex Learning Center at the EPFL in Lausanne (Switzerland, 2009). Current work of SANAA includes the new building of the Louvre in Lens (France, 2009–12). The Inujima Art House Project (Okayama, Japan, 2009–10, published here) was the work of Sejima's original firm, Kazuyo Sejima & Associates.

Die 1956 in der Präfektur Ibaraki geborene **KAZUYO SEJIMA** absolvierte 1981 ihren M.Arch an der Japanischen Frauenuniversität und begann noch im selben Jahr für Toyo Ito zu arbeiten. 1987 gründete sie in Tokio ihr Büro Kazuyo Sejima & Associates. Ryue Nishizawa wurde 1966 in Tokio geboren und schloss sein Studium 1990 an der Nationaluniversität in Yokohama ab. Noch im selben Jahr begann er, mit Sejima zu arbeiten. Gemeinsam gründeten sie 1995 das neue Büro Kazuyo Sejima + Ryue Nishizawa / SANAA. 2010 wurde SANAA mit dem Pritzker-Preis ausgezeichnet. Zum Werk von SANAA zählen das Museum für Kunst des 21. Jahrhunderts (Kanazawa, Ishikawa, 2002–04) und, erstmalig im Ausland, der Glaspavillon am Toledo Museum of Art (Ohio, USA, 2003–06) sowie ein Theater und Kulturzentrum in Almere (De Kunstlinie, Niederlande, 2007). Größere Medienpräsenz gewann das Team durch das New Museum of Contemporary Art an der Bowery in New York (USA, 2007) und die weitläufigen, offenen Räume des Rolex Learning Center an der EPFL in Lausanne (Schweiz, 2009). Aktuelle Projekte von SANAA sind u.a. ein Neubau für den Louvre in Lens (Frankreich, 2009–12). Das Inujima Art House (Okayama, Japan, 2009–10, hier vorgestellt) ist ein Entwurf von Sejimas ursprünglichem Büro, Kazuyo Sejima & Associates.

Née dans la préfecture d'Ibaraki en 1956, **KAZUYO SEJIMA** obtient son M. Arch. de l'Université féminine du Japon en 1981 et est engagée par Toyo Ito la même année. Elle crée l'agence Kazuyo Sejima & Associates à Tokyo en 1987. Ryue Nishizawa, né à Tokyo en 1966, est diplômé de l'Université nationale de Yokohama (1990). Il a commencé à travailler avec Sejima la même année avant qu'ils ne fondent ensemble Kazuyo Sejima + Ryue Nishizawa / SANAA en 1995. SANAA a reçu le Prix Pritzker en 2010. Parmi les réalisations de l'agence figurent : le Musée d'art contemporain du XXIe siècle (Kanazawa, Ishikawa, 2002–04) ; le Pavillon de verre du Musée d'art de Toledo (Ohio, 2003–06), première de leurs réalisations à l'étranger, et un théâtre et centre culturel à Almere (De Kunstlinie, Pays-Bas, 2007). Leur notoriété internationale s'est imposée avec des œuvres comme le New Museum of Contemporary Art sur le Bowery à New York (2007) ou les vastes espaces ouverts du Rolex Learning Center à l'EPFL de Lausanne (Suisse, 2009). Actuellement, SANAA a en chantier les nouvelles installations du musée du Louvre à Lens (France, 2009–12). Le projet de la maison d'art Inujima (Okayama, Japon, 2009–10, publié ici) est l'œuvre de l'agence d'origine de Sejima, Kazuyo Sejima & Associates.

INUJIMA ART HOUSE PROJECT

Inujima, Okayama, Japan, 2009–10

Address: 327-5 Inujima, Higashi-ku, Okayama 7048153, Japan, +81 86 947 1112,
www.benesse-artsite.jp/en/inujima-arthouse/index.html
Area: F-Art House (114 m²); S-Art House (64 m²); I-Art House (40 m²); Nakanotani Gazebo (62 m²)
Client: Naoshima Fukutake Art Museum Foundation. Cost: not disclosed

Like the Teshima Art Museum (page 304) by Ryue Nishizawa, these structures were built on a small island in the Inland Sea of Japan for the same client as Tadao Ando's Naoshima projects. "Our project," says Sejima, "is designed to breathe new life into this village by making exhibition spaces in and around the existing townscape." The exhibition spaces are created by renovating abandoned houses and their surroundings. Some houses were rebuilt using translucent acrylic and aluminum because their structure was no longer viable. These art exhibition spaces are scattered around the village and are meant to blend into the existing landscape. Mirror-finish aluminum is used in the case of row houses "so that the surrounding houses and lives therein are reflected into the exhibition spaces." Sejima explains that the whole becomes "a new landscape including the various previous existing residences; architecture and art become one with the peaceful local scenery. We aimed to create a new type of museum where the whole village is a museum and the environment itself brings new scenery," she concludes.

Wie auch das Teshima Art Museum (Seite 304) von Ryue Nishizawa wurden diese Bauten auf einer kleinen Insel in der Seto-Inlandsee in Auftrag gegeben – vom selben Bauherrn, der auch Tadao Andos Projekte in Naoshima beauftragt hatte. „Unser Projekt", so Sejima, „wurde konzipiert, um dem Dorf neues Leben einzuhauchen, indem es Ausstellungsflächen in und um die bestehende Dorflandschaft herum schafft." Die Ausstellungsräume entstanden durch die Sanierung verlassener Häuser und deren Umfeld. Manche Häuser wurden mithilfe von transparentem Acrylglas und Aluminium neu errichtet, weil ihr Tragwerk nicht mehr belastbar war. Die Ausstellungsräume sind im ganzen Dorf verstreut und sollen mit der Landschaft verschmelzen. Bei einigen Reihenhäusern arbeitete Sejima mit spiegelnd poliertem Aluminium, „sodass sich die Nachbarbauten und die darin Lebenden in den Ausstellungsräumen spiegeln". Sejima erklärt, das Ganze füge sich zu „einer neuen Landschaft, zu der auch viele ältere Wohnbauten gehören, Architektur und Kunst werden eins mit der friedlichen Umgebung. Wir wollten eine neue Form von Museum schaffen, bei der das gesamte Dorf zum Museum wird und die Umgebung selbst für eine stets neue Kulisse sorgt."

Comme le Musée d'art de Teshima (page 304) de Ryue Nishizawa, ces constructions sont situées sur une petite île de la Mer intérieure du Japon et ont été réalisées pour le même client que celles de Tadao Ando à Naoshima. « Notre projet », explique Sejima, « est conçu pour insuffler une vie nouvelle dans ce village par la présence de lieux d'exposition dans et autour de l'urbanisation existante. » Les espaces d'exposition occupent des maisons abandonnées rénovées, ainsi que leur environnement. Certaines ont été reconstruites en aluminium et panneaux d'acrylique transparents quand leur structure était trop vétuste. Ces petits espaces d'exposition se répartissent dans le village tout entier et se fondent dans le paysage. Pour certaines maisons alignées, l'architecte a utilisé des panneaux d'aluminium poli miroir « pour que les maisons voisines et leur vie se reflètent dans les espaces d'exposition ». Sejima explique que l'ensemble devient « un nouveau paysage qui comprend diverses maisons existantes… l'art et l'architecture ne forment plus qu'un avec ce cadre villageois paisible. Nous avons voulu créer un nouveau type de musée dans lequel le village tout entier devienne musée et l'environnement lui-même un nouveau cadre », conclut l'architecte.

The F-Art House has an unusual undulating garden gallery added on to its rectangular volume. This element is seen in the image below.

Das rechteckige Volumen des F-Art House wurde um eine ungewöhnliche, geschwungene Gartengalerie ergänzt. Unten ein Blick auf dieses bauliche Element.

La maison F-Art de plan rectangulaire a reçu une étonnante galerie de jardin de forme ondulée (photographie ci-dessous).

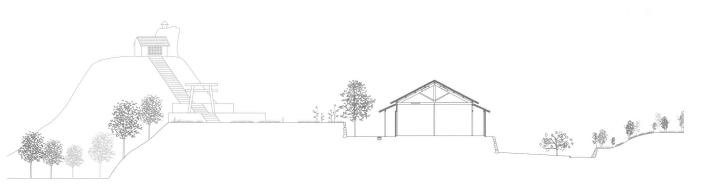

Below, a section drawing of the S-Art House in its site. Above, a covered walkway runs near the S-Art House.

Unten ein Querschnitt des S-Art House in seinem Umfeld. Oben ein überdachter Gang, der unweit des S-Art House verläuft.

Ci-dessous une coupe de la maison S-Art sur son terrain. Ci-dessus, passerelle couverte près de la maison.

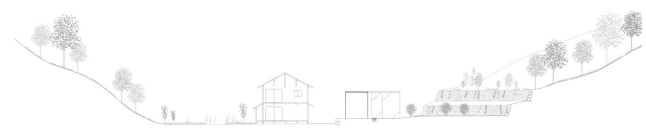

On this page an image and a section drawing of the gazebo structure designed for Inujima by Kazuyo Sejima.

Auf dieser Seite eine Ansicht und ein Querschnitt des Gartenpavillons, den Kazuyo Sejima für Inujima entwarf.

Photographie et dessin de coupe du belvédère conçu par Kazuyo Sejima pour Inujima.

STUDIO MUMBAI

Studio Mumbai Architects
561/63 N. M. Joshi Marg
Byculla West
Mumbai
Maharashtra 400 001
India

Tel: +91 22 6577 7560
Fax: +91 22 2302 1973
E-mail: contact@studiomumbai.com
Web: www.studiomumbai.com

BIJOY JAIN was born in Mumbai, India, in 1965 and received his M.Arch degree from Washington University in Saint Louis in 1990. He worked in Los Angeles and London between 1989 and 1995, and returned to India in 1995 to found his practice. As the architects define their firm: "The essence of the work lies in the relationship between land and architecture. The endeavor is to show the genuine possibility of creating buildings that emerge through a process of collective dialog, a face-to-face sharing of knowledge through imagination, intimacy, and modesty." Recent projects of the firm include the Reading Room (Nagaon, Maharashtra, 2003); Tara House (Kashid, Maharashtra, 2005); Palmyra House (Nandgaon, Maharashtra, 2006–07, published here); Leti 360 Resort (Leti, Uttaranchal, 2007); House on Pali Hill (Bandra, Mumbai, 2008); Utsav House (Satirje, Maharashtra, 2008); Belavali House (Belavali, Maharashtra, 2008); Copper House II (Chondi, Maharashtra, 2010); "In-Between Architecture," Victoria & Albert Museum (London, UK, 2010); and the exhibition "Work-Place," Venice Biennale (Venice, Italy, 2010), all in India unless stated otherwise.

BIJOY JAIN wurde 1965 in Mumbai, Indien, geboren und schloss sein Studium an der Washington University in Saint Louis 1990 mit einem M.Arch ab. Von 1989 bis 1995 arbeitete er in Los Angeles und London und kehrte 1995 nach Indien zurück, wo er sein Büro gründete. Die Architekten beschreiben ihr Profil wie folgt: „Das wesentliche Element unserer Arbeit ist das Verhältnis von Landschaft und Architektur. Unser Ziel ist es zu zeigen, dass es tatsächlich möglich ist, Bauten zu schaffen, die aus einem Prozess des kollektiven Dialogs entstehen, durch persönliches Teilen von Wissen, mithilfe von Fantasie, Vertrautheit und Bescheidenheit." Jüngere Projekte des Büros sind u.a. der Reading Room (Nagaon, Maharashtra, 2003), das Tara House (Kashid, Maharashtra, 2005), das Palmyra House (Nandgaon, Maharashtra, 2006–07, hier vorgestellt), die Hotelanlage Leti 360 (Leti, Uttaranchal, 2007), ein Haus auf Pali Hill (Bandra, Mumbai, 2008), das Utsav House (Satirje, Maharashtra, 2008), das Belavali House (Belavali, Maharashtra, 2008), das Copper House II (Chondi, Maharashtra, 2010), *In-Between Architecture*, Victoria & Albert Museum (London, GB, 2010), sowie die Ausstellung *Work-Place*, Biennale Venedig (Venedig, Italien, 2010), alle in Indien, sofern nicht anders angegeben.

BIJOY JAIN, né à Mumbai en 1965, a obtenu son M. Arch. à l'université Washington à Saint Louis (1990). Il a travaillé à Los Angeles et Londres de 1989 à 1995, puis est revenu en Inde en 1995 pour y fonder son agence dont il définit ainsi les objectifs : « L'essence de notre travail réside dans la relation entre la terre et l'architecture. Notre préoccupation constante est de montrer qu'il est véritablement possible de créer des constructions issues d'un processus de dialogue collectif, d'un échange personnel de connaissances, où l'imagination, l'intimité et la modestie ont leur place. » Parmi les projets récents de l'agence, essentiellement en Inde, figurent : une salle de lecture (Nagaon, Maharashtra, 2003) ; la maison Tara (Kashid, Maharashtra, 2005) ; la maison Palmyra (Nandgaon, Maharashtra, 2006–07, publiée ici) ; l'hôtel de tourisme Leti 360 (Leti, Uttaranchal, 2007) ; la maison sur la colline de Pali (Bandra, Mumbai, 2008) ; la maison Utsav (Satirje, Maharashtra, 2008) ; la maison Belavali (Belavali, Maharashtra, 2008) ; la maison Copper II (Chondi, Maharashtra, 2010) ; l'exposition « In-Between Architecture », Victoria & Albert Museum (Londres, 2010), et l'exposition « Work-Place » à la Biennale de Venise 2010.

PALMYRA HOUSE

Nandgaon, Maharashtra, India, 2006–07

*Area: 300 m². Client: not disclosed. Cost: not disclosed
Collaboration: Jeevaram Suthar, Punaram Suthar, Pandurang Malekar*

In this house, air and light are filtered through two louvered wood boxes set on stone plinths within a coconut plantation situated outside Mumbai. The louvers are made from the trunks of local palmyra palms, whence the name of the residence. These louvers naturally supply passive cooling, as do the neighboring trees. Water from three on-site wells is stored in a water tower that arrives through force of gravity in the house. The architects write: "Sky, sea, and landscape overlap as one moves between and through the spaces of the home. A network of stone aqueducts, inhabited by moss, lichen, and ferns, irrigate the plantation, drawing water from artesian wells as has been the practice for generations." The plan of the house is made up of a series of strict, long rectangles. This is a two-story timber house built as a weekend retreat south of Mumbai.

Bei diesem Haus werden Luft und Licht durch eine Gebäudehülle aus Lamellen gefiltert, die die zwei hölzernen Boxen auf ihrem Steinfundament umfangen. Das Haus liegt inmitten einer Kokosnussplantage außerhalb von Mumbai. Die Sonnenschutzblenden wurden aus dem Holz der heimischen Palmyra-Palme gefertigt, von der sich auch der Name des Hauses ableitet. Die Blenden sorgen für natürliche passive Kühlung, zu der auch der Baumbestand beiträgt. Wasser für das Haus wird auf dem Gelände in drei Brunnen gesammelt, gefiltert und in einem Wasserturm gespeichert, der das Haus durch natürlichen, gefällebedingten Wasserdruck versorgt. Die Architekten schreiben: „Himmel, Meer und Landschaft gehen ineinander über, sobald man sich zwischen den Bauten und durch die Räume des Hauses bewegt. Die Plantage wird durch ein Netzwerk steinerner Aquädukte voller Moos, Flechten und Farne bewässert, die durch artesische Brunnen gespeist werden, eine seit Generationen bestehende Praxis." Der Grundriss des Hauses besteht aus einer Reihe strenger, lang gestreckter Rechtecke. Die zweistöckige Holzkonstruktion wird als Wochenendhaus südlich von Mumbai genutzt.

Dans cette maison située au milieu d'une palmeraie de cocotiers au sud de Mumbai, l'air et la lumière sont filtrés par les persiennes des deux structures en bois reposant sur leurs socles en pierre. Les persiennes sont en palmier de Palmyre local, d'où le nom de la résidence. Elles assurent un rafraîchissement naturel passif qui complète celui fourni par les arbres environnants. L'eau tirée de trois puits est conservée dans un château d'eau qui alimente la maison par simple gravité. « Le ciel, la mer et le paysage semblent se superposer lorsqu'on se déplace à l'intérieur des volumes de la maison. Un réseau de petits aqueducs de pierre, où poussent des mousses, des lichens et des fougères, irrigue la plantation. Il est alimenté par des puits artésiens selon des pratiques qui remontent à des générations », précisent les architectes. Le plan de cette maison de week-end se compose de deux parallélépipèdes allongés, de deux niveaux chacun, construits en bois.

The two very light wooden box structures are seen with their sliding walls opened to the warm environment. Sitting lightly on the earth, they might almost appear to be temporary structures.

Ein Blick auf die zwei besonders leichten Baukörper aus Holz mit Schiebewänden, die sich im heißen Klima nach außen öffnen lassen. Die Bauten greifen kaum in den Baugrund ein und wirken fast wie temporäre Bauten.

Photo des deux parties de la maison composée de deux structures très légères en bois, à parois coulissantes ouvertes sur l'environnement tropical. Elles sont si délicatement posées sur le sol qu'elles pourraient faire penser à des constructions temporaires.

To the right, a site plan shows that the two structures are slightly skewed apart. The rectangular basin separates them and forms a third rectangle in the plan.

Ein Lageplan rechts zeigt die leicht schiefwinklige Anordnung der beiden Bauten. Das rechteckige Wasserbecken, das sie trennt, erscheint als drittes Rechteck auf dem Grundriss.

À droite, plan du terrain montrant que les deux constructions ne sont pas parallèles. Le bassin rectangulaire qui les sépare forme le troisième rectangle du plan.

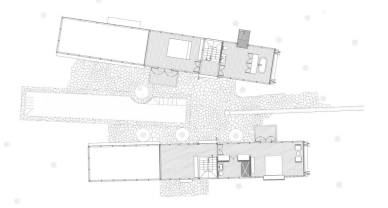

With the folding louvered walls in the open position, the interior of the house and its generous volumes are fully open to the natural setting. In elevation (below) the structure remains just as simple and rectilinear.

Sind die Lamellentüren aufgeklappt, öffnet sich das großzügige Interieur des Hauses vollständig zur Landschaft. Im Aufriss (unten) wirkt der Bau ebenso schlicht und geradlinig.

Parois à persiennes ouvertes, l'intérieur de la maison aux généreux volumes s'inscrit pleinement dans son cadre naturel. L'élévation ci-dessous illustre la forme simple et rectiligne de chaque pavillon.

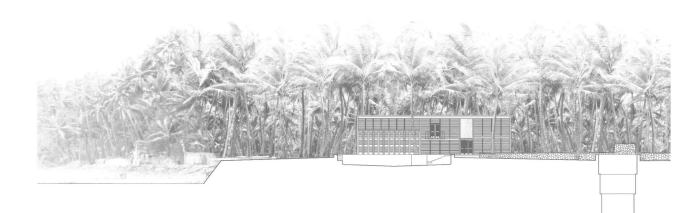

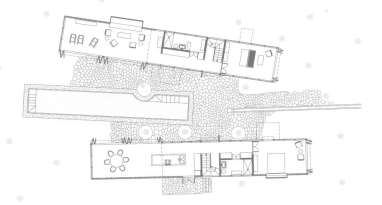

Floor plans reveal the basic simplicity of the interior design, echoing the architecture itself, as can be seen in the image below.

Etagengrundrisse zeugen von der grundlegenden Schlichtheit des Interieurs, die sich auch in der Architektur des Hauses spiegelt, wie die Ansicht unten belegt.

Les plans au sol expriment la simplicité élémentaire de l'aménagement intérieur qui vient en écho à l'architecture extérieure, comme le montre l'image ci-dessous.

TERRAIN

Terrain: Loenhart & Mayr
Marienplatz 28
Munich 80331
Germany

Tel: +49 89 51 99 71 10
E-mail: info@terrain.de
Web: www.terrain.de

KLAUS LOENHART was born in 1969. He studied architecture at the University of Applied Science FHM Munich (1994), and the Harvard Graduate School of Design (1999–2000). He worked in the office of Herzog and de Meuron, before founding Terrain in 2004 with **CHRISTOPH MAYR**, born in 1969. Mayr studied architecture at the University of Applied Sciences FHM Munich (1993). Their most significant projects include the TUEV SUED Testing Facility Prototype (Mering, Germany, 2004); Orang-Utan Large Outdoor Enclosure, Hellabrunn Zoo (Munich, Germany, 2006); the Olympic Ski Jump (Garmisch-Partenkirchen, Germany, 2009); and the Mur River Nature Observation Tower (Southern Styria, Austria, 2009, published here).

KLAUS LOENHART wurde 1969 geboren. Er studierte Architektur an der FHM München (1994) und an der Harvard Graduate School of Design (1999–2000). Er arbeitete im Büro von Herzog und de Meuron, bevor er 2004 mit **CHRISTOPH MAYR** sein Büro Terrain gründete. Mayr, geboren 1969, studierte Architektur an der FHM München (1993). Zu ihren wichtigsten Projekten zählen eine Anlage für Prototypentests für den TÜV SÜD (Mering, Deutschland, 2004), ein großes Orang-Utan-Freigehege im Zoo Hellabrunn (München, 2006), die neue Olympia Skisprungschanze (Garmisch-Partenkirchen, 2009) und der Murturm (Südsteiermark, Österreich, 2009, hier vorgestellt).

KLAUS LOENHART, né en 1969, a étudié l'architecture à l'Université des sciences appliquées FHM à Munich (1994) et à la Harvard Graduate School of Design (1999–2000). Il a travaillé pour Herzog et de Meuron avant de fonder l'agence Terrain en 2004 en association avec **CHRISTOPH MAYR**. Né en 1969, Mayr a étudié l'architecture à l'Université des sciences appliquées FHM de Munich (1993). Parmi leurs réalisations les plus significatives : un prototype d'installations d'essais TUEV SUED (Mering, Allemagne, 2004) ; l'enclos des orangs-outans au zoo d'Hellabrunn (Munich, 2006) ; le tremplin de saut à ski olympique (Garmisch-Partenkirchen, 2009) et la tour d'observation de la nature de la Mur (Styrie méridionale, Autriche, 2009, publiée ici).

MUR RIVER NATURE OBSERVATION TOWER

Southern Styria, Austria, 2009

Address: Gosdorf, Austria, +43 34 72 24 03, www.gosdorf.at
Height: 27 meters. Client: Gosdorf Infrastructure GmbH. Cost: not disclosed
Collaboration: osd office for structural design (Engineering)

Opened to the public in the spring of 2010, the **MUR RIVER NATURE OBSERVATION TOWER** is "based on the idea of a double helix." Visitors walking up the 168 steps of the aluminum stairway through the steel-tube structure observe the different ecological layers of the forest. The architects reveal that they were inspired by the double spiral staircase in the Graz Castle, built around 1500. The main structure is made up of supporting and load-bearing tube-shaped members that provide the stability, while cables limit oscillation and horizontal sway at the top of the tower. CNC manufacturing was used because of the complexity of the structure, which is based on a recurring joint configuration. The complexity of the nodal connections demanded detailed planning in 3D. The structure has a total weight of 87 tons and a diameter of 8.7 meters.

Der im Frühjahr 2010 eröffnete **MURTURM** „basiert auf dem Prinzip einer Doppelhelix". Beim Ersteigen der 168 Stufen der Aluminiumtreppe in der Stahlröhrenkonstruktion bietet sich den Besuchern der Blick auf verschiedene vertikale Schichtungen des ökologischen Lebensraums „Wald". Die Architekten nennen als Inspiration die doppelte Wendeltreppe in der um 1500 erbauten Grazer Burg. Die Konstruktion besteht in erster Linie aus tragenden Formrohren, die dem Bau Stabilität geben, während Kabelverspannungen Schwingungen an der Spitze des Turms reduzieren. Aufgrund der Komplexität der Konstruktion, die auf einer sich wiederholenden Knotensequenz basiert, wurde mit CNC-Fertigung gearbeitet. Die Komplexität der Knotenpunkte erforderte detaillierte 3D-Planung. Die Konstruktion hat ein Gesamtgewicht von 87 t und einen Durchmesser von 8,7 m.

Ouverte au public au printemps 2010, la **TOUR D'OBSERVATION DE LA NATURE DE LA MUR** repose « sur une idée de double hélice ». Les visiteurs qui escaladent les 168 marches de l'escalier en aluminium inséré dans une structure en tubes d'acier peuvent observer les différentes strates écologiques de la forêt. Les architectes avouent s'être inspirés de l'escalier en double spirale du château de Graz édifié vers 1500. La structure principale est en poutrelles tubulaires porteuses qui assurent la stabilité, tandis que des câbles limitent les oscillations et le balancement horizontal du sommet de la tour. La complexité de la construction, basée sur une configuration de joints répétitive, a nécessité de recourir à des techniques de fabrication des poutrelles par machines à commande numérique, et d'exécuter des plans techniques détaillés en 3D pour les connexions nodales. L'ensemble pèse 87 tonnes pour un diamètre de 8,70 mètres.

The tower seen in the setting of the forest (left page) reveals itself as a technological object, somewhat akin to the extendable platforms used in construction and maintenance, albeit here in a more sophisticated form.

Der hier im bewaldeten Umfeld zu sehende Turm (linke Seite) entpuppt sich als hochtechnische Konstruktion und erinnert an Hebebühnen, die man von Baustellen und Wartungsarbeiten kennt, auch wenn der Turm zweifellos weitaus anspruchsvoller ist.

Dans son cadre forestier (page de gauche), la tour affirme sa nature d'objet technologique et évoque les plates-formes élévatrices de chantier, bien qu'ici de forme plus sophistiquée.

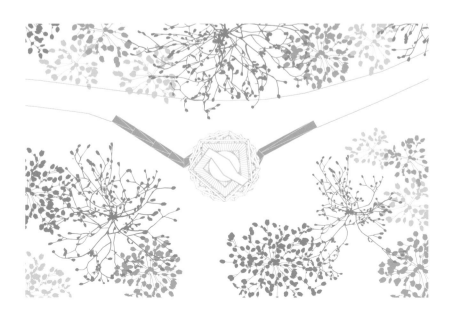

Although it appears rather complex from certain angles, the tower is carefully engineered to provide a very light and open structure, as can be seen in the images above. To the left, a site plan.

Auch wenn der Turm aus bestimmten Blickwinkeln hochkomplex erscheint, wurde er technisch bewusst so geplant, dass eine leichte, offene Konstruktion entsteht, wie auf den Ansichten oben zu sehen. Links ein Lageplan.

Apparaissant assez complexe vue sous certains angles, la tour reste une structure légère et très ouverte, comme le montrent les images ci-dessus. À gauche, un plan du site.

An elevation shows the tower at almost precisely the height of neighboring trees. Below, the view from the topmost level of the structure.

Der Aufriss zeigt, dass der Turm fast exakt dieselbe Höhe wie der angrenzende Baumbestand hat. Unten der Blick von der Spitze des Turms.

Élévation montrant la tour dont la hauteur atteint exactement celle des arbres. Ci-dessous vue prise du sommet de la tour.

UNDURRAGA DEVES

Undurraga Deves Arquitectos
Presidente Errazuriz 2999 Las Condes
Santiago, RM 7550356
Chile

Tel: +56 2 498 0655
Fax: +56 2 498 0650
E-mail: info@undurragadeves.cl
Web: www.undurragadeves.cl

CRISTIAN UNDURRAGA received his degree in Architecture from the Universidad Católica de Chile in 1977. The same year he obtained the First Prize for Young Architects at the Chilean Architectural Biennale. In 1978 he created Undurraga Deves Studio. Recent work includes La Moneda Cultural Center (Santiago, 2004); San Alberto Hurtado Solidarity Memorial (Santiago, 2008); the Horizon Houses (Zapallar, 2008–09, published here); Capilla del Retiro (Valley of the Andes, 2009); and the Violeta Parra Museum (Santiago, 2011), all in Chile.

CRISTIAN UNDURRAGA schloss sein Architekturstudium 1977 an der Universidad Católica de Chile ab. Im selben Jahr wurde er auf der chilenischen Architekturbiennale mit dem Ersten Preis für junge Architekten ausgezeichnet. 1978 gründete er Undurraga Deves Studio. Jüngere Projekte sind das La Moneda Kulturzentrum (Santiago, 2004), das Solidaritätsdenkmal San Alberto Hurtado (Santiago, 2008), die Horizon Houses (Zapallar, 2008–09, hier vorgestellt), die Capilla del Retiro (Andentäler, 2009) und das Violeta-Parra-Museum (Santiago, 2011), alle in Chile.

CRISTIAN UNDURRAGA est diplômé en architecture de l'Université catholique du Chili (1977). La même année, il a obtenu le premier prix des jeunes Architectes lors de la Biennale de l'architecture chilienne et a fondé le Undurraga Deves Studio en 1978. Parmi ses réalisations récentes, toutes au Chili : le Centre culturel de La Moneda (Santiago, 2004) ; le mémorial de la solidarité San Alberto Hurtado (Santiago, 2008) ; les maisons Horizon (Zapallar, 2008–09, publiées ici) ; la chapelle du Retiro (vallée des Andes, 2009) et le musée Violeta Parra (Santiago, 2011).

HORIZON HOUSES

Zapallar, Chile, 2008–09

Area: 433 m² (House 1); 491 m² (House 2). Client: not disclosed
Cost: not disclosed

The **HORIZON HOUSES** are located on the central coast of Chile on a site 25 meters above the ocean. Referring to the dramatic natural setting the architect states: "The formidable sum of stimuli offered by the site demanded a radical architectural decision, setting a new order in the landscape without introducing any characteristic in contradiction with the forces expressed by nature." Two large stone cavities were created. 44- and 48-meter-long post-tensioned reinforced-concrete beams supporting a bridge "are what define the character of the houses." These beams are supported by three pillars. Floor slabs are hung from these elements with steel posts. The architect explains: "Toward the south, the windows allow the view of the sea and the town of Zapallar. To the north, the windows collect sunlight, which is regulated by mobile lattices. Cross ventilation is provided for by the constant sea breezes."

Die **HORIZON HOUSES** an der Zentralküste von Chile liegen auf einem Grundstück 25 m über dem Meer. Mit Blick auf die spektakuläre Landschaft erklärt der Architekt: „Die beeindruckende Anzahl verschiedener Stimuli, die dieses Grundstück bietet, erforderte eine radikale architektonische Entscheidung, das Setzen einer neuen Ordnung in der Landschaft, ohne Elemente einzuführen, die im Widerspruch zu den Naturgewalten stehen könnten." Zwei Aushöhlungen wurden in den Fels geschlagen. 44 und 48 m lange Spannbeton-Brückenträger aus Stahlbeton „prägen den Charakter der Hausbauten". Diese Träger ruhen auf drei Säulen. Die Bodenplatten wurden mithilfe von Stahlträgern von der Konstruktion abgehängt. Der Architekt erklärt: „Nach Süden hin bieten die Fenster Blick auf das Meer und hinüber zur Kleinstadt Zapallar. Nach Norden sammeln die Fenster das Sonnenlicht, dessen Einfall durch bewegliche Sonnenschutzblenden reguliert wird. Querlüftung ensteht durch die ständige Brise vom Meer."

Les **MAISONS HORIZON** se trouvent sur la partie centrale de la côte du Chili à 25 mètres au-dessus de l'océan. Évoquant ce cadre naturel spectaculaire, l'architecte précise : « La formidable somme de stimuli qu'offrait ce terrain réclamait une décision architecturale radicale, la création d'un nouvel ordre dans le paysage, sans pour autant y introduire des caractéristiques venant en contradiction avec les forces exprimées par la nature. » Deux importantes cavités ont été creusées dans le rocher. Des poutres en béton armé postcontraint de 44 et 48 mètres de long reposant sur trois piliers qui soutiennent un pont « définissent le caractère des maisons ». Les dalles de sols sont suspendues à ces éléments par des poutrelles d'acier. « Vers le sud, les baies donnent sur l'océan et la ville de Zapallar. Au nord, la lumière du soleil est filtrée par des treillis mobiles. La brise constante de la mer permet une ventilation croisée. »

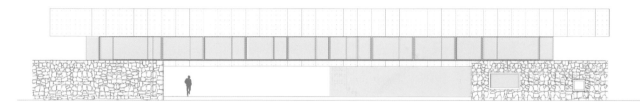

The same structure seen in a south elevation (above) and an image of the north elevation (top of page). The houses offer a spectacular view of the ocean thanks to the full-height glazing employed.

Dasselbe Gebäude auf einem Aufriss der Südfassade und einer Aufnahme der Nordseite (oben). Dank deckenhoher Verglasung bieten sich vom Haus aus dramatische Ausblicke aufs Meer.

Une maison vue en élévation côté sud et une photographie de sa façade nord (ci-dessus). Les maisons offrent des perspectives spectaculaires sur l'océan grâce au vitrage toute hauteur.

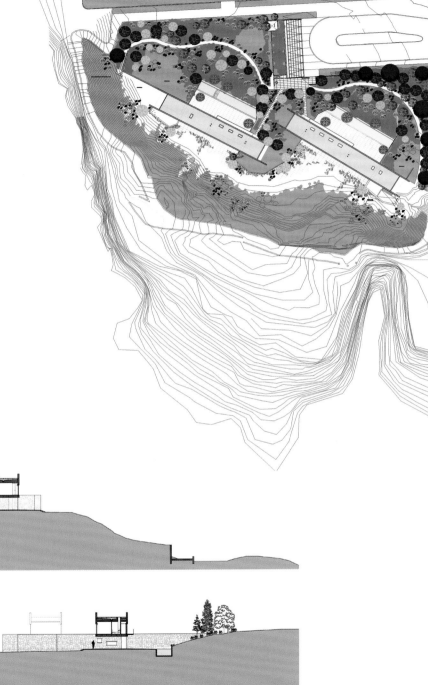

The powerful concrete beam design appears to hover over the fully glazed main level in the images on the left. To the right, a general plan shows the topographic lines of the sloped site and the two house volumes.

Die eindrucksvollen Betonträger scheinen über dem vollverglasten Hauptgeschoss zu schweben (links). Rechts ein Überblicksplan mit den topografischen Linien des Hang-grundstücks und den zwei Gebäuden.

Les puissantes poutres de béton semblent en suspension au-dessus du niveau principal entièrement vitré (image de gauche). À droite, plan de la topographie et de l'implantation des deux maisons.

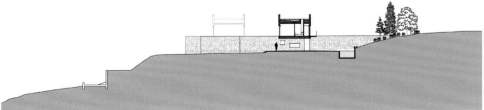

Section drawings show the way in which only the narrow pool is notched into the site, while the rest of the volume sits on the flat area overlooking the sea.

Wie auf den Querschnitten zu sehen, wurde der schmale Pool in den Boden eingelassen, während die übrigen Baukörper flach auf dem Grundstück am Meer aufliegen.

Des coupes montrent la façon dont l'étroit bassin a été creusé dans la pente, les maisons ayant été construites sur un petit plateau donnant sur la mer.

The double full-height glazing makes the interior space seem almost as though it is in a continuum with the exterior. To the right, stairs leading down form a strictly geometric frame for the wild beauty of the ocean.

Dank der beidseitigen geschosshohen Verglasung wirken die Innenräume fast wie ein fließendes Raumkontinuum in ihrer Umgebung. Eine nach unten führende Treppe (rechts) wird zum streng geometrischen Rahmen für die ungezähmte Schönheit des Ozeans.

Le vitrage toute hauteur des deux côtés donne l'impression d'une continuité entre l'intérieur et l'extérieur. À droite, la cage de l'escalier qui conduit au niveau inférieur offre un cadrage sur la beauté sauvage de l'océan.

UNSTUDIO

*UNStudio
Stadhouderskade 113
1073 AX Amsterdam
The Netherlands*

*Tel: +31 20 570 20 40
Fax: +31 20 570 20 41
E-mail: info@unstudio.com
Web: www.unstudio.com*

BEN VAN BERKEL was born in Utrecht, the Netherlands, in 1957 and studied at the Rietveld Academy in Amsterdam and at the Architectural Association (AA) in London, receiving the AA Diploma with honors in 1987. After working briefly in the office of Santiago Calatrava in 1988, he set up his practice in Amsterdam with Caroline Bos. As well as the Erasmus Bridge in Rotterdam (1996), Van Berkel & Bos Architectural Bureau has built the Karbouw and ACOM (1989–93) office buildings, and the REMU Electricity Station (1989–93), all in Amersfoort; and housing projects and the Aedes East Gallery for Kristin Feireiss in Berlin, Germany. Projects include the Möbius House (Naarden, 1993–98); Het Valkhof Museum (Nijmegen, 1998); and NMR Laboratory (Utrecht, 2000), all in the Netherlands; a Switching Station (Innsbruck, Austria, 1998–2001); an Electricity Station (Innsbruck, Austria, 2002); VilLA NM (Upstate New York, USA, 2000–06); and the Mercedes-Benz Museum (Stuttgart, Germany, 2003–06). Recent work includes a Teahouse (Groot Kantwijk, Vreeland, The Netherlands, 2005–07); a Music Theater (Graz, Austria, 1998–2008); a Research Laboratory at Groningen University (Groningen, The Netherlands, 2003–08); Star Place (Kaohsiung, Taiwan, 2006–08); Burnham Pavilion (Chicago, Illinois, USA, 2009); the Art Collector's Loft (New York, USA, 2007–10, published here); and Arnhem Station (The Netherlands, 1986–2014).

BEN VAN BERKEL wurde 1957 in Utrecht geboren und studierte an der Rietveld-Akademie in Amsterdam sowie an der Architectural Association (AA) in London, wo er 1987 das Diplom mit Auszeichnung erhielt. Nach einem kurzen Arbeitseinsatz 1988 bei Santiago Calatrava gründete er mit Caroline Bos sein eigenes Büro in Amsterdam. Neben der Erasmusbrücke in Rotterdam (1996) baute Van Berkel & Bos Architectural Bureau die Büros für Karbouw und ACOM (1989–93) sowie das Kraftwerk REMU (1989–93), alle in Amersfoort, und realisierte in Berlin Wohnbauprojekte sowie die Galerie Aedes East für Kristin Feireiss. Zu den Projekten des Teams zählen das Haus Möbius (Naarden, 1993–98), das Museum Het Valkhof (Nijmegen, 1998) und das Labor NMR (Utrecht, 2000), alle in den Niederlanden, ein Umspannwerk (Innsbruck, 1998–2001), ein Elektrizitätswerk (Innsbruck, 2002), die VilLA NM (bei New York, 2000–06) und das Mercedes-Benz-Museum (Stuttgart, 2003–06). Jüngere Arbeiten sind u.a. ein Teehaus (Groot Kantwijk, Vreeland, Niederlande, 2005–07), ein Musiktheater in Graz (1998–2008), ein Forschungslabor an der Universität Groningen (2003–08), Star Place (Kaohsiung, Taiwan, 2006–08), der Burnham-Pavillon (Chicago, 2009), ein Loft für eine Kunstsammler (New York, 2007–10, hier vorgestellt) und der Bahnhof Arnhem (Niederlande, 1986–2014).

BEN VAN BERKEL, né à Utrecht en 1957, a étudié à l'Académie Rietveld à Amsterdam et à l'Architectural Association (AA) de Londres, dont il est sorti diplômé avec mention en 1987. Après avoir brièvement travaillé pour Santiago Calatrava en 1988, il a créé son agence à Amsterdam en association avec Caroline Bos. Accédant à la notoriété grâce au pont Erasmus à Rotterdam (inauguré en 1996), Van Berkel & Bos Architectural Bureau a réalisé les immeubles de bureaux Karbouw et ACOM (1989–93) et la centrale électrique REMU (1989–93) à Amersfoort, ainsi que des immeubles de logements et la galerie Aedes East pour Kristin Feireiss à Berlin. Plus récemment, l'agence a signé la maison Möbius (Naarden, 1993–98) ; le musée Het Valkhof (Nijmegen, 1998) ; le laboratoire NMR (Utrecht, 2000), tous aux Pays-Bas ; une station de transformation (Innsbruck, Autriche, 1998–2001), une centrale électrique (Innsbruck, Autriche, 2002) ; la VilLA NM (Upstate New York, 2000–06) et le musée Mercedes-Benz (Stuttgart, Allemagne, 2003–06). UNStudio a également réalisé une Maison de thé (Groot Kantwijk, Vreeland, Pays-Bas, 2005–07) ; une salle de concerts (Graz, Autriche, 1998–2008) ; un laboratoire de recherches pour l'université de Groningue (Pays-Bas, 2003–08) ; le centre commercial Star Place (Kaohsiung, Taïwan, 2006–08) ; le pavillon Burnham (Chicago, Illinois, 2009) ; le loft d'un collectionneur d'art (New York, 2007–10, publié ici) et la gare d'Arnhem (Pays-Bas, 1986–2014).

ART COLLECTOR'S LOFT

New York, New York, USA, 2007–10

Area: 439 m². Client: not disclosed. Cost: not disclosed
Collaboration: Arjan Dingsté, Marianthi Tatari, Colette Parras

By emptying the middle of the volume and adding curved walls, the architect provides a spectacular space for the exposition of contemporary art.

Durch die Öffnung des zentralen baulichen Volumens und den Einbau geschwungener Zwischenwände schafft der Architekt einen dramatischen Raum für die Präsentation zeitgenössischer Kunst.

En vidant la partie centrale du volume et en y intégrant des murs incurvés, l'architecte délimite un espace spectaculaire qui permet d'exposer des œuvres d'art contemporain.

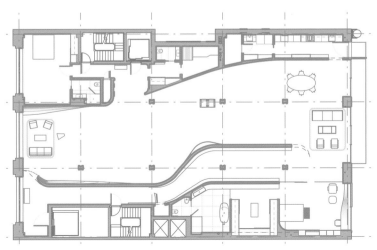

In the floor plan to the left and the image above, it is apparent how the architect has carved out the central space and located the other parts of the 439-square-meter apartment at the periphery of the art exhibition area.

Auf Grundriss (unten) und Ansicht (oben) wird deutlich, wie der Architekt den zentralen Bereich ausgespart und die übrigen Nutzflächen des 439 m² großen Apartments in die Randzonen der Ausstellungsfläche verlegt hat.

Le plan au sol à gauche et l'image ci-dessus explicitent comment l'architecte a modelé le nouvel espace central d'exposition et réparti en périphérie les autres pièces de cet appartement de 439 m².

This design for an existing loft in Greenwich Village in Manhattan "explores the interaction between a gallery and living space." The main walls in the loft flow through the space, allowing exhibition areas to merge into living areas. The space is long, wide, and low. The "meandering" walls made of double-curved glass-fiber-reinforced-gypsum paneling added by the architects create ample exhibition space. The ceiling varies between luminous and opaque surfaces. The luminous areas are back-lit by 18 000 LEDs. UNStudio has also used full floor-to-ceiling windows and a glass balcony to frame views of downtown Manhattan. A Douglas fir floor with wide planks is used throughout the loft.

Bei diesem Entwurf für ein Loft in Greenwich Village in Manhattan ging es darum, „mit dem Zusammenspiel von Galerie und Wohnraum zu experimentieren". Die zentralen Wände des Lofts fließen durch den Raum und ermöglichen gleitende Übergänge zwischen Ausstellungs- und Wohnbereichen. Der Raum ist gestreckt, breit und niedrig. Durch die vom Architekten eingezogenen, „mäandernden" Wände aus zweifach geschwungenem, glasfaserverstärkten Gipsbauplatten entstanden großzügige Ausstellungsflächen. Die Decken sind wechselweise opak oder lichtdurchlässig. Die lichtdurchlässigen Zonen sind mit 18 000 LEDs hinterleuchtet. Darüber hinaus rahmte UNStudio den Ausblick über Manhattan mit deckenhohen Fensterflächen und einem gläsernen Balkon. Die breiten Bodendielen im gesamten Loft sind aus Douglasie.

Ce projet de rénovation d'un loft dans Greenwich Village à New York « explore l'interaction entre une galerie et un espace de vie ». Les longs murs principaux qui traversent l'espace provoquent la fusion des zones d'exposition et de celles de séjour. Le vaste volume en longueur est relativement bas de plafond. Rajoutés par les architectes, les murs « en méandres » constitués de fibre de verre et de panneaux de plâtre à double courbure, offrent de vastes espaces d'exposition. Le plafond est tantôt lumineux (éclairé par 18 000 DEL) tantôt opaque. UNStudio a disposé des baies toute hauteur et un balcon de verre qui cadrent des perspectives sur le centre de Manhattan. Les sols sont en parquet de pin de Douglas à larges lattes.

Adept at the art of using computers to imagine very contemporary spaces, UNStudio uses the marked tracks in the ceiling to give a feeling of movement and continuity to the space.

UNStudio, geschult in der Kunst, dezidiert zeitgenössische Räume digital zu entwerfen, nutzt die Markierungen an der Decke, um dem Raum Dynamik und Kontinuität zu geben.

Adepte de l'ordinateur pour imaginer des espaces très contemporains, UNStudio renforce l'impression de mouvement et de continuité par des filets tracés au plafond.

A library space emerges from the curves generated for the art while an opening in the ceiling provides light in the same spirit.

Zwischen den geschwungenen Wänden, die zur Präsentation von Kunst eingezogen wurden, findet sich eine Bibliothek. Eine ähnlich geschwungene Deckenöffnung sorgt für Belichtung.

Une bibliothèque a été aménagée au détour d'une des courbes de l'espace d'exposition, éclairée par une verrière zénithale dont la forme reprend le principe de flux.

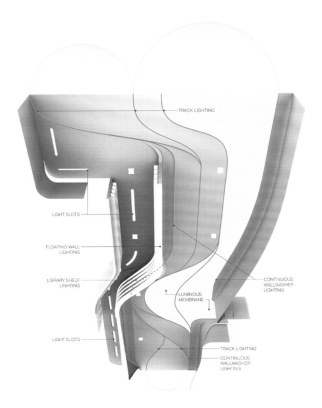

TRACK LIGHTING

LIGHT SLOTS

FLOATING WALL
LIGHTING

LIBRARY SHELF
LIGHTING

LUMINOUS
MEMBRANE

CONTINUOUS
WALLWASHER
LIGHTING

LIGHT SLOTS

TRACK LIGHTING

CONTINUOUS
WALLWASHER
LIGHTING

The diagram on the left shows the care taken by the architects in the conception of the lighting scheme for the apartment. Below, a bedroom with glass walls. Right page, curves are lit to emphasize the flow of the spaces.

Das Diagramm (links) veranschaulicht die sorgsame Lichtplanung der Architekten für das Apartment. Unten ein Schlafzimmer mit Glaswänden. Die Beleuchtung der geschwungenen Wandflächen betont den fließenden Raumeindruck (rechte Seite).

Le diagramme de gauche illustre l'attention apportée à la disposition de l'éclairage de l'appartement. Ci-dessous, une chambre à murs de verre. Page de droite, l'éclairage des courbes met en valeur l'idée de flux spatial.

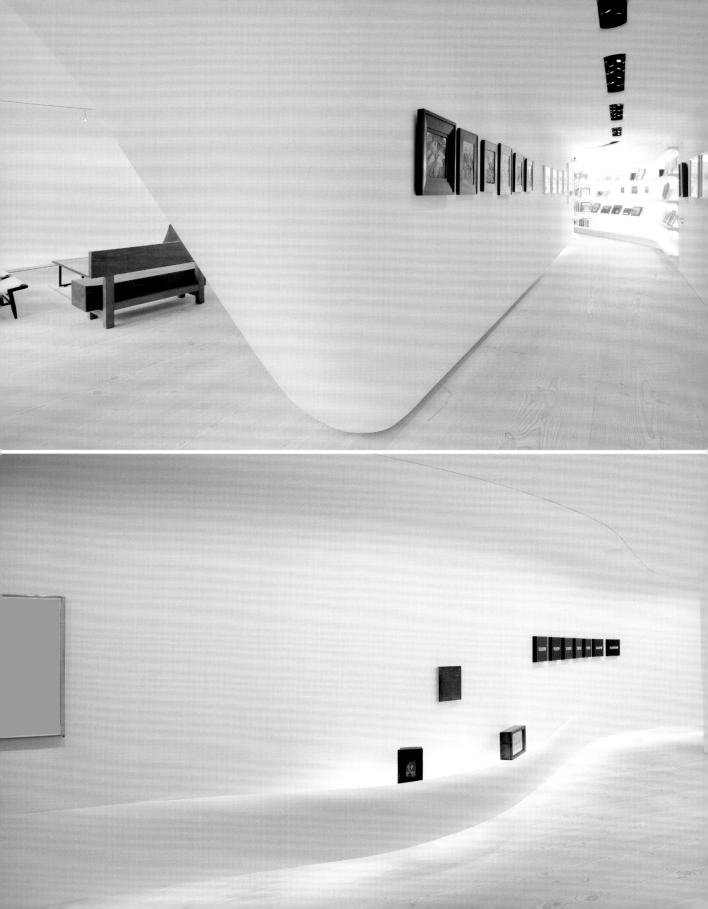

URBANA

URBANA
House 56, Road 5A
Dhanmondi
Dhaka 1209
Bangladesh

Tel: +88 02 967 1500
E-mail: contacturbana@gmail.com

KASHEF MAHBOOB CHOWDHURY was born in Dhaka, Bangladesh, in 1970. He received a B.Arch degree from the Bangladesh University of Engineering and Technology (BUET) in 1995. He participated in a Master Class with Glenn Murcutt in Sydney in 2006. He established URBANA in partnership in 1995 but since 2004 has continued as the sole principal of the firm. His work includes his own residence (Lalmatia, Dhaka, 1995–2001); BEN Bangladesh Factory Building (EPZ, Dhaka); the Chandgaon Mosque (Chittagong, 2006–07, published here); and a residence (Baridhara, Dhaka, 2007–10). Ongoing work includes the Friendship Training Center (Gaibandha, 2009–); Gulshan Mosque (Dhaka, 2010–); and the EHL Premium Apartments (Dhaka, 2010–), all in Bangladesh.

KASHEF MAHBOOB CHOWDHURY wurde 1970 in Dhaka, Bangladesh, geboren. Seinen B.Arch absolvierte er 1995 an der Universität für Ingenieurwissenschaften und Technik von Bangladesh (BUET). 2006 nahm er an einer Meisterklasse bei Glenn Murcutt in Sydney teil. Nachdem er URBANA 1995 zunächst als Partnerschaft gegründet hatte, betreibt er das Büro seit 2004 unter eigener Regie. Zu seinen Projekten zählen sein eigenes Wohnhaus (Lalmatia, Dhaka, 1995–2001), ein Fabrikgebäude für BEN Bangladesh (EPZ, Dhaka), die Chandgaon-Moschee (Chittagong, 2006–07, hier vorgestellt) und ein privater Wohnbau (Baridhara, Dhaka, 2007–10). Laufende Projekte sind u.a. das Friendship Training Center (Gaibandha, 2009–), die Gulshan-Moschee (Dhaka, 2010–) sowie die EHL Premium Apartments (Dhaka, 2010–), alle in Bangladesh.

KASHEF MAHBOOB CHOWDHURY, né à Dhaka (Bangladesh) en 1970 a obtenu son B. Arch. à l'Université d'ingénierie et de technologie du Bangladesh (BUET) en 1995. Il a participé à une *master class* animée par Glenn Murcutt à Sydney en 2006. Il a fondé l'agence URBANA en partenariat avec d'autres architectes en 1995 mais est depuis 2004 l'unique dirigeant de l'agence. Parmi ses réalisations, toutes au Bangladesh : sa propre maison (Lalmatia, Dhaka, 1995–2001) ; l'usine BEN Bangladesh (EPZ, Dhaka) ; la mosquée de Chandgaon (Chittagong, 2006–07, publiée ici) et une maison individuelle (Baridhara, Dhaka, 2007–10). Il travaille actuellement au Friendship Training Center (Gaibandha, 2009–) ; à la mosquée de Gulshan (Dhaka, 2010–) et à l'immeuble EHL Premium Apartments (Dhaka, 2010–).

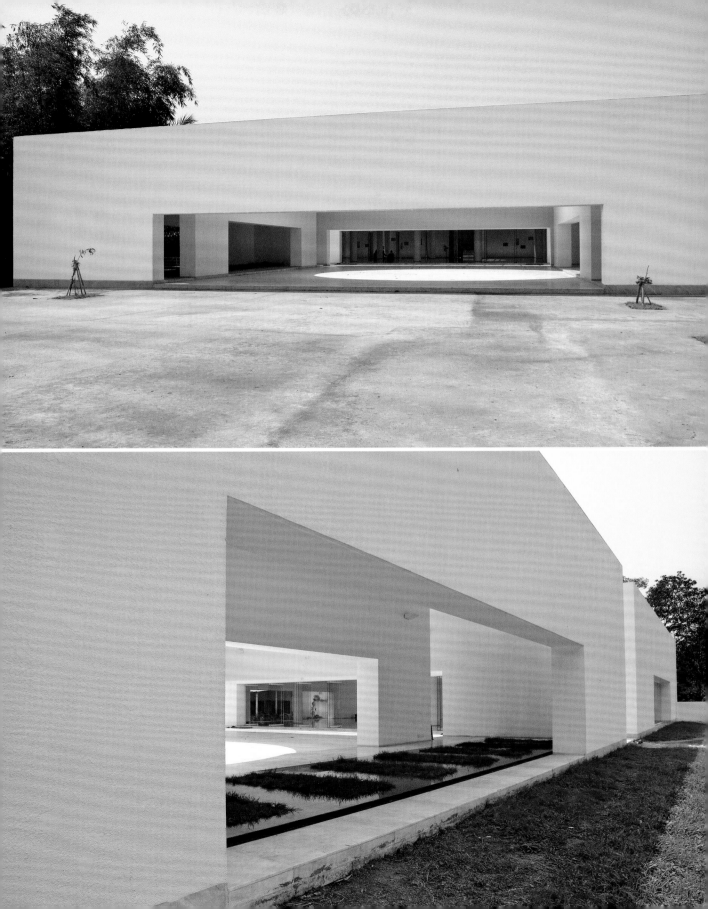

MOSQUE IN CHANDGAON

Chittagong, Bangladesh, 2006–07

Address: Chandgaon, Chittagong, Bangladesh
Area: 925 m². Client: M. Morshed Khan, Faisal M. Khan and family. Cost: $285 000

The architect sought to seek both a place of worship and a place for meditation. He started by identifying the "essential" elements of the mosque. "The design," he explains, "consists of two identical cuboid volumes, one as the front court and the mosque proper as the other. The traditional courtyard in front of a mosque, which serves as spillover area during larger congregations, therefore manifests itself in the first structure—open to the elements and offering a preparation before entry to the mosque proper. The design pivots around the tension between the horizontal sweep of the low, wide openings and the gathering people (earthbound) and the vertical reference to zenith of the circular opening or cut dome (spiritual)." The cut dome, open to the sky, differentiates this from most other mosques. The architect has also sought to reinstate this mosque to the traditional role of community gathering place.

Dem Architekten ging es darum, einen Ort des Gottesdienstes und der Meditation zu schaffen. Ausgangspunkt war für ihn die Bestimmung der „wesentlichen" Elemente einer Moschee. „Der Entwurf", so der Architekt, „besteht aus zwei identischen kubischen Volumina, einem Vorhof und der eigentlichen Moschee. Der traditionelle Vorhof einer Moschee, der dazu dient, Besucher aufzunehmen, die bei großen Gottesdiensten keinen Platz mehr in der Moschee finden, ist damit das erste bauliche Element – offen den Elementen ausgesetzt und zudem ein Ort der Vorbereitung vor dem Betreten der Moschee. Dreh- und Angelpunkt des Entwurfs ist die Spannung zwischen den horizontal ausgreifenden, niedrigen, weiten Öffnungen und den versammelten Besuchern (erdverbunden) und der vertikalen Referenz zum Zenith durch das runde Oberlicht und die gespaltene Kuppel (spirituell)." Die zum Himmel offene, gespaltene Kuppel unterscheidet den Bau von den meisten Moscheen. Darüber hinaus ging es dem Architekten darum, der Moschee wieder ihre überkommene Rolle als nachbarschaftlichen Versammlungsort zurückzugeben.

L'architecte a cherché à créer ici un lieu de culte qui soit aussi un lieu de méditation. Il a commencé par identifier les éléments qui constituent l'essence de la mosquée. « Le projet », explique-t-il, « consiste en deux volumes cuboïdes, l'un étant une cour, l'autre la mosquée proprement dite. La cour que l'on trouve traditionnellement devant une mosquée et qui sert aussi à accueillir les fidèles lors des grandes fêtes religieuses, est ouverte aux éléments et permet d'accomplir les rites qui précèdent l'entrée dans la grande salle. Le projet joue sur la tension entre l'ampleur des vastes ouvertures surbaissées et la réunion des fidèles (la terre) et la référence verticale au zénith par l'ouverture centrale découpée dans la coupole (le spirituel). » Cette coupole tranchée qui s'ouvre sur le ciel, différencie ce projet de la plupart des mosquées existantes. L'architecte a également cherché à redonner au lieu son rôle traditionnel de rassemblement de la communauté des croyants.

Not readily identifiable as a mosque
from the exterior, the structure adopts
the configuration of gateways that
lead into gardens such as those seen
on the left.

Der von außen nicht sofort als
Moschee erkennbare Bau wurde als
Abfolge verschiedener Torgänge
geplant, die unter anderem zu Gärten
wie links im Bild führen.

De prime abord, le bâtiment n'évoque
pas une mosquée. Il intègre une série
de portails qui mènent vers des
jardins, tels ceux visibles à gauche.

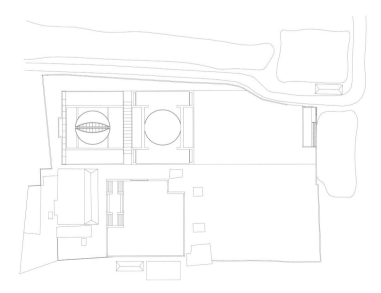

Although mosque architecture is codi-
fied to some extent, there is a great
deal of leeway which the architect
has made use of to create a modern,
inspiring space.

Trotz typologischer Vorgaben für den
Bau von Moscheen versteht es der
Architekt, vorhandene Freiräume zu
nutzen und einen modernen, inspirie-
renden Raum zu schaffen.

Si l'architecture des mosquées est
codifiée dans une certaine mesure, il
reste une grand liberté d'interpréta-
tion, dont l'architecte a profité pour
créer un espace moderne et inspiré.

The dome, seen in the elevations below and in the photos on this double page, brings natural light into the mosque.

Die auf den Aufrissen unten und den Aufnahmen dieser Doppelseite erkennbare Kuppel lässt Tageslicht in die Moschee.

La coupole tranchée en deux parties (coupes ci-dessous et photos de cette double-page) laisse pénétrer la lumière naturelle dans l'intérieur de la mosquée.

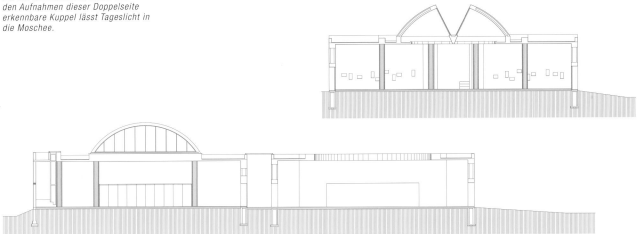

VARIOUS ARCHITECTS

Tatiana Bilbao S.C.
Paseo de la Reforma 382–301, Colonia Juárez
Delegación Cuauhtémoc, México DF 06600, Mexico
Tel/Fax: +52 55 8589 8822
E-mail: info@tatianabilbao.com / Web: www.tatianabilbao.com

Dellekamp Arquitectos
Celaya 26 Loc.2
Col. Hipodromo, México DF 06100, Mexico
Tel: +52 55 5264 1557
E-mail: press@dellekamparq.com / Web: www.dellekamparq.com

Curated by **TATIANA BILBAO** and **DEREK DELLEKAMP**, Ruta del Peregrino (Route of the pilgrim, published here) is a 117-kilometer pilgrimage route where the architects Tatiana Bilbao (Mexico), Christ & Gantenbein AG Architekten (Switzerland), Dellekamp Arquitectos (Mexico), Elemental (Chile), Godoylab (Mexico), Fake Design (China), HHF architects (Switzerland), Periférica (Mexico), and Taller TOA (Mexico) have each participated in the design and construction of stopping points or small buildings on the route. The project is unusual in that it involves architects from Mexico, China, and Switzerland, and also in that, despite its relative abstraction, it serves large numbers of pilgrims.

Die von **TATIANA BILBAO** und **DEREK DELLEKAMP** kuratierte Ruta del Peregrino (hier vorgestellt) ist ein 117 km langer Pilgerweg. Entlang der Route entwarfen und realisierten die Architekten Tatiana Bilbao (Mexiko), Christ & Gantenbein AG Architekten (Schweiz), Dellekamp Arquitectos (Mexiko), Elemental (Chile), Godoylab (Mexiko), Fake Design (China), HHF architects (Schweiz), Periférica (Mexiko) und Taller TOA (Mexiko) Pilgerstationen bzw. kleinere Bauten. Das Projekt ist insofern ungewöhnlich, als Architekten aus Mexiko, China und der Schweiz beteiligt waren und es trotz seines vergleichsweise abstrakten Charakters von vielen Pilgern genutzt wird.

Sous la direction de **TATIANA BILBAO** et de **DEREK DELLEKAMP**, la route du Pèlerin (Ruta del Peregrino, publiée ici) est un chemin de pèlerinage de 117 kilomètres de long ponctué de points d'arrêts ou de petites constructions signées de divers architectes : Tatiana Bilbao (Mexique), Christ & Gantenbein AG Architekten (Suisse), Dellekamp Arquitectos (Mexique), Elemental (Chili), Godoylab (Mexique), Fake Design (Chine), HHF architects (Suisse), Periférica (Mexique) et Taller TOA (Mexique). Ce projet, qui innove par l'implication d'architectes de pays aussi variés que le Mexique, la Chine et la Suisse, est utilisé par un grand nombre de pèlerins malgré son caractère relativement abstrait.

RUTA DEL PEREGRINO (ROUTE OF THE PILGRIM)

from Ameca to Talpa de Allende, Jalisco, Mexico, 2009–11

Address: from Ameca to Talpa de Allende, Jalisco, Mexico
Area: 117 kilometers (length of Ruta). Client: Secretaría de Turismo de Jalisco
Cost: not disclosed

Each year, approximately two million people come from different areas of Mexico to walk through the mountain range of Jalisco, starting in Ameca, and ascending to el Cerro del Obispo at an altitude of 2000 meters, crossing the peak of Espinazo del Diablo to descend to their final destination in the town of Talpa de Allende to pay homage to the Virgin of Talpa as an act of devotion, faith, and gratitude. This ceremonial procession has taken place since the 17th century as a form of penitence. The architects state: "This project aims to provide the historical route with better conditions for the pilgrims as well as to maximize the social and economical profit for this area by taking advantage of this massive event." The master plan is a kind of "ecological corridor" with infrastructure and some iconic architecture—each piece by a different team. The works concerned are Gratitude Open Chapel (Lagunillas) by Dellekamp Arquitectos and Tatiana Bilbao, 2009; Sanctuary (Estanzuela) by Ai Weiwei (Fake Design), 2009; Shelters (Estanzuela and Atenguillo) by Luis Aldrete, 2009; Lookout Point (Espinazo del Diablo) by HHF architects, 2010; Lookout Point (Las Cruces) by Elemental, 2009; Void Temple (Cocina) by Dellekamp Arquitectos and Periférica, 2009; Mesa Colorada Sanctuary (Mixtlán) by Tatiana Bilbao, 2010; and Viewpoint (Cerro del Obispo) by Christ & Gantenbein, 2010.

Jahr für Jahr kommen rund zwei Millionen Menschen aus den verschiedensten Gegenden Mexikos, um durch die Berge in der Region Jalisco zu wandern, von Ameca bis hinauf nach el Cerro del Obispo auf einer Höhe von 2000 m, weiter über den Gipfel des Espinazo del Diablo bis hinab zum Ziel der Weges, dem Städtchen Talpa de Allende, um der Jungfrau von Talpa die Ehre zu erweisen, ein Akt der Verehrung, des Glaubens und der Dankbarkeit. Diese religiösen Wanderungen finden bereits seit dem 17. Jahrhundert als Form der Buße statt. Die Architekten erklären: „Bei diesem Projekt ging es darum, den Pilgern auf diesem historischen Weg bessere Bedingungen zu schaffen und zugleich den sozialen und ökonomischen Nutzen für die Region zu steigern, indem man das gewaltige Ereignis aufgreift." Als Masterplan für das Projekt diente eine Art „ökologischer Korridor" mit Infrastruktur und verschiedenen architektonischen Landmarken – jede Intervention wurde von einem anderen Team realisiert. Die einzelnen Arbeiten sind: Gratitude Open Chapel (Lagunillas), Dellekamp Arquitectos, Tatiana Bilbao, 2009; Andachtsort (Estanzuela), Ai Weiwei (Fake Design), 2009; Schutzräume (Estanzuela und Atenguillo), Luis Aldrete, 2009; Aussichtspunkt (Espinazo del Diablo), HHF architects, 2010; Aussichtspunkt (Las Cruces), Elemental, 2009; Void Temple (Cocina), Dellekamp Arquitectos, Periférica, 2009; Andachtsort Mesa Colorada (Mixtlán), Tatiana Bilbao, 2010; Aussichtspunkt (Cerro del Obispo), Christ & Gantenbein, 2010.

Chaque année, deux millions de personnes environ, venues de tout le Mexique, traversent à pied la chaîne de montagnes de Jalisco à partir d'Ameca, montent au Cerro del Obispo (2000 mètres d'altitude) et franchissent le pic d'Espinazo del Diablo avant de redescendre vers leur destination finale, Talpa de Allende, pour rendre hommage à la Vierge de Talpa et manifester leur foi et leur gratitude. Ce pèlerinage, qui est aussi une épreuve de pénitence, se déroule ainsi depuis le XVIIe siècle. « Ce projet vise à offrir aux pèlerins de meilleures conditions de déplacement le long de ce chemin historique, mais aussi d'optimiser le profit social et économique que peut tirer la région de cette manifestation de masse », expliquent les architectes. Le plan directeur est une sorte de « corridor écologique » ponctué d'infrastructures et de réalisations emblématiques, chacune signée par une équipe différente. Les œuvres réalisées sont : La chapelle ouverte de la Gratitude (Lagunillas) par Dellekamp Arquitectos, Tatiana Bilbao, 2009 ; le sanctuaire (Estanzuela) par Ai Weiwei (Fake Design), 2009 ; les abris (Estanzuela et Atenguillo) par Luis Aldrete, 2009 ; un observatoire (Espinazo del Diablo) par HHF architects, 2010 ; un observatoire (Las Cruces) par Elemental, 2009 ; le Temple vide (Cocina) par Dellekamp Arquitectos, Periférica, 2009 ; le sanctuaire de la Mesa Colorada (Mixtlán) par Tatiana Bilbao, 2010 ; le point de vue (Cerro del Obispo) par Christ & Gantenbein, 2010.

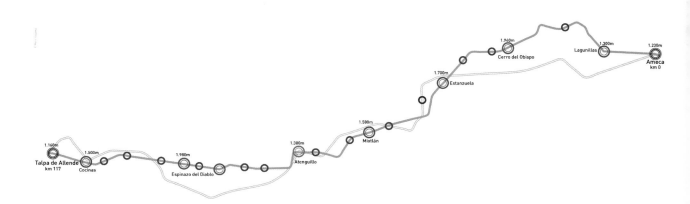

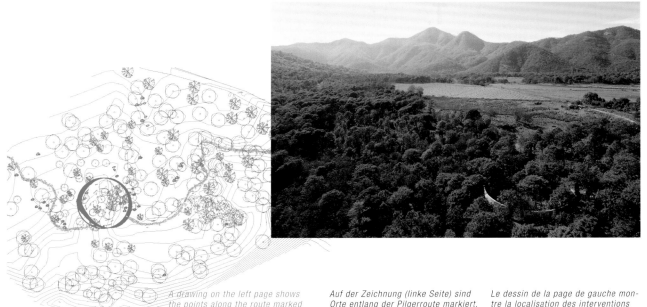

A drawing on the left page shows the points along the route marked by architectural interventions. Below, the Void Temple by Dellekamp Arquitectos and Periférica (2009).

Auf der Zeichnung (linke Seite) sind Orte entlang der Pilgerroute markiert, an denen architektonische Interventionen zu finden sind. Unten der Void Temple von Dellekamp Arquitectos und Periférica (2009).

Le dessin de la page de gauche montre la localisation des interventions architecturales le long de la route du pèlerinage. Ci-dessous le Temple vide de Dellekamp Arquitectos et Periférica (2009).

Above, the Las Cruces Lookout Point (Elemental, 2009) located at one of the highest points of the route.

Oben der Aussichtspunkt Las Cruces (Elemental, 2009) an einem der höchst gelegenen Punkte des Wegs.

Ci-dessus, l'observatoire de Las Cruces (Elemental, 2009) situé sur l'un des points les plus élevés du parcours.

Above and in the broader view on the left page, the Espinazo del Diablo Lookout Point designed by the Swiss architects HHF (2010).

Oben und auf einer größeren Ansicht links der Aussichtspunkt Espinazo del Diablo des Schweizer Büros HHF architekten (2010).

Ci-dessus et page de gauche en bas : l'observatoire de l'Espinazo del Diablo conçu par l'agence suisse HHF (2010).

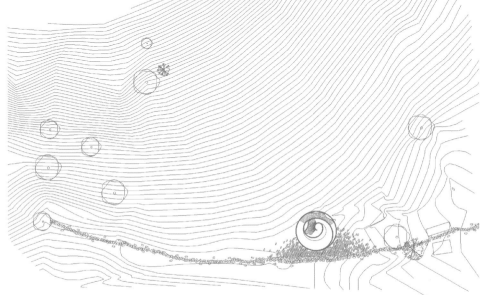

The Estanzuela Shelter by Luis Aldrete (2009) is made with adobe clay bricks stacked in two different ways. It is intended as a "base module" that can be used elsewhere to structure the route.

Luis Aldrete baute seinen Estanzuela Shelter (2009) aus Lehmziegeln, die in zwei Laufrichtungen gemauert wurden. Das Konzept ist als „Basismodul" gedacht, das auch an anderen Stationen des Wanderwegs realisiert werden kann.

L'abri d'Estanzuela par Luis Aldrete (2009) est en briques d'adobe empilées en deux sens différents. C'est un « module de base » qui pourrait être repris ailleurs tout le long du parcours.

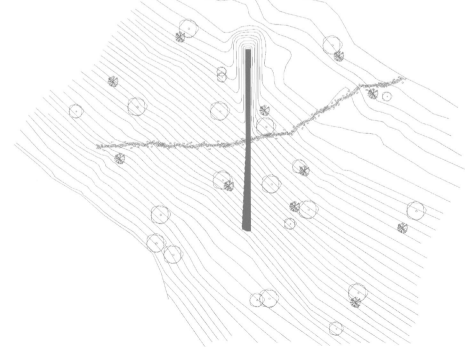

On this page, and also in the broader view on the left page, the Estanzuela Sanctuary by Ai Weiwei (Fake Design, 2009). A straight line is "both submerged in the landscape and elevated above it."

Auf dieser Seite und auf einer größeren Ansicht (links) das Estanzuela Sanctuary von Ai Weiwei (Fake Design, 2009). Die gerade Linie ist „in die Landschaft eingelassen und wächst zugleich über sie hinaus".

Ci-dessus et page de gauche, en bas : le sanctuaire d'Estanzuela par Ai Weiwei (Fake Design, 2009), ligne droite qui est « à la fois submergée par le paysage et s'élève au-dessus de lui ».

VO TRONG NGHIA

Vo Trong Nghia Co., Ltd.
85 bis Phan Ke Binh, Dakao, Dist.1
Ho Chi Minh City
Vietnam

Tel: +84 8 3829 7763
Fax: +84 8 3911 0103
E-mail: info@votrongnghia.com
Web: www.votrongnghia.com

VO TRONG NGHIA was born in Quang Binh Province, Vietnam, in 1976. He attended Ha Noi Architecture University (1994) and received a B.Arch degree from the Nagoya Institute of Technology (Japan, 2002), followed by a Master of Civil Engineering from Tokyo University (2004). His major works are the Ho Chi Minh City University of Architecture (HUA, with Kazuhiro Kojima and Daisuke Sanuki, Ho Chi Minh City, Mekong Delta, 2006), won by an international design competition in 2006; the wNw Café (Binh Duong, 2006); wNw Bar (Binh Duong, 2008, published here); Trung Nguyen Coffee Culture Center (Hanoi, 2008); the Vietnam Pavilion for the Shanghai Expo (Shanghai, China, 2010); Stacking Green (Ho Chi Minh City, 2011); and Stone Villa (Quangninh, 2011), all in Vietnam unless stated otherwise.

VO TRONG NGHIA wurde 1976 in der Quang Binh Provinz, Vietnam, geboren. Er studierte an der Architekturhochschule Ha Noi (1994) und absolvierte einen B.Arch am Nagoya Institut für Technik (Japan, 2002) sowie einen Master in Bauingenieurwesen an der Universität Tokio (2004). Seine wichtigsten Projekte sind die Architekturhochschule Ho Chi Minh City (HUA, mit Kazuhiro Kojima und Daisuke Sanuki, Ho Chi Minh City, Mekongdelta, 2006), nachdem das Team 2006 einen internationalen Wettbewerb gewonnen hatte, das wNw Café (Binh Duong, 2006), die wNw Bar (Binh Duong, 2008, hier vorgestellt), das Trung Nguyen Coffee Culture Center (Hanoi, 2008), der vietnamesische Pavillon für die Expo in Shanghai (Shanghai, China, 2010), Stacking Green (Ho Chi Minh City, 2011) sowie die Stone Villa (Quangninh, 2011), alle in Vietnam, sofern nicht anders angegeben.

VO TRONG NGHIA, né dans la province de Quang Binh (Vietnam) en 1976, a étudié à l'Université d'architecture d'Hanoï (1994). Il a obtenu son B. Arch. à l'Institut de technologie de Nagoya (Japon, 2002) et un mastère en ingénierie civile à l'université de Tokyo (2004). Ses réalisations les plus importantes, essentiellement au Vietnam, sont l'Université d'architecture d'Hô Chi Minh-Ville (HUA, avec Kazuhiro Kojima et Daisuke Sanuki, Hô Chi Minh-Ville, delta du Mékong, 2006), projet remporté lors d'un concours international en 2006 ; le café wNw (Binh Duong, 2006) ; le bar wNw (Binh Duong, 2008, publié ici) ; le Centre de la culture du café Trung Nguyen (Hanoï, 2008) ; le pavillon du Vietnam pour Shanghaï Expo (Shanghaï, 2010) ; la maison Stacking Green (Hô Chi Minh-Ville, 2011) et la Villa de pierre (Quangninh, 2011).

WNW BAR

Binh Duong, Vietnam, 2008

Address: 6/28T, Zone 3, Phu Tho district, Thu Dau Mot Town, Binh Duong, Vietnam, +84 65 0381 3085
Area: 270 m². Client: Wind and Water Joint Stock Company. Cost: not disclosed

The **WNW BAR** is located in an artificial lake next to the wNw Café, which is an open café made of bamboo. By way of contrast, the bar was designed as an enclosed space which can be used for different purposes such as concerts, shows, or ceremonies. A structural bamboo arch system was designed for the 10-meter-high, 15-meter-wide dome. The main frame is made up of 48 prefabricated units, each of them consisting of several bamboo elements bound together. The building uses wind energy and cool water from the lake to create natural ventilation. On the top of the roof there is a 1.5-meter hole for the evacuation of hot air from the interior. The architect states: "The two wNw buildings originated from nature. They now merge in harmony with nature. With time they will return to nature."

Die **WNW BAR** liegt in einem künstlichen See neben dem wNw Café, einem offenen Café aus Bambus. Im Gegensatz hierzu wurde die Bar als geschlossener Raum konzipiert. Er lässt sich für verschiedene Zwecke nutzen, etwa für Konzerte, Aufführungen oder Feiern. Für die 10 m hohe Kuppel mit einem Durchmesser von 15 m entwarf der Architekt eine Bogenkonstruktion aus Bambus. Das Haupttragwerk besteht aus 48 vorgefertigten Elementen, die wiederum aus mehreren zusammengebundenen Bambuselementen bestehen. Mithilfe von Windenergie und Kühlwasser aus dem See wird der Bau natürlich belüftet. In der Mitte des Dachs dient eine 1,5 m große Öffnung als Auslass für Warmluft aus dem Innern der Bar. Der Architekt führt aus: „Die beiden wNw-Bauten entwickelten sich aus der Natur. Inzwischen verschmelzen sie harmonisch mit ihr. Mit der Zeit werden sie wieder zu Natur werden."

Le **BAR WNW** se trouve sur un lac artificiel près du wNw Café, petit établissement de plan ouvert en bambou. Par contraste, le bar forme un espace clos également utilisé pour des concerts, des spectacles ou des cérémonies. La coupole de 10 mètres de haut et 15 mètres de diamètre repose sur un système structurel d'arcs en bambou. L'ossature principale se compose de 48 éléments préfabriqués, chacun composé de plusieurs tiges de bambou liées ensemble. Le petit bâtiment bénéficie d'une ventilation naturelle grâce à la fraîcheur de l'eau du lac et aux vents. Au sommet de la coupole, un oculus de 1,50 mètre de diamètre permet l'évacuation de l'air chaud intérieur. « Le café et le bar wNw sont issus de la nature. Ils fusionnent avec elle, en harmonie. Avec le temps, ils retourneront à la nature », conclut l'architecte.

The thatched volume of the bar appears to sit directly on the water. Though it does evoke more "primitive" types of shelter, the building is in fact quite sophisticated in its design.

Der reetgedeckte Rundbau der Bar scheint unmittelbar auf dem Wasser aufzuliegen. Obwohl die Konstruktion an „primitive" Hütten erinnern mag, ist sie bautechnisch vergleichsweise anspruchsvoll.

Le pavillon du bar recouvert de chaume semble posé directement sur l'eau. Bien qu'il évoque des types d'abris plus « primitifs », le projet relève en fait d'une conception sophistiquée.

The complex bamboo structure was made with prefabricated elements whose assembly phase, seen here, created an elegant and stable overall design.

Die komplexe Bambuskonstruktion besteht aus vorgefertigten Elementen, deren Aufbau hier zu sehen ist. Mit ihrer Hilfe konnte der elegante und stabile Entwurf realisiert werden.

La structure complexe en bambou a été réalisée à partir d'éléments préfabriqués dont l'assemblage a permis de créer une forme élégante et stable.

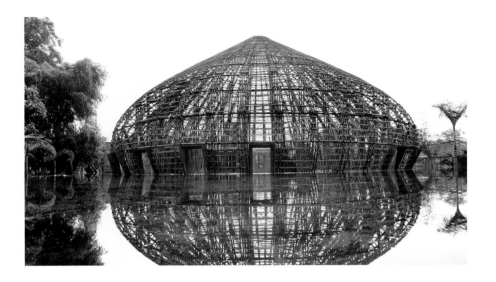

The architect states: "The building gives a luxurious feeling but at the same time remains gentle in its atmosphere. The bar is now also used for town meetings and other social activities."

Der Architekt erklärt: „Die Atmosphäre des Baus ist luxuriös und dennoch nicht aufdringlich. Die Bar wird inzwischen auch für Gemeindetreffen und andere Veranstaltungen genutzt."

« Le bâtiment donne une impression de luxe, tout en conservant une atmosphère agréable. Le bar est aussi utilisé pour des réunions municipales et diverses activités sociales », explique Vo Trong Nghia.

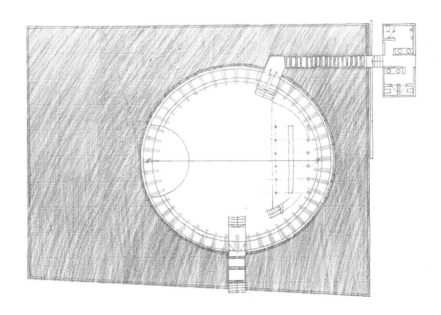

ISAY WEINFELD

Isay Weinfeld
Rua Wisard 305, 7° andar
05434–080 São Paulo, SP
Brazil

Tel: +55 11 3079 7581
Fax: +55 11 3079 5656
E-mail: contato@isayweinfeld.com
Web: www.isayweinfeld.com

ISAY WEINFELD was born in 1952 in São Paulo, Brazil. He graduated from the School of Architecture at Mackenzie University in São Paulo in 1975. In an unusual mixture of careers, Weinfeld has also worked in cinema since 1974, making 14 short films that have received numerous international awards. In 1988, he wrote and directed his first full-length movie, Fogo e Paixão, considered to be one of the ten best comedies produced that year worldwide. In 1989, the São Paulo Art Critics' Association awarded him the Prize for Best New Director. Weinfeld has completed dozens of private homes, commercial projects, banks, advertising agencies, discotheques, a bar, a restaurant, an art gallery, and the Hotel Fasano (São Paulo, 2001–03). He has worked with Marcio Kogan on numerous projects, including the 2001 exhibit "Arquitetura e Humor" at the Casa Brasileira Museum. Recent work includes Livraria da Vila (São Paulo, 2006–07); the Sumaré House (São Paulo, 2007); Kesley Caliguere Antique Shop (São Paulo, 2007); Havaianas (São Paulo, 2008–09); Grecia House (São Paulo, 2008–09, published here); the Midrash Building, for the Jewish Congregation of Brazil (Rio de Janeiro, 2009); Fasano Las Piedras Hotel (Punta del Este, Uruguay, 2008–11); and the 360° Building (São Paulo, under construction), all in Brazil unless stated otherwise.

ISAY WEINFELD wurde 1952 in São Paulo, Brasilien, geboren. 1975 schloss er sein Architekturstudium an der Mackenzie Universität in São Paulo ab. Weinfeld verbindet zwei Laufbahnen auf ungewöhnliche Weise: Seit 1974 ist er auch Filmemacher – seine 14 Kurzfilme wurden mit zahlreichen internationalen Preisen ausgezeichnet. 1988 schrieb er das Drehbuch für seinen ersten Spielfilm, Fogo e Paixão, bei dem er auch Regie führte und der als eine der zehn besten Komödien gilt, die in diesem Jahr produziert wurden. 1989 zeichnet ihn der Kunstkritikerverband São Paulo als „Besten neuen Regisseur" aus. Weinfeld realisierte Dutzende von privaten Wohnbauten, gewerbliche Projekte, Banken, Werbeagenturen, Diskotheken, eine Bar, ein Restaurant, eine Galerie sowie das Hotel Fasano (São Paulo, 2001–03). Bei zahlreichen Projekten kooperierte er mit Marcio Kogan, etwa für die Ausstellung Arquitetura e Humor am Casa Brasileira Museum (2001). Jüngere Arbeiten sind u.a. die Livraria da Vila (São Paulo, 2006–07), das Haus Sumaré (São Paulo, 2007), der Antiquitätenladen Kesley Caliguere (São Paulo, 2007), Havaianas (São Paulo, 2008–09), das Haus Grecia (São Paulo, 2008–09, hier vorgestellt), das Midrasch-Gebäude für die jüdische Gemeinde in Brasilien (Rio de Janeiro, 2009), Hotel Las Piedras Fasano (Punta del Este, Uruguay, 2008–11) und das 360° Building (São Paulo, im Bau), alle in Brasilien, sofern nicht anders angegeben.

ISAY WEINFELD, né en 1952 à São Paulo (Brésil), est diplômé de l'école d'architecture de l'université Mackenzie à São Paulo (1975). Sa carrière étonnamment variée l'a conduit à s'intéresser au cinéma. Depuis 1974, il a réalisé 14 courts métrages qui ont reçu de nombreux prix internationaux. En 1988, il a écrit et dirigé son premier long métrage Fogo e Paixão, considéré comme l'une des dix meilleures comédies produites dans le monde cette année-là. En 1989, l'Association des critiques d'art de São Paulo lui a remis son prix du meilleur nouveau metteur en scène. Weinfeld a réalisé des dizaines de résidences privées, de projets commerciaux, de banques, d'agences de publicité, de discothèques, un bar, un restaurant, une galerie d'art et l'hôtel Fasano (São Paulo, 2001–03). Il a collaboré avec Marcio Kogan sur de nombreux projets dont une pièce critique « Arquitetura e Humor » pour le Musée de la maison brésilienne (2001). Parmi ses réalisations récentes, la plupart au Brésil : la librairie da Vila (São Paulo, 2006–07) ; la maison Sumaré (São Paulo, 2007) ; le magasin d'antiquités Kesley Caliguere (São Paulo, 2007) ; le magasin Havaianas (São Paulo, 2008–09) ; la maison Grecia (São Paulo, 2008–09, publiée ici); l'immeuble Midrash pour la congrégation juive du Brésil (Rio de Janeiro, 2009) ; l'hôtel Fasano Las Piedras (Punta del Este, Uruguay, 2008–11) et le 360° Building (São Paulo, en construction).

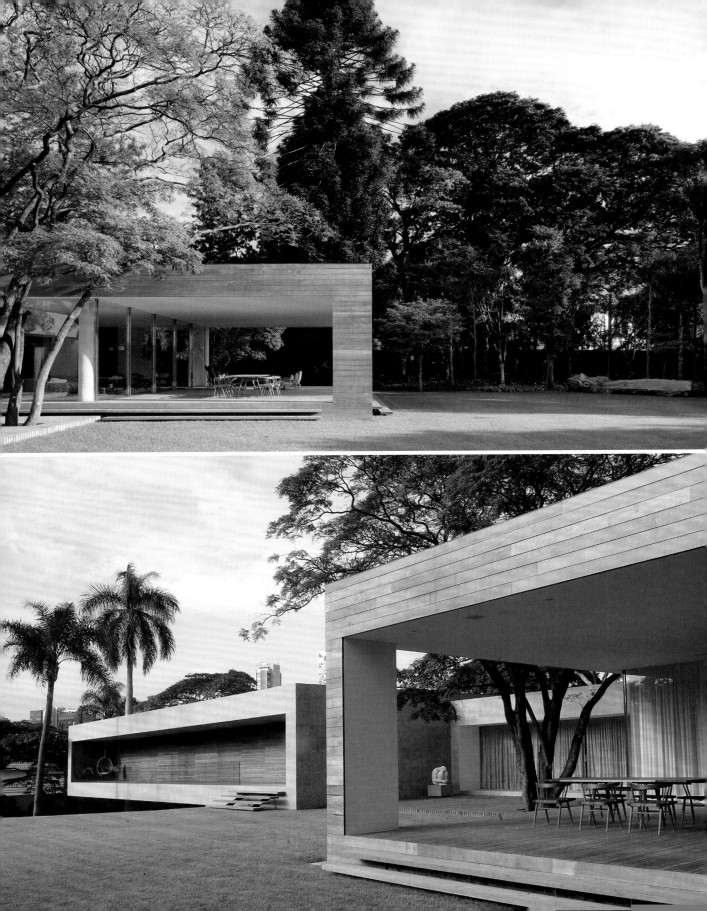

GRECIA HOUSE

São Paulo, Brazil, 2008–09

Area: 1920 m². Client: not disclosed
Cost: not disclosed

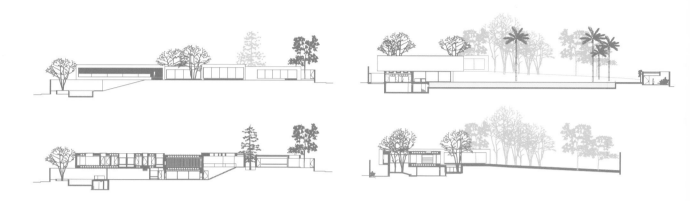

The most evident element in the design of the Grecia House is its powerful horizontality, underlined by a geometric composition made of concrete and wood.

Auffälligstes Merkmal des Grecia House ist seine beeindruckende Horizontalität. Die geometrische Komposition des Wohnbaus aus Beton und Holz betont die horizontalen Linien zusätzlich.

La caractéristique la plus évidente de la maison Grecia est sa puissante horizontalité soulignée par une rigoureuse composition en bois et béton.

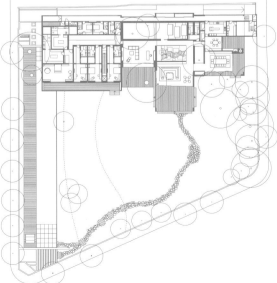

A long, narrow pool is placed perpendicular to the volumes of the house in a garden that is certainly generous by São Paulo standards.

Ein langer schmaler Pool verläuft lotrecht zum Baukörper des Hauses und liegt in einem Garten, der für São Paulo zweifellos großzügig ist.

Le long couloir de natation perpendiculaire à la maison se développe vers un jardin de proportions généreuses selon les standards de São Paulo.

GRECIA HOUSE is located on a 4830-square-meter corner plot in a residential area of São Paulo. The client asked for such facilities as a cinema room, a recreation area for the children, a sauna, a large gym, and a long swimming lane. Set back in a garden in a location determined by large existing trees that were preserved, the house is made up of four joined but distinct blocks, respectively covered with pebble-blasted concrete (living quarters), exposed concrete (office), wood planks (entertainment area), and sand-blasted concrete plaques (dining and service areas). The main floor houses the main living areas, with the gym and recreation areas below. Small patios and gardens were created around the old trees, allowing light and air to flow past them into the house.

Das **HAUS GRECIA** liegt inmitten eines 4830 m² großen Eckgrundstücks in einem Wohngebiet von São Paulo. Der Bauherr gab unter anderem ein Heimkino, einen Freizeitbereich für die Kinder, eine Sauna, ein großes Fitnessstudio und ein Langschwimmbecken in Auftrag. Das Haus liegt zurückgesetzt in einem Garten, dessen alter Baumbestand erhalten wurde. Der Bau besteht aus vier separaten Blöcken mit jeweils unterschiedlicher Verblendung: Beton mit grobem Kieseleinschluss (Wohnbereich), Sichtbeton (Büro), Holzbeplankung (Unterhaltungsbereiche) und sandgestrahlte Betonplatten (Ess- und Versorgungsbereiche). Im Hauptgeschoss befinden sich die Hauptwohnbereiche, das Fitnessstudio und Freizeitbereiche liegen im Untergeschoss. Im Außenbereich wurden kleinere Terrassen und Gärten um die alten Bäume herum angelegt, durch die Licht und Luft ins Haus gelangen.

La **MAISON GRECIA** a été construite sur une parcelle d'angle de 4830 mètres carrés dans un quartier résidentiel de São Paulo. Le client souhaitait disposer d'une salle de cinéma, d'un espace de jeux pour les enfants, d'un sauna, d'une grande salle de sport et d'un long couloir de natation. Implantée en retrait dans un jardin dont les grands arbres ont été préservés, la résidence se compose de quatre blocs distincts, mais reliés, dont les façades sont respectivement en béton sablé au gravier (séjour), béton brut (bureau), lattes de bois (loisirs) et dalles de béton sablé (salle à manger et commodités). Le niveau principal est réservé aux pièces de séjour, au-dessus de la salle de sport et de l'espace de jeux. Des petits patios et des jardins ont été créés autour des arbres conservés, en faisant en sorte que la lumière et la brise puissent pénétrer dans la maison.

Living spaces naturally echo the overall horizontality of the house, but volumes open into each other, creating a feeling of unity in the design.

Die Wohnbereiche greifen die horizontalen Linien des Hauses auf. Doch gehen die einzelnen Räume ineinander über, wodurch ein fließender harmonischer Gesamteindruck entsteht.

Les espaces de séjour font naturellement écho à l'horizontalité du plan de la maison, mais les volumes restent interconnectés, créant un sentiment d'unité.

The dining room space is shown here entirely open to the garden, a device frequently seen in this warm equatorial climate.

Der Essbereich ist gänzlich offen zum Garten, ein häufig anzutreffendes Element in heißen Klimazonen um den Äquator.

Ici, la salle à manger est montrée entièrement ouverte sur le jardin, possibilité fréquente sous ce climat équatorial chaud.

The architect reverses the usual relationship of interior and exterior by creating the winter garden seen on the left.

Mit dem Wintergarten links stellt der Architekt das Verhältnis von Innen und Außen auf den Kopf.

L'architecte a inversé la relation habituelle entre l'intérieur et l'extérieur en créant un jardin d'hiver (à gauche).

Cloud 360° (Floating Observatory)

CHANGKI YUN

KyungAm Architects Associates Ltd.
5F Myungjin Bldg.
234–27 Nonhyon-dong
Gangnam-gu
Seoul 135–830
South Korea

Tel: +82 10 8889 3130
Fax: +82 2 508 6313
E-mail: ckyun@kaanp.com
Web: www.kaanp.com

CHANGKI YUN was born in 1970 in Seoul (South Korea) and graduated from the Architectural Association (London) and Konkuk University Seoul. He worked at Aum & Lee Architects (1996–2001), and was a partner of Dowoo Architects Associates (2002–05) and principal of ZAACK (2006–08). He founded KyungAm Architects Associates Ltd. in Seoul (2008). His recent work includes Cloud 360° (Floating Observatory), Daewon Park (Songnam, Seoul, 2008, published here); the Floating Stage (Yeouido, Seoul, 2009); Han River International Cruise Terminal and Floating Hotel (2009 Yeouido, Seoul, 2009); Wave Soul Marina Club (Dduksum Park, Seoul, 2009); Mirage Residential and Resort Hotel (Abu Dhabi UAE, 2009); Landmark Tower (Mongolia, 2009); Ogdon Condominium (Los Angeles, USA, 2010); and Seoul City Tour Ship (Seoul, 2010), all in South Korea unless stated otherwise.

CHANGKI YUN wurde 1970 in Seoul (Südkorea) geboren und schloss sein Studium an der Architectural Association (London) und Konkuk Universität in Seoul ab. Er arbeitete bei Aum & Lee Architects (1996–2001), war Partner bei Dowoo Architects Associates (2002–05) und Direktor bei ZAACK (2006–08). 2008 gründete er KyungAm Architects Associates Ltd. in Seoul. Zu seinen jüngeren Projekten zählen Cloud 360° (Schwebender Aussichtsturm) im Daewon Park (Songnam, Seoul, 2008, hier vorgestellt), Floating Stage (Yeouido, Seoul, 2009), ein Schiffsterminal und schwimmendes Hotel am Hangang (2009 Yeouido, Seoul, 2009), der Yachtclub Wave Soul (Dduksum Park, Seoul, 2009), die Mirage Apartment- und Hotelanlage (Abu Dhabi VAE, 2009), der Landmark Tower (Mongolei, 2009), Ogdon Eigentumswohnungen (Los Angeles, USA, 2010) sowie ein Schiff für Flussrundfahrten in Seoul (Seoul, 2010), alle in Südkorea, sofern nicht anders angegeben.

CHANGKI YUN, né en 1970 à Seoul (Corée du Sud), est diplômé de l'Architectural Association (Londres) et de l'université Konkuk à Séoul. Il a travaillé chez Aum & Lee Architects (1996–2001), a été partenaire chez Dowoo Architects Associates (2002–05) et a dirigé l'agence ZAACK (2006–08). Il a fondé KyungAm Architects Associates Ltd. à Séoul en 2008. Parmi ses réalisations récentes : Cloud 360° (Observatoire flottant), Daewon Park (Songnam, Séoul, 2008, publié ici) ; la Scène flottante (Yeouido, Séoul, 2009) ; le terminal international de croisières et hôtel flottant de la rivière Han (2009 Yeouido, Séoul, 2009) ; le Wave Soul Marina Club (Dduksum Park, Séoul, 2009) ; l'hôtel résidentiel et de vacances Mirage (Abou Dhabi, EAU, 2009) ; la tour Landmark (Mongolie, 2009) ; le condominium Ogdon (Los Angeles, 2010) et la tour Ship (Séoul, 2010).

CLOUD 360°
(FLOATING OBSERVATORY)

Daewon Park, Songnam, Seoul, South Korea, 2008

Area: 939 m². Client: Songnam City. Cost: $7 million
Collaboration: Seungjoong Yang, Taehyung Lim

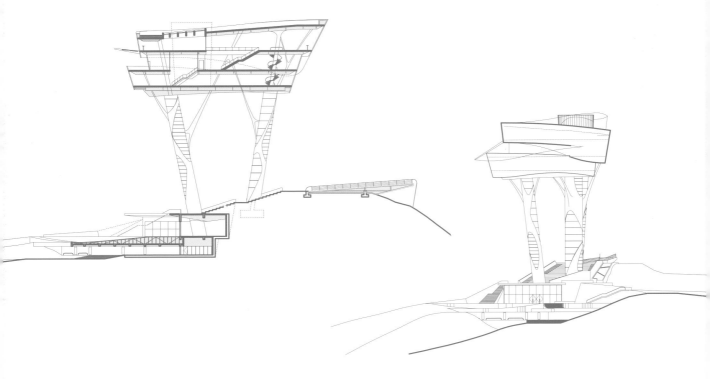

The drawings above show that the Floating Observatory is very much a carefully thought-out architectural idea, despite its unusual form.

Die Zeichnungen oben belegen, dass der schwebende Aussichtsturm trotz seiner ungewöhnlichen Form tatsächlich eine sorgsam ausgearbeitete architektonische Idee ist.

Les plans ci-dessus montrent la réflexion concrète et approfondie qui a présidé à ce curieux projet d'Observatoire flottant.

"The dream of flight is blissful," says the architect, evoking this unbuilt project. This observatory and restaurant is reached via two main elevators, intended to "transport visitors to the sky." The restaurant, cafe, and media facilities are located in upper levels of the cloud observatory. Modestly, the architect concludes: "This new observatory is sure to become the new landmark of any district." This is an interesting association between a kind of architectural fantasy and the idea of flight or transport to the sky, which surely has something to do with the traditions of science fiction or cartoon design.

„Der Traum vom Fliegen ist pures Glück", so der Architekt im Hinblick auf sein nicht realisiertes Projekt. Erschlossen wird der Aussichtsturm mit Restaurant über zwei zentrale Aufzüge, die die Besucher „in den Himmel tragen" sollen. Restaurant, Café und mediale Einrichtungen sind auf den oberen Ebenen des Cloud Observatory (Wolken-Aussichtsturm) untergebracht. Bescheiden merkt der Architekt an: „Dieser neue Aussichtsturm wird zweifellos zum neuen Wahrzeichen, in welchem Viertel er auch stehen mag." Diese interessante Verknüpfung einer architektonischen Utopie mit der Vorstellung vom Fliegen oder der Reise in den Himmel hat ohne Frage etwas mit Genres wie Sciencefiction oder Comics zu tun.

« Rêver de voler est un bonheur extrême », commente l'architecte en évoquant ce projet non réalisé. Ce restaurant-observatoire est accessible par deux ascenseurs principaux censés « transporter les visiteurs dans le ciel ». Le restaurant, un café et des installations médias sont installés au sommet de cette tour dans les nuages. « Ce nouvel observatoire pourrait certainement devenir un point d'attraction dans n'importe quel lieu », fait remarquer l'architecte avec modestie. Il s'agit là d'une intéressante association entre une architecture d'esprit utopique et l'idée de vol ou de transport vers le ciel, qui n'est pas sans rapport avec l'imaginaire de la science-fiction ou de la bande dessinée.

In this computer-generated perspective drawing the observatory might seem to have come directly out of a science-fiction movie, and yet both materials and engineering have been studied in the context of real construction.

Auf dieser computergenerierten Ansicht könnte der Aussichtsturm unmittelbar einem Sciencefiction-Film entsprungen sein. Dennoch wurden Baumaterialien und Statik im Hinblick auf eine tatsächliche Realisierung geplant.

Dans cette image de synthèse, l'observatoire semble tout droit sorti d'un film de science-fiction. Néanmoins, l'ingénierie et le choix des matériaux ont fait l'objet d'études très concrètes.

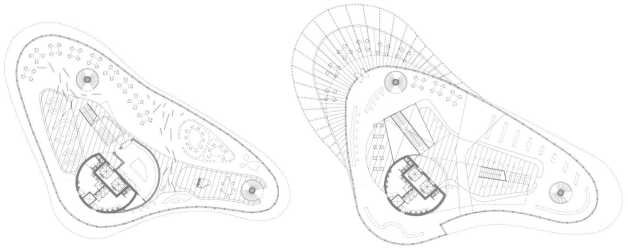

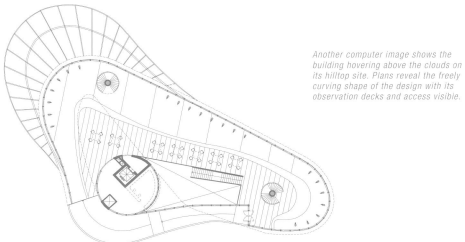

Another computer image shows the building hovering above the clouds on its hilltop site. Plans reveal the freely curving shape of the design with its observation decks and access visible.

Eine weitere Computersimulation zeigt den Bau auf einem Hügel über den Wolken schwebend. Auf Grundrissen ist die frei geschwungene Kontur des Entwurfs mit Aussichtsplattformen und Erschließungswegen zu sehen.

Autre image de synthèse montrant l'observatoire en suspension au sommet d'une colline au-dessus des nuages. Les plans montrent la forme libre du projet, ses plates-formes d'observation et ses accès.

PETER ZUMTHOR

Peter Zumthor
Atelier Zumthor
Süsswinkel 20
7023 Haldenstein
Switzerland

Tel: +41 81 353 28 06
Fax: +41 81 353 30 59

PETER ZUMTHOR was born in 1943 in Basel, Switzerland. In 1958, he worked as an apprentice carpenter. He graduated from the Schule für Gestaltung in Basel in 1963 and then attended the Pratt Institute in New York, studying architecture and design. From 1968 to 1977, he worked as an architect for the preservation of historic monuments in the Graubünden region of Switzerland. He served as tutor at the University of Zurich in 1978 and created his own firm in the town of Haldenstein, also in the Graubünden, in 1979. He has taught at SCI-Arc in Santa Monica, the Technical University of Munich, Tulane University in New Orleans, and at the Academy of Architecture in Mendrisio, beginning in 1996. Peter Zumthor won the 2009 Pritzker Prize. His major buildings include Protective Housing for Roman Archaeological Excavations (Chur, 1986); Sogn Benedetg Chapel (Sumvitg, 1988); Gugalun House (Versam, 1994); the Thermal Baths in Vals (1996); the Kunsthaus in Bregenz (Austria, 1997); and the Swiss Pavilion in Hannover (Germany, 2000), all in Switzerland unless stated otherwise. More recently he completed the Bruder Klaus Field Chapel (Wachendorf, Germany, 2007); Kolumba Art Museum (Cologne, Germany, 2007); the Steilneset Memorial to the Victims of the Witch Trials in the Finnmark region (Vardø, Norway, 2011); and the Serpentine Gallery Summer Pavilion (Kensington Gardens, London, UK, 2011, published here).

PETER ZUMTHOR wurde 1943 in Basel, Schweiz, geboren. Nach einer Lehre als Möbelschreiner (1958–62) studierte er Gestaltung und Architektur an der Schule für Gestaltung in Basel (1963–67) sowie am Pratt Institute in New York. Ab 1967 arbeitete er als baulicher und planerischer Berater für den Erhalt historischer Dörfer im Kanton Graubünden. 1979 gründete er sein eigenes Büro in Haldenstein, Graubünden. Er war Gastprofessor am SCI-Arc (1988), an der Technischen Universität München (1989) und dem Harvard GSD (1999) sowie Professor an der Akademie für Architektur in Mendrisio (Universität Lugano, 1996–2008). 2009 wurde Peter Zumthor mit dem Pritzker-Preis ausgezeichnet. Zu seinen wichtigsten Bauten zählen Schutzbauten über Ausgrabungen der Römerzeit (Chur, 1986), die Kapelle Sogn Benedegt (Sumvitg, 1988), das Haus Gugalun (Versam, 1994), das Thermalbad Vals (1996), das Kunsthaus Bregenz (Österreich, 1997) und der Schweizer Pavillon auf der Expo Hannover (Deutschland, 2000), alle in der Schweiz, sofern nicht anders angegeben. In jüngerer Zeit fertiggestellt wurden die Bruder-Klaus-Kapelle (Wachendorf, Deutschland, 2007), das Kunstmuseum Kolumba (Köln, Deutschland, 2007), das Steilneset-Mahnmal für die Opfer der Hexenprozesse in der Region Finnmark (Vardø, Norwegen, 2011) sowie der Sommerpavillon der Serpentine Gallery (Kensington Gardens, London, GB, 2011, hier vorgestellt).

PETER ZUMTHOR, né en 1943 à Bâle (Suisse), débute comme apprenti-menuisier en 1958 et sort diplômé de l'école de design de Bâle en 1963. Il étudie ensuite l'architecture et le design au Pratt Institute à New York. De 1968 à 1977, il travaille comme architecte pour la préservation des monuments historiques du canton des Grisons en Suisse. Tuteur à l'université de Zurich en 1978, il crée son agence à Haldenstein, dans les Grisons, en 1979. Il a été professeur invité à SCI-Arc à Santa Monica, à l'Université technique de Munich, à l'université Tulane de La Nouvelle-Orléans, et à l'académie d'architecture de Mendrisio (1996). Il a reçu le prix Pritzker en 2009. Parmi ses réalisations majeures, essentiellement en Suisse : un abri de protection pour des fouilles archéologiques romaines (Chur, 1986) ; la chapelle de Sogn Benedetg (Sumvitg, 1988) ; la Maison Gugalun (Versam, 1994) ; les Thermes de Vals (1996) ; la Kunsthaus de Bregenz (Autriche, 1997) ; le Pavillon suisse à Hanovre (Allemagne, 2000) ; une résidence familiale (Grisons, 1997–2003) et, plus récemment, la chapelle de Frère Klaus (Wachendorf, Allemagne, 2007) ; le Musée d'art Kolumba (Cologne, Allemagne, 2007) : le Mémorial de Steilneset aux victimes des procès en sorcellerie de la région du Finmark (Vardø, Norvège, 2011) et le Pavillon d'été de la Serpentine Gallery dans les jardins de Kensigton (Londres, 2011, publié ici).

SERPENTINE GALLERY SUMMER PAVILION

Kensington Gardens, London, UK, 2011

Address: Kensington Gardens, London W2 3XA, UK, +44 20 74 02 60 75, www.serpentinegallery.org
Area: 350 m². Client: Serpentine Gallery. Cost: not disclosed

Peter Zumthor has designed a "Hortus Conclusus": a dramatic enclosed garden featuring an elegant structure that surrounds a planted space with covered walkways around it for the 2011 **SERPENTINE SUMMER PAVILION**. After the many other well-known architects, from Zaha Hadid to Jean Nouvel, selected for the design of these temporary structures in Kensington Gardens, near the building of the Serpentine Gallery itself, Zumthor has succeeded in creating an original work. Used for summer events organized by the gallery, this design is more enclosed than many of the previous pavilions, and perhaps more contemplative. The rectangular structure is roughly 35 meters long, 10 meters wide, and 4.5 meters high.

Peter Zumthors Entwurf ist ein „Hortus Conclusus": ein dramatischer geschlossener Garten. Es ist ein eleganter Bau, der einen begrünten Raum mit überdachten Gängen umschließt und 2011 als **SOMMERPAVILLON FÜR DIE SERPENTINE GALLERY** realisiert wurde. Nach zahlreichen bekannten Architekten, von Zaha Hadid bis Jean Nouvel, die in der Vergangenheit ausgewählt wurden, um temporäre Pavillons in Kensington Gardens neben der Serpentine Gallery zu bauen, gelingt es Zumthor, eine ganz eigene Lösung zu finden. Der Pavillon, der für Sommerveranstaltungen der Galerie genutzt wird, wirkt geschlossener als viele seiner Vorgängerbauten und wohl auch kontemplativer. Der rechteckige Bau ist rund 35 m lang, 10 m breit und 4,5 m hoch.

Pour le **PAVILLON D'ÉTÉ DE LA SERPENTINE GALLERY** de 2011, Peter Zumthor a conçu un *hortus conclusus*, spectaculaire jardin clos prenant la forme d'une élégante structure entourant un espace planté entouré de passages couverts. Après de nombreuses autres célébrités de l'architecture – de Zaha Hadid à Jean Nouvel – également sélectionnées pour concevoir un de ces pavillons temporaires dans les jardins de Kensington, près de la Serpentine Gallery, Zumthor a réussi à créer une œuvre particulièrement originale. Utilisé pour les manifestations estivales organisées par la galerie, ce projet est plus fermé que ses prédécesseurs et d'esprit peut-être plus contemplatif. La structure de plan rectangulaire mesure 35 mètres de long, 10 mètres de large et 4,50 mètres de haut.

Zumthor's pavilion contrasts with
those seen in previous years in front
of the Serpentine Gallery because it
appears to be essentially closed and
austere. Drawings show the enclosed
garden.

Zumthors Pavillon ist ein Kontrastprogramm zu Pavillons früherer Jahre
vor der Serpentine Gallery, er wirkt
streng und geschlossen. Zeichnungen
zeigen den umbauten Garten.

Le pavillon de Zumthor contraste par
son austérité et son aspect fermé
avec ceux réalisés précédemment
devant la Serpentine Gallery. Les
dessins illustrent le jardin clos.

The enclosed garden seen shortly after the opening of the pavilion in the summer of 2011. The dark architectural forms contrast with the lightness of the garden.

Der umbaute Garten kurz nach Eröffnung des Pavillons im Sommer 2011. Die dunkle Architektur bildet einen Kontrast zum hellen Garten.

Le jardin clos vu peu après l'ouverture du pavillon au début de l'été 2011. L'aspect sombre de l'architecture contraste avec la légèreté des plantations.

The contemplative and protected nature of the space allows visitors to enter a different environment than that of the surrounding park or the often more extroverted Serpentine Summer Pavilions.

Die kontemplative und geschützte Natur im Pavillon bietet Besuchern ein anderes Umfeld als der angrenzende Park oder die oft wesentlich extrovertierteren Sommerpavillons der Serpentine Gallery.

La nature contemplative et protégée de cet espace accueille les visiteurs dans un environnement différent de celui du parc de Kensington ou des pavillons de la Serpentine généralement plus extravertis.

INDEX OF BUILDINGS AND PLACES

INDEX OF BUILDINGS AND PLACES

CREDITS